COURBET'S LANDSCAPES

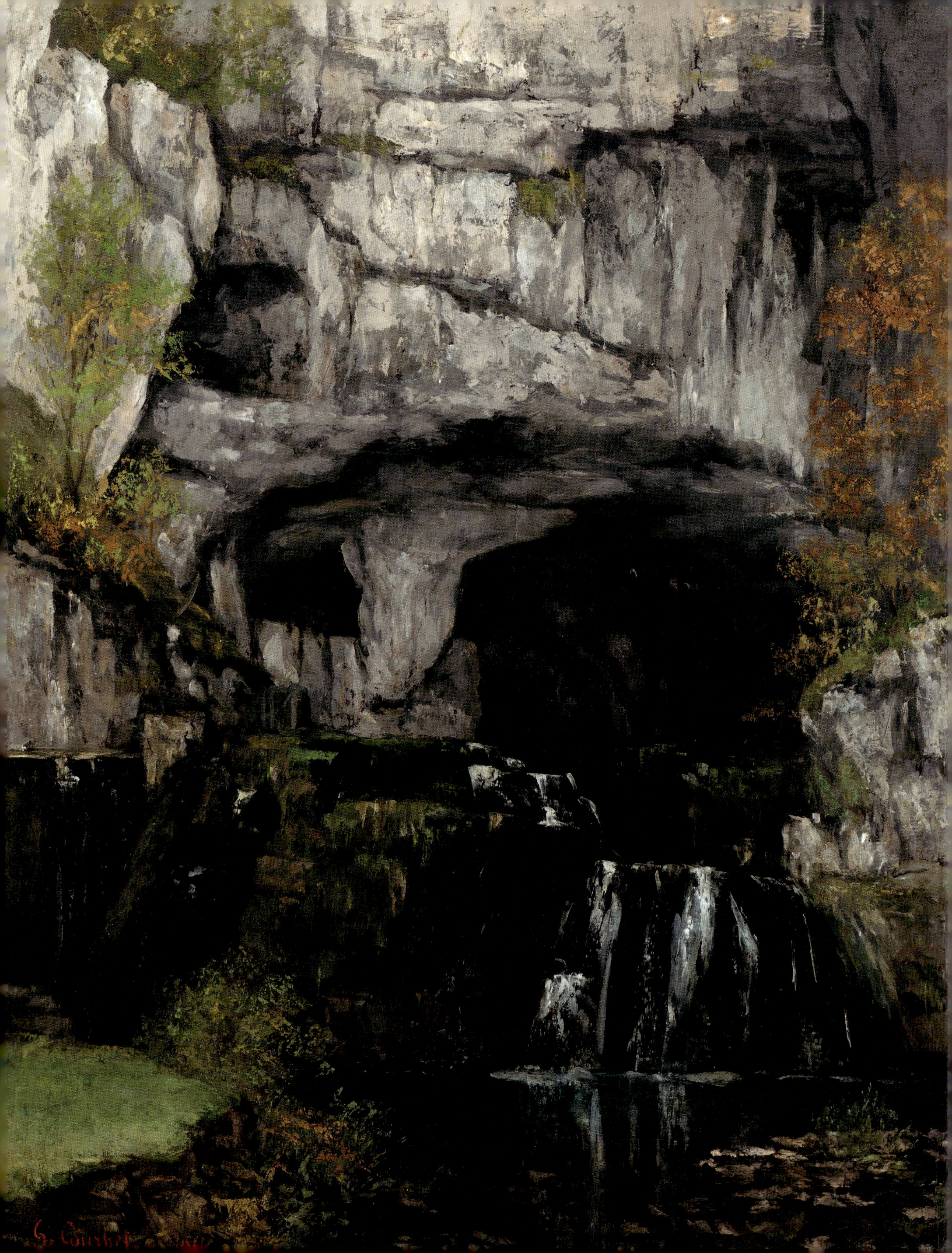
G. Courbet.

COURBET'S LANDSCAPES

THE ORIGINS OF MODERN PAINTING

PAUL GALVEZ

Yale University Press New Haven and London

First published by Yale University Press 2022
302 Temple Street, P. O. Box 209040, New Haven CT 06520-9040
47 Bedford Square, London WC1B 3DP
yalebooks.com | yalebooks.co.uk

ISBN 978-0-300-24413-7 HB
Library of Congress Control Number: 2021947381

10 9 8 7 6 5 4 3 2 1
2026 2025 2024 2023 2022

Designed by Studio Noel
Copyedited by Rosalind Neely
Printed in Slovenia by DZS-Grafik d.o.o.

Front cover: Gustave Courbet, *Beneath the Trees at Port-Berteau: Children Dancing*, *ca.*1862. Oil on canvas, 66.5 × 52.1 cm. The Fitzwilliam Museum, Cambridge, England

Frontispiece: Gustave Courbet, *Source of the Lison*, 1864. Oil on canvas, 91 × 73 cm. Private collection, Minnesota Marine Art Museum, Winona, Minnesota

p. 24: Gustave Courbet, *Stream in the Forest*, *ca.*1862. Oil on canvas, 156.8 × 114 cm. Museum of Fine Arts, Boston

p. 56: Gustave Courbet, *Le Gour de Conche*, 1864. Oil on canvas, 74 × 60 cm. Musée des Beaux-Arts et d'Archéologie, Besançon

p. 84: Gustave Courbet, *Wave* (detail), 1869. Oil on canvas, 65.8 × 90.5 cm. Musée des Beaux-Arts, Lyons

p. 128: Paul Cézanne, *Uncle Dominique with a Turban*, 1866–67. Oil on canvas, 44 × 37 cm. Private collection

p. 162: Camille Pissarro, *The Climb, Rue de la Côte-du-Jalet, Pontoise* (detail), 1875. Oil on canvas, 54 × 66.7 cm. Brooklyn Museum of Art, New York

FSC www.fsc.org
MIX
Paper from responsible sources
FSC® C106600

CONTENTS

7 **INTRODUCTION**

25 **CHAPTER 1: BAGS OF PAINT IN GLASSY SKINS**

57 **CHAPTER 2: WHEN LANDSCAPE BECAME LANGUAGE**

85 **CHAPTER 3: MILK OF THE SEA**

129 **CHAPTER 4: CUT WITH A PALETTE KNIFE**

163 **CODA: ANTI-IMPRESSIONISM**

177 *List of Abbreviations*

178 *Notes*

193 *Select Bibliography*

200 *Index*

206 *Acknowledgments*

208 *Picture Credits*

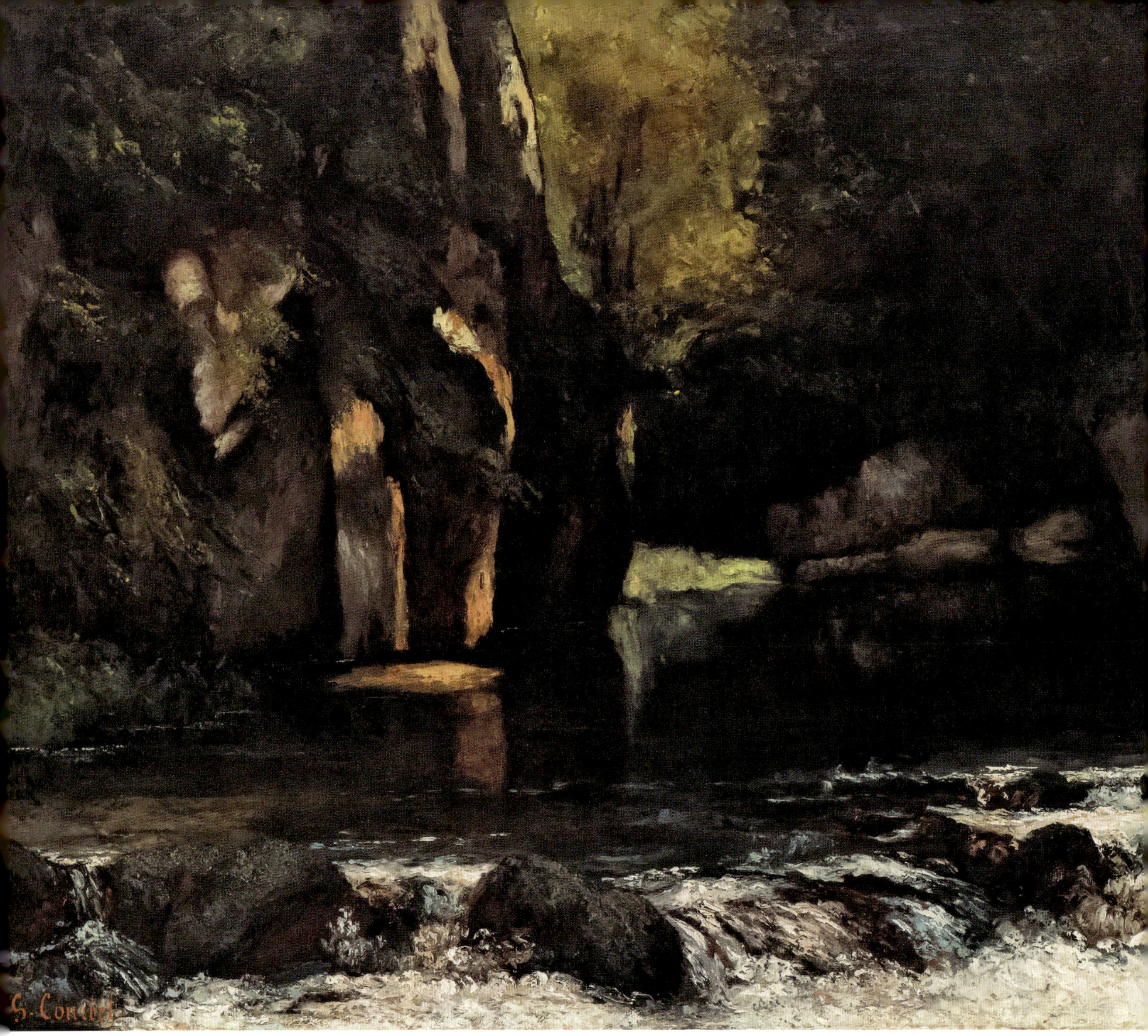

1 | *The Stream of the Puits noir*, 1864. Oil on canvas, 82.1 × 96.5 cm. Phillips Art Holdings LLC

INTRODUCTION

The Stream of the Puits noir (fig. 1) by Gustave Courbet (1819–1877) depicts a site in his native region of Franche-Comté in eastern France as if it were a dark primordial world. In this penumbra solid forms are hard to make out. Moving a step closer, what was just a nascent glimmer in the shadows morphs into a jutting rock face. Time has carved into it many crags, whose edges now catch light. One of the most salient facets, just left of center, hovers above its own reflection. A patch of lit earth divides the stony protuberance from what now appears to be a limpid pool. Attention momentarily nestles here, at the point where water splits from earth. This initial bifurcation gives us a foothold in the landscape; we expect the rest of the picture to come into focus. Yet a quick look around and things remain stubbornly unresolved. As we peer more closely, we see that the rock is mottled and screened by foliage. However, the true shape of the outcropping and the extent of its bulk are still unknown. As we look to the right in search of clarification, boulders become clear on the far embankment. For a moment they determine a background before they regress back into the depths. Suddenly, a blaze of luxuriant verdure erupts between the projecting cliff and the distant riverbank. Light has finally managed to pierce the landscape's seemingly impenetrable shroud. Common sense says that this enlivened area should lie behind the escarpment. Yet, visually, its luminosity nudges it forward, and our perceptual grip on this world once again loosens.

At even closer quarters, the threshold of legibility seems to have been reached at last. All those protrusions, greeneries, and rock surfaces now reveal themselves to be as thick and viscous as paint itself. At this point, the illusion should fall apart, devolving into pure matter—but it doesn't. Because nature here is humid and dark, leaves, rocks, and earth plausibly appear to be covered in a moist

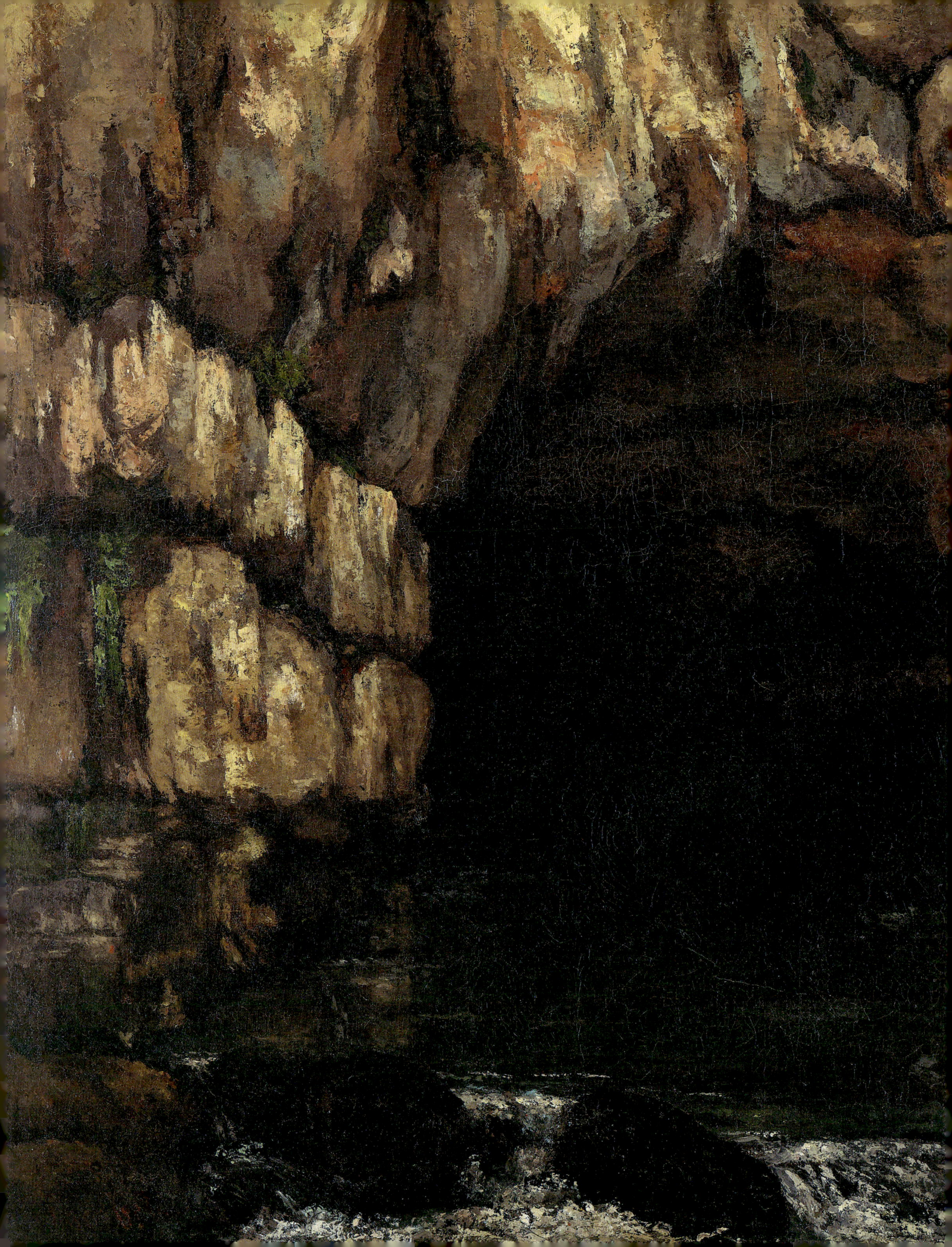

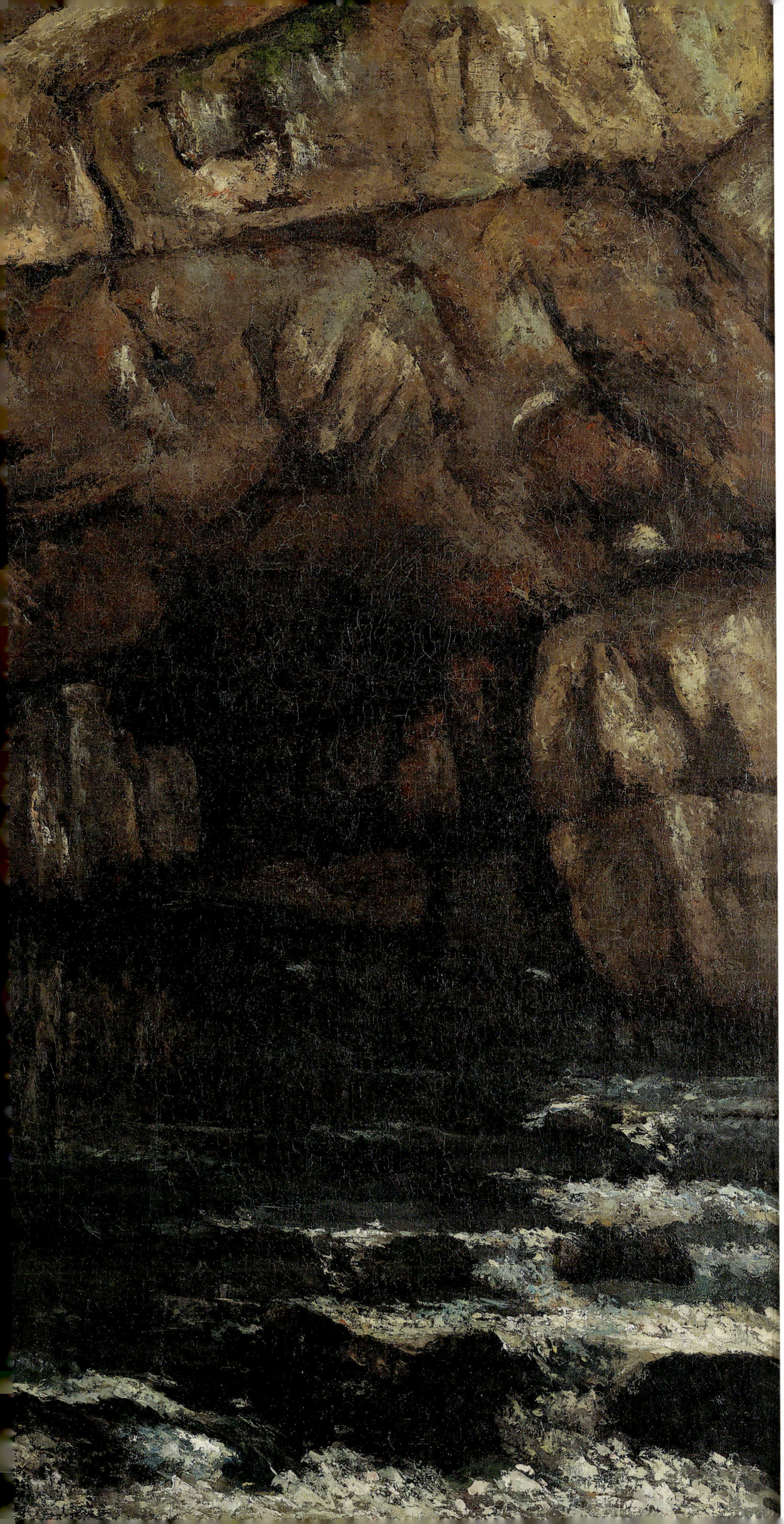

2 *The Source of the Loue*, ca.1864.
Oil on canvas, 107.3 × 137.4 cm.
Albright-Knox Art Gallery,
Buffalo

slime. Uncharacteristically, this close attention to the physical accumulation of paint here does not threaten the cohesiveness of the scene. Zooming in only entices us further into a universe of soggy, paint-like substance. The result of our prolonged entry into the landscape is an experience of an environment of ill-defined dampened forms coming into being at a glacial pace. Viewing time is so dilated in *The Stream of the Puits noir* that it seems the true subject of the painting is not the exact description of nature but rather the protracted *process* of trying to make sense of it.

Courbet later re-created again and again the slow, sensuous experience of a landscape, one that, embracing obscurity in place of clarity and context, seems to offer the viewer nothing but the birth of form itself. *Courbet's Landscapes* is the story of when, how, and why Courbet made the material origins of the world, in all its substantive immediacy, a subject for art. The artist's landscapes—which comprise more than half his known oeuvre—date to as early as the 1840s. Although Courbet achieves landscape backgrounds of the highest quality in several of his figure paintings from the early 1850s, it is during the 1860s that he truly comes into his own as a landscapist. At this time, Courbet paints a series of landscapes—mostly grottoes, riverbeds, and seascapes—that can best be described as originary worlds of pure substance and that, as depictions of sheer matter, have few precedents in the history of European painting. He paints nature almost everywhere he travels during this period, from the forests of the Saintonge near Bordeaux to the beaches at Trouville and Étretat on the Normandy coast. Around 1864, he is also temporarily drawn, even more than usual, to the geological oddities unique to his native Franche-Comté; the representations of the cavernous sources of the Loue and Lison rivers and the area around the Puits noir are perhaps Courbet's greatest achievements in the genre (fig. 2).

Courbet often painted the same motif in intense, energetic spurts, usually lasting no more than a couple of months. In accordance with the artist's own working rhythm, this book is also episodic. Chapters are organized around significant moments: the 1862–63 trip to the Saintonge, the 1864 stay in Franche-Comté, and the visits to Normandy in 1865, 1866, and 1869. Concentrating on these periods allows for a deeper analysis of the landscapes than might have been achieved in a broad survey. At the other end of our time frame, the artist's period of inventiveness in the genre effectively ended in the 1870s. After he was held responsible for the demolition of the column in the Place Vendôme with a statue of Napoleon during the Paris Commune, he went into exile in 1873 and undertook formulaic compositions to pay his bills. Rather than dwelling on the years of exile, the book concludes with a chapter on Courbet's impact on the next generation of artists. The Impressionists appreciated more than anyone the break with past ways of seeing the world found in Courbet's landscapes. Instead of inspiring younger artists to imagine an unseen origin deep in the past, this development in Courbet's art stimulated them to rewrite nature on their own terms. They accepted as a fait accompli that pictorial material unabashedly existed in the real world, not the world of the image. Now that the tension between actual and depicted matter so evident in Courbet's landscapes was broken, the new painting embraced the artificiality of art. All subject matter was now, by definition, also matter. Materialization in painting would no longer be a question of bridging the gap between the imaginary and the real, as it was for Courbet in his landscapes, but of how to destabilize, undo, and overthrow the current order of reality by means of another.

Courbet's reputation rests primarily on the large, imposing canvases of provincial scenes that he painted in the aftermath of the 1848 French Revolution, works such as *A Burial at Ornans* (1849–50; Musée d'Orsay, Paris) and *The Stonebreakers* (1851; destroyed). They were understood to be "materialist" to the extent that they gave visual form to socioeconomic forces then transforming French society. The increasing visibility of lower social classes within politics and everyday life set the tone for the hostile reception of the works in Paris. Courbet's Salon paintings, in which the artist made the provincial heroic in scale but decidedly unidealized in tone and execution, gave expression to a destabilizing threat to the civil order. Courbet thus became a lightning rod for ideological critiques that resonated well beyond the artistic sphere. This argument is so familiar to the narrative of nineteenth-century French art that it hardly bears repetition.[1] But if we are to fully comprehend Courbet's approach to depicting the material world, it is important to disentangle it from this earlier historical "materialism."

By the 1860s, Courbet's "materialism" took on a completely different character. The landscapes are less concerned with the effect of changing systems of production on the subject matter of art than on the basic process at the heart of painterly labor itself: the transformation of raw materials into an image. Traditionally, if artists wanted to depict something from the real world, they painted an illusion of one; in general, the more the obtrusive physical qualities of paint—its thickness, texture, and pastiness—were hidden and denied, the more convincing the illusion. Even in the obvious cases in the history of art when the rule is broken—think of the bravura flourishes of Titian, Rembrandt, and Goya—the disobedience was palatable, and even encouraged, on the condition that the illusion ultimately came together at a distance. Courbet is perhaps the first figure in post-Renaissance painting to challenge in a deliberate and lasting way the hierarchy of illusionistic form over matter. Unlike his predecessors in this endeavor, who more often than not would limit matter overtaking the image to select areas of drapery and clothing, or in backgrounds and foregrounds, Courbet pursued this approach across the entire pictorial field. The historical significance of this accomplishment should not be underestimated; henceforth, artists of any ambition would have to contend with, positively or negatively, the physical presence of paint. There was no going back to licked surfaces and invisible glazes as an unquestioned norm. Moreover, this interrogating of the means of representation did not arise, as was so often the case, in scenes of urban life or in the open air, but, on the contrary, from their almost exact opposite: a somber and uninhabited landscape.

Courbet's problem was this: how does one show brute matter to maximum effect, using the full resources of painting as raw stuff, in a medium that has historically denied its own substance? In brief, his answer was to paint sites evocative of some sort of origin—unfathomable caves, endless oceans—where nature appears as wet and dense as fresh paint. The return to the origin pictured in what could be called Courbet's "landscapes of origin" sought to overcome the distance that society had placed between observer and nature by imagining a place where human structures and other people would not obstruct the tactile experience of one's surroundings. Moreover, Courbet was not only aiming to get us closer to nature. He wanted us to feel as if we were experiencing the world at an earlier stage in its creation, like plunging into the depths of a prehistoric cave or testing the waters of a primordial sea. The perceived movement initiated by his landscapes was thus meant to be both temporal and physical. The paintings present an *experience* as much as a specific location—virtually moving forward in space but conceptually backward in time.

To maintain the illusion of such lush environments, without the image falling apart at close range, the depicted locales had to appear as rich in substance as the painter's material. In these originary situations, wet sand oozes as if emulsified, sea foam coagulates into a thick paste, rocks develop a moist skin not unlike that of colors on a fresh palette. The unique spatiotemporal dynamics of Courbet's landscapes of origin depend intimately on our perception of materials. The works suspend us at a moment in which painting, briefly, offers itself at one and the same time as illusion *and* matter. In other words, the pictured image (landscape) and the material used to picture it (paint) become co-substantial. The relationship between the real world and the painted one is no longer metaphorical; the chasm separating original nature from its handcrafted copy is no longer unbridgeable. Instead, the two approach a condition of material equivalence, sharing the same physical make-up, the same qualities of liquidity and solidity. Matter from our world can be credibly present in the depicted one because the world depicted is itself paint-like. Courbet's enduring invention was to find a way of declaring matter, *real* matter, the kind we can touch and feel and not just see, within a world of illusion hostile to such a declaration.[2]

The task Courbet set himself was difficult, if not impossible. There were few motifs that could satisfy its narrow set of criteria. The signs of civilization—pathways, buildings, agriculture, and even people—had to be largely absent or minimized. These elements humanized primeval nature, diverting attention away from the substance of landscape and directing it toward the activities taking place within it: living, farming, walking, etc. Deprived of such basic building blocks of narrative and pictorial space, the artist had to find alternative modes of composition. In order to foreground nature's substance, the viewer had to be close enough to the landscape elements to apprehend their texture but far enough away to be able to take in the landscape as a whole. The painter endeavoring to imagine such a sensuous plenum had to somehow combine, within a single picture, the proximate, zoomed-in view of still life with the more distanced and all-encompassing view of landscape. Such views were fundamentally at odds with one another. The genre of still life tended to focus on graspable objects and touchable surfaces, on what could fit on a tabletop and be set up indoors, with little else allowed to compete for attention. Landscape, by contrast, sacrificed the individual object, the tactile detail, for broad swaths of space organized into open fields, bodies of water, or distant mountains. There are few, if any, precedents in the history of painting for the merging of the perceptual modalities of still life and landscape that we observe in a Courbet. In order to achieve this unlikely combination of genres, nature had to appear humid, darkened, with no overly dominant focus. Courbet repeatedly found solutions to this problem by utterly transforming existing landscape models. It is hard to think of an earlier grotto painting as eerie as one of Courbet's source paintings, where the center is often nothing but a gaping void. We would be equally hard-pressed to find a marine painting that exhibits the same unsettling combination of turbulence, stillness, and heft found in the artist's waves.

The co-substantiality of image and matter at work in Courbet's landscapes is a phenomenon that has increasingly drawn critical attention from art historians. James D. Herbert, for instance, accords a special place to it in the modern history of painterly gesture: "Courbet selects for inclusion in his canvas only those aspects of the world that physically resemble his paints."[3] Historically, critical references to Courbet's singular approach to the pictorial representation of matter are less explicit, and analyses of it certainly less thorough, than in contemporary art history. The fusion of picture and material induced by Courbet's unique mark-making is often unwittingly registered at the more prosaic level of written description. In a given text about one of Courbet's landscapes the same words are often used to characterize both a particular site painted by Courbet *and* the manner in which it was painted. When a contemporary such as the art critic Jules-Antoine Castagnary praises Courbet for his "fresh and striking" landscapes, where elements happily combine to produce a breath of cool air, it is unclear whether it is Courbet's paint or the depicted site that is fresh and striking, whether it is the painter or nature that is organizing the combination, and whether it is the paint application or the represented environment that is responsible for the feeling of a breeze.[4] Such verbal slippages are too widespread in the literature to be attributed solely to poor writing. Their frequency suggests that the descriptive conflation of scene and substance is an effect propagated by the works themselves. And so, while great care has been taken throughout this book to be precise about whether it is a thing or a picture of a thing under discussion, a certain amount of semantic overlap is inevitable when talking about a body of work that deliberately plays on the possibility for aspects of a *place* (the Puits noir outside Ornans) to have the same physical properties (pastiness, thickness, fluidity, etc.) as elements of a *painting of that place* (the artwork known as *The Stream of the Puits noir*; see fig. 1).

One further comment on the language employed in this book. Until this point, "materialism" has appeared in quotation marks. The term is notoriously tricky to define, its meaning usually dependent on the particular context of its utterance.[5] To avoid confusion, "materialism" and its variant, "matter," have specific meanings throughout this study. "Materialism" denotes the philosophical tradition, resurgent in France from the eighteenth century onward, claiming that all phenomena are reducible to the action of particles of matter. As the German philosopher Friedrich Lange put it in the chapter of his 1866 *History of Materialism* on the ancient Greek philosopher Democritus (the subject, along with his counterpart Epicurus, of Marx's doctoral thesis): "nothing exists but atoms and empty space: all else is only opinion."[6] Materialism sought to eliminate from its systematic account of the world anything not grounded in observed reality. Transcendental entities for which there was no physical proof, such as God or the soul, were to be considered "only opinion." The threat this thinking was to pose over the course of the nineteenth century to institutions claiming spiritual or metaphysical authority is familiar enough. In the arts, this insurgent attitude coalesced around mid-century in the movement known as Realism and frequently took the form of protests against the restrictive standards of the Académie des Beaux-Arts and the jury of the Salon, its official exhibition in Paris, set up to protect the artistic heritage of France. We can hear not-so-faint echoes of it in Courbet's rallying cry to aspiring artists: "I also maintain that painting is an essentially concrete art form and can consist only of the representation of real and existing things.... An abstract object, not visible, nonexistent, is not within the domain of painting."[7] Or, as he wrote to the socialist philosopher Pierre-Joseph Proudhon, "Banish the mysterious, the miraculous, don't believe in the incomprehensible."[8] Courbet's public statements and large figure paintings understandably oriented themselves toward materialism's social dimension. However, Courbet's landscapes address another aspect: the fundamental axiom that the world is composed of building blocks of matter. We know from Courbet's adolescent notebook that he was exposed to thinkers such as Democritus and Epicurus in his youth.[9] But even if he had never studied philosophy, his landscapes realize, by painterly means, the materialist's atomic world.

To distinguish it from its "higher" philosophical relative, "materialism," the term "matter"—along with the analogous term "substance"—refers to crude, unstable, or as-yet-unsolidified materials such as seawater, syrup, mucus, mud, blood, and, of course, paint. Given the play in Courbet's landscapes between depicted and actual matter, most substances discussed in this study are of the dense, emulsified, or coagulated variety, as opposed to the nonconcentrated and dilute, or, at the other end of the spectrum of moistness, the brittle, desiccated kind. As a sometime stand-in for not only "materialism" and "matter" as defined above but also adjacent concepts such as "corporality" and "tactility," the term "materiality" is to be avoided, because it has proved frustratingly vague in discussions of the materials and technique of painting. This study does not shy away from more abstract considerations of the form-matter distinction that normally fall under this rubric. But it addresses the issue only on the basis of detailed analyses of specific works by specific artists at specific historical moments—that is to say, the approach taken here is highly localized. Only then can Courbet's landscapes be seen to arise at a pivotal moment in the history of painting when the substantive qualities of paint, after centuries of repression, emerged as a fundamental and unavoidable condition, and not just an isolated case or technical problem, for art.

If materialism was, in highly mediated ways, the conceptual underpinning of Courbet's approach to matter, Romanticism was its primary source of pictorial models. The myth of the return to nature, whose classic formulations had already been developed by the Swiss-born philosopher Jean-Jacques Rousseau and others during the previous century, had by the first decades of the nineteenth century trickled down through the institutions of art. The Académie des Beaux-Arts, the entity that historically oversaw artistic education and exhibition practice, established the grand prize in historical landscape in 1816 to elevate and honor, but also to limit and control, the prospering genre. In the world of letters, treatises such as the French painter Pierre-Henri de Valenciennes's influential *Élémens de perspective pratique à l'usage des artistes, suivis de réflexions et conseils à un élève sur la peinture et particulièrement sur le genre du paysage* (1800) had advised landscapists to veer off familiar paths in search of motifs. The growth of provincial excursions, artist's colonies, and day-trips to the suburbs over the course of the century showed that this advice had been heeded. Thus, when Courbet arrived in Paris in the 1840s, the critics had already divided the large group of landscape painters into schools. The poet Charles Baudelaire, to take just one example, identified three such groupings in his "Salon of 1846."[10] One tendency consisted of painters working in the mode of the Dutch and English landscapists, John Constable foremost among them. The critic astutely identified Jean-Baptiste-Camille Corot as the outstanding practitioner of a second current, *paysage historique* (historical landscape), so called because it took as its model the Roman *campagna*, considered the most appropriate setting for classicizing, historical subjects.

The third trend comprised the painters of the Barbizon School—Jean-François Millet, Charles-François Daubigny, Constant Troyon, Jules Dupré, Narcisse-Virgilio Diaz de la Peña, and, above all, Théodore Rousseau—a loosely knit group who each spent some or all of their lives dwelling in and around the

Forest of Fontainebleau, where the village of Barbizon is located. It is the work of the third "school" that came closest to anticipating Courbet's landscapes in form and spirit. These artists also exploited the freedom of expression that landscape, of all the genres, was historically granted in the representation of matter. Inventive in technique and unclassical (i.e. local and non-Italianate) in choice of motif, the Barbizon painters gave phenomena such as storms and twilight and elements such as mountains and trees a physical presence rarely encountered until that point in European landscape painting outside of Holland and England. However, none of the artists were able to produce landscape painting like Courbet, who traveled beyond forests and fields to the deepest recesses of the earth, to the ends of the ocean, until he reached a point at which all structure, all form, was reduced to a pure, all-constituting, ubiquitous substance, where even the most basic distinctions between form and matter appeared to be on the verge of breaking down.

Given the circulation of materialist ideas and the proliferation of landscape styles by mid-century, it may seem surprising that Courbet should be the first to fuse the two tendencies. After all, the cave, the forest, and the ocean were not entirely unknown motifs in his day. At some point, we could conjecture, another landscapist must have been bold enough to transform a vigorous study into a finished painting without suppressing, as tradition demanded, noticeable physical texture. However, the various woodland and beach scenes of Courbet's contemporaries typically include a path or figure or sky preventing the complete tactile submersion in matter that we experience before a Courbet. Such elements either distance the viewer from the scene or focus attention on select points at the expense of the experience of the whole. And even at its most subtle, contemporaneous landscape painting was executed in such a way that the illusion of nature inevitably broke down as soon as the viewer approached the canvas, denying the possibility of continuing to see raw paint as part of the image—which, of course, was the unique effect of Courbet's landscapes.

By 1863, Courbet had all the tools necessary—essentially, his celebrated palette-knife technique and a passion for landscape—to re-create a scene of natural origins. The convergence of a materialist attitude and Romantic landscape required a historical trigger. What made Courbet start depicting origins at this particular moment? As discussed in Chapter 2, Courbet painted such pictures as *The Stream of the Puits noir* (see fig. 1) and *The Source of the Loue* (see fig. 2) in 1864 because his closest associates at the time, working in a wide variety of fields—linguistics, archeology, geology—were at the same moment also investigating the problem of origins.

Perhaps the most noteworthy example was his friend Max Buchon, who upon his return to Franche-Comté in 1856 after years of political exile wrote a series of articles, booklets, and anthologies, almost all of which made direct or indirect reference to Courbet or mentioned sites he painted in 1864, including the sources of the Loue and Lison rivers, the Roche pourrie outside Salins, and a waterfall called Gour de Conche. Buchon's publications—*Noëls et chants populaires de la Franche-Comté* (1863), *Revue littéraire de la Franche-Comté* (1864), *Salins-les-Bains* (1862 and 1866), and articles in the newspaper *Le Salinois*—all shared a common theme: the need to create a truly popular literature from original and soon-to-be-lost patois. To this end, Buchon believed it important to study the early development and structure of Franc-comtois dialects, which would reveal a hidden history of the region and its people, just as, in his view, contemporary geology was uncovering hitherto-unknown layers of earth history. This explains, for example, Buchon's glee upon telling Charles Thuriet, the editor of *Revue littéraire de la Franche-Comté*, about an eighteenth-century patois songbook he had discovered in the possession of the Courbet family during a visit to Ornans in 1864, just as Courbet was painting his grottoes and riverbeds.[11] Thuriet himself characterized Buchon's project as doing "in poetry what Courbet, another of our compatriots, does in painting."[12] What Buchon wanted to do for language—to trace it back to its origins—Courbet did for landscape. While Courbet's landscapes of origin entered the history of art, Buchon's "popular literature," based on similar ideas, has been all but forgotten. The artist, unlike the writer, had been able to transform the notion of peeling back layers of history from a metaphor into an integral part of the work. Buchon introduced old forms of speech into his stories by using the rather traditional form of the provincial tale to narrate scenes of villagers speaking patois. Courbet, by contrast, created a new kind of landscape in which the viewer, by means of a seemingly endless voyage through layers of paint-like substance toward an unknown origin, experienced, within perception, the visual equivalent of the *longue durée* of deep historical time.[13]

Once unleashed, painting substance took over Courbet's practice at other key moments. Most spectacularly, and also most surprisingly, Courbet adapted what he had achieved in the land-locked recesses of the Franche-Comté region to the maritime environment of the Normandy coast. As a motif, nothing could be more unlike a cave than the sea. Whereas the former is rocky, hollowed out, and subterranean, the latter is fluid, mobile, and expansive. Yet when Courbet first visited the beach town of Trouville in 1865 (to be followed by subsequent trips to even more fashionable Deauville in 1866, and to Étretat further up the coast in 1869), he decided to turn away from the vibrant social life of boardwalks, concerts, and casinos made possible by the arrival of the railway from Paris in 1863 in order to focus on a depopulated view toward the horizon. Often composed of three broad zones representing sand, sea, and sky and little else, Courbet's oceanic vistas at first glance appear unsettlingly desolate; in terms of narrative and figurative content they are some of the "emptiest" landscapes ever produced up until this point. But from the standpoint of matter, they are also some of the "fullest." For each tripartite division appears impossibly dense: the shore is permeated with seawater, turning it into a sludge; the sea is a maelstrom of foam; the sky is pregnant with vapor.

In Normandy, Courbet's painterly intuition had brought him to a stunning realization: that the most primordial landscape is the sea. Unlike the search for origins in Franche-Comté, Courbet's practice on the coast would proceed independently of a specific intellectual milieu. But what was carried over from the 1864 landscapes was the direct, immersive experience of nature. Taking in the ocean became for Courbet a kind of bodily pleasure distinct from the superficial one of modern leisure. In this pursuit, he was not alone. For to conceive the ocean as a matrix of origination—in direct response to the alienation of modern life—was a theme that resonated well beyond the visual arts. It fascinated, for instance, two of the leading literary figures of the Second Empire, the exiled poet-novelist-critic Victor Hugo (with whom Courbet had a brief correspondence) and the repatriated historian Jules Michelet.[14] Michelet's best-selling *La Mer* (1861) and Victor Hugo's equally successful *Les Travailleurs de la mer* (1866) rival Courbet's seascapes in their evocation of the physicality of the sea. (Indeed, Hugo even made extraordinary ink drawings demonstrating that physicality.)

Chapter 3 addresses Courbet's seascapes in the broader context of contemporary literature, especially the worldviews expressed in the works of Hugo and Michelet. For Hugo, the impenetrable ocean represented the limits of knowledge, a frontier he explored at multiple levels in both his writing and drawing. For Michelet, seawater is practically an ur-substance—to which belong an entire class of similarly behaving substances such as blood, cream, and oil—vividly described throughout his writing, whatever the genre (history, natural history, travelogue) or subject (the French Revolution, medieval saints, insects). This basic substance is associated with everything from the blood of medieval relics to the grease of Napoleon's hair, from the pivotal events of human history to the remotest landscape, and the sea is its most supreme manifestation. Unlike Hugo, Michelet did not work out his oceanic vision materially as art. But the hypersubstantial universe permeating his writing nevertheless strongly mirrors the one realized in Courbet's painting. Reference to the physical consistency of the world runs like an undercurrent or subtext throughout the oeuvres of both men. For both the artist and the historian, the world—human and inhuman—is a highly saturated, corporeal one through which a paint-like, all-pervading substance flows, like blood through a body.

These historical connections have been little examined for so long because of the overwhelming attention given to figure painting in Courbet studies.[15] Much current thinking traces its roots to the middle of the twentieth century. When Meyer Schapiro wrote in his landmark essay "Courbet and Popular Imagery" that Courbet moved from "an originally aggressive conception of realism, with something of the social preoccupations of the second Republic, towards a more personal, aestheticized view," the tone was set for future scholars.[16]

For Schapiro, the subversive, threatening aspect of the popular (as opposed to the benign, conciliatory version of the Realist writer Champfleury, or the critics who, in the decade after the artist's death, tried to cleanse Courbet's oeuvre of politics) was embodied in Courbet's earlier Salon paintings. The landscapes of the 1860s, by contrast, ignored radical politics in favor of depoliticized art. Once set in stone, this strict opposition of History to Nature was hard to dislodge, and almost all subsequent readings of the landscapes, consciously or not, took this approach.

A full summary of the voluminous scholarship on the artist is beyond the scope of this or perhaps any one book. However, it is appropriate to set out the differences between this study and previous surveys right at the beginning. The literature on Courbet's landscapes can be summarized in five arguments:

1. *The landscapes have no subject.* The most severe way to deal with the organicism of Courbet's landscapes has been to ignore or outright dismiss it. It would be hard to find a blunter statement than that of T. J. Clark, who commented:

> "Courbet's landscape style was in fact an integral part of his Realism. Its failure, for it seems to me the weakest part of Courbet's art, is almost necessary to the figure paintings' success.... In the landscapes—and this is in direct and limiting contrast to the greatest figure paintings—individual shapes and surfaces and weights tend to recede into the thick paste of paint. The palette knife takes over, the things themselves are lost. Foliage and cliff-face blur into a froth of pigment, indefinite without being in any effective sense ambiguous, since the paint is never precise enough to invite any one reading, or even suggest finite alternatives."[17]

There is much to agree with here. In *The Stream of the Puits noir* (see fig. 1) forms recede, get lost, blur; they do indeed become indefinite, ambiguous, and imprecise—except that we could argue that they do so, contra Clark, in an incredibly effective sense.

In the quoted passage the vacillation between image and matter that a work such as *The Stream of the Puits noir* so often produces is deemed a loss for art. Courbet does not "invite any one reading" and even forestalls all "finite alternatives." Why are open-endedness and multiplicity deemed so threatening? Because they mean that the artist "rejected the most fertile tradition in landscape painting ... the record of a human presence, the painting of landscapes thick with the remains of a human past, landscape created by man."[18] Depopulated, with all traces of human activity removed from view, *The Stream of the Puits noir* has little to offer a landscape tradition that privileges humans' relationship to nature above all. It has no place in a conception of the genre that is essentially anthropocentric. However, not more than once have these works been characterized as pictures of places as yet untouched by society where only animals have lived. By emptying his landscapes of all traces of civilization and by shifting their point of emphasis from concrete visual mastery over the world to a more fluid somatic experience of it, Courbet goes further than any landscapist before him in displacing the civilized mind from the center of their universe—a decentering that can be construed in its own way as a challenge to tradition.

2. *The landscapes embody an idea.* As if to compensate for this uncertainty regarding the landscapes' subject, critics often turned to broad overarching concepts in order to stamp upon the works a more stable, more readily accessible "meaning." In the strongest form of this approach, all formal and iconographic elements of the work are reduced to a master theme or idea. Thus, for Klaus Herding, Courbet's landscapes show democratic overtones at a symbolic level (because they picture universally accessible lands rather than elite historical subjects), while "equality" also permeates them at the level of their pictorial construction: "If the visual transformation of primal nature into a symbol of social authenticity and promise required clearly contoured objects as vehicles of meaning, the attempt to convey this message by means of egalitarian structure also required removal of borders between objects, a search for unifying characteristics, links, and analogies."[19] In this view, consistent handling of paint across the canvas, no matter how insignificant the area in question, constitutes a form of egalitarianism, a democratization of art at the level of technique. Henceforth, all aspects of the image, its formal realization as well as its metaphorical

associations, are subsumed by the new generic descriptor, "equality."

Certain problems arise in this mode of interpretation. First, in order to be valid, the primary theme must be discovered everywhere (or at least in a significant number of cases). Take the example of pictorial "equality." According to such a reading, it is seen to permeate not just the Franche-Comté scenes but also the Normandy seascapes, the hunting and animal pictures, and even some of the early landscapes. The result is that works produced under vastly different historical circumstances are reduced to a common denominator (albeit a high-minded one). Moreover, even if this symbolic reading were true—in theory nothing prevents this from being the case—it falls under considerable strain once works by other artists are considered. If Claude Monet and Édouard Manet paint intensely across the entire surface of their canvases, does that mean that they, too, are realizing pictorial "democracy"? Such a reading seems to fly in the face of the paintings themselves, for instance those depicting the outskirts of Paris, which visualize the breakdown of social relations rather than some ideal version of them. Finally, the symbolic interpretation often does not even hold up on its own terms. However equally distributed paint may be in the Salon paintings, for example, the very presence of a dominant person means that the figure will inevitably receive the viewer's main attention and therefore that the painting will be decidedly inegalitarian (even "authoritarian"). The same might be said of some of the landscapes. When Courbet isolates in his compositions a tree or a set of buildings, or even just accentuates certain areas by means of traditional devices such as receding planes and atmospheric perspective, these parts of the canvas inevitably garner more attention than others. The existence of such focal points belies the argument for an even distribution of attention.

3. *The landscapes are about paint itself.* While some acknowledge the landscapes' deliberate ambiguity only to decry their meaninglessness, and others try to neutralize that ambiguity by making all content and form reflective of a single grand idea, a third approach turns Courbet's breaking down of the barriers between form and matter into a proto-modernist gesture. In a review of a Courbet exhibition at Wildenstein & Co., New York, in 1949, Clement Greenberg contended that Courbet, by painting "with body color, using very little medium and pressing masses of pigment to the canvas with his palette knife ... emphasized the *corporeality of the picture itself* as well as that of nature [my emphasis]."[20] The phrase "the corporeality of the picture itself" encompasses two important ideas: first, that Courbet's impasto is quasi-organic, as if belonging to a body; and, second, that this substantiveness characterizes not only the scene represented but also something the critic calls the "picture itself."

Underlying Greenberg's seemingly abrupt move from thickness to picture-ness is a staunch formalist point of view that he had been developing since the 1930s. Nine years before the Courbet review, in the essay "Towards a Newer Laocoön," published in *Partisan Review* (July–August 1940), the art critic famously argued that the only way for painting to maintain its cultural value in an age of debased mass entertainment was to divest itself of anything that was too literary (Greenberg regarded literature as the mass medium of the nineteenth century par excellence). This would include anything with too much message, too much anecdote, and, ultimately, subject matter at all. The corollary to this anti-literariness was a pro-painterliness, and, to stave off contamination from other arts such as literature, painting would henceforth have to deal with only what was unique to it as a physical medium. As is well known, Greenberg would eventually prioritize one particular mode of self-definition in painting: the declaration of flatness. Thus, formal developments such as the elimination of depth, all-over composition, and color fields, because they highlighted the planarity of the canvas support, were understood by Greenberg to be emblematic of a heroic, and medium-specific, self-consciousness in art. There are glimpses of this argument in the 1940 essay when the critic states that "a new flatness begins to appear in Courbet's painting, and an equally new attention to every inch of the canvas, regardless of its relation to 'centers of interest.'" By the time of the 1949 review, Greenberg's conception of Courbet's modernism now included knife-pressed pigment, for, like visible brushstrokes and, later, Cubist grids, it was in the critic's view a way of emphasizing painting's essential condition as a flat surface. Privileging matter in order to turn it into a sign of the "picture itself," Greenberg overlooked the complex and highly nuanced interplay between image and matter in Courbet's painting in order to pursue his true goal: to define all pictorial and material elements of a work, including that of "paint itself," as forms of self-reference.

4. *The landscapes are naturalized myth.* The spectacular rise of landscape painting in the nineteenth century meant that the precise workings of Courbet's landscapes often became lost in critical debates. Critics frequently spoke about Courbet's landscapes in exactly the same way they talked about any other landscape, classical, Romantic, Realist, or otherwise. Champfleury, for instance, asserted that every landscapist is "a kind of moral counselor who slips into the businessman's office and the homes of the gentleman and the courtesan to freshen their spirits."[21] With such lack of discrimination, it was easy for Champfleury to argue that landscapists as different as Corot and Courbet, to cite his own examples, could be reduced to serving the same comforting function.

It is difficult for us today to think of Nature as anything other than just this sort of reassuring myth. Indeed, one of the most extensive texts on Courbet's landscapes, Anne M. Wagner's "Courbet's Landscapes and Their Market," takes the artist to task on precisely these grounds.[22] Following in Champfleury's footsteps but turning the critic's value system on its head, this interpretation condemns landscape as a form of escapism, a condition to which Courbet, no less than other landscapists of the time, had all too readily succumbed. Certainly, there is plenty of evidence for this. Courbet *did* paint for Parisian collectors; he often accommodated specific requests for figures, animals, or the depiction of a particular mood; he was clearly excited about how much money he made from sales; and, at the end of his career, in his landscapes, he did try overly hard to please in order to pay his debts.

An unfortunate outcome of a devil's pact made with well-heeled middle-class collectors, the packaged image of Nature, according to this line of argument, had another sinister underside. It was not just the image of Nature that was palliative; the way it was painted was soothing and therefore complicit with uncritical, acquiescent taste.[23] Yet certain unnamed works by the artist are absolved of this sin, specifically "those few canvases which aim at an awkward, slow, seemingly uncomposed description of things observed, pictures where materiality is neither first nor last the fiction of paint."[24] These unspecified, "slow" paintings, which by the author's own admission resist commercialism, are the landscapes of origins that are the subject of this book. The enigmatic phrase used to describe them, "pictures where materiality is neither first nor last the fiction of paint," also deserves further comment. For if we agree that "materiality" should not be reduced to the "fiction of paint," i.e. the fictive condition of "paint itself" proposed by high modernism, then how exactly should we define it? What makes the exceptional landscapes so different, materially, from those simply following the whims of the market? Wagner is careful to distinguish Courbet's greatest works in the genre from lesser ones that merely promote "the materiality of Courbet's pictures, their paint and brushstrokes, as the ultimate vehicle of meaning, and in a sense, as meaning itself."[25] But that still leaves us with the problem of how to historicize and describe the "materiality" of the greatest landscapes without reducing it to "paint and brushstrokes." This is the question that this study tries to answer.

5. *The landscapes are bodies.* No book about Courbet and the origins of the world can ignore the small, close-up, cropped view of a woman's genital area, known by the title *Origin of the World* (1866; Musée d'Orsay, Paris) that the artist painted for the retired Turkish diplomat and art collector Khalil Bey. But the earliest evidence of its current title only dates to 1929, that is, well after its creation.[26] Its notorious reputation belies its modest size and outlying role in Courbet's oeuvre (the constant stream of publications on it since its rediscovery in the late 1980s says as much, if not more, about current attitudes toward sexuality as it does about those of the Second Empire). It would not even warrant mention here except that it seemingly supports a gynemorphic interpretation of the artist's landscapes. For, according to a certain train of logic, if the *Origin of the World* is a body, then so is every origin that Courbet painted. This would seem to bolster the habit of reading *The Source of the Loue* (see fig. 2) as a not-so-veiled representation of the female sex, or of

discerning figures and body parts in the rocks surrounding the grotto.[27] Yet, to the best of our knowledge, there is only one painting with a clearly anthropomorphic element, a late painting of a Swiss site known as *Grotto of the Giants near Saillon, Switzerland* (1873; Musée de Picardie, Amiens), and on this occasion the body was not hidden there by Courbet but already present in the motif.

The anthropomorphic reading seems to satisfy two overlapping desires: a wish to return to the womb; and a need for a clearly identifiable figurative subject as a basis for interpretation. True, Courbet painted several nudes in a landscape that fit between the allegorical nude and the contemporary model. The association of matter and *mater* is in those cases inescapable.[28] But in the most stunning landscapes, mostly figureless, it is precisely the nonidentification of matter with *any* permanent and whole form, human or natural, that constitutes their unique contribution to the history of art. Any attempts to unearth a body or allegorize the landscapes run counter to the inherent openness and ambiguity of the work. And even if we take the route of anthropomorphism, a case could be made for a grotto or riverbed representing an ungendered orifice, a mouth or anus (and thus neither solely gynemorphic *nor* andropomorphic, strictly speaking), rather than genitalia. At this early stage of development, before the advent of sexual differentiation, the body is more self-generating tissue than miniature human being. Following this line of reasoning, it could be argued that the dissolution and de-differentiation of the body suggested by the landscapes culminate in the seascapes, which are universes of substance unbound by any fixed bodily form.

In summary, Courbet's landscape painting is less about the representation of individual bodies and more about the bodily *experience* of landscape, one in which viewing is recast as a return to the origin through layers of substance. As Michael Fried, who has pursued the experiential component of the landscapes most thoroughly, puts it:

> "An experience of duration is also strongly posited by Courbet's version of dark-ground painting, with its implicit temporal metaphorics of light emerging from darkness and form from formlessness: indeed some paintings in which that technique is most in evidence, most notably certain landscapes of forest scenes, allow their representational content to be fully made out only gradually, in and through acts of attention, of reading, that need time to achieve their ends. There may be no *slower* picture in all Western art than the magnificent *Stream of the Puits noir, Valley of the Loue (Doubs)*" (also known as *The Stream*; fig. 3).[29]

Not only is this an outstanding characterization of what one undergoes in front of a Puits noir painting, its insights also open the door to issues that a cruder investigation of Courbet's paint might have glossed over. For instance, it diverts critical attention away from the thickness of Courbet's painting (which is easy enough to see) and instead channels it toward the much less easily defined visual effect of the dilated viewing time upon which his painting insists, as if the landscape were leading us to some faraway unknown origin.

It is tempting to consider, following Fried, this deceleration of the gaze as the overarching principle of Courbet's entire oeuvre. Such a reading could help overcome the sometimes overly strict division drawn between the artist's figure and landscape painting. But it would also have the disadvantage of all too easily eliding works done in different genres, made at different times and at different scales, under the same all-encompassing rubric. Taken to an extreme, details as diverse—and as incommensurable—as back-turned figures, hand gestures, and signatures could all be co-opted as signs of slow advance, the only limit to such totalizing allegorization being the interpreter's own imagination.

It is therefore striking that the one aspect of Courbet's painting that seems to have escaped this kind of figurative reading is precisely the one that is most responsible for the feeling of deceleration in the first place: Courbet's unique handling of paint. The artist's deliberate touch-by-touch construction, his singular use of the palette knife and spatula, the surprising lack of heavy impasto, his use of hue and close value juxtapositions—none figure in the most imaginative and authoritative analysis of the landscapes' unusually distended temporality. Indeed, it is clear that, because knife-strokes and paint layering do not easily lend themselves to allegorical interpretation as figures of forward progression—the way people looking or moving

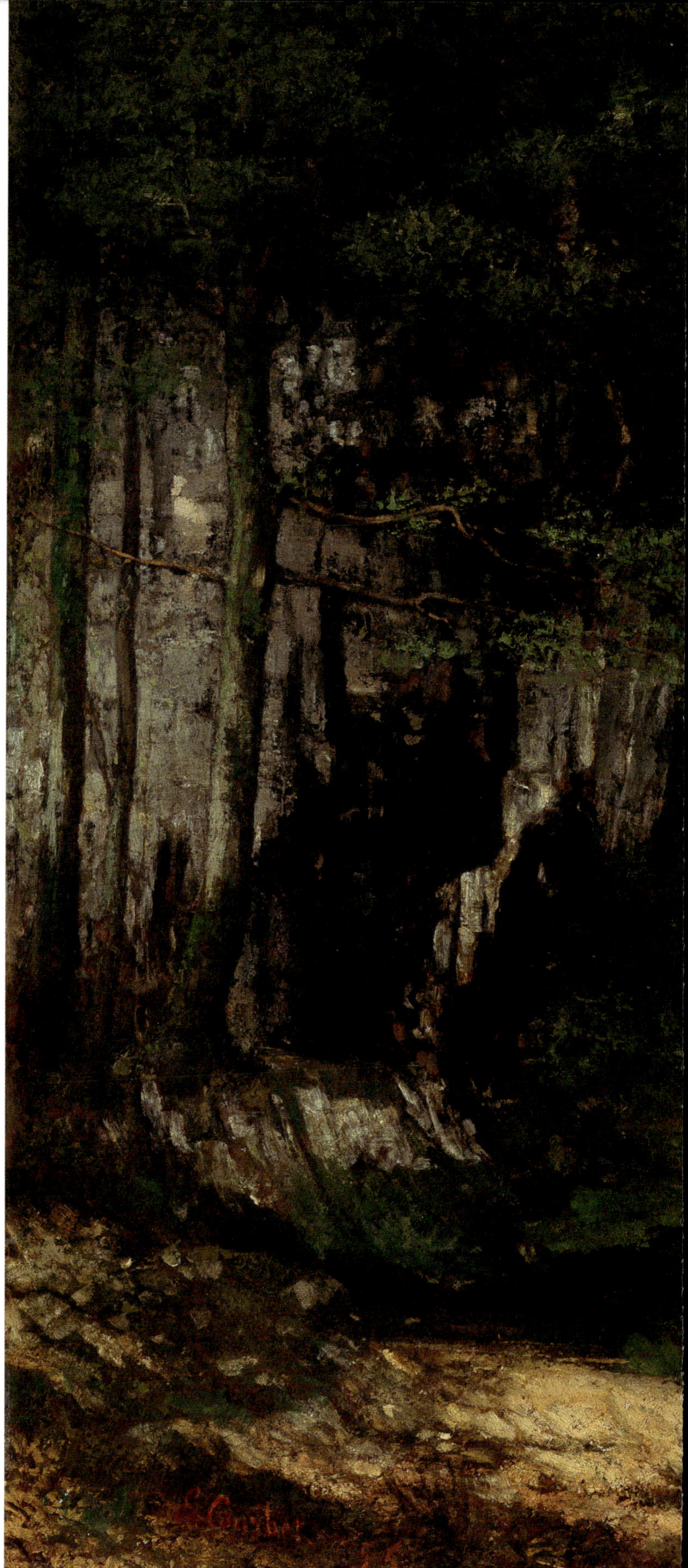

3 | *The Stream*, 1855. Oil on canvas, 104 × 137 cm.
National Gallery of Art, Washington, D.C.

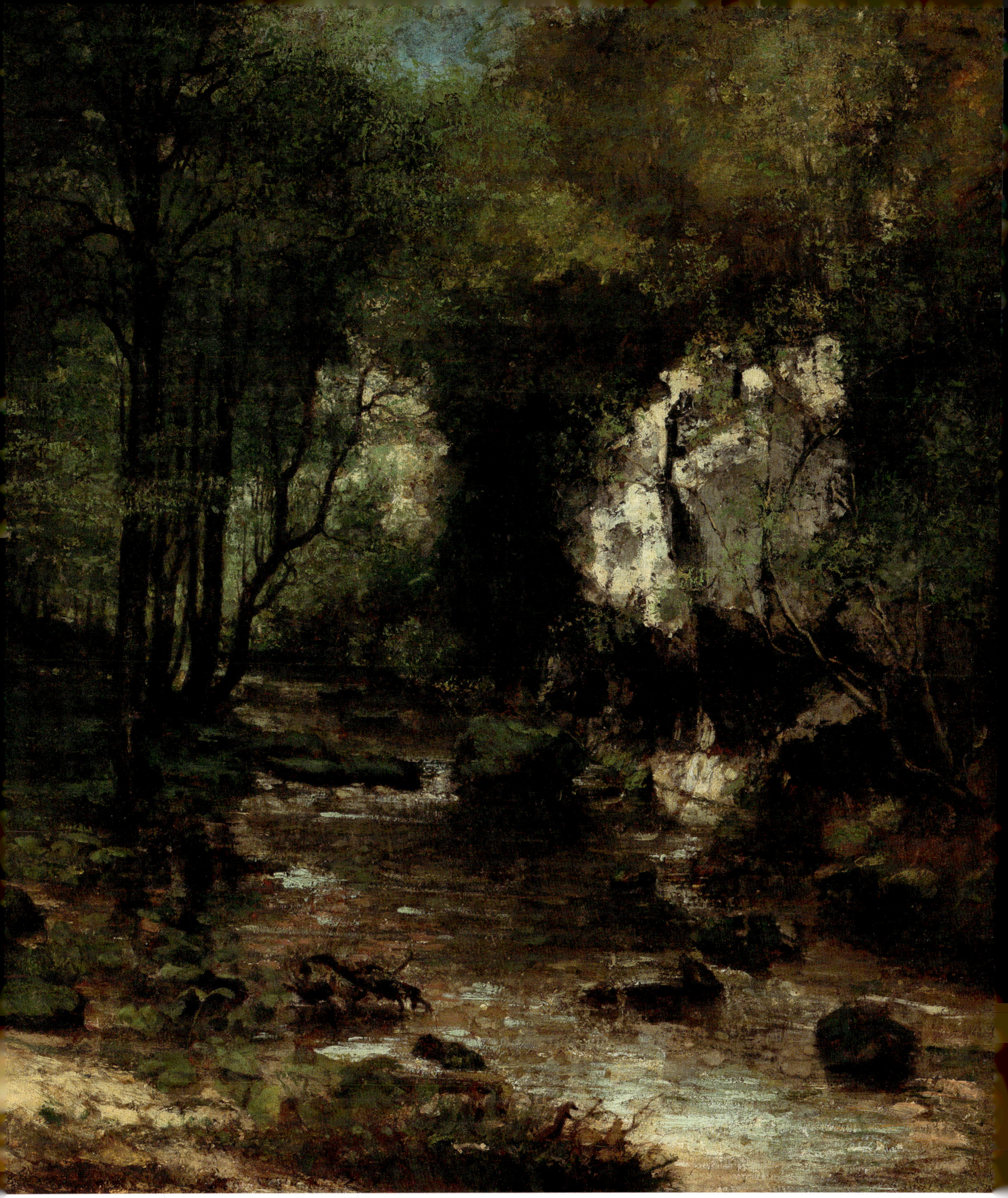

in a certain direction do, or, less obviously, traces of the artist's presence in front of the canvas—they are left out of the discussion. By contrast, this study emphasizes the means of representation at the level of the pictorial mark. It is key for understanding not only the illusion of imagined entry but also the two related yet slightly different features of Courbet's landscape painting discussed at the beginning of the Introduction: the extraordinary co-substantiality of image and paint, as well as the impression of returning to an origin.

For this reason, this book concentrates on the material construction of individual works. Painstaking analysis of brushstrokes, knife-marks, paint layers, and surface textures is crucial to understanding Courbet's technique of evoking origins and substances. At the time Courbet was painting, the public was interested in the "bigger picture," so to speak, rather than the "technical details," and art historians writing about the period have followed suit. However, in Courbet's landscapes the minute processes by which an entire world (and not just select objects from it, as in still life) materially comes into being have become for the first time precisely the bigger picture, i.e. the subject matter of the work. If the analysis of visual form proposed here at times verges on the overemphatic, it is only because Courbet placed equal emphasis on the creation of form in his own paintings.

Collaborations between conservators and art historians will hopefully continue to shed light on Courbet's technique, just as technology will hopefully improve the quality of reproductions (the landscapes' unique visual effects are notoriously difficult to capture). But for the time being, given the relative paucity of technical studies, arguments throughout the book have been based primarily, though not exclusively, on visual observation.[30] Skeptics might object that the paintings have been damaged and treated beyond repair, making any conclusion about their original state at best speculative. This would be especially true of landscape, a genre in which texture and tone often figure more prominently than composition and contour, which are essentially elements of drawing. Despite the inevitable ravages of time, the last two are usually easy to pinpoint long after their creation. It is often simple to decipher the outline of a tree or edges of a riverbank in a landscape painting, no matter how old the canvas (a process that infrared reflectography has made even more straightforward). By contrast, the desaturation (or even outright change in hue) of pigments over time and alterations to the paint layers because of restoration are more difficult to analyze, especially in the cases of such technically inventive artists as Courbet. It would be reasonable to suppose, for instance, that the lack of sharp, raised edges in Courbet's knife-marks can be understood in terms of the harsh treatments that have sucked the life out of them. However, following this line of argument, any painting of the period, subjected to the same process, should in theory undergo the same sort of flattening. Yet this is not the case. Many contemporaneous paintings, since lined, retain visible traces of the tool. Moreover, there are a small number of unlined Courbets—which according to this view should have fresh and unadulterated impasto—where marks appear nonetheless purposefully flattened, just as in treated canvases. In summary, despite some inevitable damage to the surfaces of Courbet's paintings over time, there is still much to be gleaned from them.

Nowhere is this more relevant than in the study of Courbet's signature palette-knife technique. As the name implies, the *couteau à palette* (palette knife) is a handheld blade used to manipulate paint on the palette before its application onto a physical support. Anthea Callen, Matthias Krüger, and Frédérique Desbuissons have greatly expanded our knowledge of its use in the nineteenth century and its characterization in the press.[31] A close cousin of the spatula and trowel, the palette knife came in assorted shapes and sizes. Throughout the book "palette knife" will stand for any metal-edged implement for applying paint, except in cases where more precise identification is called for. The task of identifying Courbet's implement is less challenging than describing its effects. Courbet studies suffer from the poverty of the language used to describe his signature technique.[32] Did Courbet paint thinly or thickly? How many layers did he use? Why did he choose knife over brush and vice versa? Any attempt to answer such questions must sort through the period's often divergent assessments of his painting in terms of form, texture, and thickness. Accordingly, the book's opening chapter briefly examines the artist's use of the palette knife through the eyes of his contemporaries and successors. Rather than favoring one of the various views, Chapter 1 proposes that the opposing descriptions of Courbet's knife-painting result from the inherently contradictory nature of knife-painting itself. Courbet used the tool to create with paint various effects, alternatively flat or bulbous, thin or thick, opaque or translucent, and much of the impact of the landscapes derives from the artist's expert harnessing of the implement. Courbet began to realize the full potential of those effects only in the early 1860s, in such landscapes as *Stream in the Forest* (see fig. 10) and *Source of the Lison* (see fig. 17), where it is evident that he was breaking away from the era's leading practitioners of classical and Romantic landscape, Camille Corot (with whom Courbet painted side by side in 1862) and Théodore Rousseau (who depicted some of the same sites as Courbet).

Finally, in addition to studying Courbet's works closely, this book engages with Cézanne scholarship. Among the next generation, Paul Cézanne took on the search for origins and the world-building evident in Courbet's landscapes. It is hard to think of another painter to whom the gradual material construction of the world mattered more. The two artists shared in particular a fascination with geology and the idea of a vastly expanded global timescale or deep time—admirably dissected in Cézanne's case by Nina Athanassoglou-Kallmyer, John Elderfield, and Faya Causey.[33] In addition, both lay bare process and technique in their paintings. To a far greater extent than their peers, Courbet and Cézanne demonstrate the way in which their marks are assembled, as if each was vital for the structure of the whole. For this reason, much of this study's terminology—touch-by-touch technique, unitary mark-making, constructive strokes, and so forth—will have a distinctly Cézannean ring. Of course, there are obvious differences between the painters from Ornans and Aix-en-Provence. First, Courbet could materially re-create the world only under peculiar conditions, the deepest grottoes, the most expansive oceanic horizons. What Courbet endeavored to observe at the world's limits, Cézanne found outside his doorstep, in his studio, or almost wherever he looked. Second, Courbet was driven to make the world pictured in his landscapes viscous and paint-like, somber and encroaching. Cézanne, by contrast, knew no such limits. A distant mountain, a sun-drenched rock, an arid Provençal field, the bay of l'Estaque: all these were fair game for his particular brand of pictorial realization through touch and color. By turning a limit case into an everyday perception, Cézanne updated Courbet's technique for the Impressionist age.

If the first three chapters of this book constitute perhaps a Cézannean reading of Courbet's landscapes, Chapter 4 looks at Cézanne's 1865–66 palette-knife paintings as fully realized responses to Courbet's sensuous, substantive universe. Developed in dialogue with his close friend Émile Zola, Cézanne's creative interpretation of Courbet led to an internally conflicted palette-knife technique with a propensity to both create a world and destroy it, something we hardly ever witness in Courbet's landscapes. While at first glance this reading may seem to isolate Cézanne's early palette-knife painting from his later work, this is not the case. Indeed, Chapter 4 and the final Coda insist on its relevance, even prescience, in regard to the "mature" work of the 1880s and later. For if the scholarship of Clark and Kathryn A. Tuma has suggested that, far from discovering the bedrock of his sensations, what Cézanne was demonstrating in his last decades was the impossibility of establishing any kind of secure base or ground, be it perceptual, pictorial, or material, then this deconstructive project was in retrospect already present at the beginning of his career in the earliest palette-knife paintings.[34] Impressionism may have subsequently steered that impulse in certain directions—to be revisited, for instance, in the 1870s at Auvers-sur-Oise and Pontoise—but picturing a world caught simultaneously in a state of making and undoing is something already broached, albeit in an almost deliberately infantile fashion, in Cézanne's early work. With Cézanne, the possibility—but also the ultimate impossibility—of an absolute ground zero as a kind of uncompromised origin is installed as a dream of modernism, to be discovered and rediscovered at periodic intervals throughout its subsequent history. As the works where Cézanne first realized this condition were direct responses to Courbet, the latter's landscapes are in turn revealed to be, fittingly, the origin of the *problem of the origin* in modern painting.

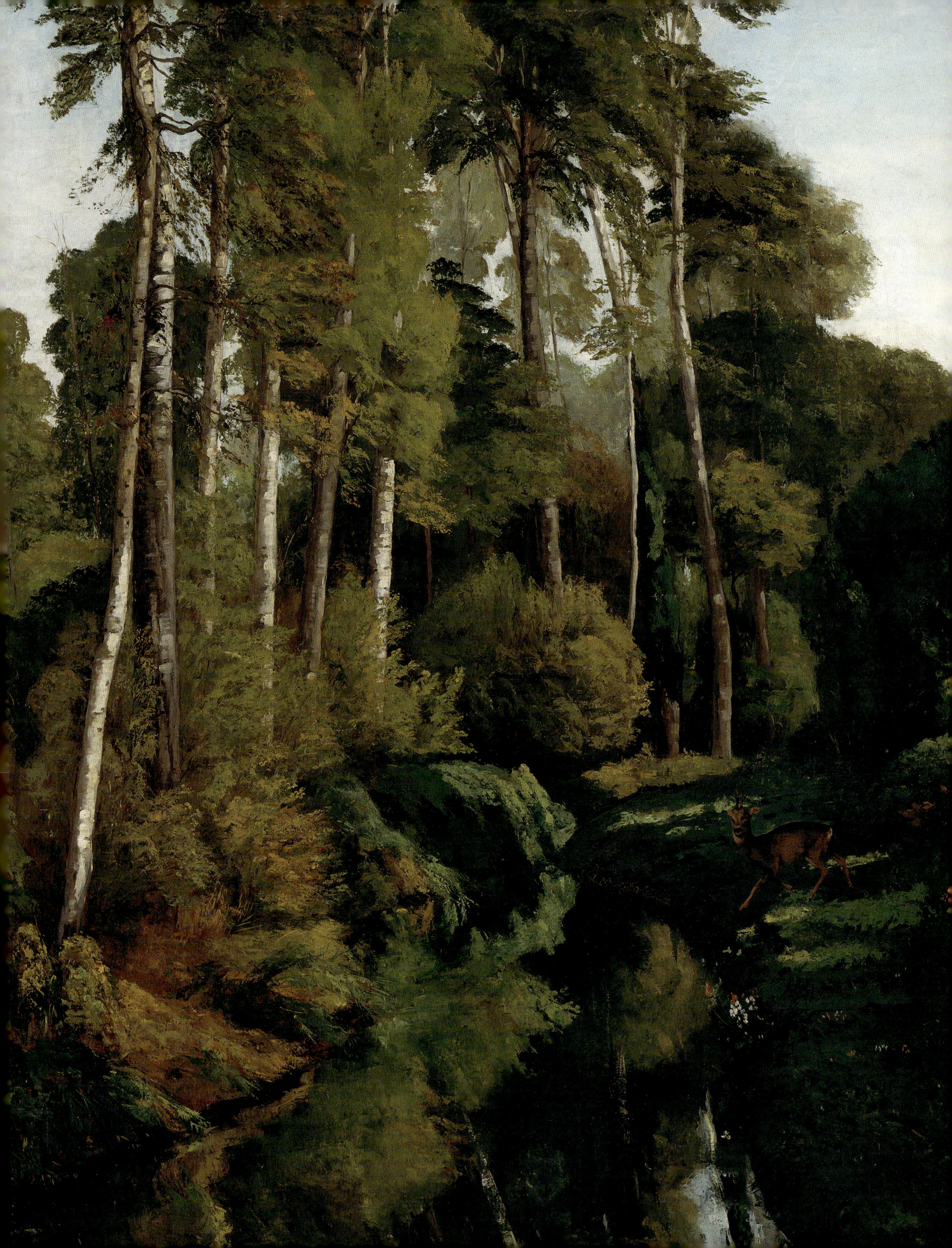

Chapter 1

BAGS OF PAINT IN GLASSY SKINS

Courbet's first ambitious landscape of origin was *The Stream* (see fig. 3). At over a meter wide, it would have been perhaps the most impressive of the three landscapes accepted to the 1855 Universal Exhibition. As first showings go, the timing was opportune. In addition to the 11 works in the official exhibition, visitors would have been able to see 42 more in Courbet's *Pavilion of Realism*, a private exhibition organized outside the government-sponsored Universal Exhibition. Inside the pavilion, Salon-scale canvases such as *A Burial at Ornans* and *The Peasants of Flagey Returning from the Fair* (1850; Musée des Beaux-Arts et d'Archéologie de Besançon), because of their sheer size and scale, would have dominated visually. Roughly a third of the works listed in the catalogue were landscapes. What's more, landscape was at the heart of one of the show's most spectacular works, the monumental *The Artist's Studio* (1854–55; Musée d'Orsay, Paris). Within a grand studio, Courbet, life-size and flanked by friends and characters who in his own words summed up seven years of his artistic life, can be seen at his easel, painting a landscape.

For the purposes of this book, what is most curious about this landscape—a composite Franc-comtois river-plus-cliff scene with a judicious balance of sky, water, and land—is how *unlike The Stream* it is. Eugène Delacroix, the doyen of the Romantic School, had complained that the landscape in *The Artist's Studio* had the effect of putting "too much true sky in the middle of the painting"; no such danger lurked when it came to *The Stream*.[1] The latter pictured an altogether different kind of landscape: a view of the Brême River 3 kilometers outside Ornans as it passes a deep natural well known as the Puits noir and funnels through a heavily shaded narrow gorge framed by rich foliage and rocky crags, producing in the viewer a disturbing sense of physical isolation, of being plunged alone into an uninhabited world so full of substance that escape from it seems futile.

When Courbet, after an eight-year hiatus, revisited the site, known as the Puits noir even though the well itself never appears in the paintings, as the subject of a series of stunning canvases painted between 1863 and 1865, he kept many aspects of the 1855 prototype intact—the material lushness, the point of view from practically mid-stream, and a certain eerie timelessness brought about by an almost complete lack of direct sunlight. Yet the new versions differed noticeably in other respects. For landscapes that appeared to be bursting with matter, there was a surprising economy of means in terms of their painterly execution. Whereas in the 1855 *Stream*, Courbet did not hesitate to accumulate details as necessary—extra brushed-in leaves in the foreground, dark branches and patches of shadow painted over rocks, further layers of encrustation—the later examples were painted with minimal fuss, the strategy apparently being to apply the most assured of brush- and knife-strokes in as few layers as possible to avoid overelaboration. Courbet also began to compress space by making the distance between viewer and background collapse even more dramatically and by eliminating visual hurdles such as the cluster of trees dividing the 1855 composition in two.

By 1864, Courbet had learned how to coax matter into being in his landscapes without excessive retouching. Two important events had led the painter to this point: first, the representation of natural origins had become important enough to him to warrant an entire series of landscapes on the subject; and second, he had gained the technical means to achieve their extraordinary organicism. Landscapes such as *Stream of the Puits noir* (see fig. 1) would have been impossible without either: without an altered technique, the later, smaller versions of the site would have appeared overworked rather than materially sumptuous and incredibly thick; without an interest in origins, Courbet might never have returned to the motif of the Puits noir and instead looked elsewhere for inspiration. In the case of his originary landscapes, the invention of the new technique (a novel way of wielding the palette knife and brush to mold form) historically preceded the discovery of new motifs (the depiction of origins). In order to lay the groundwork for the discussion of origins in Chapter 2, this chapter will examine the shift in Courbet's painterly methods around 1862–63, when the surfaces of his landscapes begin to take on an organic, skin-like appearance. The argument is that Courbet's heightened attention to the transparency, color, size, and thickness of his pictorial marks at this time belies conventional readings of his painting as a kind of blunt masonry. Taking into account the complexities of his technique provides us in turn with a more nuanced way of distinguishing his landscape painting from that of the leading practitioners of his day, Camille Corot and Théodore Rousseau.

SIDE BY SIDE

During a long residence in the Saintonge from 1862 to 1863—that is, during the period immediately preceding his *Puits noir* series of mid-decade—Courbet came into the orbit of a community of artists and patrons that would push his art in new and unexpected directions, eventually leading him fundamentally to alter his approach to painting landscape. The impetus was meeting the collector Étienne Baudry in 1861. At the time of their first encounter, Courbet could not have imagined that he would soon spend almost a year in the Saintonge province at Baudry's invitation. Like his old friend and fellow Saintongeais, the art critic Jules-Antoine Castagnary, Baudry had abandoned law school after arriving in Paris and began fraternizing with the group of Realist artists and writers who were often found gathering at the Brasserie Andler in the capital. The meeting between artist and collector, most likely facilitated by Castagnary (who himself had met Courbet only the previous year), was highly positive. Baudry acquired some works practically on the spot and secured the friendship of an artist whose sensibilities, if not politics, matched his own; Courbet gained a young, rich, and passionate patron whose advocacy on his behalf, like that of Castagnary, would extend well beyond the artist's death in 1877.[2] In 1848, at the age of 18, Baudry had inherited vineyards and land from his father, a *notaire* (legal administrator) during the government of the July Monarchy (1830–48). This inheritance included the property of Rochemont in the commune of Fontcouverte next to the main town of Saintes. Beyond the agrarian interests on which his income depended, Baudry committed much time and energy to two other activities: art and politics.

Courbet was neither the first artist invited to Rochemont nor the last. From 1860 to 1861, the landscape painter Louis-Auguste Auguin had temporarily lived and worked on the grounds in a specially built studio before eventually settling in the nearby hamlet of Port-Berteau. Camille Corot, whom Auguin cited as his teacher, would come in August 1862 for a brief stay of around two weeks, a couple of months after Courbet's own arrival in May 1862. All three painters would contribute works to an exhibition in Saintes for the benefit of the poor from January to February 1863, an event that perhaps marks the high point of Courbet's visit, at least as far as artistic matters are concerned.[3] The chateau at Rochemont was also an unofficial meetinghouse for those opposed to the imperial regime of Napoleon III. In addition to Castagnary, frequent guests included: Phoedora Gaudin, lawyer and founder in 1844 of the radical *L'Union* (suppressed after the 1851 coup d'état); Frédéric Mestreau, republican member of the municipal council and future prefect under the Third Republic; Victor Vallein, ex-Bonapartist turned liberal editor of the local newspaper *L'Indépendant de la Charente-Inférieure*; and Baudry's cousin, the art critic Théodore Duret.[4]

Surrounded by kindred spirits and supported by Baudry, Courbet had almost ideal working conditions. Although he integrated himself into local society, the political situation of the time had surprisingly little impact on his landscapes. Courbet's paintings of the Parc de Rochemont, the banks of the Charente, La Roche Courbon, and other local sites are seemingly light-hearted works tailored to the tastes of men of means

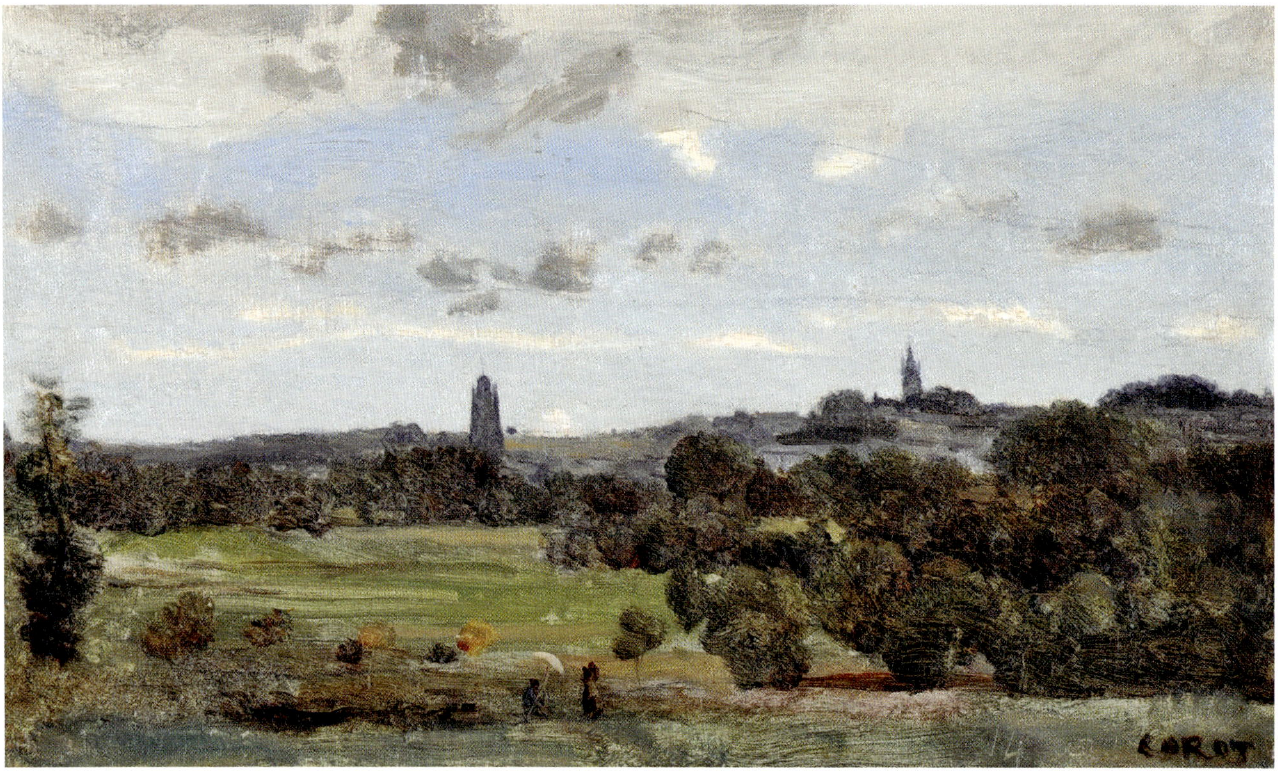

4 | Jean-Baptiste-Camille Corot, *Saintonge Landscape. View of Saintes from the Route of St. Jean d'Angely*, 1862. Oil on canvas, 22 × 36 cm. Musée des Beaux-Arts de la Boverie, Liège

whose privileged position in society had granted them unfettered access to nature—just as it had to Rochemont's previous chatelains, except that now the views spoke less to the patron's noble status and more to a much-needed respite from the stresses of modern life. Indeed, this is exactly how the Realist critic Champfleury would define the role of landscape in 1862: "if a man feeling blasé were to have in front of his eyes a foggy morning by Corot or a rock casting a shadow on the grass by Courbet, he would feel refreshed and would think about being able to find, just two leagues away, the fresh sensations denied to him by the art of the Rue Laffite."[5]

The Saintonge views seem to do little to dissuade us from the veracity of Champfleury's argument: that landscape offers nothing but escapist relief to the modern bourgeoisie, confirming their absolute control over Nature, in the sense of defining it and limiting others' access to it. Any attempt to rethink Nature would have to go to even further extremes than previous incarnations of Romanticism had in order to have any hope of success. Courbet's landscapes of origin appeared just at the historical moment when such a redefinition seemed all but foreclosed. In a move that might be considered the last gasp of a certain kind of naturalism within the European pictorial tradition, Courbet dared to imagine an intense somatic relationship to Nature that might resist alienation, however temporarily, a kind of bodily pleasure that was not (yet) the one of modern leisure.

Such an ambition could never be achieved in a single work or series. It would take Courbet several years to realize it. Nevertheless, one of the key moments in its development took place in the Saintonge period, in whose leisurely landscapes we would least expect it. Picking up where Champfleury's diagnosis of landscape left off, we can ask if the "fresh sensations" of a Corot or a Courbet were simply yet another temporary panacea

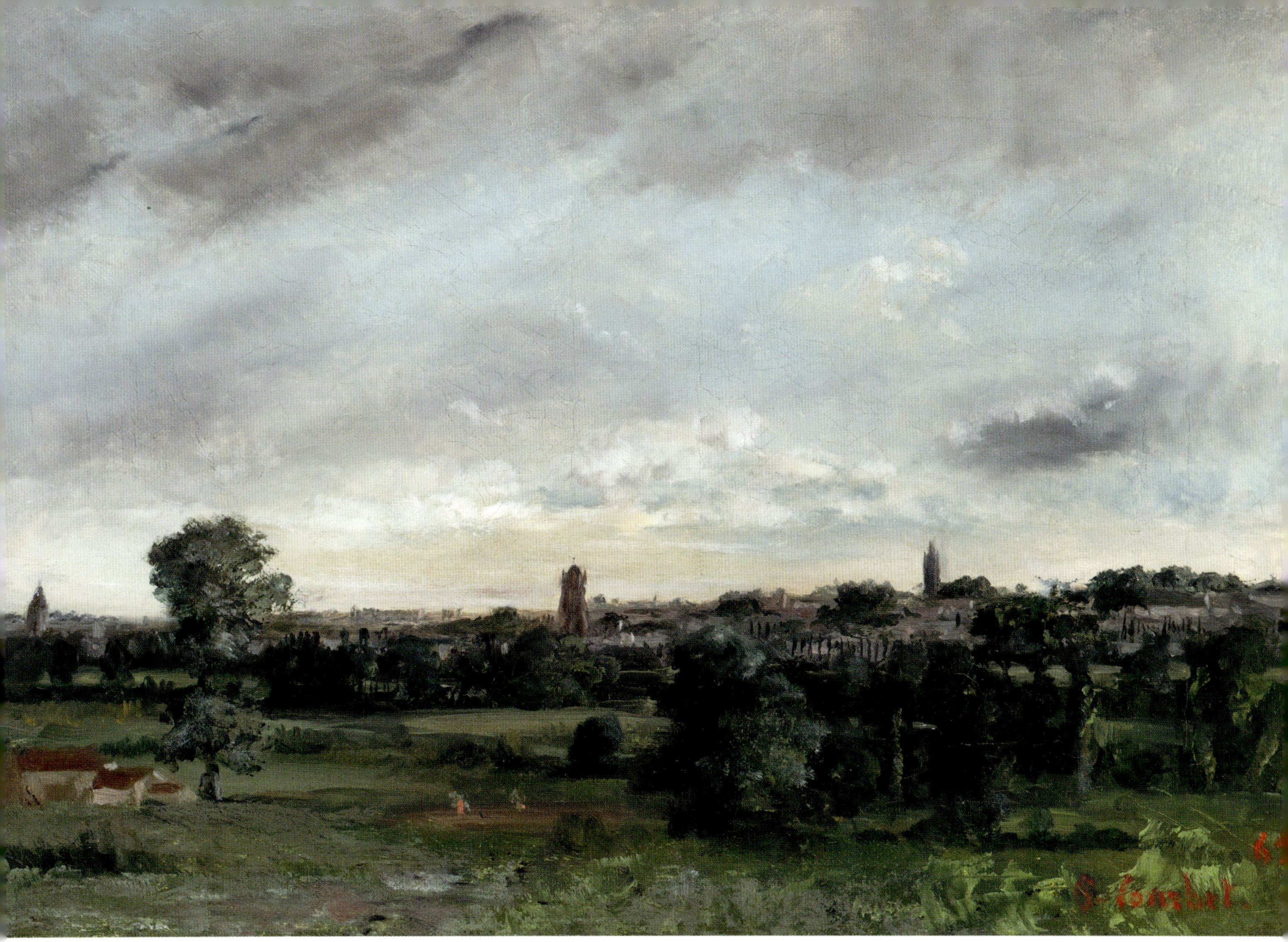

5 | *View of Saintes, from Lormont*, 1862. Oil on canvas, 32 × 46 cm. Galerie Talabardon & Gautier, Paris

6 | Jean-Baptise-Camille Corot, *Corner of the Park at Port-Berteau, near Rochemont (Charente-Intérieur)*, 1862. Oil on canvas, 46 × 38.2 cm. National Museum of Serbia, Belgrade

to urban malaise or if, on the contrary, they proposed an alternative, hopefully more permanent cure to it—a form of experience still rooted in the material world but not yet disenchanted with it. The question is not merely hypothetical; Corot and Courbet painted landscapes side by side in the summer of 1862. Their interaction therefore gives us a concrete historical example against which to test Champfleury's claim.

Surviving examples of side-by-side painting before Impressionism are exceedingly rare. While depictions of popular sites such as Bas-Bréau and the Gorges d'Apremont in the Forest of Fontainebleau abound, few were painted by two different artists at the exact same time. All the more reason, then, to examine closely the two extant pairs of side-by-side paintings by Corot and Courbet.[6] According to Duret, the two painters followed certain self-imposed conditions when working side by side in the Saintonge that summer: each painted before the motif on similarly sized canvas or supports and for the same amount of time, with easels set close enough to permit discussion but far enough away to hide what each artist was painting (figs. 4 and 5).[7]

When Duret came across paired views of Saintes for sale in Paris, he noted, "These two paintings certainly reveal the two artists' individual manners, more tender in Corot, more severe in Courbet."[8] Duret's assessment carries some weight, as he claimed to have been present at the moment of their creation. The tenderness that he discerns in the Corot is no doubt a function of the picture's light and even tone, a quality that has done much to guarantee the painter a place in art history. The exposure of an underlayer here and there does much to brighten certain sections, for instance in the striated middle ground and the clouds above it. But what is "more severe" about the slightly larger Courbet? Perhaps not only its more solemn greens but also its pastose upper half, seemingly thick with pressed pigment, at times knifed, unlike Corot's brushed sky.

Yet a comparison of the Saintes paintings and the entire oeuvres reveals the similarities, not the differences between the work of the two artists. Over the course of their joint experiment, Corot at times strayed far from his more familiar sun-baked Roman studies and Salon *paysages historiques* and toward the dark, enclosed *sous-bois* (undergrowth) preferred by Courbet. For his part, Courbet sometimes drastically reduced and lightened his palette, techniques that are the hallmark of Corot. The meeting of the two painters brought together two seemingly opposed artistic paradigms.

A second surviving pair shows Nelly Auguin, the painter's wife, promenading in a Fort-Berteau forest: with children in the Courbet, without them in the Corot (figs. 6 and 7). From the placement of details—the forked tree in the mid-ground left of center, the leafy trunk on the right, the bright sunlit patch in the central foreground—Corot's easel was positioned slightly higher and to the right of Courbet's. As with the twin city views of Saintes, the two painters worked side by side. Let us first look at Corot's contribution, the small sketch-like *Corner of the Park at Port-Berteau* (fig. 6). At first glance, nothing could be further from his imposing Salon paintings, such as *The Bath of Diana* (fig. 8), which had been acquired at the Salon de la Société des Amis des Arts de Bordeaux in 1858 and was on view at the

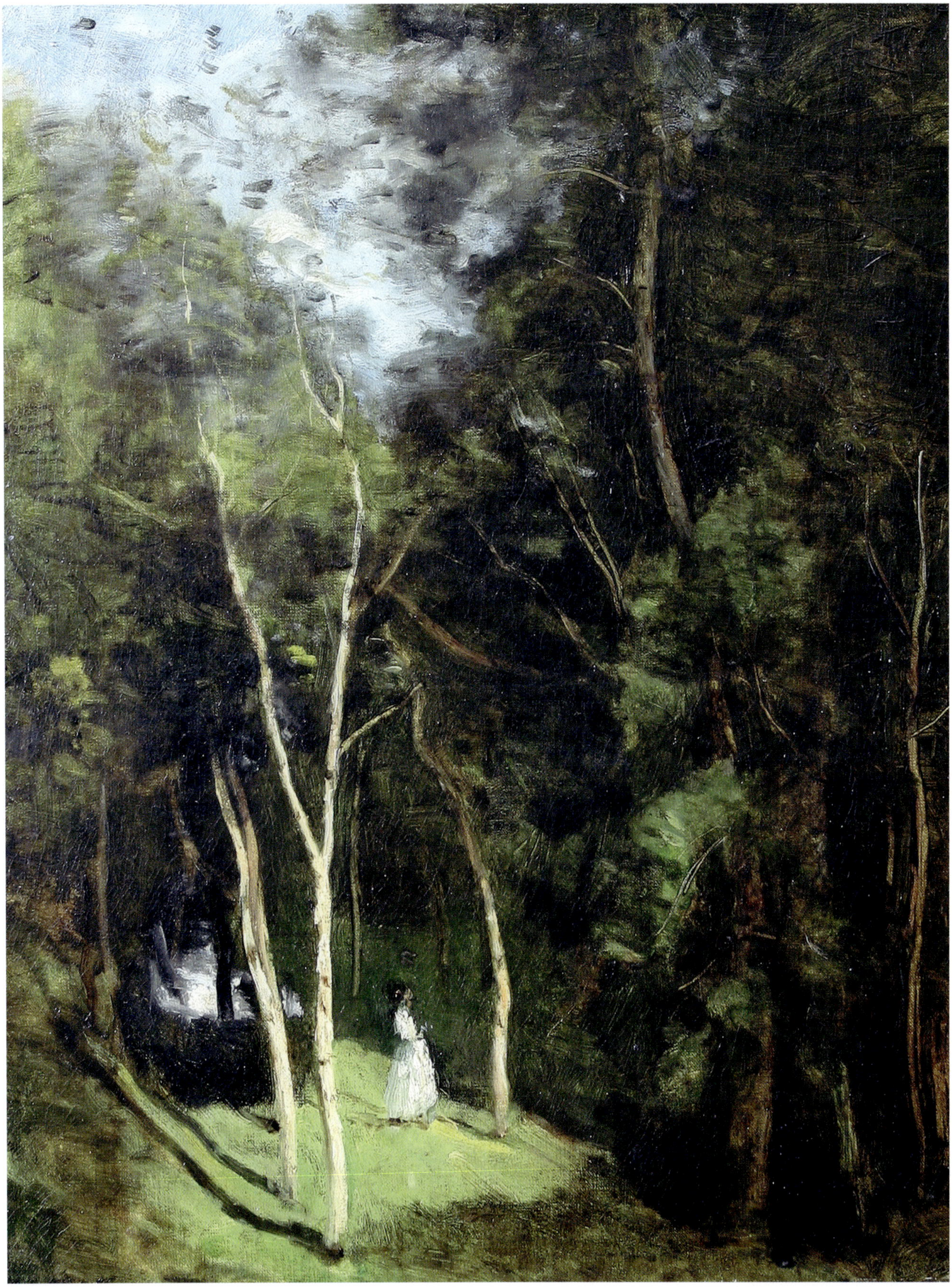

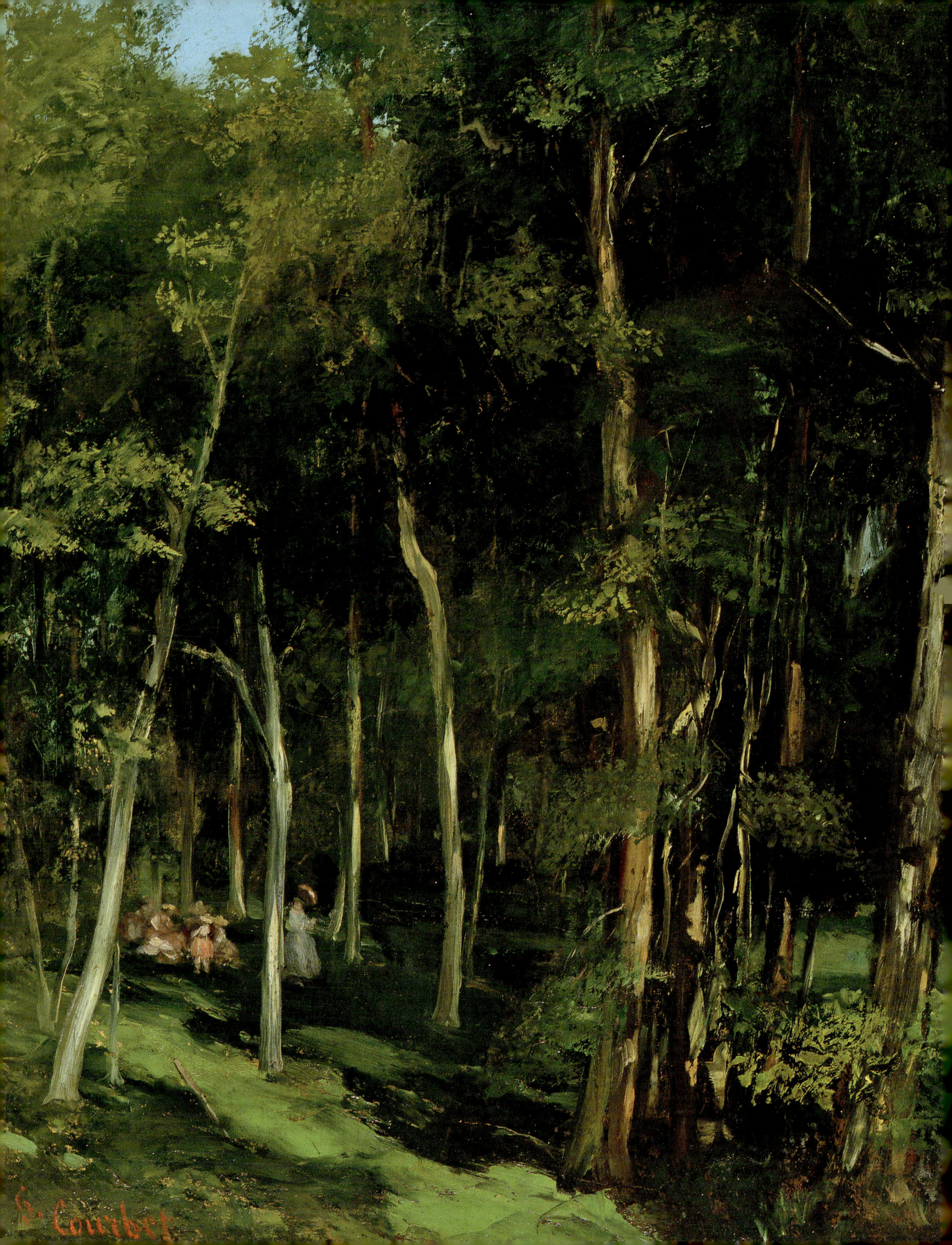
G. Courbet

7 | *Beneath the Trees at Port-Berteau: Children Dancing*, *ca.*1862. Oil on canvas, 66.5 × 52.1 cm. The Fitzwilliam Museum, Cambridge, England

museum in that regional city. The grand classicizing landscape dwarfs the open-air study in size, scale, and ambition, as would be expected of a work from the 1855 Universal Exhibition. Yet they also have something in common. The right-hand side of *Bath of Diana* prefigures in many respects the composition of *Corner of the Park at Port-Berteau.* Towering trees encroach upon nymphs standing in a spot-lit patch of riverbank. Although the forest appears all-encompassing, there is just enough of an opening at upper right to let light pierce the thicket, bathing the figures in a glow and casting what lay on either side into shadow. The silvery atmosphere permeating this part of the scene is made possible by making the forest canopy semi-transparent, almost feathery. These elements—a blue aperture, a bright patch of earth, dramatic shadows, and tall surrounding trees—can be found in Corot's *Port-Berteau*, just in the cruder form befitting of a sketch.

Yet at the same time, the scene's cropping and paint handling suggest a Courbetian influence. The painter from Ornans had a predilection for shaded undergrowth with little to no sky. His landscapes were described on at least one occasion as "unlivable for those who like to breath fully from their breast," where "currents that should flow freely through the air from sky to valley are replaced by the thick atmosphere of the rue Hautefeuille studio."[9] Perhaps Corot likewise felt suffocated by the "thick atmosphere" of the *sous-bois* (which might explain the addition of an indecipherable blue-and-white patch at the rear of his landscape). Whatever the case, the general disposition of the picture is dark for Corot. Even the solitary patch of light-green ground cover does not brighten the scene so much as render its shaded parts all the more mysterious. If Corot was gravitating toward his partner's cropping and color, Courbet likewise took elements from Corot. In Courbet's contribution to their game, *Beneath the Trees at Port-Berteau: Children Dancing* (fig. 7), Courbet rotated his support from his usual horizontal landscape orientation to the vertical one adopted by Corot, a simple change of axis that immediately opens up the picture. In terms of color, Courbet makes a gesture toward Corot's lighter palette (although Courbet's greens are still much more saturated—that is, they have not acquired a softer Corotian pallor through the addition of extra gray or white).[10]

Although Corot's and Courbet's approximation of each other's styles might seem a predictable outcome of working next to each other, it was not always the case, as the work of one of their less-heralded companions testifies. The Alsatian painter Hippolyte Pradelles opened a studio in Saintes in 1855 and soon attracted a local clientele, including Baudry. By 1862, he was a regular at Rochemont and joined Courbet and Corot on painting expeditions upon their arrival. In Pradelles's *Moonlight Promenade by Boat* (also known as *L'Echo interrogé*; fig. 9), Courbet stands in a boat guided by Pradelles, with (probably) Charlotte Pradelles, the partner of Hippolyte, and Nelly Auguin seated together in the middle and Auguin taking up the rear.[11] However, *Moonlight Promenade by Boat* is more than just a minigroup portrait of a "band of brothers" (and sisters).[12] Like *Corner of the Park at Port-Berteau* and *Beneath the Trees at Port-Berteau: Children Dancing*, Pradelles's picture also combines different aspects of Corot and Courbet. Pradelles uses

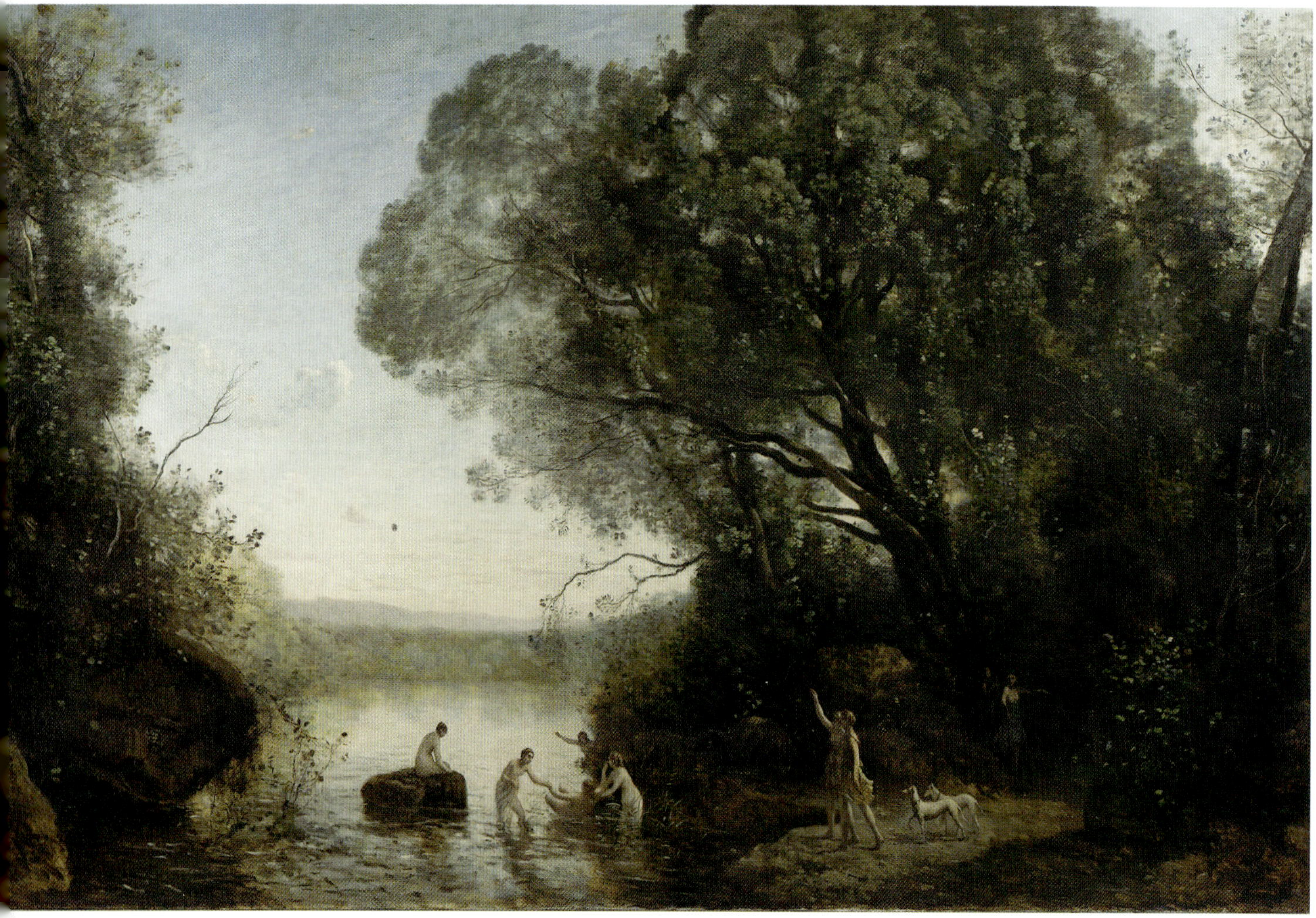

the template of the close view of the forest set against a body of water from Corot's *Bath of Diana* (albeit with less distance between viewer, tree, and background). However, *Moonlight Promenade by Boat* does not benefit from Corot's tone or Courbet's *sous-bois* composition. Instead, Pradelles fuses the compositional principles and scale of Corot's Salon painting (but not its tonal subtlety) with Courbet's demonstrative handling of paint. Pradelles's attempt to replicate the master's touch, however, is clumsy and uneconomical. Light and dark touches are mixed and applied in a rushed rather than a restrained and considered way.[13]

8 Jean-Baptiste-Camille Corot, *The Bath of Diana*, 1855. Oil on canvas, 168 × 257 cm. Musée des Beaux-Arts, Bordeaux

9 Hippolyte Pradelles, *Moonlight Promenade by Boat* (also known as *L'Echo interrogé*), 1863. Oil on canvas, 117 × 89 cm. Musée des Beaux-Arts, Strasbourg

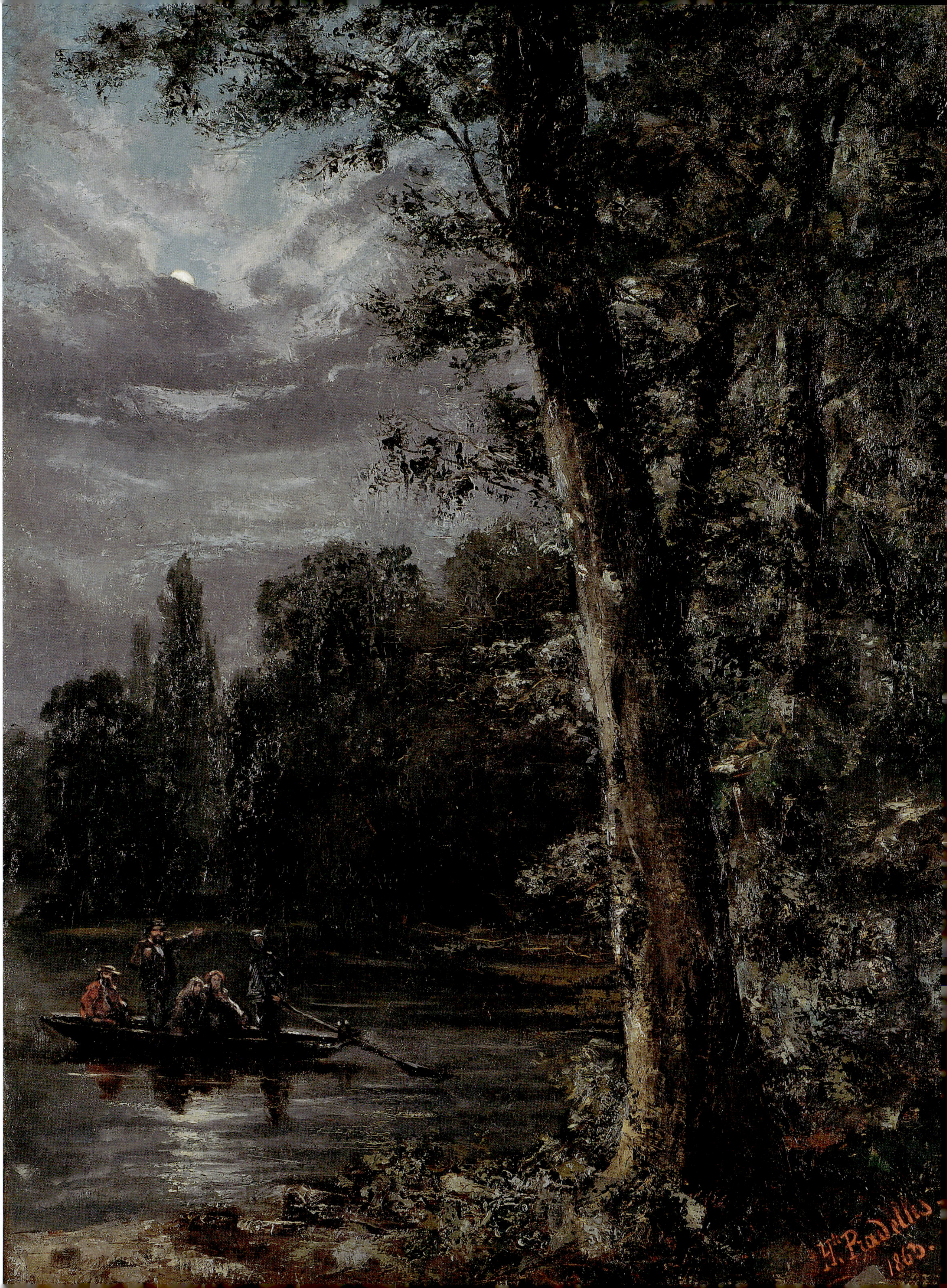

AT AN IMPASSE

By the end of the summer of 1862, Corot had left Rochemont and Courbet had moved to the nearby hamlet of Port-Berteau. There was talk of a fall exhibition of their work (along with that of Auguin and Pradelles). The show that eventually opened on 15 January 1863 comprised over 200 works spread out across four rooms on the ground floor of the Saintes town hall, including 48 by Courbet, 35 of which were landscapes.[14] Courbet's shadow loomed large over proceedings. "The broad manner of Courbet" would have been there for all to see, for instance, in Pradelles's *Moonlight Promenade by Boat*, one of the artist's 42 submissions.[15] As for Auguin's work, a review from *L'Indépendant de la Charente-Inférieure* said that there was "a lot of Courbet and little Auguin" in it.[16]

We do not know if Courbet exhibited the large vertical landscape *Stream in the Forest* in Saintes (fig. 10). Its dimensions alone, exceeding those of Pradelles's *Moonlight Promenade by Boat*, would have certainly provided an argument for its inclusion in the exhibition. But, most of all, it would have merited a place as a striking example of the new attitude toward color first broached in his side-by-side paintings. Perhaps the most stunning landscape of the Saintonge period, *Stream in the Forest* is a tour de force, demonstrating how to animate a landscape with minimal chromatic variation. The scene is mostly green, ranging from the dark, almost transparent layers in the undergrowth right of center to the bright yellowish and light greens next to them. Because he restricts his use of color, Courbet is forced to make some unusual choices. For example, the yellowish green to the left of the stream is repeated, in equal-size strokes, in the upper foliage. Whereas common sense says that the leafy cover in the far distance should be less clear and precise than the nearby shrubbery, here top and bottom are impossibly equivalent.[17]

Beneath the Trees at Port-Berteau: Children Dancing had already hinted at this deployment of green. In that smaller work, almost the exact same shade of light green is used in three different sections: the canopy at upper right, the foliage at lower left, and the streak of light raking across the foreground. This equivalence may have been acceptable in an open-air sketch, the making of which allowed only so many colors and only so much time for painting. But a studio picture such as *Stream in the Forest* demanded further refinement on the landscapist's part. For example, the laws of atmospheric perspective prescribed that outlines far from the eye become steadily less distinct as the landscape recedes into the distance and, conversely, that the parts of the landscape closest to the eye be more detailed, rules that Courbet did not follow.

In addition to adjusting color and focus, another tried-and-true way of arranging pictorial space was to erect framing elements at the edges (*coulisses*) and in the foreground (*repoussoirs*) in order to choreograph the movement of the viewer's gaze into the picture. However, such visual guideposts are largely absent from *Stream in the Forest*. Instead, our gaze hits an impasse at the central point where the stream disappears mysteriously into the landscape. At this nexus, a swath of light green

10 | *Stream in the Forest, ca.*1862. Oil on canvas, 156.8 × 114 cm. Museum of Fine Arts, Boston

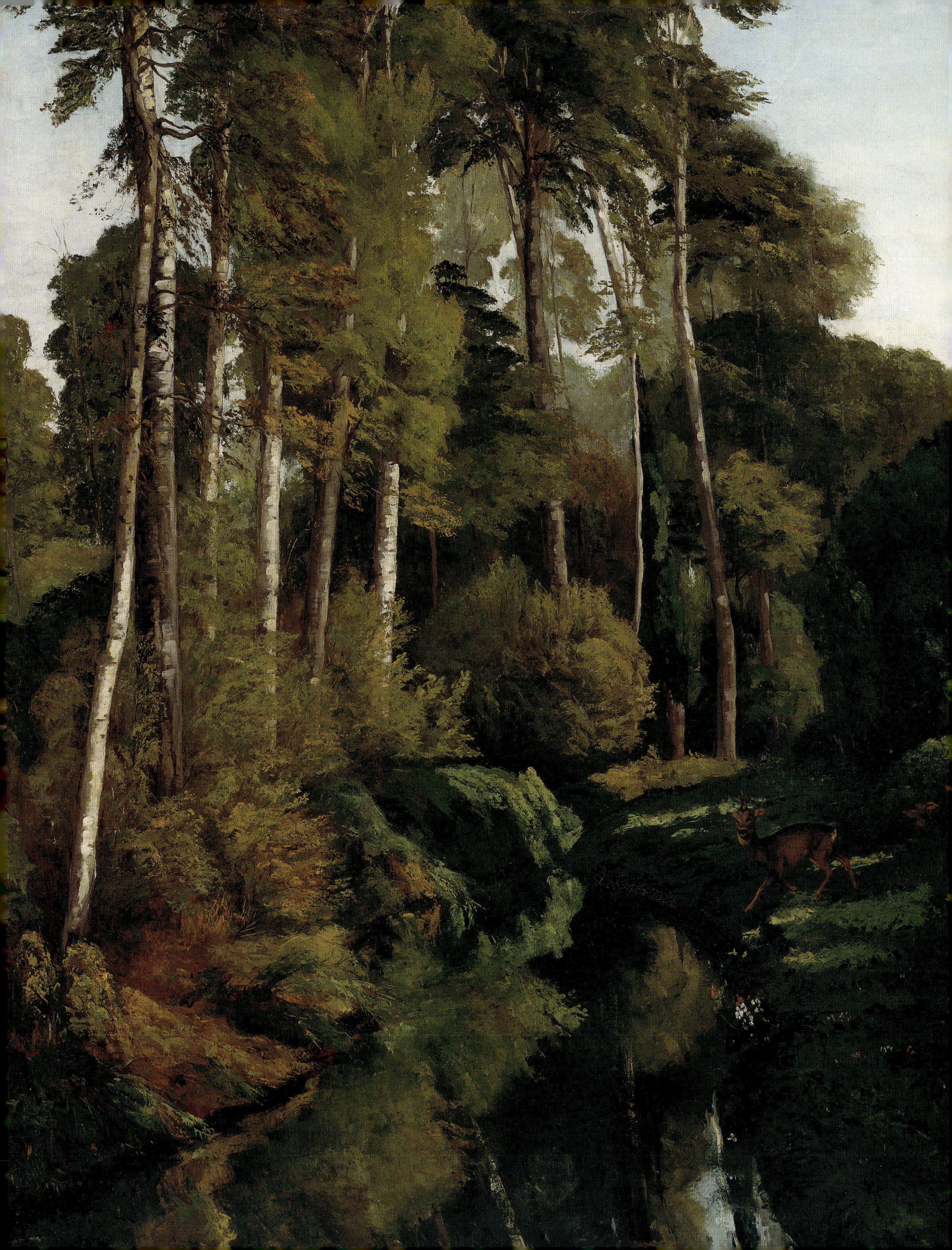

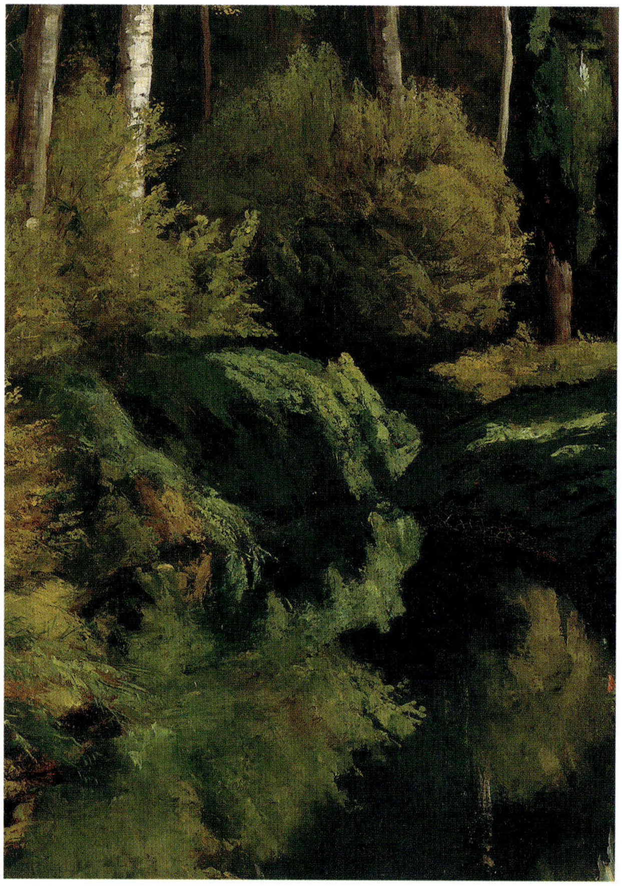

11 | *Stream in the Forest* (detail), *ca.*1862. Oil on canvas, 156.8 × 114 cm. Museum of Fine Arts, Boston

rises from the watery depths. This vigorously painted patch is supposed to represent an evanescent reflection in the water, a pale mirror image, not a solid entity in its own right, like its similarly colored counterpart on the riverbank. On closer inspection, we see that this effect is not an isolated occurrence; the entire surface of the stream (particularly the green touches along the stream's left bank) seems to have materialized.

As the reflected world solidifies, the real world becomes unhinged. The more we delve into the forest, the more we realize that it is barely holding itself together. Bushes, leaves, and grass, viewed at close range, never disclose an architecture of stems and branches. They float in, around, and on top of each other. The only stable features in this landscape are the tall gray tree trunks that, not coincidentally, are the only objects not painted in green, brown, or blue. But even *their* earthly moorings are cloaked, their stalks partially obscured, their leafy crowns decapitated. Courbet's scene is not a serene, unified view, but one breaking under pressure.

At this point, we can turn to the crucial and complicated issue of Courbet's mark-making—and how it does, or does not, relate to Corot's. Painterly gesture would seem to be the area where the painter from Ornans was most resistant to Corot's influence. There is nothing, for example, in Corot's *Corner of the Park at Port-Berteau* as thick as the light-green paint applied with a knife across the left foreground of Courbet's *Beneath the Trees at Port-Berteau: Children Dancing*. And there is nothing in the Courbet that evokes the silvery, ethereal mood of Corot's most recent works, all those poetic morning and twilight landscapes or *souvenirs* that had garnered him nearly universal admiration. But the story is different if we instead compare Courbet's facture to that of the early Italian Corot.

Consider the following review of *Corot: An Exhibition of Paintings, Drawings and Prints* (held in Edinburgh and London in 1965) by Lawrence Gowing:

> Nothing is visible except by grace of definite tonal intervals, and they are transcribed in pastes of a certain definite viscosity. Following the process, we become aware of still another aspect of the emotion that seized the painter, a feeling for the oil medium itself. The brush deposits its message without the slightest display of deftness or bravura. Rather, with its adhesive burden, it stumbles a little, minutely hesitant or precipitate.[18]

Although addressing Corot's work, the description corresponds most elegantly to Courbet's *Stream in the Forest*: an array of carefully modulated greens form "definite tonal intervals"; discrete, thick paint marks generate a sense of "definite viscosity," the surface seems to call attention to the "oil medium itself." The exception is the last part: "The brush deposits its message without the slightest display of deftness or bravura," the handling is "minutely hesitant." Although these words can be applied to Corot's modest touches, they seem inappropriate for Courbet's brazen marks, which are more than just "adhesive" covering; the extra heft has rendered them *physically palpable*. Instead of subtle gradations, viewers are confronted with, in works such as *Stream in the Forest*, block-like accumulations of distinct tones, seemingly unblended and bare, whose ancestors are the "definite tonal intervals" made up of "pastes of a certain definite viscosity" that Gowing identified in the work of Corot. Whereas Corot's brushstrokes are too "hesitant," all caution is discarded, by contrast, in Courbet's *Stream in the Forest*. Take again, for instance, the painting's epicenter. On the left bank, just as the stream seems to disappear around a bend, semi-transparent dark-green touches conjure up the faint traces of ground cover (fig. 11). Above these marks lies a more opaque, light-green pigment coalescing into a sort of sloping plant life whose direction and thickness suggests it was painted with a dry brush (notice how the paint drags across the surface instead of seamlessly blending into the underlayers, as a wet-on-wet application might yield). The same goes for its aqueous mirror image. Next observe the yellow-green bushes (or perhaps small trees) that hide, like a dirty veil, our view of the tree trunks where they hit the riverbank. These microdeposits are so individualized, and yet so consistent in thickness, that we can imagine Courbet painting them only with either a sponge or rag.[19] With three different greens, applied in three different touches, Courbet not only generates a sense of maximum density from minimum material, he also manages to make his landscape buckle, as if convulsing from within. The illusion of dense and hallucinatory matter, an illusion that is born from very little pictorial matter and seemingly even less painterly effort, is such an incredible—and unprecedented—accomplishment that it would take Courbet several years to come to terms with it.

The interaction with Corot caused Courbet to take this new direction. But there was also a stimulus from an unexpected source: flowers. That year, again and again, in sizes small and large, Courbet experimented with the capacity of brushwork to render, in loving detail, all sorts of petals, pistils, and stamens. Scholars have attributed this sudden burst of still-life production to the influence of Baudry and Gaudin and the richness of Rochemont's gardens. But what must have also captivated Courbet in this body of work was the pleasure of painting at small scale. Like every painter of flowers, Courbet was confronted with the problem of how to control, in something as intimate as a bouquet, the seemingly unlimited range of color and texture that floral arrangements make available to the artist. Part still life, part portrait, and by far the largest of the group of flower paintings made at Saintes, the impressive *The Trellis* (fig. 12) can be considered one particularly inventive solution. In the face of two competing demands—to emphasize the figure or the flowers— Courbet defied the convention that situated still life below figure painting in the hierarchy of the genres and focused on the flower display rather than the young woman (he was more in love with the hollyhocks than the peasant, said one critic).[20]

If we look long enough at *The Trellis*, we begin to detect some unusual features. First, the shape of the arrangement. It is neither a vased bouquet nor a wreath. "Body cavity" or "orifice" are better terms to describe the indented space from which a lone red hollyhock protrudes like a stuck-out tongue.[21] And where are the stems and the crisscrossed rods of the trellis itself? Some signs of physical support—natural or artificial—would counter the sense of weightlessness experienced in front of these blooms. Courbet has withheld from us the stability of anchorage, leaving us adrift among the petals.

Finally, there are the flowers themselves. Consider the pink double hollyhocks on top. Each petal is rendered by a single brushstroke of translucent pigment. The dark ground visually seeps into each one. Whereas an opaque color would appear flat if applied with such an individualized touch (or become carved into relief by a particularly heavy one), the translucency makes each petal appear as if emerging from the ground itself. The ability of translucent layers to model form is, of course, not new. But what the Old Masters took several painstakingly thin layers of glaze to achieve, Courbet accomplished with a few confident strokes, and sometimes even a single one. The more we look at *The Trellis*, the more we notice the sheer diversity of touch: A wispy curve of an orange lily; a collection of dots concentrated into multicolored umbellifers at lower left. Courbet handled his brush with such agility that a simple manual adjustment is enough to completely alter a flower's personality. A pair of white hollyhocks at lower right are outwardly exploding fans of striated brushstrokes. The examples of the same species visible just left of the central depression have an altogether different character. The petals are soft, the paint more

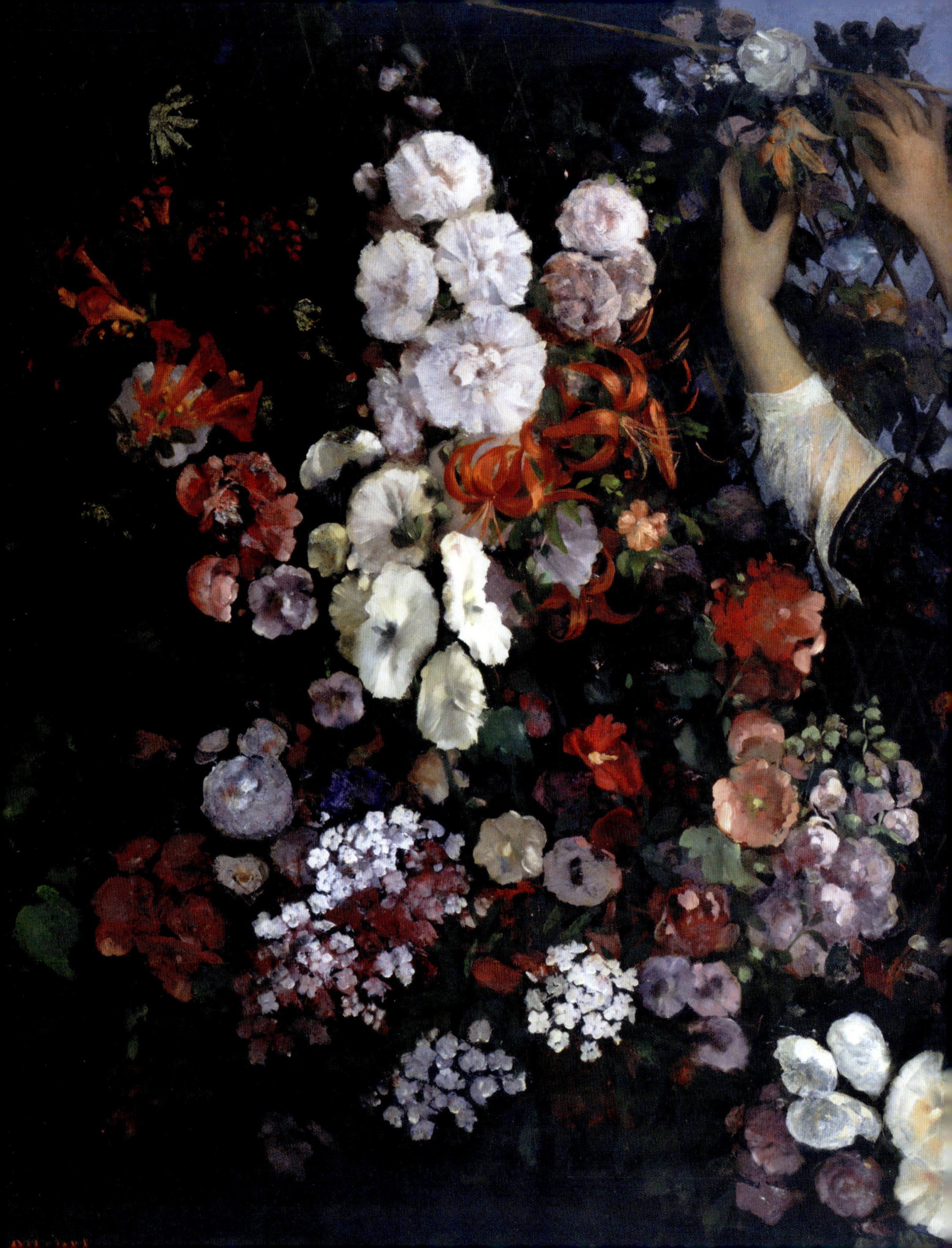

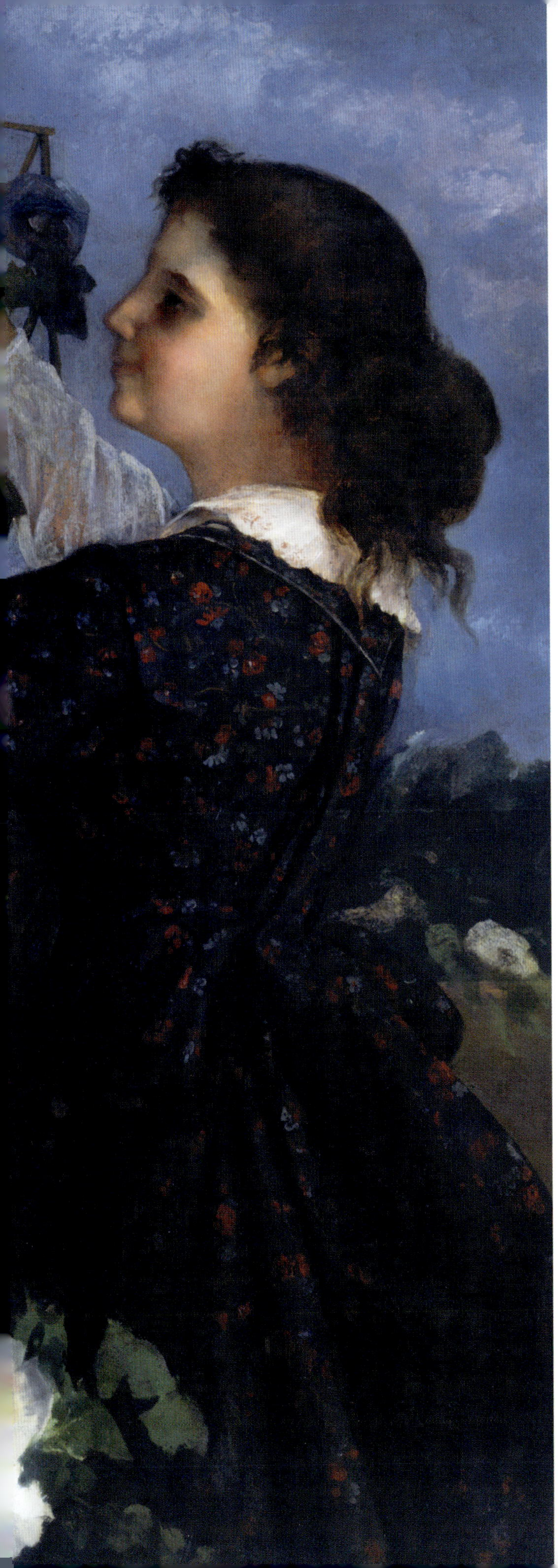

blended, the point of view more oblique. The result is a flower that is as much bodily organ as botanical specimen.

If we return to *Stream in the Forest* and compare it to *The Trellis*, we can take stock of the most pertinent lessons learned from this brief flirtation with flowers: the creation of the illusion of volume from a minimum of textureless, translucent touches against a dark ground; the spatial disorientation produced by the withdrawal of a stable architecture or ground of support; the organic, hovering quality of the subsequent painted forms. Had Courbet not passed through this apprenticeship in which he learned to summon natural elements from the depths of the pictorial field in carefully controlled and discrete units, he might never have attained the control of the mark necessary for his later, more accomplished landscapes.

12 | *The Trellis*, 1862. Oil on canvas, 109.8 × 135.2 cm. Toledo Museum of Art

BETWEEN ENAMEL AND MORTAR

The artist as exacting materialist demiurge is not the usual image we have of Courbet as a painter of substance. Many may imagine him, as did the French caricaturist André Gill, wielding the palette knife in the way a mason handles a trowel (fig. 13). Another example from Gill's *Stock Album* pictures the artist's knife as a thick chef's blade laden with whipped cream (fig. 14).[22] The Courbet of legend does not simply handle paint, he manhandles it. This chorus of jest—one certainly not limited, as Matthias Krüger has shown, to Courbet[23]—has had the unfortunate effect of drowning out the evidence of the paintings themselves. For if everyone agrees that Courbet had "made the palette knife an instrument all his own,"[24] it must also be said that this most recognizable aspect of Courbet's art has been among its least analyzed until recently, and most notably in the work of Anthea Callen and Krüger.[25] The lack of firsthand accounts is partly responsible for this situation; nineteenth-century descriptions of the artist at work are rare and even then seldom rise above the level of generality. True, there are some accounts, mostly by close friends, that delve into details—such as his choice of colors, the order in which they were applied—and these will be examined in due course. But even when description verges on real interpretation, we may be left frustrated. More often than not, as soon as a text discusses Courbet's manner of working, it either descends into hyperbole or changes topic, without addressing the inventiveness of the artist's technique. The recollection of Jean Gigoux, a fellow Franc-comtois painter, is typical: "Indeed, the painting was so thick that the bladders [containing paint] were just crushed against the canvas. 'Oh, Monsieur,' [Courbet] cried, 'Oh Monsieur! This *paaaint* ["*pâââte*"] is rough plaster!"[26]

A study of "technical details" is therefore all the more necessary in the case of a painter such as Courbet for whom technique was a matter of artistic identity. In his landscapes, the artist built up form slowly, touch by touch, economically executed with discrete, almost floating, brushstrokes, knife-marks, and rag-marks. There were a few critics who occasionally saw past the caricatural Courbet, writers who in good faith tried to explain what they saw rather than repeat what they read. And it is in their writings that the subtle nuances of Courbet's way of representing matter come to the fore. Here are three examples:

> His painting is alchemical, at times brusque, impacted, like a plaster wall, and at others delicate, fine, and transparent. Sometimes the colors applied form a mass, sometimes on the contrary they are laid out like irregular crystals.[27]
>
> He handles it [the palette knife] with incomparable skill and draws from it surprising effects. Thus a tone laid flat acquires a transparency and intensity without equal.... Courbet paints in full impasto but without excess or bumps; His paintings, where color unites with the canvas, are as polished as glass, shine like enamel, and are just as solid.[28]
>
> The palette knife, Goya used it.... The tone was placed without concern for smudging and its projecting relief had the advantage of giving the canvas something even more vibrant. In Courbet, certain surfaces are too smooth, agate-like, and look like they have undergone vitrification.[29]

What is most interesting about these descriptions is the apparent contradiction built into all of them between a "rude" and "fine" paint application. On the one hand, Courbet's painting (like Goya's in the third example) is "impacted," wall-like, "in full impasto," and "projecting relief"; and, on the other hand, it is "delicate," "transparent," "without excess or bumps," and has "undergone vitrification," like agate, glass, and enamel.

Looking at materials such as glass and agate normally involves two distinct visual experiences: there is the sparkle as light bounces off a polished surface. There is also a sense of something beyond the surface that draws the beholder in, what lies on the other side of a window, for instance, in the case of a glass pane, or what can be discovered in the crystalline depths of a stone, in the case of agate.[30] What a flat patch of paint shares with glass and agate, then, is the capacity to cast attention across a surface while simultaneously drawing attention to something solid beyond or underneath that surface. As Courbet's paint marks are relatively oily and pressed flat, they reflect light like a jewel or piece of lacquerware. However, they are also discrete units of noticeable thickness, not yet integrated with the canvas surface, making us aware of their physical density. Courbet's subtle touches are unique in their ability to put the two competing perceptions into productive tension: they attract us to the twinkle of a reflective surface and compel us to dive past that surface into the inner substance of things.

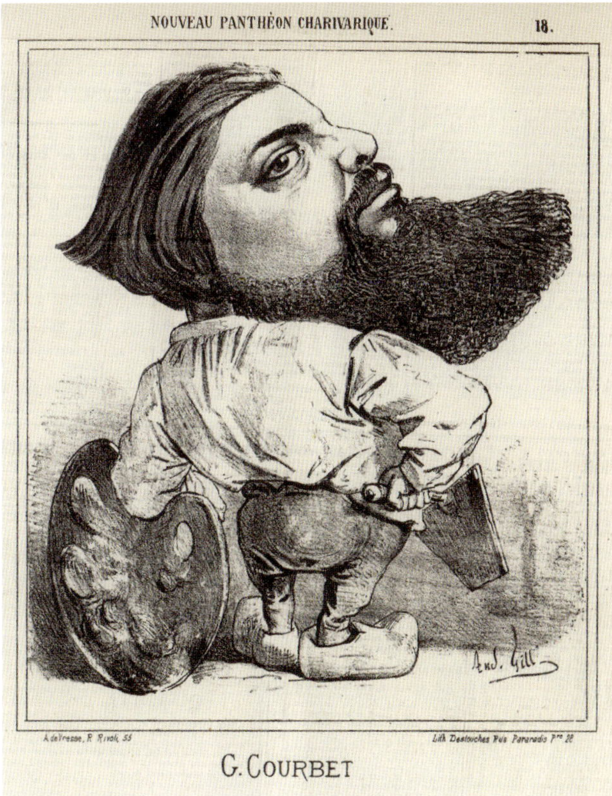

13 | André Gill, "G. Courbet," *Le Charivari* (6 February 1867)

This comparison suggests that the overly strict opposition between thin and thick, brushed and knifed, academic and avant-garde technique that has determined much of the writing on Courbet's working methods ignores many of his painting's subtleties. As well as the persistent misunderstanding of his paint's thickness, there has been confusion about his choice of tool. The "thickness" of his surfaces is not due solely to the use of the palette knife. On closer inspection, what we often perceive in his landscapes as "knife-marks" are not even knifed. Instead, they were painted with a brush. Writing about two early Salon paintings, *Young Ladies of the Village* (1851–52; The Metropolitan Museum of Art, New York) and *The Wrestlers* (1853; Museum of Fine Arts, Budapest), the critic Théophile Silvestre observed that "[Courbet] makes great use of the knife, which deposits color on the canvas with a striking and brutal frankness, while the brush-hairs bore small furrows where light is subdued and fades away, as in velvet fabric."[31] Courbet became so celebrated for his knife's "striking and brutal frankness" that critics and viewers alike all but assumed that every perceived instance of such "frankness" resulted from the artist using this signature tool (as the caricatures presented earlier attest). "Thickness" became synonymous with "knifed"; Courbet was a victim of his own success with the implement. However, in his landscapes, the artist does not create the illusion of thickness by replacing all brushstrokes with knife-strokes. Rather, he makes use of both kinds of mark simultaneously (following a certain logic to be analyzed over the course of this study).

How is it that the interplay of knife-work and brushwork in Courbet's landscapes has gone unnoticed for so long (or, at best, been underexamined)? It has already been proposed that the public image of the artist as an unskilled artisan is partly responsible. But this does

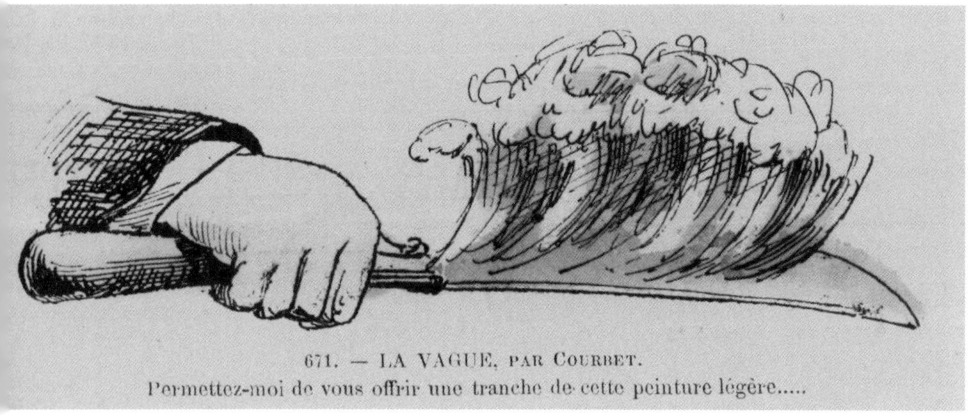

14 | André Gill, *The Wave*, 1870. Caricature of Courbet from *Stock Album*, no. 1, 1870

not really explain why experienced artists and writers did not also recognize or appreciate the near equivalence of knife-mark and brushstroke. Another, and perhaps more significant, reason is that the artist himself suppressed certain physical signs of their difference as he painted. Knives (and spatulas) and brushes usually leave behind tell-tale traces of their use—hard, metal-carved edges for the former, toothed grooves or hair-wisps for the latter. Yet in Courbet's landscapes these signs are often missing. In order to accomplish this effect, Courbet had probably gone over his initial touches with an implement—a rag, sponge, knife, an unloaded brush—to obliterate the clues of their making.[32] Consequently, in his painting, rather than ridges of relief, the kind generated when a blade forces paint against canvas, we discover calibrated deposits, strangely razed.[33] What we inevitably encounter to some degree in almost all of Courbet's best landscapes is the deliberate *slimming of impasto*. A serious effort has been made to cancel the more obvious signs of handiwork, to de-authorize the painter's touch (without, however, eliminating its identity *as touch* altogether, i.e. without letting the picture surface assimilate it entirely). Instead of a thickly knifed mark, in his painting we find a pseudothick, knifed or brushed, de-marked mark. This presents a challenge to the critic seeking a technical description of this "palette-knife effect," let alone a historical account of it. Even Courbet's most fervent and perceptive supporters, such as fellow painter Adolph Menzel, tended to view his work primarily through the stark dichotomy of brush vs. knife, thin vs. thick. After visiting Courbet's pavilion outside the 1867 Universal Exhibition, Menzel remarked that "one should take away all of Courbet's paintbrushes. As long as he paints with a palette knife he is excellent. But when he takes up the brush, the work is poor."[34] Criticism was ill-equipped to deal with something so paradoxical—and stunningly novel—as a picture surface that had both something of the roughness of Realist painting and something of the smoothness of Old Master pictures.

To conclude this sampling of critical reactions to Courbet's painting technique, the artist Walter Sickert also complained about Courbet's major flaws as an artist, when reviewing *The Impressionist School and Some Great French Painters of the 19th Century* at the Lefèvre Galleries, London, in 1923. In addition to "painting after nature," Courbet was accused of misusing the palette knife. The review is explicit about the tool's defects:

> Good painters have sometimes dallied with this trick [of painting with the palette knife instead of with the brush]. But to the extent that they have, such passages have suffered. Their avoidance of it may be said to be the measure of their aesthetic instinct. That instinct has told them, firstly, that the knife cannot draw with the sensitiveness of the brush. Their knowledge of the very stuff of their craft has also told them that oil painting needs air—that a surface spread with a knife produces two things, *a bag of wet paint sealed up in a glassy skin* [my emphasis].[35]

In one innocuous phrase, Sickert hits on a metaphor—that of a "glassy skin"— capable of conveying the double nature of the Courbetian pictorial unit, i.e. its simultaneous flatness *and* substantiality. Where his assessment goes astray is in his description of this skin as encapsulating a "bag of wet paint." As has been demonstrated, the mark in Courbet's hands never attains such pronounced three-dimensional relief; it never sags or bulges from the canvas; it is a thin, palpable epidermis, not a bulbous wart. Perhaps Sickert exaggerates the plumpness of Courbet's paint in order to put distance between himself and an artist whose painting he despised for the artist's refusal to subsume all paint layers into a single, totalizing surface. By calling Courbet's laid-on touches "bags of wet paint," Sickert emphasizes that they will never be fully assimilated by their underlayers.

Sickert commented that, in addition to their lack of aesthetic appeal, these "glassy skins" posed long-term technical problems:

> The wet paint within [knifed paint] dries too slowly and shrivels, and the impervious skin darkens [whereas] the painter's traditional instrument produces, with its bristles, the minute furrows in the surface of the painting which have a double effect. The air has access to the paint and dries it soundly through and through. And secondly, the tooth thus given by the brush to the surface gives a hold to each subsequent coat of paint.[36]

According to Sickert, the uneven drying time of knife-painting would lead to chips and cracks, forever risking damage to the surface of the painting. Following this logic, we would have expected Courbet's landscapes to have suffered significant paint loss. Yet the surfaces of his paintings are remarkably stable (even when unlined). This is because they are often not nearly as built up as their apparent heft suggests—there are usually no more than two or three overlapping touches at any given point (if any)—and the danger of uneven drying posed by multiple layers of "bags of paint" is minimized. Similarly, as Courbet applies paint with such skill and economy, aerating brush-grooves are no longer essential for stability. Part of what makes Courbet's surfaces unique is the quality of one oily layer hovering above another, as if in a state of suspended animation, so producing a surface that is not a single integument but rather consists of overlapping, separate, shiny yet solid skins, one floating atop another.

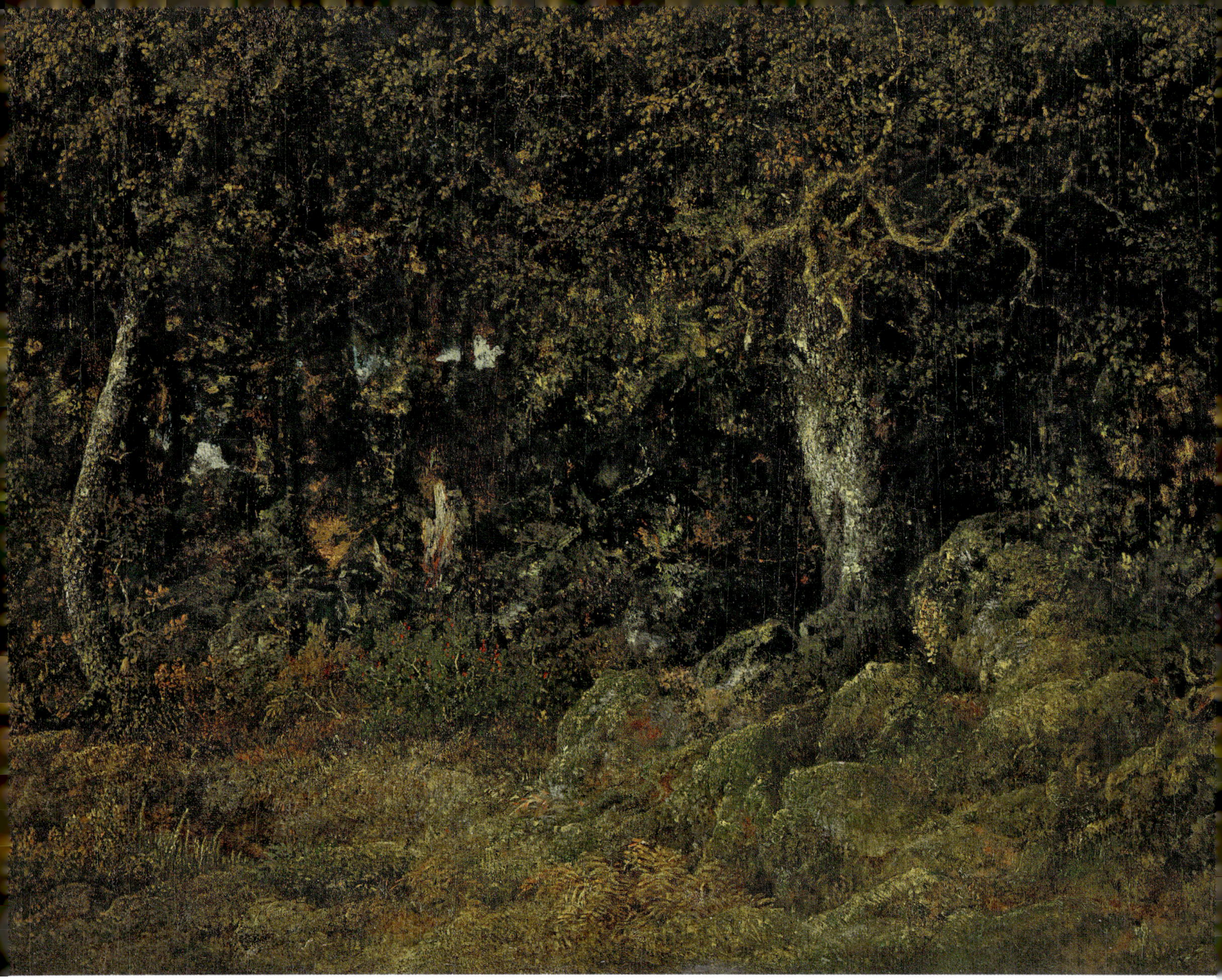

15 Théodore Rousseau, *The Rock Oak*, 1860–61. Oil on panel, 88.9 × 116.8 cm. Ny Carlsberg Glyptotek, Copenhagen

Rousseau
Barbizon School

SALIENT POINTS

Courbet left the Saintonge province in May 1863 with newly found confidence in the use of the pictorial mark to depict substance. In *Stream in the Forest*, he had imaginatively fused two modes: the intimate mark-making of still life with the broad tonal organization of landscape. And he did so in a way that would have been scarcely possible for a historical landscape artist such as Corot. But surely, we might retort, it *would* have been possible for the other great landscapist of the era, Théodore Rousseau—or one of his fellow Barbizon painters, such as Jean-François Millet, Constant Troyon, Jules Dupré, or Narcisse-Virgilio Diaz de la Peña, to name only the most well known, all of whom resisted the charms of the bright, Italianate countryside for moodier, more melancholic sites in their native France. For Rousseau, too, energized his landscapes by means of a highly inventive, idiosyncratic technique, one also heavily invested in the representation of natural textures, and in Rousseau's case, one that also blurred the boundaries between drawing and painting. Yet on both these points—texture and drawing—Rousseau's approach stood in stark contrast to Courbet's to the same landscape subjects.

After numerous rejections from the Salon during the 1830s, Rousseau settled permanently in the late 1840s in the village of Barbizon on the edge of the Forest of Fontainebleau, where he became the mainstay of a loose-knit colony of resident and visiting painters today referred to as the Barbizon School. In 1849, a more liberal Salon jury under the Second Republic welcomed him back from the wilderness. Six years later, 13 of his paintings were accepted for the Universal Exhibition (where he was member of the jury). From this point on he was held up as a model for aspiring painters of landscape, the genre to which he devoted himself almost exclusively.

In 1861, a year before Corot and Courbet's side-by-side experiments in the province of Saintonge, Rousseau presented his own *sous-bois* painting, *The Rock Oak* (fig. 15) at the Salon. The Forest of Fontainebleau played a central role in Rousseau's oeuvre, but rarely was it so gloomy and overgrown. Even his friends were struck by this. The republican critic and former exile Théophile Thoré (under the pseudonym Willem Bürger) found it mysterious; Alfred Sensier, Rousseau's biographer, imagined it the setting for a Dantesque witches' sabbath. Sensier attributed its haunting quality to a reductive color scheme: "The general tone was green and modulated all the greens of the forests, from the grasses and ferns to the oak branches, to the general 'greenish-ness' of realities ["'*verdaturre*' *des réalités*"], as well as the half-tones and the shadows."[37] Sensier's language, its description of Rousseau's almost one-note palette, suggests a possible point of comparison with Courbet's hyperverdant *Stream in the Forest.*

However, when looking at *The Rock Oak*, it is the words of Robert L. Herbert, one of Rousseau's most insightful interpreters, that come to mind:

> Shortly after mid-century, memory knowledge of touchable, solid masses yielded to the optical, so purged of non-visual experience that the dabs of pigment began to float free of imaginary substance. When that occurred, the artist became as much interested in the dabs as in what they represented, and by the early sixties they were all painting in a variety of small strokes whose colors, no longer blended one with another, took on new life.[38]

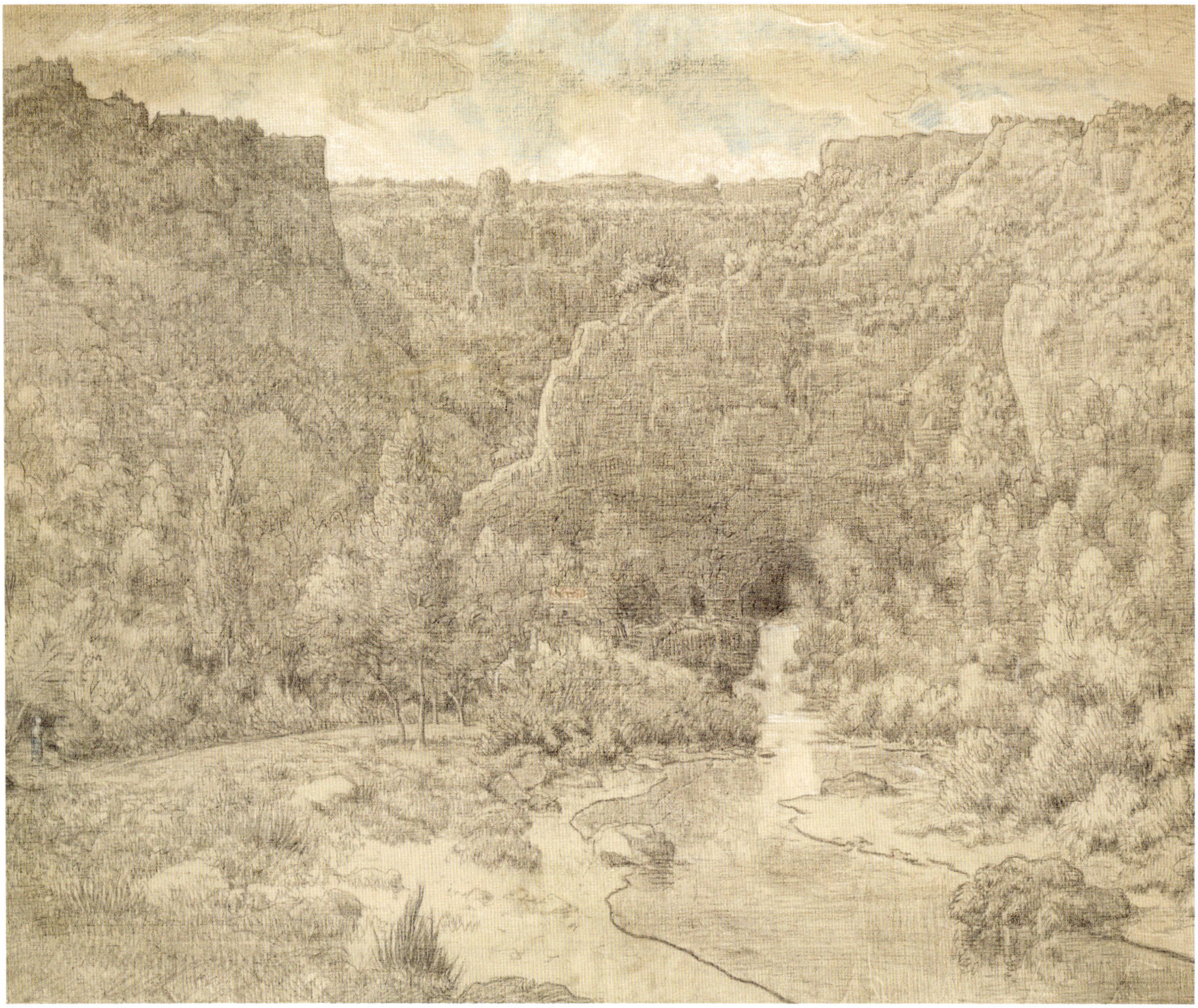

16 | Théodore Rousseau, *Source of the Lison (Doubs)*, *ca.*1862. Charcoal and pastel on canvas, 89 × 116 cm. Musée du Louvre, Paris

Though addressing the Barbizon School's output as a whole, the passage aptly describes how paint functions in *The Rock Oak*. One of its most striking features is what one could call a molecularization of the mark. Gone are the "touchable, solid masses" of Corot's Italian studies or Courbet's *Stream in the Forest*. Instead, *The Rock Oak* is a panoply of minutely dabbed surfaces: reddish brambles roll across the foreground like a dense carpet; its sponge-like texture is taken up on the right, in a more verdant key, by the velvety moss covering the rocks around the oak; the intense brushstrokes continue above in the arboreal canopy too dense for the eye to pierce, save for the speck of sky peeking through the undergrowth left of center; even the object that should be the most solid, the sturdy trunk of the dominant oak tree, is speckled with white lichen.

We are far from the steady, patchwork build-up of tones in Courbet's *Stream in the Forest*. As Herbert put it in the above quotation: "a variety of small strokes whose colors, no longer blended with another, took on new life." This phenomenon was noticed even in Rousseau's day. Already in 1861—that is, well before optical mixing would become central to contemporary art theory—critics compared Rousseau's flickering specks to multi-tiled mosaics and tapestry weaving.[39] But instead of fusing to form "light" in anticipation of Neo-Impressionism, Rousseau's atomized units condense into a kind of creeping fog that covers everything in its path.

Herbert is therefore correct in claiming that "dabs of pigment began to float free of imaginary substance." It is not that Rousseau's painterly particles have lost all their weight; they are still recognizable as "dabs of pigment." It is rather that those dabs are no longer so tightly bound with the individual objects that they define. For instance, in the ground cover of *The Rock Oak*, individual paint marks no longer denote *this* patch of grass or *that* outcropping of rock. They are much too small to define an entire landscape element on their own. Instead, they combine with surrounding marks to form a sort of natural carpeting, a literal ground cover, that "floats" above the "substantive" reality now imagined as lying underneath it. We have a sense, when looking at this superficial layer, that if a strong wind were to sweep it away, the objects hidden beneath that covering would be revealed.

This is not the case in Courbet's *Stream in the Forest*, whose overall effect is not surface volatility, but bulky accumulation. The skinlike quality of Courbet's touches means that individual marks appear to adhere to a larger substantive mass. The patches of paint at the center of *Stream in the Forest*, for instance, do not simply cover the bushes, riverbank, and water. Rather, they appear to constitute their very material being. The light-green paint mark *is* the bush, the slightly darker one *is* the sloping ground upon which the bush sits; the green in the water *is* their reflection. Courbet's touches function here much as they do in the still lifes. In both cases brushstrokes work to materialize whole entities, flowers in the still lifes, landscape elements in *Stream in the Forest*. To eliminate such marks would be tantamount to gouging something out of the landscape or bouquet, an excavation of matter, and not, as appears to be the case in *The Rock Oak*, a sweeping away of cover. The Courbetian dab is no mere surface treatment; quite the opposite, it is *co-substantial* with the object it represents.

Ultimately, Rousseau and Courbet moved in opposite directions: Rousseau deployed many small touches to diminish the perception of solid substance; Courbet used a few relatively large ones to promote it.[40] Although, as far as we know, Rousseau and Courbet never painted side by side, Rousseau had family connections with Courbet's region of Franche-Comté. Rousseau's father, Pierre-Claude-Catherine Rousseau, came from Salins (a town we will revisit in the next chapter). The young Théodore had worked for a family friend outside Besançon, the capital of Franche-Comté and hometown of his future wife Elisa Gros (where she would often recuperate during times of illness), and so visited the region several times, as numerous drawings of the surrounding countryside attest.[41] One bout of sketching in the area, likely in the early 1860s, led to an *ébauche* (preliminary drawing) of a local grotto known as the source of the Lison (fig. 16). In 1864, Courbet also painted the source (fig. 17), so it is possible to contrast their different attitudes toward landscape. Although the Rousseau is not a painting, and therefore can't be analyzed in terms of mark-making, it does invite comparison with the Courbet: in the relationship of drawing to painting in landscape.

Source of the Lison is typical of Rousseau in panoramic mode. From a high vantage point above the Lison River, the artist portrays the wide expanse of the landscape. Usually, Rousseau's sketches either isolate a small landscape area for focused examination or capture an overall mood, glossing over individual details. The highly developed composition of *Source of the Lison* combines both features. It is at once a microscopic study of tiny details and a macroscopic view of the world at large. Though Rousseau locates our viewpoint at considerable distance from the water-spouting cavern for which the drawing is named, there is hardly any part of the composition upon which the artist has not lavished care, as if we were observing each landscape element from up close. We can make out single blades of grass in the foreground, tree trunks and branches in the middle ground, and even leafy outgrowths on the distant cliffs. Moreover, in case the detail distracts

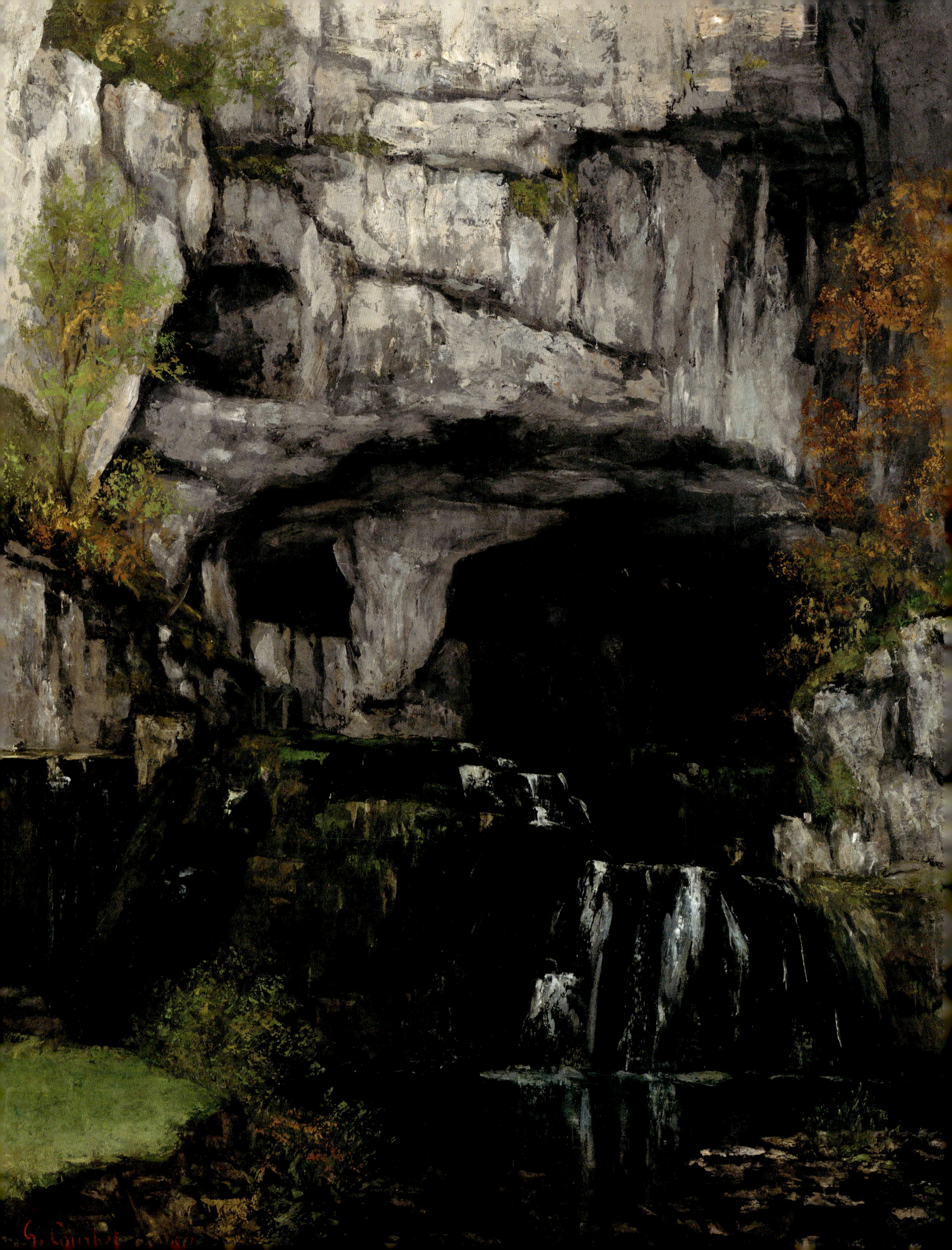

us too much from the whole, Rousseau has delineated the landscape's primary contours, as if revealing a hidden template: dark black lines define the banks of the river as it courses out of the picture; the right-hand cliff is clearly marked at its top and side edges where it meets sky and ground. So fastidious are the artist's tracings that one observer has gone so far as to call it a "drawing on canvas" instead of an "unfinished painting."[42]

Because the scene is sketched on a canvas almost a meter in height and even more in width, it is likely that at some point *Source of the Lison* would have led to a finished work.[43] But we need not have the final picture before us to see that Rousseau's working process follows two phases: first, draw with charcoal and pastel; second, complete with oil pigments. This is not to say that the distinction was absolute. Rousseau often allowed the initial drawing to show through subsequent paint layers. Indeed, he was a master of conjuring weather effects from the interaction between the two media. But *The Rock Oak* and *Source of the Lison* testify to the general thrust of his work in that the application of paint is secondary; it is something added on to a delineated, drawn prototype that precedes painting both formally and conceptually. As Herbert notes: "[Rousseau's] paintings were built on a structure of hard lines, almost like engravings, because he had to have the certainty that he had penetrated the vitals of nature."[44]

The difference with Courbet's *Source of the Lison* of 1864 is so dramatic that it is easy to overlook that they depict the same site.[45] It is not as if Courbet was unaware of, or had never been interested by, the panoramic view. A drawing (fig. 18) from one of his early sketchbooks testifies to a youthful fascination with just the kind of delineation pursued by Rousseau (notice the doubly

17 | *Source of the Lison*, 1864. Oil on canvas, 91 × 73 cm. Private collection, Minnesota Marine Art Museum, Winona, Minnesota

18 | Folio 30 recto from Courbet sketchbook, 1840–50. Musée du Louvre, Paris

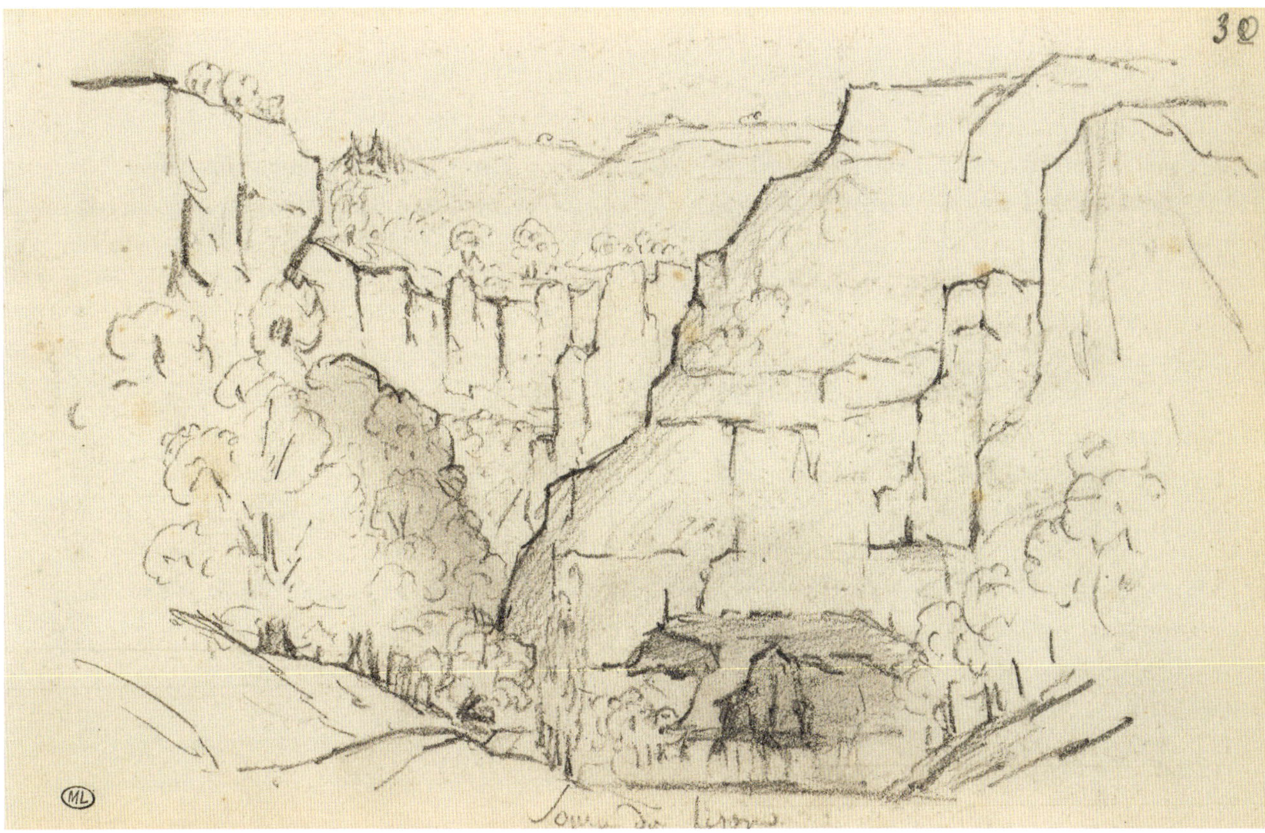

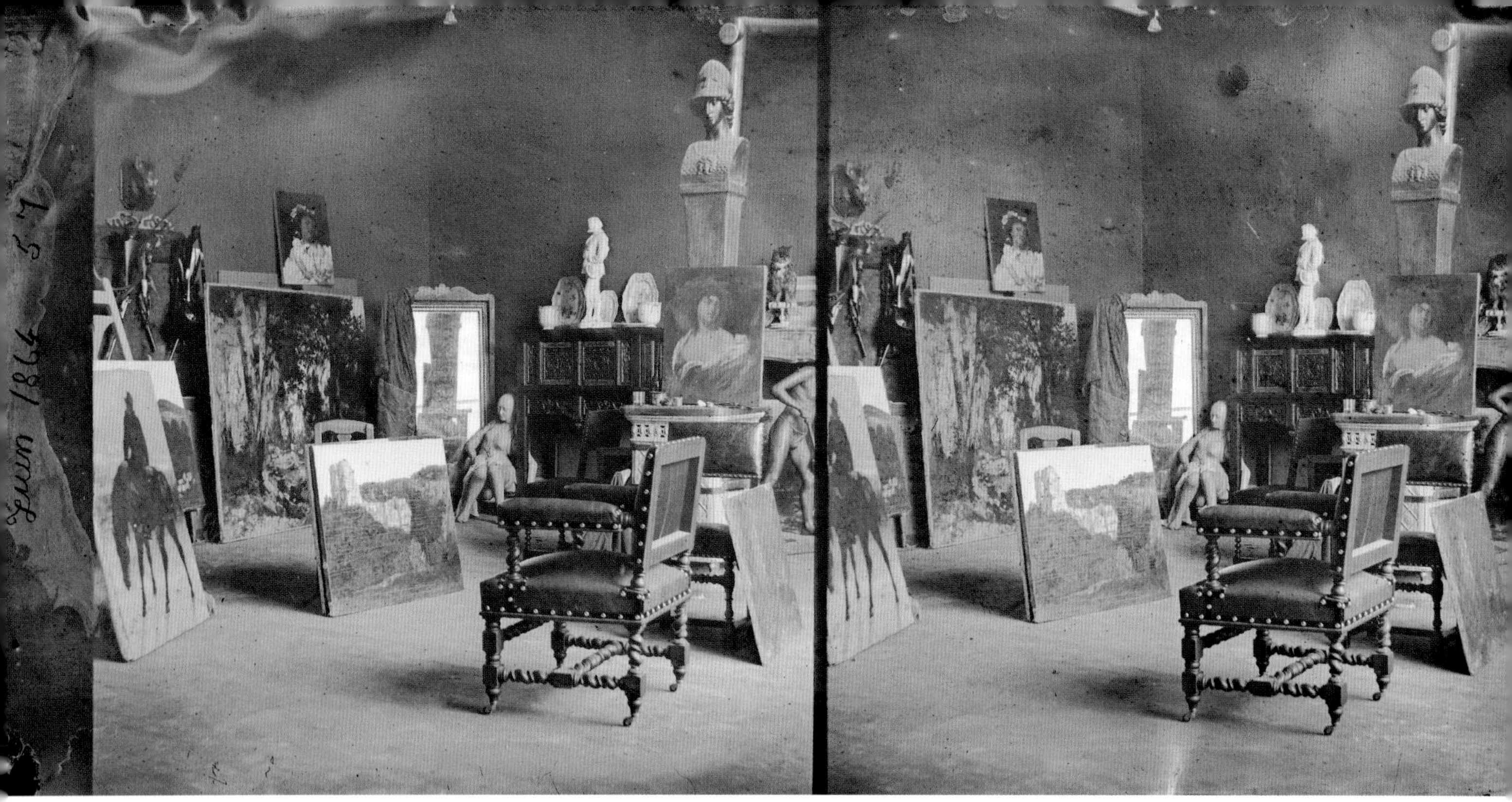

19 Eugène Feyen, *Interior of Courbet's Studio at Ornans*, 1864. Stereoscopic photograph (albumen print). Institut Gustave Courbet, Ornans

thick left edge of the rock formation housing the source, strikingly similar to the same feature in the Rousseau). In Rousseau's drawing from a bird's-eye view, the artist surveys the landscape down to the last detail. One of Rousseau's details—an obscure, almost negligible black patch—metamorphoses in Courbet's version into a cavernous tunnel to nowhere. Courbet's *Source of the Lison* transplants the viewer from the far view atop the valley to the near view slightly below and to the left of the grotto's mouth, thereby producing a disturbing sense of physical proximity. Deprived of the usual spatial markers of pathways, receding planes, the horizon, and without the intermediary of distance or drawing, we are forced to contemplate a gaping hollow at the center of the visual field.

In his memoirs, the young sculptor Max Claudet reveals what Courbet had told him while painting the *Source of the Lison*:

> "It surprises you that my canvas is black," he said. "Nature without sunlight is black and obscure. I do just as the light does, I illuminate the salient points, and the painting is done." And with his knife he took some white, yellow, red, and black from some glass paint containers in a box. He mixed them on the palette. Then, with his knife, he spread the mixture on the canvas and scraped it with a sure and firm stroke.... "Some more trees here, a little green grass in the foreground, and we will soon be finished," he said. He constantly ran his knife across the canvas. At four o'clock, the painting was done, and one sensed in it the master's hand and his powerful breath. We were amazed at the speed with which he executed it. Hardly two hours of work to cover a meter of canvas![46]

In a few sentences, Courbet's identity as a painter is distilled into three aspects: he paints to illuminate; he paints primarily with the palette knife; and he paints quickly. Most interesting for our discussion is the comparison with sunlight. Courbet's words (via Claudet) emphasize the imperceptibility of nature, that it is "black and obscure" without sunlight. We may know that there is a world out there waiting to be revealed, but we do not see it yet. The painter, light patch by light patch, slowly extracts landscape forms from obscurity, like the sun at dawn. Over time the illuminated points accumulate until finally a landscape is born, not by means of a premeditated drawing but rather through a steady massing of skinlike near tones.

Earlier in this chapter it was clear that our vision hit an impasse near the center of Courbet's 1862 *Stream in the Forest* (see fig. 10). This is not what happens at the heart of *Source of the Lison*. The center of the 1864 painting is now an opening that beckons the beholder, however unnervingly. What happened between the 1863 Saintes exhibition and the making of *Source of the Lison* at the end of 1864 to trigger this desire to plunge, free of obstacles, into the depths of the landscape is the subject of the next chapter.

An extended stay in the Saintonge did not prevent Courbet from preparing for the Salon. On the contrary, a building on Baudry's property was exclusively set aside for the task. The fate of the painting eventually submitted, *Return from the Conference* (1863; destroyed), is well known. The scene of drunk clergymen was rejected from that year's Salon (as well as from its offshoot, the Salon des Réfusés, Paris, in the same year). In anticipation of this exclusion, Courbet planned to show the picture elsewhere, first in his studio and then later in England, to be accompanied by a pamphlet by the philosopher Pierre-Joseph Proudhon.[47] Later that year, Courbet prepared another painting in a humorous vein for the Salon of 1864. *Hippocrene Spring* was meant to depict a mythical spring (in reality a Franc-comtois landscape) tended by an all-too-realistic nude, from which several recognized poets (Alphonse de Lamartine, Charles Baudelaire, Pierre Dupont, Gustave Mathieu, Charles Monselet, Théophile Gautier) are seen being poisoned by the source's tainted waters. The large painting was accidentally damaged in the studio and did not make it to the annual exhibition. There is no doubt that, just as with *Return from the Conference*, Courbet had banked on controversy. As he wrote to Castagnary in January of that year: "Farewell nasty reviews, farewell recriminations, farewell to poetry's hatred of Realism. The next Exhibition will once more lack gaiety. If, by chance, I am wronging my critics, it is not my fault! My intentions were good!"[48] Castagnary, for his part, was secretly relieved. He understood that what Courbet had done was simply replace one object of ridicule with another: "I ignore it [i.e., *Hippocrene Spring*]. I believe Courbet accepted the accident as an act of fate and abandoned the enterprise. Maybe he understood that after having put the priests in their place it would not be in his best interest to alienate the poets."[49]

With *Hippocrene Spring* damaged, Courbet sent a painting of two female nudes, *Study of Women*, also known as *Venus in Jealous Pursuit of Psyche* (1864; probably destroyed) to the Salon instead, just in time for the deadline. Between his preparations for the Salon of 1864 and the beginning of work on the portrait *Pierre-Joseph Proudhon and His Children in 1853* (1865; Musée du Petit Palais, Paris) the following January, Courbet stayed, practically without interruption, in Franche-Comté for the first time in years. There, in his new studio on the outskirts of Ornans, he devoted much of his energy to painting landscape. In a photograph of the studio dated June 1864, the canvas destined to have become *Hippocrene Spring* sits against the back wall (fig. 19). Now there was only a landscape, which eventually became the background of *Covert of Roe-Deer by the Stream of Plaisir-Fontaine*, exhibited at the Salon of 1866 (fig. 20). Courbet may have bid adieu to the poets, to the critics, to Paris. But with the unfinished painting as a daily reminder he embraced what was left—a Franc-comtois landscape—with open arms.

20 *Covert of Roe-Deer by the Stream of Plaisir-Fontaine*, 1866. Oil on canvas, 174 × 209 cm. Musée d'Orsay, Paris

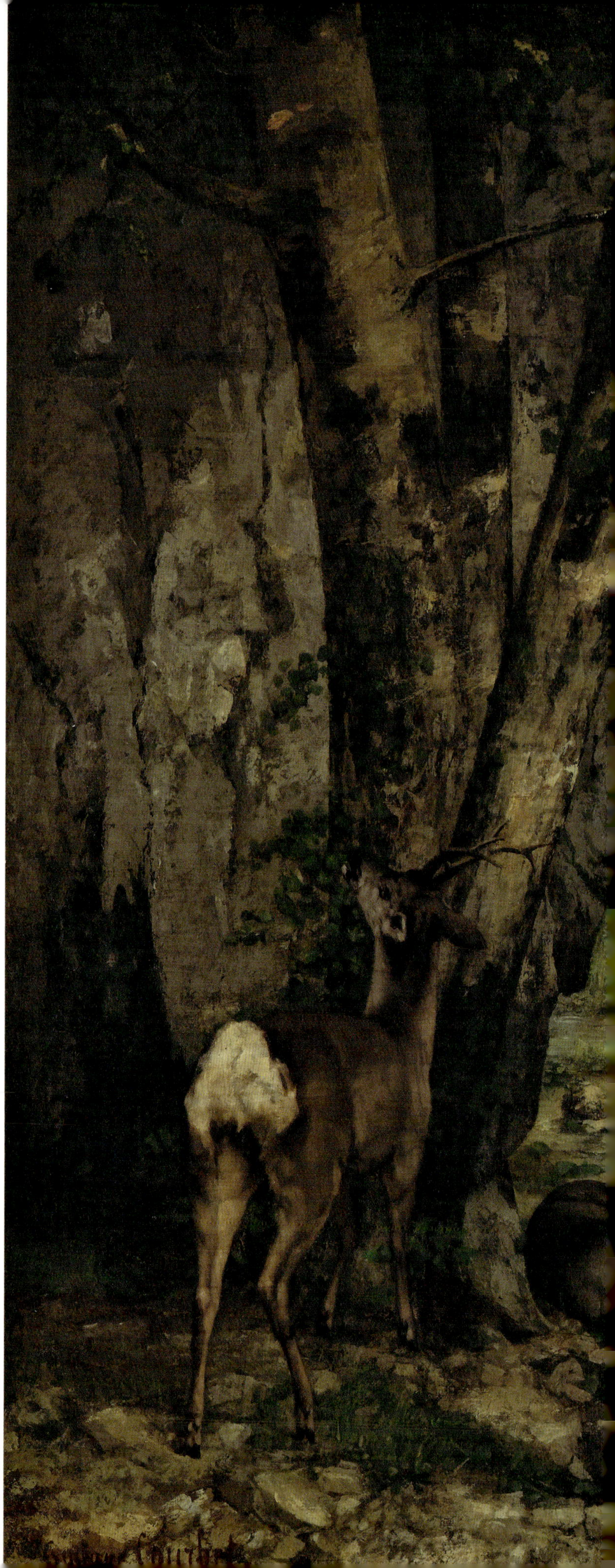

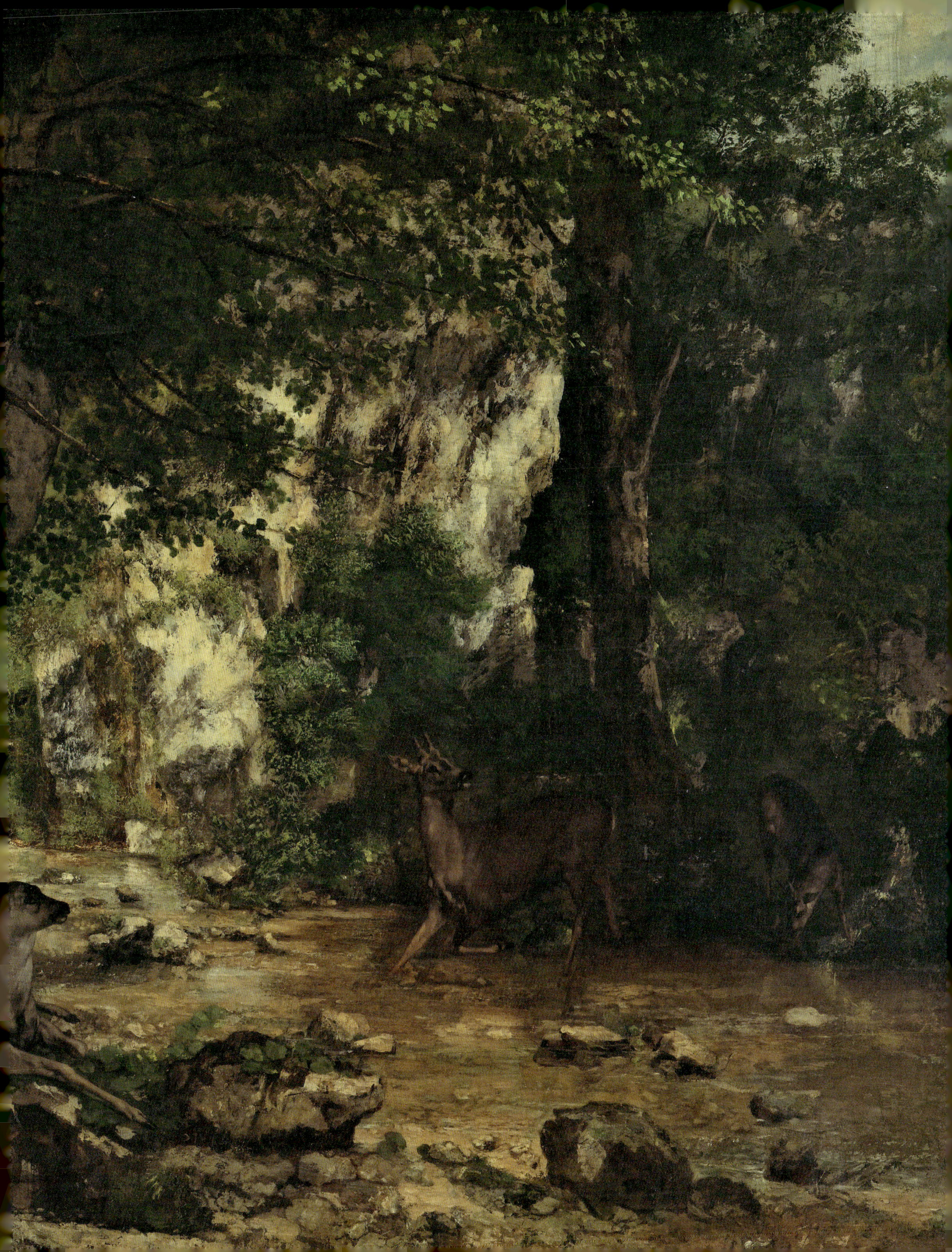

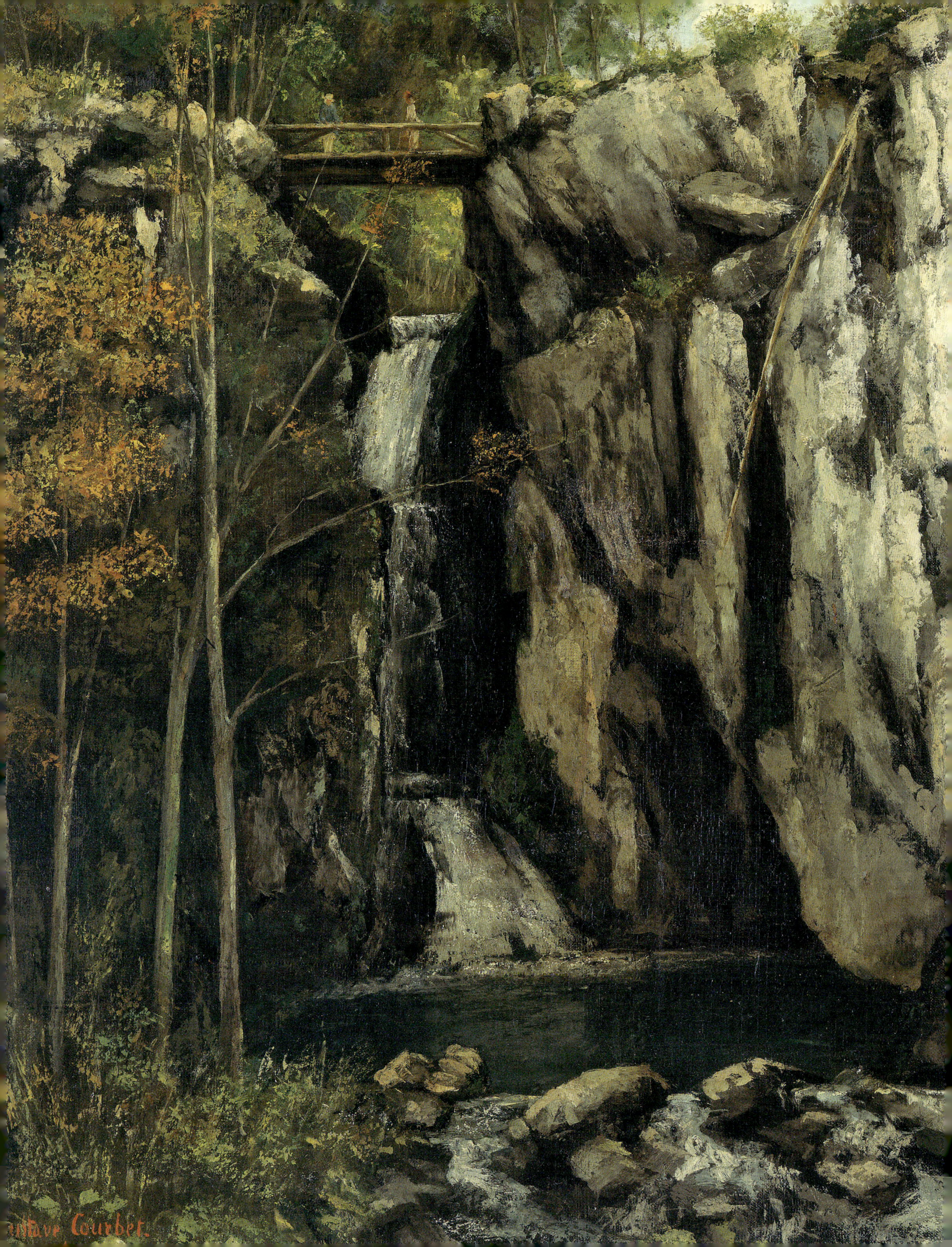
Gustave Courbet.

Chapter 2

WHEN LANDSCAPE BECAME LANGUAGE

After almost a year in the Saintonge, Courbet returned to Paris in May 1863 during the opening weeks of the Salon. His main submission to that year's exhibition was the satirical, anticlerical *Return from the Conference*, a large painting of drunken priests stumbling through a Franc-comtois landscape. It was a deliberate provocation. He had anticipated its refusal and the public controversy that would ensue. Instead, he showed the work in his Rue Hautefeuille studio, where he reaped the rewards of the carefully targeted publicity. That fall, he moved back to Ornans, as his business in the capital was mostly done and there was talk of *Return from the Conference* being sold and exhibited abroad. A new studio was waiting for him along the Route de Besançon. The area became his main place of residence practically without interruption from fall 1863 to spring 1865. This would be the first time since 1860 that he would commit to such a long-term stay in his native region.

Courbet's homecoming would have profound implications for his art. Landscape would come to the fore in his work as never before in terms of both quality and quantity. The area around Ornans—essentially a massive limestone block into which epochal erosion has carved a network of underground and surface waterways—furnished the artist with a plethora of landscape subjects: flatlands on the plateaus, bird's-eye views into the valleys, resplendent cliffs, all sorts of cascades and riverbends. However, Courbet was at his creative best when he addressed the area's subterranean grottoes and dark, secluded streams head-on and up close, sites that his friend, the art critic Jules-Antoine Castagnary, once described as mysterious nooks that you are seemingly the first to have entered.[1] The outstanding examples of this type—*The Source of the Loue* (see figs. 2 and 23), *Source of the Lison* (see fig. 17) and *The Stream of the Puits noir* (see fig. 1)—all date to this period. Compared to the Corot-inspired Saintonge pictures of 1862–63 discussed in the previous chapter, the grotto and stream paintings of 1864 are even more ambitious in composition and even more visceral in physical impact. They were the perfect subject matter for Courbet's recently developed technique of small-scale, piecemeal painting in palette knife and brush. Depositing close-valued paint in a relatively minimal number of discrete touches allowed him to give these landscapes an unprecedented organic density that creates the startling effect on the beholder of having traveled back to some prehistoric terrain.

Provincial pride undoubtedly played its part in Courbet's renewed commitment to landscape painting. He told the critic Edgar Monteil that "to paint the country, one must know it. I know my country, I paint it. These undergrowths, they're from home. This river, it's the Loue, that one, the Lison. These rocks, they're from Ornans and the Puits noir. Go see them, and you will recognize all my paintings."[2] However, his connection to the landscape was more than physical or spiritual; for a short while in 1864, it was intellectual. As Petra ten-Doesschate Chu was the first to emphasize, Courbet's interlocuters in the area included learned Franc-comtois thinkers, many of whom were at this moment also investigating, within their own areas of expertise, the problem of origins.[3] For his longtime friend, the writer Max Buchon, it was the linguistic origins of patois; for the antiquarian Charles Toubin, it was the historical origins of the French nation; for the geologist Jules Marcou, it was the geological origins of the earth. Despite the diversity of their respective fields of inquiry—language, classical antiquity, natural science—each in his own way sought to uncover within his object of study traces of that object's historical formation over time. For each of these men, studying the world meant unearthing the often-invisible forces that shaped its appearance, such as the hidden rules governing language change or laws of geological development. Courbet's contribution was to invent a kind of landscape painting in which Nature, too, would be made to reveal to the viewer its formative material processes, those that have seemingly been in existence since prehistoric times. By depicting the progressive unfurling of layers of form and substance within Nature, his landscape painting thus joined other historicizing discourses of the nineteenth century. Although Courbet and his associates all studied different things, they practiced, fundamentally, the same mode of analysis: to unearth the internal stages of an object's creation. Courbet's great achievement in the 1864 landscapes was to have visualized *as art* this revelation of process.

THE LANGUAGE OF THE PEOPLE

Before delving deeper into the intellectual activity of the Courbet milieu—that of Buchon, Toubin, and Marcou—it helps to look at the series of originary 1864 landscapes that we know the most about: the various depictions of the source of the Loue River. Located near the village of Mouthier, 14 kilometers southeast of Ornans, the source is a large cavern situated at the base of a domineering 100-meter-high cliff. The underground waters feeding the Loue initially coalesce into a glassy pool within the grotto. Eventually they overflow their stone basin and spill out in a series of thundering waterfalls to form the river proper. The site was of both economic and geological interest; since medieval times, its waters have driven wheels powering mills and forges along the Loue. A passage from the venerable *Voyages pittoresques et romantiques dans l'ancienne France* (1825) is typical of more emotional reactions to the source: "the gloom one feels is a strange mix of admiration and terror, an inexplicable and unknown malaise."[4]

Such sentiments drew nineteenth-century artists to the local landscape, including the young Courbet, whose early sketchbooks of the 1840s contain several drawings of sites mentioned in contemporary travel literature. By the 1860s, the source of the Loue was just as likely to figure in regional poetry as it was in legal disputes about water rights.[5] It is therefore at first surprising that none of the major known paintings of the source of the Loue from this period are especially picturesque or documentary in spirit. Besides the picture in New York (the exception that proves the rule; fig. 21), none intimates that the source of the Loue was also a source of preindustrial power. Courbet at all other times deliberately excluded the formidable stone-and-wood construction running along the left-hand side of the Metropolitan Museum canvas. To put this dramatic exclusion into perspective, an illustration from *Voyages pittoresques et romantiques dans l'ancienne France* (fig. 22) reveals an entire complex downstream. Except for the lone example of the solitary figure in the picture in Washington, D.C. (fig. 23), Courbet seems to have made it something of a mission to exclude all traces of society.

The earliest work in the series, dated 1863 and now in Zurich (fig. 24), shows that from the beginning Courbet had another, far more inspired reason to paint the source: to conjure a singular, close-up encounter with nature that prioritized the natural over the built. In the Zurich picture, we approach the cave from the left. Although this means that we are practically inside the cave, we are not totally trapped. At such close range and from such an angle, the waters of the Loue do not spill out toward us but off to the right. At this early stage in his treatment of the subject, which still followed the layout of the site to a large degree, Courbet was trying to resolve a tricky issue: how to depict being near enough to the source so as to be almost inside it while at the same time being far away enough to witness the full force of its water-spurt. That Courbet had not yet solved the problem explains the awkwardness of the explosive river-foam on the right of the Zurich picture that is at odds with the rest of the scene. At this point, Courbet could paint a claustrophobic source or a materially aggressive one but not both at the same time.

By summer 1864, Courbet was eagerly telling the art dealer Jules Luquet about four paintings focusing

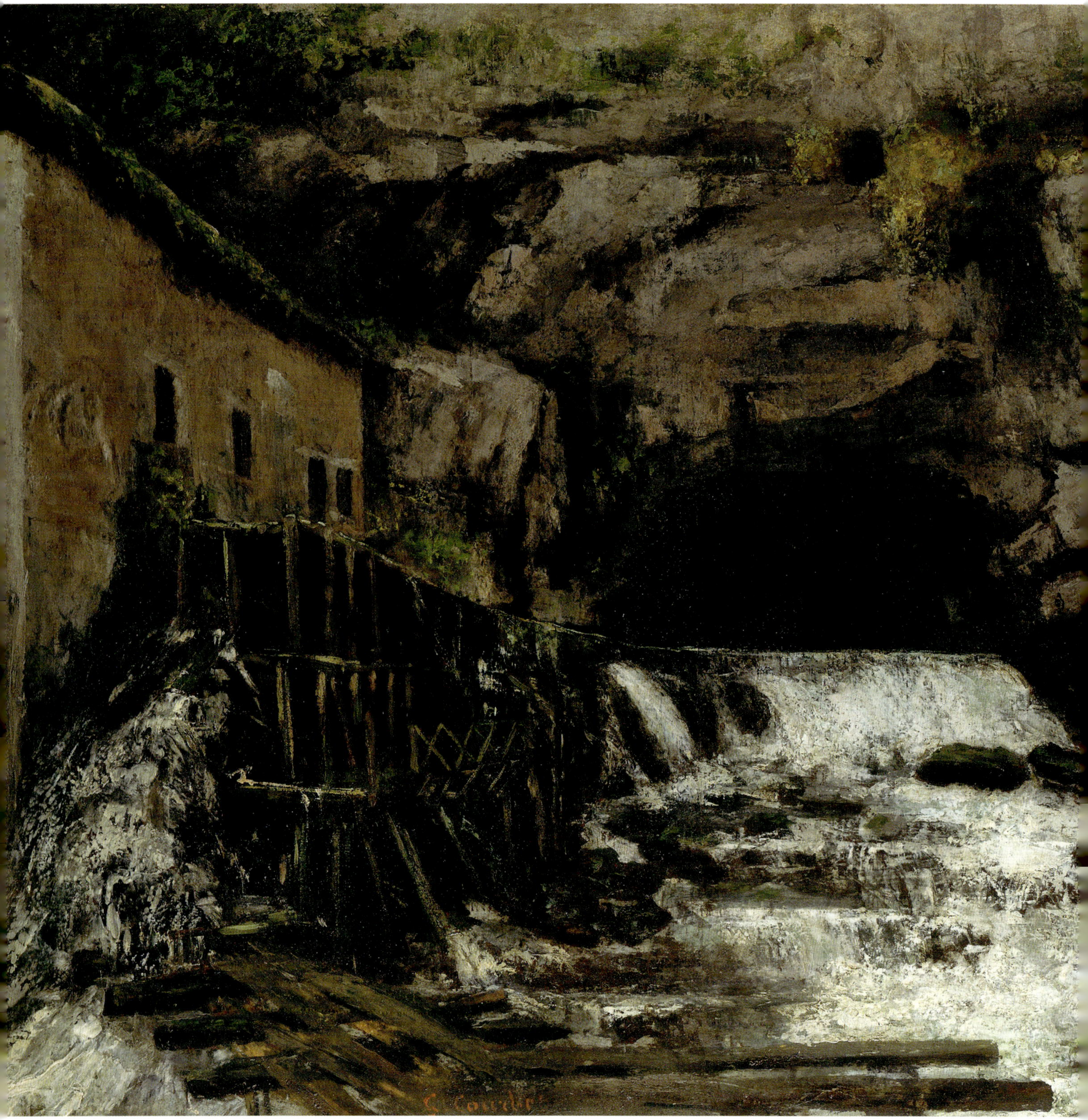

21 | *The Source of the Loue*, 1864. Oil on canvas, 99.7 × 142.2 cm. The Metropolitan Museum of Art, New York

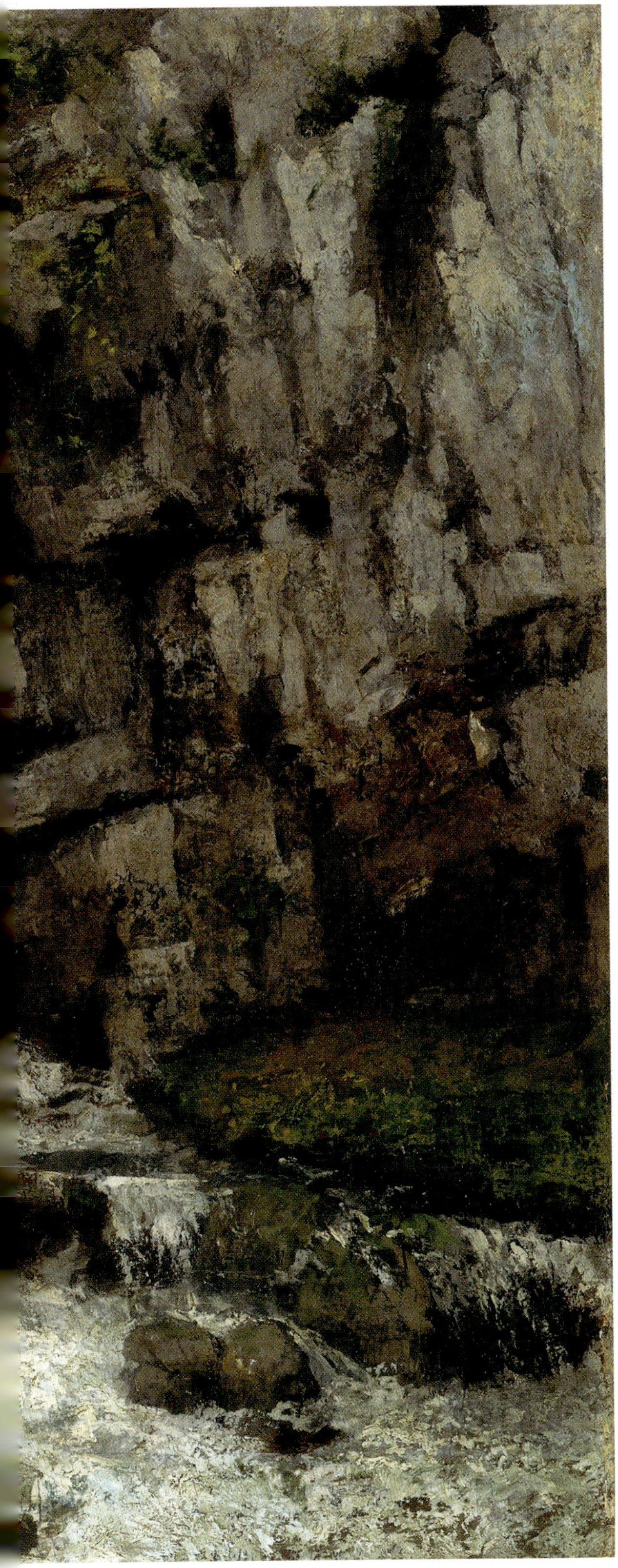

on the source of the Loue, each over a meter wide.[6] If, as Lorenz Eitner argues, these are the versions in the Albright-Knox Art Gallery, Buffalo (see fig. 2), the Musées royaux des Beaux-Arts de Belgique, Brussels, plus one in private hands and another lost painting, then Courbet had apparently solved his initial problem within months.[7] By removing the wooden pier from the left of the Zurich picture and re-orienting the cascading water so that it now fell toward the viewer rather than to the side, Courbet eliminated the last vestiges of lateral movement from his depiction of the source. The grotto is now approached head-on. We are positioned, seemingly in defiance of gravity, in front of the basin-pool, hovering above the waterfall in the lower part of the canvas, poised to take in the gushing water while simultaneously answering the cavern's summons. Or, in the words of Michael Fried, "Without exception, caves and grottos in Courbet's paintings are not simply enclosing spaces toward which the artist regressively was drawn; they are also sources of water coursing outward toward the painter-beholder."[8]

Parallels in art or literature for this intensely visceral journey into the recesses of the earth are few and far between. Travel writings could sometimes appreciate the rawness of nature at the source. But, like the *Voyages pittoresques et romantiques dans l'ancienne France*, they inevitably exalted the sublime and the soul-inspiring at the expense of the material or prehistoric. Given the relative dearth of comparable texts, it is striking that more has not been made of the texts that Max Buchon produced around the time of the artist's stay in Franche-Comté. Buchon, an early collaborator and political kindred spirit of Courbet's, had been exiled to Switzerland in 1852 for being the chief "demagogic spirit among his political brothers" in Poligny during the Second Republic.[9] In 1856, he returned to his native Salins, a day's journey from Ornans, where he would remain until his death in 1869, supposedly in Courbet's arms. In negotiating this return, Buchon had agreed to occupy himself "uniquely with literature and administration."[10] Between 1862 and 1864, that literature would include a book of verse, a collection of popular songs, a translation of German poetry, a guidebook for tourists, articles in local newspapers, and the launching of a new literary journal.[11]

22 Illustration from Charles Nodier, Justin Taylor, and Alphonse de Cailleux, *Voyages pittoresques et romantiques dans l'ancienne France*, 1825

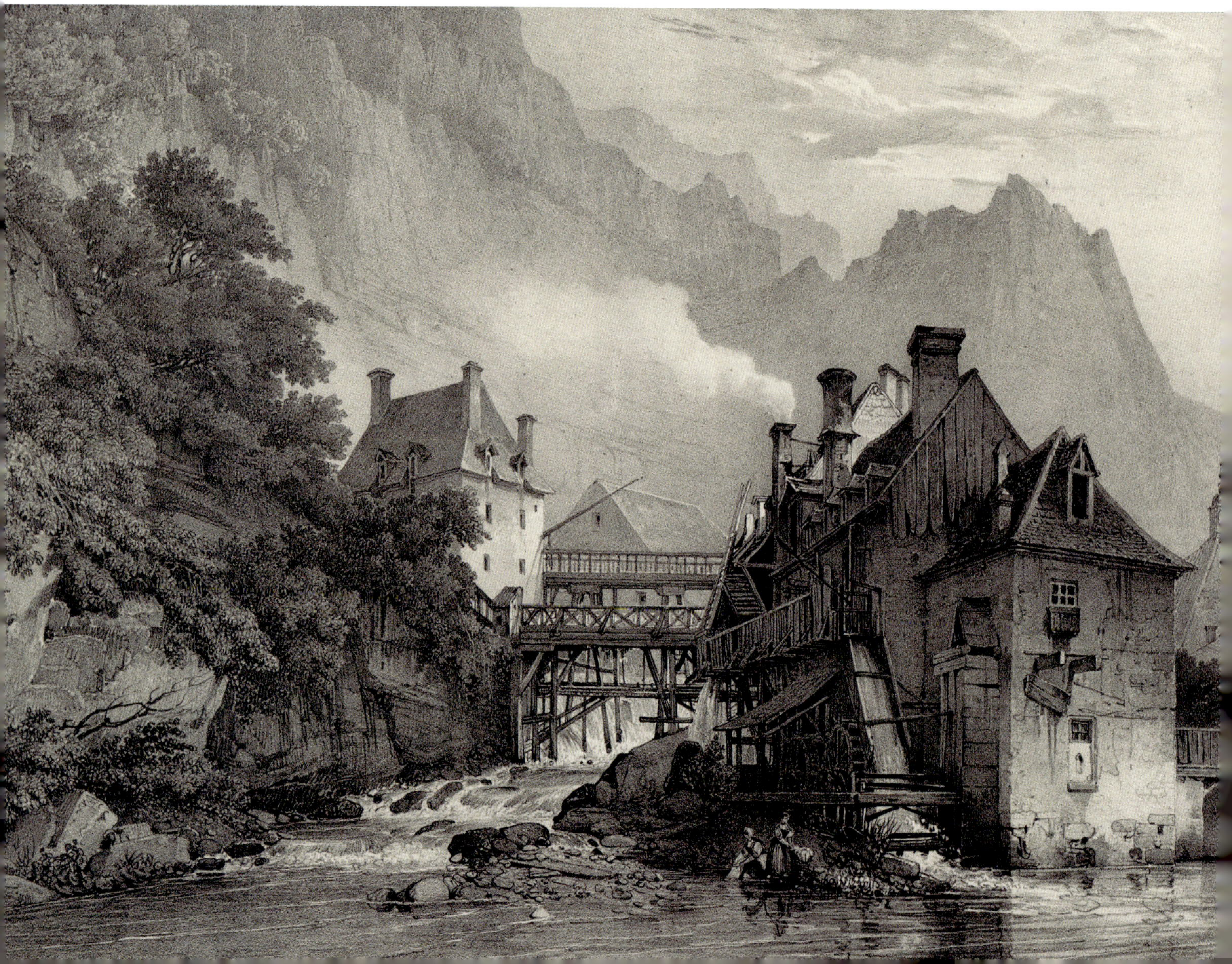

Studies of Courbet's intellectual concerns in the mid-1860s have tended to make the philosophy of Pierre-Joseph Proudhon their primary frame of reference. There are good reasons for this: Courbet and Proudhon at this time corresponded about the latter's forthcoming magnum opus of art criticism, *Du Principe de l'art et de sa destination sociale* (1865), and Proudhonian thinking also informed two major Salon paintings, the anticlerical (and rejected) *Return from the Conference* of 1863 and the great 1865 portrait of the recently deceased thinker and his family. And Courbet vouched for their association himself, as in an oft-quoted letter to his father: "At the moment I am corresponding with Proudhon; We are producing an important work together that attaches my art to his philosophy and his work to mine."[12]

Yet Courbet's friendship with Buchon, it can be argued, was just as intense—if not more so—over the same period.[13] To cite one little-known example, in the months that Courbet was painting his source paintings, Buchon was working on an article on popular song for the new journal *Revue littéraire de la Franche-Comté*. Writing to his collaborator Charles Thuriet on 8 March 1864, Buchon stated his desire to do another piece for the journal on the sculpture of Max Claudet and the painting of Courbet (he had just seen the painter in Ornans). Given the critic's joy, expressed in the same letter, on discovering a rare eighteenth-century patois songbook owned by the Courbet family, it is safe to say that Courbet was aware of his friend's scholarly pursuits by early 1864 at the latest, that is, in the months the artist was painting his river and grotto scenes.[14]

Buchon's search for linguistic origins of the regional dialect and Courbet's interest in the natural origins of the local landscape shared the same motivation in revealing a hitherto-lost or unknown past through painstaking study and observation of material that was usually overlooked. Until this point, Buchon had used patois primarily as source material for his fiction and verse. However, after reading Champfleury's *Chansons populaires des provinces de France* (1860), he adopted a more analytical attitude toward the subject.[15] Between 1862 and 1864 Buchon tracked the historical development of patois through a comparative analysis of Franc-comtois song lyrics, folklore, sayings, and place names. The Courbet family songbook was one of many sources, oral and written, that formed the basis for his study. The book that Buchon published on the topic, *Noëls et chants populaires de la Franche-Comté* (1863), was his answer to Champfleury's *Chansons populaires* and often stressed patois's counterofficial character:

> Our patois are not, as one might think, jargon generated from altered French. They are true languages that began at the same time as French and have marched alongside it. In the wake of invasions and religious or secular relations, they have obeyed general laws of formation, but have developed independently of one another such that each language has its own particular rules, always logical and consistent to the least details.[16]

The alleged superiority of French over patois was not a given, but a matter of social convention established "in the wake of invasions and religious or secular relations." Patois had survived the official Romanization of culture by hiding "underground" in the speech of village, family, and home. By gathering colloquialisms, idiomatic expressions, and folktunes, Buchon hoped to rescue patois from centuries of linguistic suppression to serve as the basis of popular literature. He understood this project in political terms: "by nature, man is too mobile and independent to let a static language be imposed upon him, and thus to give up the freedom to create words according to his own whims and needs.... The study of patois is therefore the study of humanity."[17] In other words, Buchon saw his task as being not only to compare patois to French but also to liberate it from French.

By the time of his discovery of the Courbet family songbook in 1864, Buchon had acquired a trove of patois words and phrases but did not know how to use them in his writing. Buchon would never solve the problem of the form popular literature should take. But in two years he had come a long way with his linguistic project. He could not have failed to convey his excitement to his friends, including, of course, Courbet (to whom he had devoted an entire chapter of *Noëls*). What he would have told them is that even the tiniest details of their local environment—a word here, a rock there—were all potential cornucopias of knowledge about the past, if only people concentrated hard enough on them. Scrutinizing the "least detail" could potentially rescue

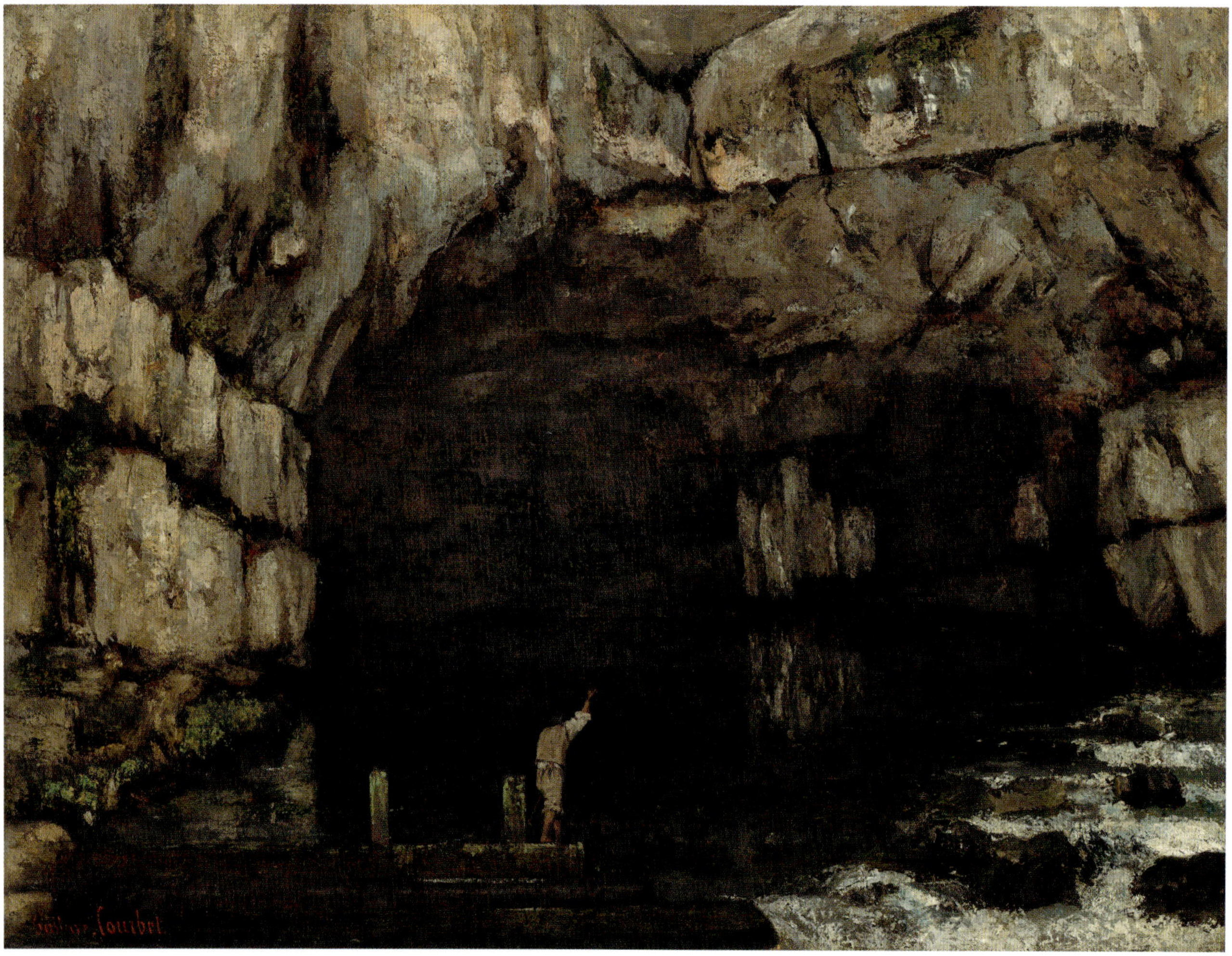

23 | *Source of the Loue*, 1864. Oil on canvas, 98.4 × 130.4 cm. National Gallery of Art, Washington, D.C.

ways of life and forms of knowledge that had been hidden, lost, or suppressed. Whereas a Buchon would have focused his attention on such things as a traditional children's game from Ornans, Courbet, a much more visual person at heart, would have turned his gaze to the landscape surrounding the town.[18] Courbet's association with Buchon did not lead, as we might have expected, given his earlier work, to paintings of after-dinner drinks and town gatherings, situations where patois could have been heard. Instead, he took landscape itself as his object and gravitated toward sites that were both old and seemingly never-ending, where sustained observation was rewarded like nowhere else with a constant offer of more to see, and thus more natural history to be revealed, as one was drawn further and further into a prehistoric core. This could not happen in scenes foregrounding people, or in landscapes that showed no signs of being epochs old, no traces of having been gouged out by eons of erosion, for instance, or of having been formed by the shifting of tectonic plates. Nor could it happen in landscapes with a broad expanse of sky, or any other kind of visual escape route save for one leading directly toward an obscure, as-yet-unknown origin. Ancient grottoes and shrouded riverbeds fulfilled all the necessary criteria—they were uninhabited, primeval, and up-close felt almost inescapable, which is why Courbet painted them.

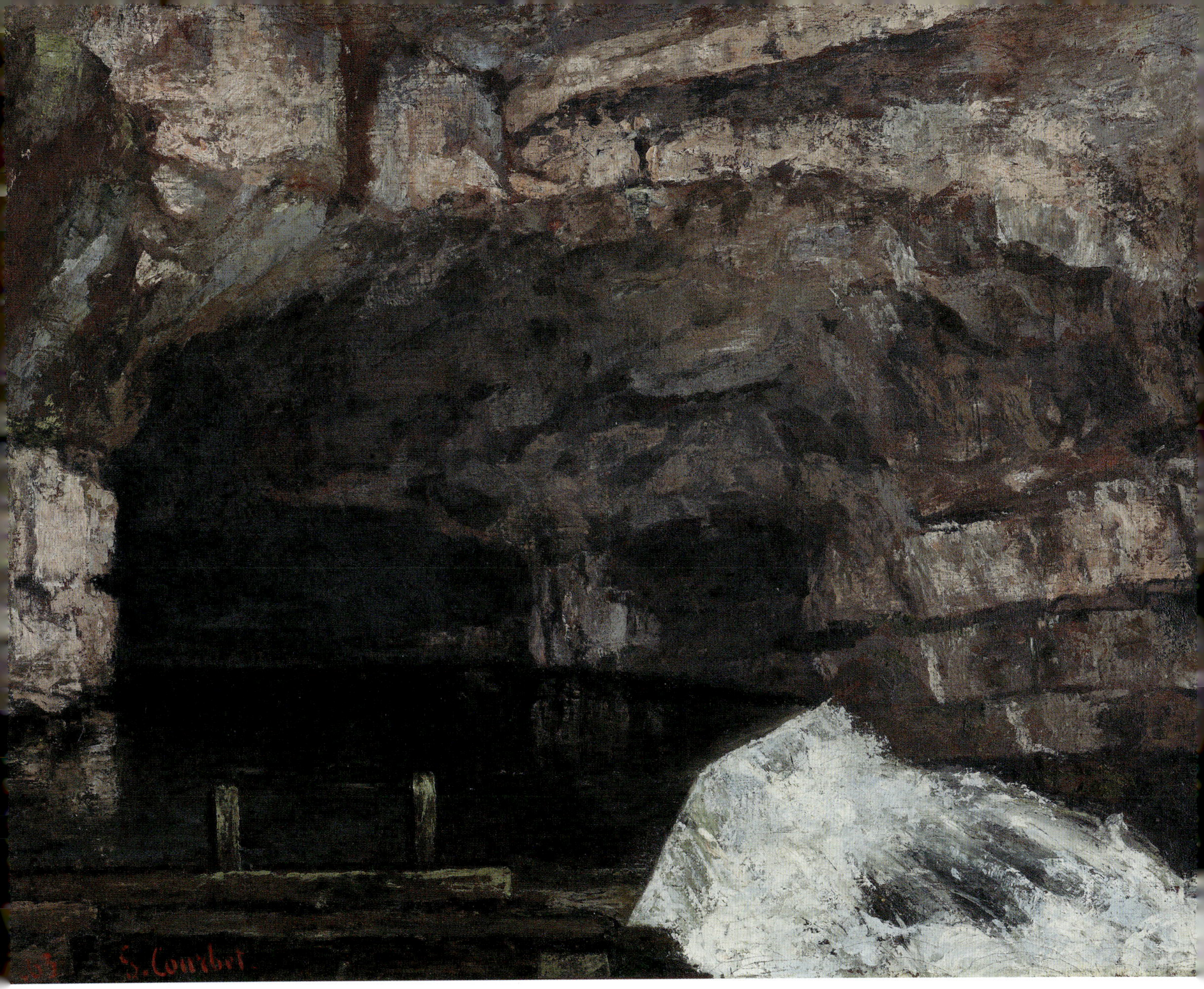

24 | *Source of the Loue*, 1863. Oil on canvas, 84 × 106.5 cm. Kunsthaus Zürich, Zurich

BATTLES OF ALESIA

For Courbet and his circle, exploring the deep historicity of words and places had ramifications beyond art and literature. Indeed, at the moment that Courbet was painting his river sources and Buchon was collecting his songs, a national debate about the history of a certain Franc-comtois landscape was raging across the country, from the meetings of provincial learned societies to the schools of Paris to the highest levels of government. The dispute, which brought historical investigations such as Buchon's to bear on contemporary issues, informed two Courbet landscapes at this time, one of a waterfall near Salins and one of a large oak on the plateau of Flagey. The central point of contention was the true location of the historic Battle of Alesia, the epic conflict that finally delivered Gaul to Rome at the end of the Gallic wars in 52 BCE. The event takes its name from the capital of Alesia inhabited by the Mandubii, where the Gallic army led by Vercingetorix held its last stand against the forces of Julius Caesar. The Battle of Alesia's importance to French identity is on par with that of the martyrdom of Joan of Arc and cannot be overestimated. Caesar's victory extinguished Celtic influence in the area, inaugurated Latin hegemony, and secured in perpetuity France's historical link to classical antiquity. Alesia's location remained uncertain well into the nineteenth century. At that time, the choice came down to two cities: Alise-Sainte-Reine in Burgundy and Alaise in Franche-Comté, 30 kilometers southwest of Ornans.[19]

The study of the historical origins of language and landscape played a critical role in this controversy. Partisans for each city enlisted whole teams of antiquarians, philologists, and even military planners to mine their respective areas for signs of ancient Alesia.[20] This research demanded both a knowledge of old languages (to read the historical accounts and decode place names) and a familiarity with the local terrain (to match places described in the texts with actual locations). This fact was not lost upon the Courbet–Buchon group. The member of their entourage most conversant with the matter was the Salinois schoolteacher and historian Charles Toubin. A nineteenth-century polymath who often pursued research outside professional institutions and disciplines, Toubin authored texts on subjects as diverse as pre-Roman Gaul, religious sanctuaries in antiquity, and Salinois folklore. The heterogeneity of his corpus—as well as its idiosyncrasy—largely resulted from his own self-confidence as a self-taught man.[21] In 1857, Toubin had presented a paper in defense of Alaise as the site of ancient Alesia to the Société d'Émulation du Doubs (of which he was a member).[22] At a time when archeological research was still mostly philological in nature (i.e. library-based), Toubin and others used their wanderings around Alaise to produce evidence, mostly place names and topographic details, that had gone unmentioned in the written historical accounts.

Toubin was Courbet's guide to Alaise when, in late 1864, businessman Alfred Bouvet commissioned the artist to paint a site believed to have been involved in the Battle of Alesia. The locale in question was the Gour de Conche (local parlance for "gouffre de conches" or "gulf of the conch-shells"; fig. 25), a 17-meter-high waterfall formed from the descent of the Todeure River from the plateau of Alaise down to the Lison River (fig. 26). The cascade's unusual name was taken from a small stream

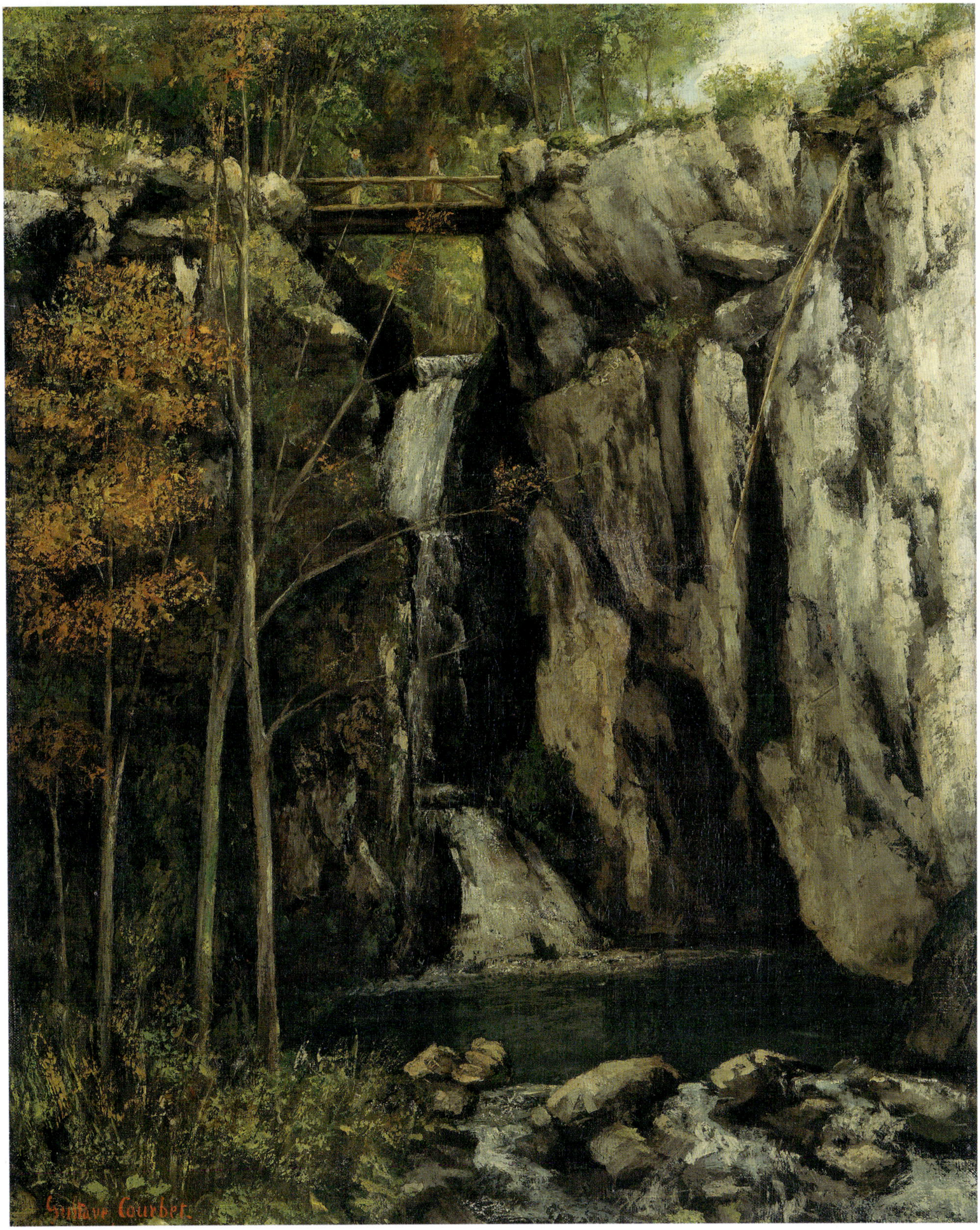

25 | *Le Gour de Conche*, 1864. Oil on canvas, 74 × 60 cm. Musée des Beaux-Arts et d'Archéologie, Besançon

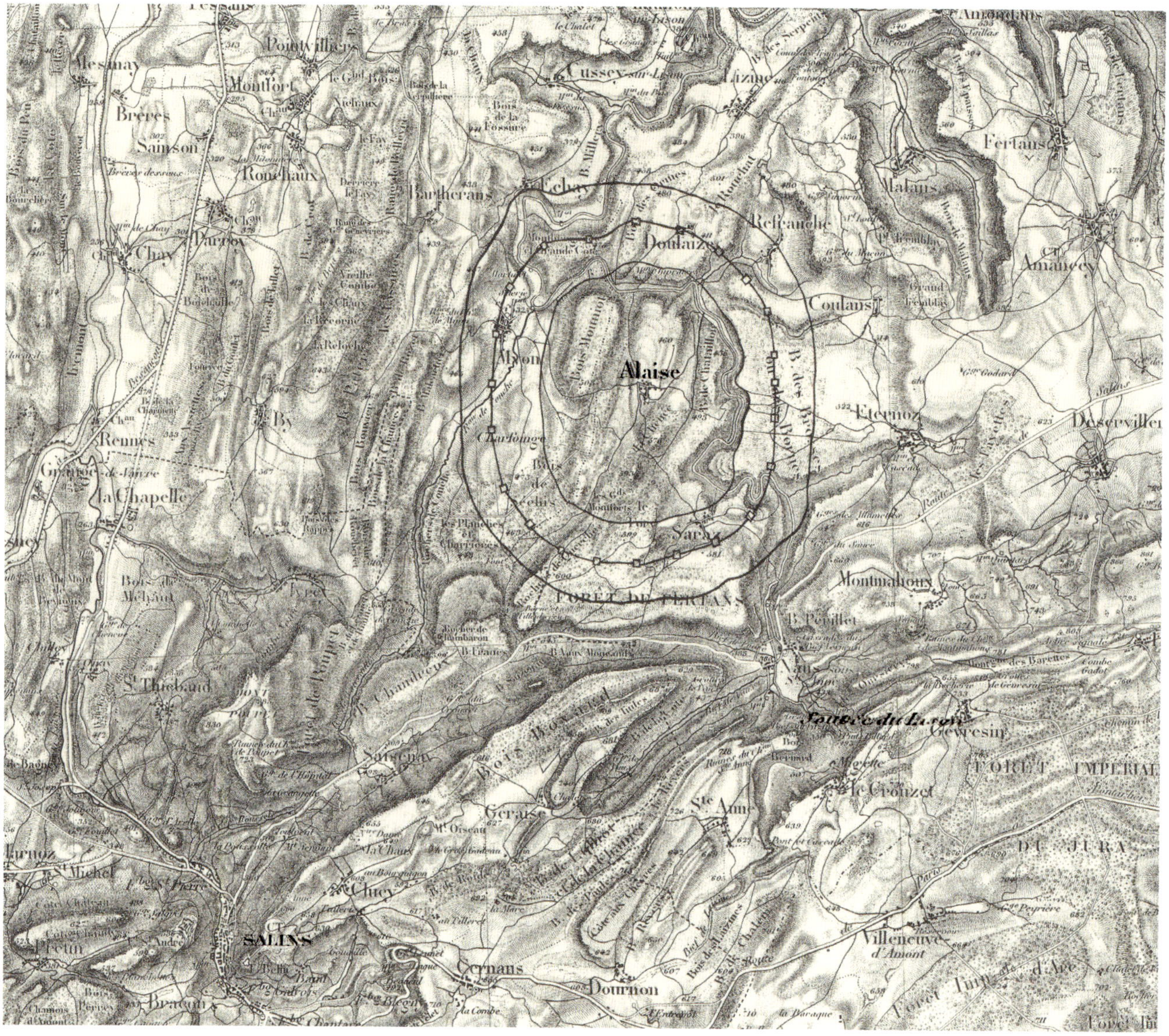

26 | Map of the area around Salins (detail), including the location of Alaise, from the *Carte d'état major*, reproduced in *Le Spectateur militaire* (1856)

that fed the Todeure River called the Conches, whose bed was lined with shells. Following the nineteenth-century Alesia specialist Alphonse Delacroix, Toubin believed that, during the siege of Alesia, the Romans had used water from the Gour de Conche to fill trenches fortifying their position. He may have shared this knowledge with Courbet in several places: at the Gour de Conche; around Alaise, at a ditch called Le Conat, where according to Delacroix the Gauls tried to escape Caesar's *conatus* (attack); or at a mountain, Les Mouniots, whose name resembles the Latin word *munitiones* (fort).[23]

As to whether Alaise was Alesia, Courbet did not need much convincing. He had already given an answer in the affirmative when he painted *Oak of Flagey* earlier that year (fig. 27). Exhibited in 1867 with the subtitle *The Vercengetorix Oak, Caesar's Camp near Alesia*, the painting referred to the Roman army encamping on the Flagey plateau opposite Alaise. According to Linda Nochlin, the massive solitary oak represents the valiant Gallic leader Vercengetorix, defiant in the face of defeat.[24] It is not difficult to see why the artist would have identified with the famous Gaul. For a Franc-comtois such as Courbet, Vercengetorix symbolized the region's independence. Furthermore, siding with Rome's historical enemy was a bold statement for Courbet to make at a time when Napoleon III was setting himself up as a modern-day Caesar (and, indeed, putting all his weight behind the resolution of the Alesia question in favor of Burgundian Alise).[25]

Courbet's anti-Napoleonic streak extended to *Gour de Conche*, though less obviously. *Gour de Conche* was a pendant to *Fort de Joux* (1864; Private collection), also painted for Bouvet.[26] The Fort de Joux, an old, recently decommissioned prison in the Jura mountains near the Swiss border, was also a symbol of intransigence in the face of authority; the prisoners incarcerated there were enemies of the state. If this political symbolism has always attached itself to *Fort de Joux*, it has almost never come up in discussions of *Gour de Conche*. Yet, like *The Oak of Flagey*, whose subtitle sets Vercengetorix against Julius Caesar, thus making clear Courbet's disagreements with the administration of the period, *Gour de Conche* depicted in its own way a site of resistance, one situated deep in the river valleys of the region instead of at its highest peaks.

Buchon was the first to report on Courbet's painting of the Gour de Conche in the 11 December 1864 edition of *Le Salinois*, where it was given the title *Gour de Conche, sur le chemin d'Alésia*.[27] By this date, Courbet had been living and working in Salins for almost three months, probably with his friend's encouragement. Two weeks later, at Courbet's invitation, Castagnary arrived in Salins, checking in at the centrally located Hôtel Sauvage, where he would lodge for the next twelve days. On arrival, he dined at the Buchons' place with a group he would later affectionally dub the *colonie réaliste*: Buchon and his wife, the "father" and "mother" of Realism; Courbet, of course, celebrating as usual in patois song; and a tall man in an American-style jacket with a hammer poking out of his pocket, the geologist Jules Marcou. During Castagnary's stay, Courbet honored a promise to give the critic a tour of "Alaise, or according to the Druids, Alesia."[28] The visitor later recalled two men, a doctor (probably the town physician Albert Germain) and an "antiquarian" (certainly Toubin), joining them on their journey. The latter's arguments must have left a deep impression on Castagnary, for long afterwards he would still remember the Gour de Conche, the etymology of village names, and the topography of the Gallic refuge.[29]

Before departing with Courbet for Ornans, Castagnary visited two other sites painted by the artist (and also reported on by Buchon): an unusual nearby cliff called the Roche pourrie, and a grotto located along the route to Ornans, the source of the Lison River.[30] Unlike the Gour de Conche, they had little to do with the Battle of Alesia. Knowledge of languages and antiquity would be useless in unearthing their secrets. A more geological approach would be required that was at ease with the vast timescale of planetary development, and no longer needing humankind as a reference point. Fortunately, someone with the necessary expertise was at hand, one of the members of the *colonie réaliste*: Jules Marcou.

27 *Oak of Flagey (The Vercengetorix Oak, Caesar's Camp near Alesia)*, 1864. Oil on canvas, 89 × 111.5 cm. Musée Courbet, Ornans

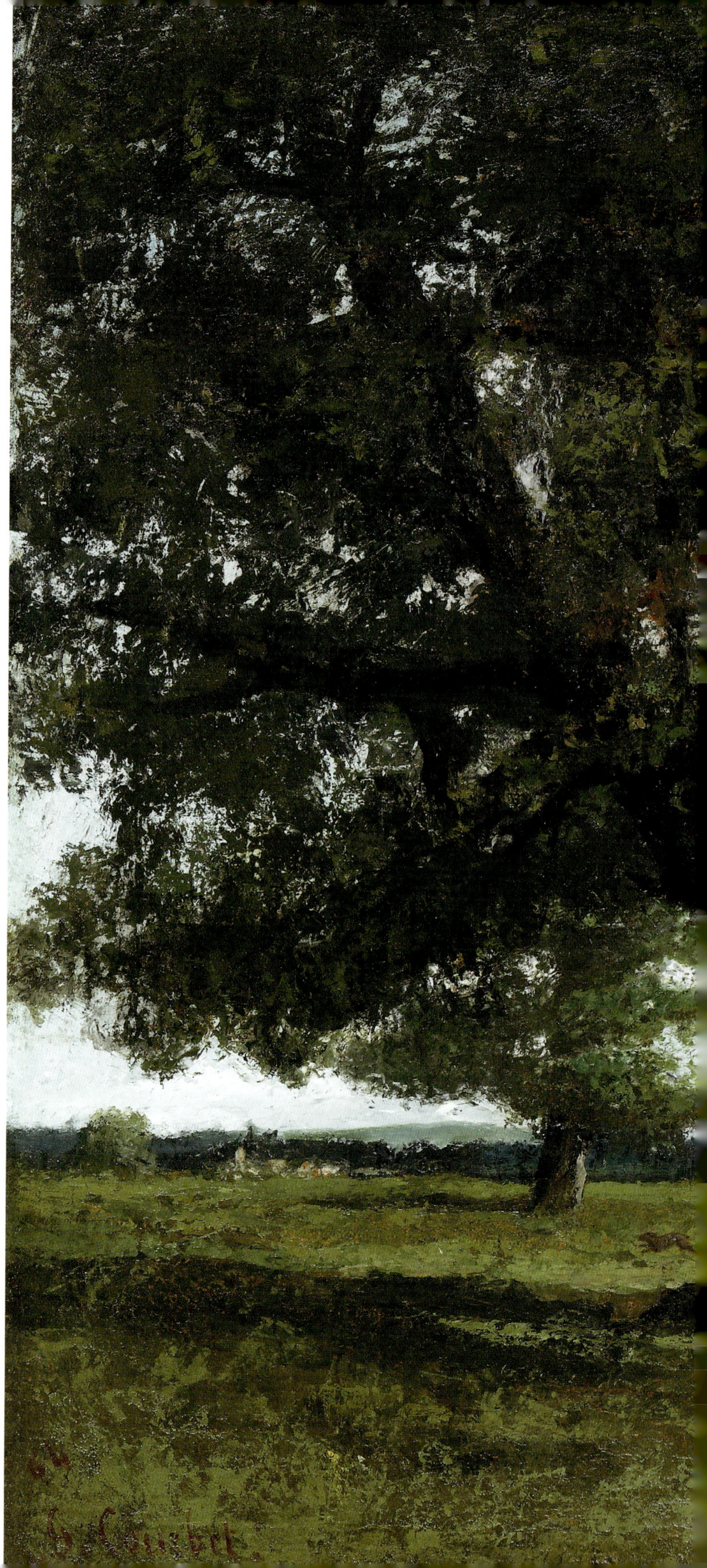

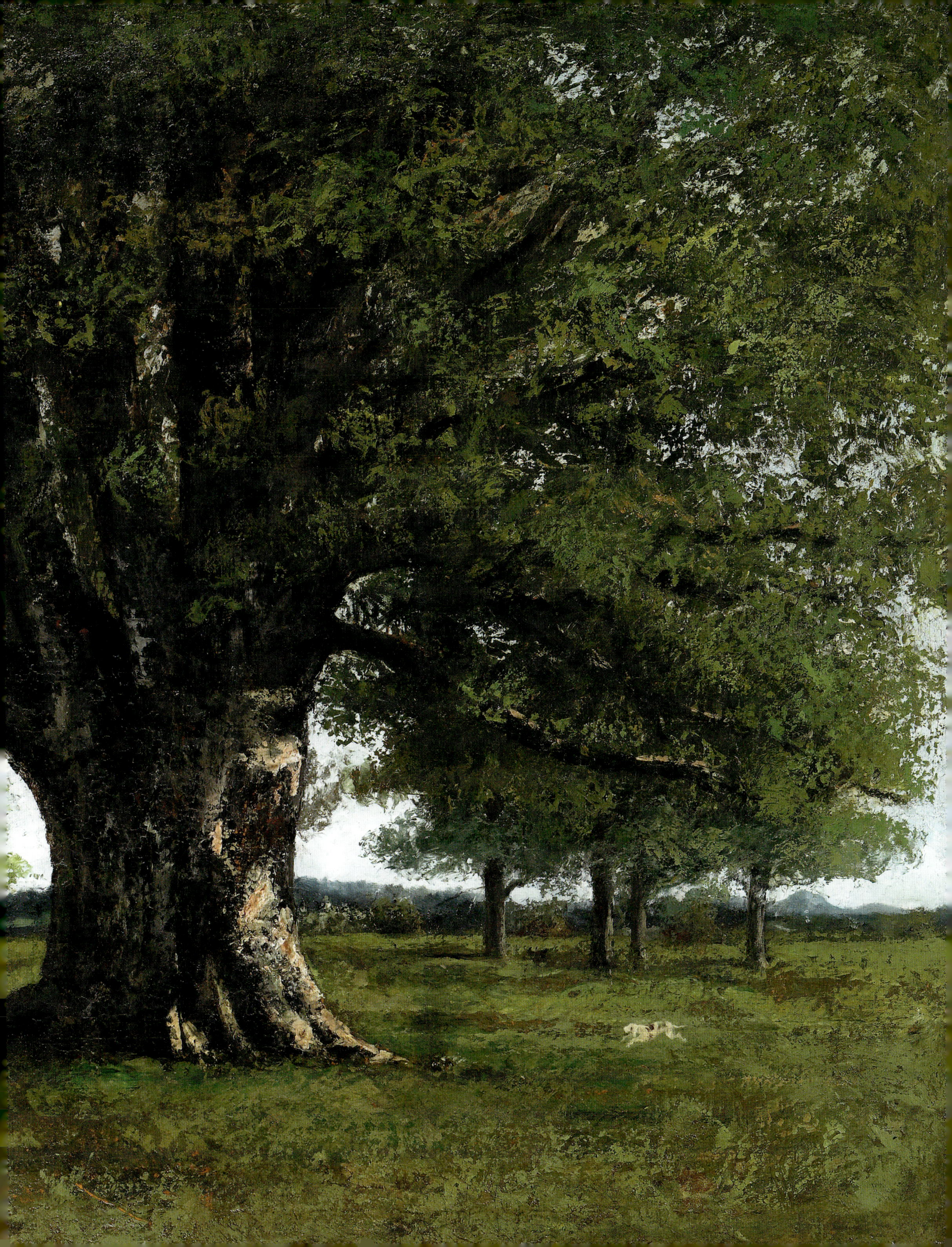

LAYERS OF MEANING

Buchon, Toubin, and Courbet all acknowledged the deeply historical character of languages and landscapes. Buchon collected patois songs in the hope of laying the foundations of a popular literature; Toubin investigated the topography and toponymy of Alaise to link France's early history with Franche-Comté, not Burgundy; Courbet reimagined picturesque caverns as prehistoric sources of origin. What Marcou would add to their collective endeavor was the knowledge and experience of a professional scientist whose main occupation was to dig up and analyze sedimented layers of history in search of the origin of his object, the earth.[31]

Marcou had initially trained to be a mathematician. But in 1844, while still a student in Paris, he fell ill and had to return to his native Salins. While recuperating, he began taking walks in the Jura with the physician and amateur naturalist Claude-Marie Germain. From this generous, almost fatherly doctor, Marcou acquired not only a passion for collecting rocks but also the most up-to-date knowledge of local land masses, for Germain was the only geologist of note in a region surprisingly understudied despite its distinctive topography. Marcou's education was rapid: within a year Germain introduced Marcou to the renowned Swiss geologists Jules Thurmann and Louis Agassiz. With help from Agassiz, Marcou published his first proper geological study, "Recherches géologiques sur le Jura Salinois," in 1845[32] and presented a revised version the following year to the Société Géologique de la France, Paris.[33] Marcou's innovative and unrivaled classification of Jurassic rock layers led to his appointment as chair of mineralogy at the Sorbonne in the city in 1846. By 1847, scarcely 23 years old, Marcou was curating the fossil collection at the Jardin des Plantes, Paris, then the world's undisputed center of geological research. By 1848, he was pursuing his research in America as the organization's chief traveling scientist. The trans-Atlantic voyage proved pivotal; Marcou would spend most of the next decade in the United States. He moved back to Salins in June 1864, where he stayed for over a decade to raise his children.

Buchon had known the geologist since at least the 1840s,[34] and within a year of Marcou's return to Salins, Buchon penned a biography of him.[35] Judging from the precise detail and almost embarrassingly hagiographic tone of his account, Buchon must have written it in close consultation with his subject. According to Buchon, Marcou was renowned for his analysis of local rock formations, those that to this day bear the region's name, the Jurassic. He was one of the few scientists at the time, Buchon noted, to have surveyed the Jurassic on multiple continents, thus making him well placed to chart a global Jurassic system (fig. 28).[36] One of the reasons why Buchon must have been drawn to Marcou, therefore, was the geologist's success in connecting something of local interest, the rock formations around Salins, with something of universal significance, the history and structure of the world.

Marcou commissioned a most unusual portrait from Courbet in 1864 when both painter and scientist were in Salins (fig. 29). Its strangeness derives from its subject, which is not, as one would expect, the geologist but the Roche pourrie. According to Castagnary, Courbet, Marcou, and Buchon joined him on a trek to the Roche pourrie between 20 December and the visiting critic's departure from Salins on 30 December.[37] While Castagnary and Buchon continued to the Fort Belin overlooking the rock, Courbet and Marcou stopped, presumably somewhere with a good view of the entire cliff, to paint the portrait. That Marcou is barely noticeable in the foreground of the painting suggests that Courbet did not spend much time capturing his sitter's features or asking him to hold a pose, especially as they were working outdoors on a winter's day. The bulk of his attention was focused on depicting the imposing rock formation.

The Roche pourrie was undoubtedly important to Marcou. He named an entire layer of the Jurassic system, the ninth one to be exact, after it. Here is how he defined it: "9. *Fer de La Rochepourrie.*—Iron hydroxide, oolitic, dark rust with patches of blackish blue. The limestone that contains it is more or less compact, and it is found superimposed and intercalated with yellowish-blue marl-limestone banded with large veins of iron oxide.—Total thickness, 10 meters [*Ammonites*] *Murchisonoe*."[38]

Reading Marcou's description, we are struck by how closely it matches aspects of the painting. Over the course of epochs rust-colored layers of iron-rich limestone alternated with light-blue layers of marl limestone to form strata that are still visible today. The layers of iron-red limestone are indeed remarkably compact, particularly in the lowest of the bluff's three large bands, where the painter's meticulous touches admirably convey a sense of layered superimposition. The painter has even stayed true to Marcou's palette, rusty red-brown interlaced with tones of blue. It is impossible to know if this remarkable correlation is due to Marcou's careful instructions or Courbet's painterly instincts. Whatever the case, *Roche pourrie* is an apt translation into paint, down to structure and color, of Marcou's recently christened substratum. Courbet did not produce such a pressurized stacking of horizontal strata again until the large painting *The Étretat Cliffs after the Storm* (1870; Musée d'Orsay, Paris).

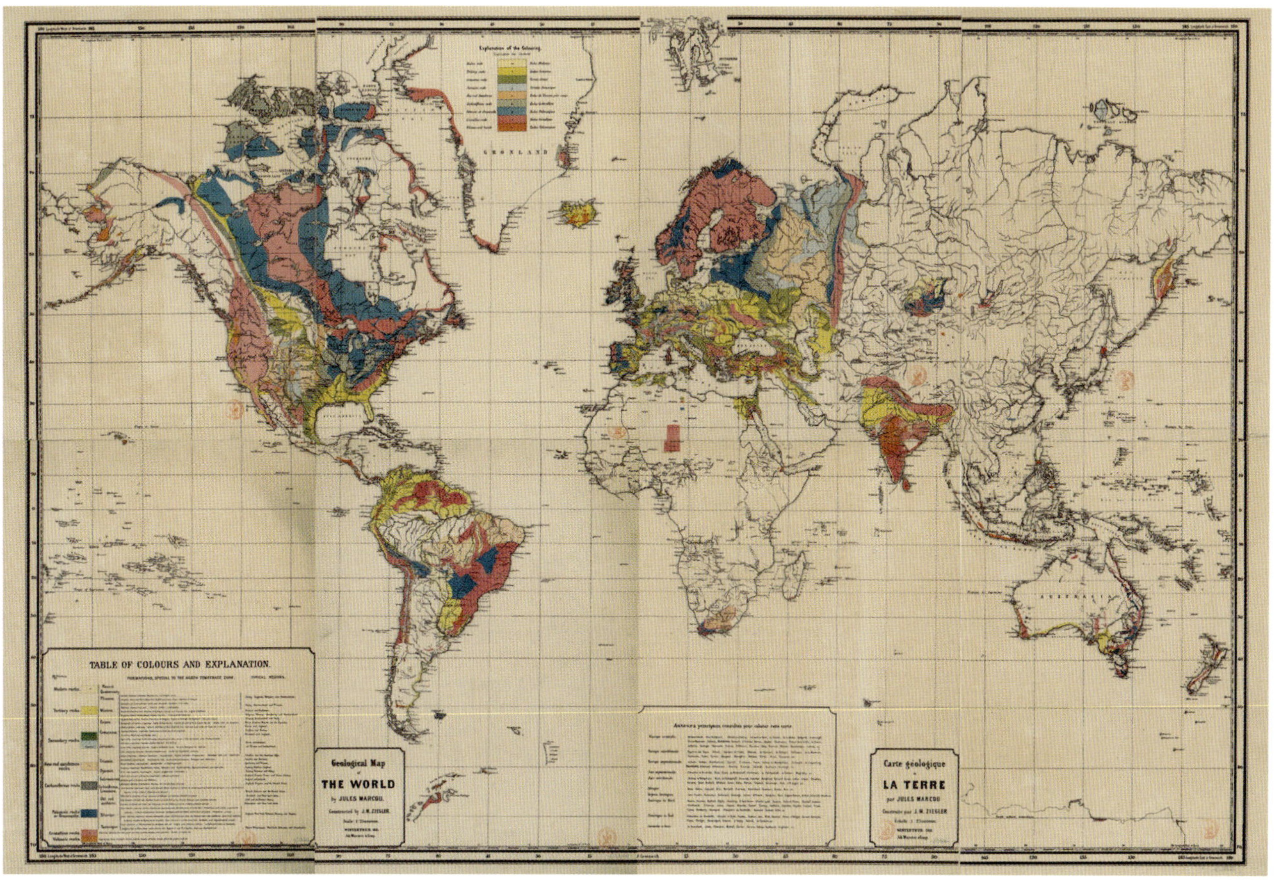

28 | Map from Jules Marcou, *Carte géologique de la terre*, 1861

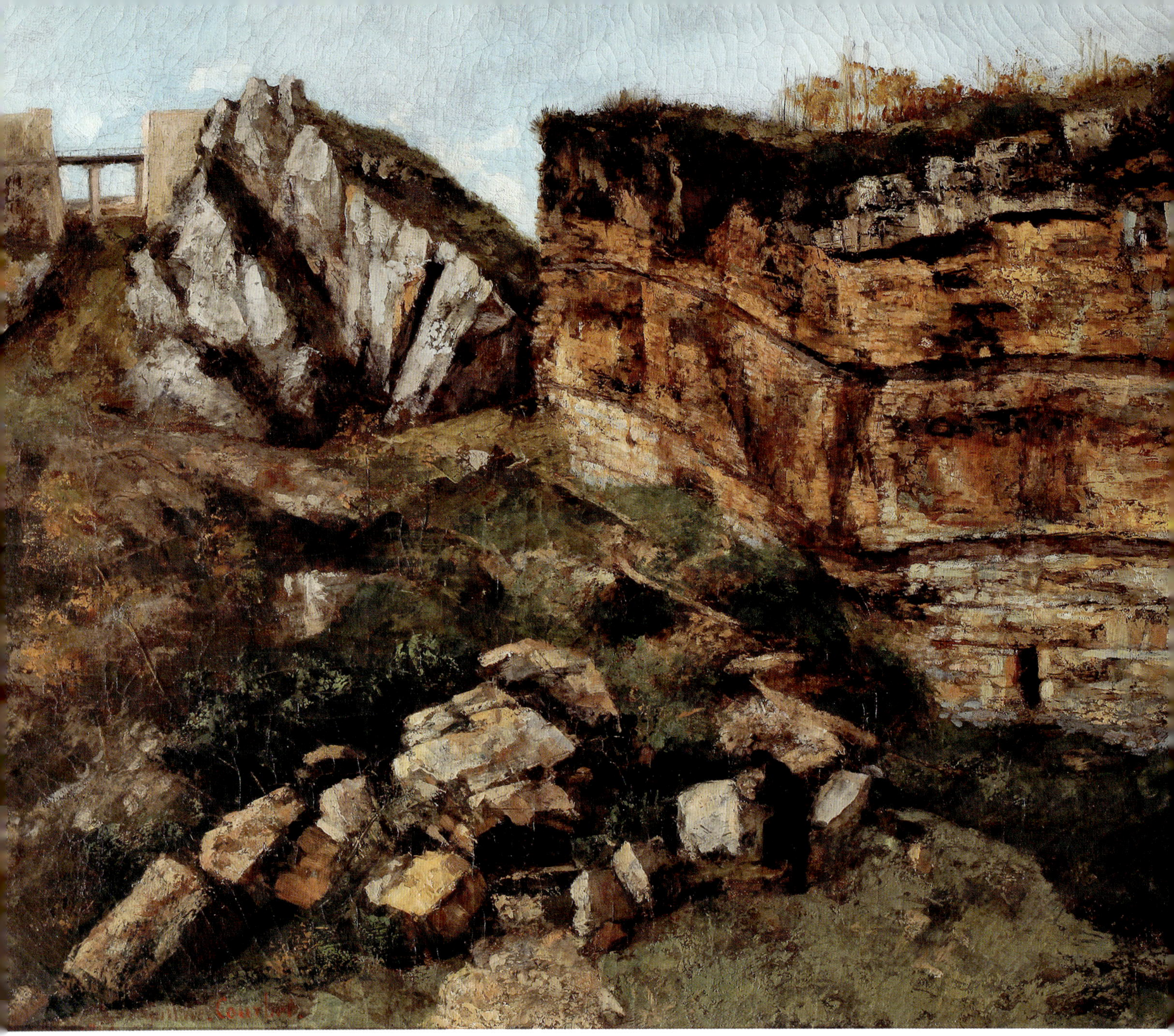

29 | *Roche pourrie*, 1864. Oil on canvas, 60 × 73 cm. Musée de la Grande Saline, Salins-les-Bains

Another reason for the selection of the Roche pourrie as the backdrop—or the subject—of the Marcou portrait is more personal. A familiar figure entered Marcou's thoughts while he devised the nomenclature "*Fer de La Rochepourrie*":

> I designated this division with the name *Fer de la Rochepourrie* first because of the large number of fossils that one could recover at the base of this mountain behind the Fort Belin near Salins and also because La Rochepourrie drew the attention of the most celebrated stratigraphic geologist France ever had. In 1817 Alexandre Brongniart drew and colored an excellent cross-section that he had framed and mounted in his celebrated collection and library.[39]

Particularly rich in strata and fossils, the Roche pourrie dated to the Jurassic period that was the subject of Marcou's early research and publications. Furthermore, it was a memorial to Alexandre Brongniart, the great innovator in the field of stratigraphy, with

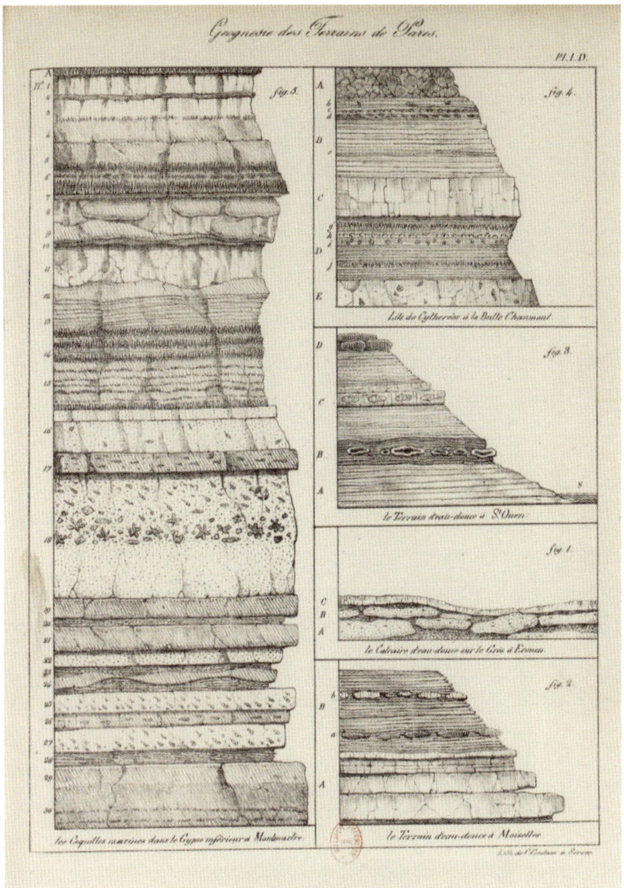

30 | Illustration from Georges Cuvier and Alexandre Brongniart, *Essai sur la géographie minéralogique des environs de Paris*, 1811

whom Marcou had discussed the Roche pourrie weeks before the elder scientist's death (fig. 30).[40]

Here it seems necessary to comment on both the outsized reputation of a canvas of such modest size and a composition of equally modest ambition. The painting was first exhibited in 1867 with the title *Roche pourrie, étude géologique*, the sole explicit reference to geological science in Courbet's oeuvre.[41] In most interpretations the comparison of the painterly process to the geological process remains almost exclusively at the level of analogy; Courbet's pictorial surfaces are similar to earth strata in that both are built up in visible layers. But this could be said of *any* painting, if examined closely enough. Instead, if Courbet's landscapes are in any way "geological," it is not necessarily because they are constructed in layers (although this is often the case), but because Courbet's painting at this particular moment shared with other nineteenth-century discourses—linguistics, archeology, and, yes, geology—a more general desire: to unravel stages of a historical process of formation in order to arrive at a lost origin somewhere in the deep past. Examining the accumulation of paint on canvas therefore can only go so far in helping us to understand the "geological" character of his painting. For Courbet's unique way of laying down paint was only a means to an end: to engage the broader field of nineteenth-century histori-comparative discourses of which his landscape painting, however temporarily, was a part.

Of all the group, Buchon was the most self-consciously aware of this discursive field. In his patois study, for instance, he explicitly compared his own project with that of a geologist:

> A man picks up a pebble, turns it over, and then, finding it worthless, shrugs his shoulders, and tosses it back. Later, he finds another, and while looking at it compares it to the first, noting the similarities and differences. Little by little, he comes to suspect deposits, more or less regular, spanning entire areas. Then come theories of alluvial sedimentation, of upheavals, and so forth until eventually the science of geology is born.[42]

For Buchon, the geologist gathering pebbles is no different from the linguist gathering words. Such activity, seemingly inconsequential in isolated cases, becomes a far-reaching science through the accumulation and cross-examination of examples. For it is only with a mass of comparative material that the history of a landscape, like the history of a language, can be reconstructed, its rules and processes revealed, its origins discovered.

The change introduced by such nineteenth-century disciplines as linguistics and geology brought about a fundamental shift in the nature and object of study. Let us first take the example of linguistics. Nineteenth-century linguists did not obsess as much as their eighteenth-century predecessors about the origins of language, which it was eventually assumed would be impossible to discover. For them, it was not crucial to explain how a primal cry or throaty grunt first became a meaningful word. Instead, it was paramount to identify an individual term's grammatical roots. Only then could it be situated within a language that itself nestled within a family tree of related languages. Over time the accumulation and analysis of roots would push comparative grammar ever closer to its true goal: the revelation of the invisible patterns and rules governing each language's internal structure as well as its historical relationship with other languages. The *process*, not the original meaning, was the object. As Michel Bréal, the first chair of comparative philology at the Collège de France, stated in his inaugural lecture of 1864, the same year Courbet was painting his Franc-comtois grottoes and streams: "Comparative grammar does not provide a new theory of the origin of language; it shows what, at its origin, language is."[43]

A similar development occurred in the sciences of the earth. In the previous century, natural historians, as they were then called, had concluded sooner than the scholars of language that the origin of *its* object, the planet, could not be traced with any certainty (barring of course the biblical explanation of the Creation). Theirs was a humbler project, to identify strata by their characteristic properties (color, mineral content, density, etc.) without passing judgment on how they came to be where they were located. In this sense, they had already reached the stage of data collection that linguists would achieve only at the beginning of the next century with the publication of the first comprehensive dictionaries and grammars. This classification of layers became mature stratigraphy once the strata, now fully surveyed and mapped, came to be understood as lines of *geo-historical* development (thus, the importance of fossils, which greatly facilitated their accurate dating). Just as the invisible processes shaping language became the linguist's true object of study, so the hidden forces shaping the earth became the preserve of the geologist. Once again it was the *process of formation*, not merely the form itself or its origin, that mattered.

This discovery of the object's internal historicity would resonate well beyond the disciplines of linguistics and geology. Several shifts took place: In philosophy, from the transcendental ego to the subject of history; in economics, from the abstract notion of wealth to the social forces of production; in natural history, from Linnean taxonomy to comparative anatomy (and later evolutionary biology); and in the nascent field of art history, from the definition of beauty to the study of historical styles. All these were part of a general historicizing discourse, to which the activities of Buchon, Toubin, and Marcou belonged. The Alesia debate proved that this type of analysis, in this case through the study of place names and actual sites, could unearth what had been lost or repressed by official history, just as the global mapping projects of geology at the time, working from the isolated pebble to the general theory, helped illuminate earth history.

Another document is even more explicit about the interrelatedness of these fields. At first glance it appears to be one of Buchon's least significant texts: a guidebook, *Salins-les-Bains: Ses Eaux minérales et ses environs*, published in two editions in 1862 and 1866. The earlier version contains familiar content: Franc-comtois poetry; patois songs; Alesia; the Todeure and Gour de Conche; Toubin and Alphonse Delacroix; and Marcou. Although written for the uninitiated, it is in some places polemical; Buchon points readers curious about Gallic history to Toubin's *Étude sur* les *champs sacrés de la Gaule et de la Grèce* (1861), encouraging them to test its written arguments against the evidence of the landscape.[44] When asked later why nothing more was written about Alaise's true identity, Buchon snidely remarks that "official history is like King Dagobert; it doesn't like to ask why."[45]

Even in the innocuous format of the tourist brochure, Buchon can convey something of his approach to history. He promotes landscape as its own kind of unwritten evidence, as the unearthing of "other," unofficial histories buried within the local. The expanded 1866 edition, with new sections on archeology, botany, and geology, makes his approach even more evident. The account of Alesia is now even more indebted to Toubin. Marcou, previously briefly mentioned, now has his own lengthy homage, including citations from his texts and a personal appreciation from Buchon. The Roche pourric, entirely absent from the previous edition, is described in glowing terms, couched in Marcousian geological terminology. And, of course, as Buchon does when he is feeling inspired, Courbet makes an appearance, in a brief cameo as Marcou's portraitist.[46]

It is tempting to think of *Salins-les-Bains* as an 1860s version of its celebrated forerunner, Nodier,

Taylor, and Cailleux's *Voyages pittoresques et romantiques dans l'ancienne France* (1825). Both travelogues take their readers on tours of Salins, Nans, and the source of the Lison River; both deliver evocative description and historical fact in equal measure.[47] But *Voyages* was a lavish illustrated tome written in an earnest, cultivated manner for the genteel reader who could have afforded it. *Salins-les-Bains*, with its more modest format and more jocular tone, targeted a different audience.

The full title, *Salins-les-Bains: Ses Eaux minérales et ses environs*, reveals much. In 1855, Jean-Marie de Grimaldi, an ambitious businessman and favorite of Napoleon III, founded a bathing establishment in Salins on part of the old saltworks to which the town owed its name. Since 1844, he had been trying to monopolize salt production in the region by merging the recently privatized saltworks of Arc-et-Senans, Salins, and Montmorot into a limited company. His intentions regarding his other main investment, transport, were just as clear, and, in 1852, Grimaldi had obtained the rights to build a railway line connecting Salins to Dôle, seizing the opportunity to join Salins to the main Besançon–Dôle–Dijon artery. The baths were extensions of a modernizing enterprise that sought to streamline production, expand markets, and promote tourism.[48]

The readership of *Salins-les-Bains* was not therefore yesteryear's gentleman traveler but someone who came to sample the Second Empire's latest fashion, the bathing resort.[49] At first glance, it seems odd that Buchon would stand behind such a guide, for history has shown that the influx of tourism can often signal the decline of local character, not its preservation. However, there are at least three reasons for his decision. First, travel to Franche-Comté had not yet reached the levels of mass tourism that we associate with places closer to Paris such as the Forest of Fontainebleau or the Normandy coast.[50] (Buchon would later reminisce that the people of Salins used to think *they* were the ones exploiting the bathers, not the other way around.) Second, the promotion of the baths gave Buchon an opportunity to spell out *his* version of the local, one that included patois, history, and geology, not just the usual sites. The third reason was economic. Salins had experienced a severe financial downturn in the second half of 1864, when it was also without a mayor. Buchon's support of the baths and the nomination of Grimaldi and his assistants as temporary municipal administrators were a stopgap in a time of crisis.[51]

Buchon's public defense of Grimaldi in *Le Salinois* linked the town's hopes to the success of the new enterprise. It is not so much that he believed in their success. Indeed, he would later claim to have remained lukewarm toward them. But, in 1864, Buchon saw only two possible remedies to Salins's problems: his friends' efforts and Grimaldi's money.[52] The guidebook combined the two, which explains its oddness. It is both learned report and leisurely travelogue, an almanac of facts for the intellectual and practical advice for the vacationer, all in easily digestible—if at times tongue-in-cheek—form. Buchon even mentions Grimaldi by name at certain points in his proposed tour: the businessman is credited with providing a mineral spring in town, building a pathway next to the mill near the source of the Lison, and, of course, underwriting the baths.[53]

In short, Buchon had every reason, high-minded as well as economic, to rewrite *Salins-les-Bains* so that he could include even more of his friends' research. It is precisely because he had to convey their complex ideas with a light—yet nonetheless serious—touch that *Salins-les-Bains* is such a revealing document. Unlike his more erudite projects, it does not read like the notes of a curious neophyte. Rather, it makes accessible areas as different as landscape, language, history, and the natural sciences. Had he become a master of any one of these fields exclusively, he might not have had the vision to see how they intertwined. This "mere" guidebook, then, had become something more: a plea for the local in a format whose existence spoke to the forces of tourism and capitalist development that threatened popular culture in general.

COURBET'S SOURCES

When Courbet arrived in Salins in September 1864, Buchon was probably the busiest he had been since returning from exile. In addition to his ongoing research on patois and popular song, he held quasi-editorial roles for *Revue littéraire de la Franche-Comté* and *Le Salinois*. In the latter, he weighed in on everything from the economics of bakeries to noise pollution to mayoral politics, seemingly pushing the limits of the "literature and administration" that had been set as the condition of his return from exile.[54] It would not be too long before the official powers would attack a seemingly innocuous library committee to which both he and Toubin belonged not only for its "socialist" acquisitions, but also for its covert assembling of opposition candidates for forthcoming elections.[55] The city's financial crisis only exacerbated matters. Courbet therefore arrived at not only a busy but also an uneasy moment for his friends.

The collective energy of the Buchon group was, of course, also channeled into art. Besides Courbet, the other practitioner was the now-forgotten sculptor Max Claudet. It is a measure of the esteem in which he was held locally that Buchon had organized a subscription to purchase Claudet's *The Grape-Picker* (1865; Salins-les-Bains) with the idea of turning it into a monument to Salinois viniculture (one of the town's chief industries, along with salt and wood production).[56] Claudet's other work included a portrait bust of Buchon and separate medallions of Courbet and Marcou.[57] For the present discussion, however, what is most pertinent are Claudet's memoirs, which describe in relative detail the creation of Courbet's most impressive Salins painting, *Source of the Lison* (see fig. 17 and quoted passage on p. 52).

According to Claudet, the day's journey from Ornans to Salins took Courbet first to Nans-sous-Sainte-Anne, a village within easy walking distance of the source. On hearing from Buchon that Courbet had arrived in the area, Claudet promptly set out from Salins for Nans. It is impossible to verify Claudet's claim that he saw Courbet paint the source in under two hours. But whether *Source of the Lison* was completed in the open air or in the studio (or, more likely, a combination of the two), Buchon considered the picture important enough to mention in one of his "Lettres salinoises" (in the same article, he revealed the connection of the Gour de Conche to Alesia).[58] His approval would have been expected; Claudet tells us that Buchon himself had acquired a version of *Source of the Lison*. Courbet later repossessed it after Buchon's death in 1869, further proof of the importance to him of both friend and painting.[59]

Like the much larger source of the Loue River, the source of the Lison is also situated at the base of a towering rocky cliff. Within its mouth, thin walls of stone, like columns in a vaulted cathedral, as Claudet put it, partition the interior into smaller recesses. From here water cascades downward through various shimmering pools before finally settling to feed the Lison River. Compositionally, *Source of the Lison* adheres to a basic template. A plate from the *Voyages pittoresques et romantiques dans l'ancienne France*, for example, is cropped and shown from roughly the same point of

31 | Illustration from Nodier, Taylor, and de Cailleux, *Voyages pittoresques et romantiques dans l'ancienne France*, 1825

J. 117.

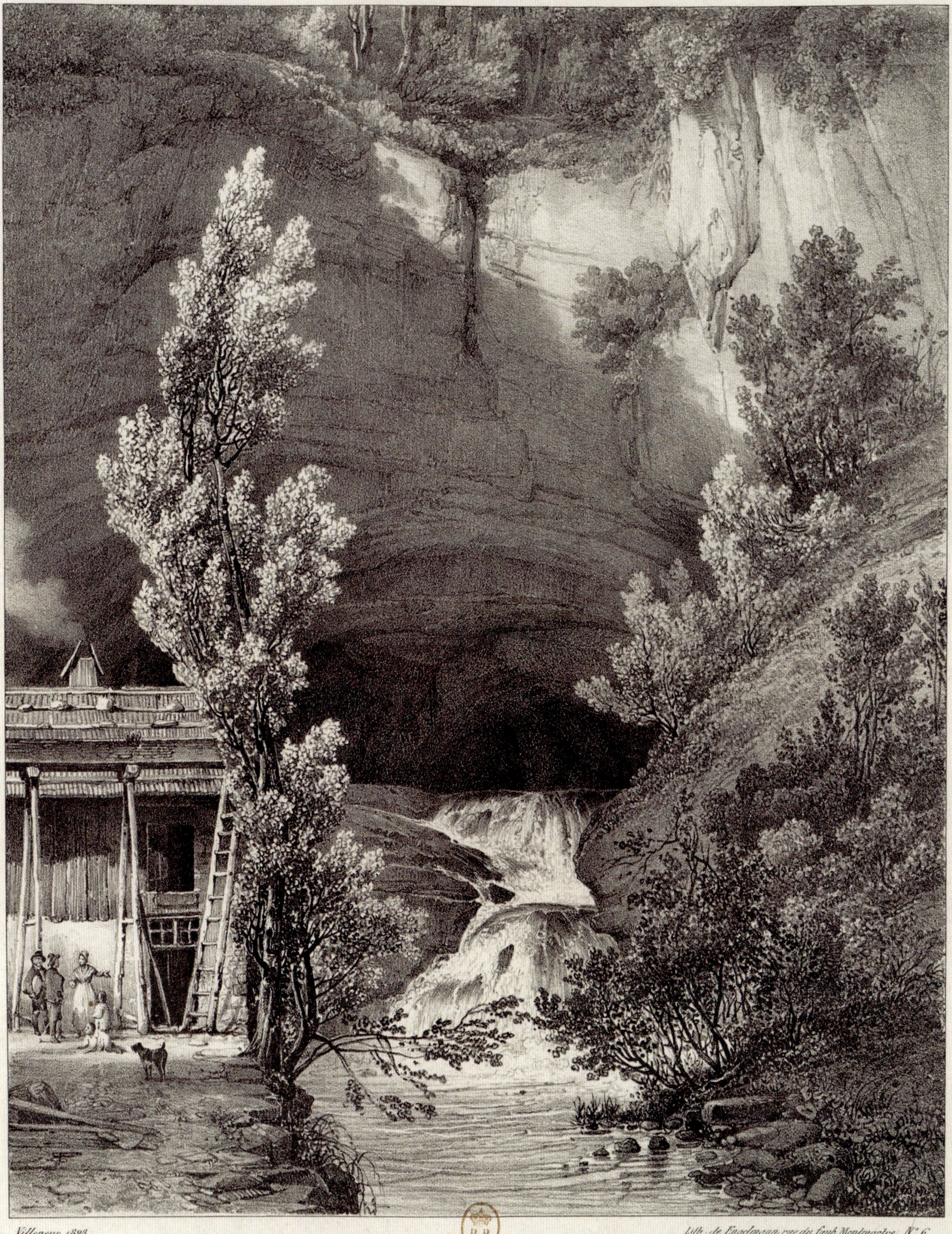

Villeneur 1828. Lith. de Engelmann, rue du faub. Montmartre N.° 6.

Grotte de la source du Léson.

view (fig. 31).[60] But Courbet has taken liberties with the Romantic prototype. Most obviously, he eliminates sentimental details such as the group in front of the shelter in the *Voyages* print. The viewer's position, while still central in the painting, is now much closer to the final waterfall. Gone, too, are the shadow cast onto the cliff and the strip of vegetation atop it. Anything that would put distance between us and the source, be it a genre scene, architecture, background, shadows, or a long trail of water, is removed or reduced. *Source of the Lison* transforms what had previously been an awe-inspiring scene of nature's grandeur into the experience of peering into an unknown crevice or examining a hole.

Claudet does not have much to say about this aspect of the painting. If anything, in celebrating the rocks' "gigantic" scale, as well as the cave's cathedral-like vault, he moves in his description closer to cliché. However, he was much more attuned to the work's painterly qualities. *Source of the Lison* is a stunning demonstration of the panoply of effects that the palette knife, sponge, and rag make possible. Claudet observed that Courbet "took with his knife some white, yellow, red and blue from his color box, mixed them on his palette, then spread and scraped them on the canvas with a sure and firm stroke."[61]

These "sure and firm strokes" can be organized into three basic types: the dab; the scrape or smear; and the deposit. All three appear throughout the painting, and they are particularly vivid when they are near each other. Let us focus on the area just right of center that is defined, moving clockwise, by the roof of the mouth, the autumn foliage at the rightmost edge, a group of gray rocks below it, and the central waterfall. We have already encountered the dab in our examination of marks in the *ca.*1862 Saintonge *Stream in the Forest* (see fig. 10). In that painting, the artist carefully pressed a paint-laden sponge or rag (or perhaps even a large, dry brush) into the canvas, creating floating clouds of greenish particles that the eye resolved into bushes and foliage. In *Source of the Lison*, Courbet used the same method in the tawny leaves to the right, but with an added twist. The dabs no longer consist of greens keyed to other lighter and darker greens around them in a system of finely graded tones, as they were in the Saintonge picture. Rather, Courbet's confidence in his technique had grown to the point that he could play with multiple colors at once, putting two dabbed colors, a light and a dark umber, for instance, close to both the gray of the rocks and the green of the grass below it.

We find a similar progression in the use of the scrape or smear. As in *Stream in the Forest*, Courbet applies drawn-out strokes to leave behind patches of paint that seem to float above their grounds. Whereas in the earlier landscape the smears, inevitably in some shade of green, are placed in small, crowded clusters, here they are much more evident. Perhaps none more so than the white and light-blue streaks at the center that represent effervescent rivulets of falling water. In less than two years, Courbet's methods had advanced to the point that he no longer needed to be so restrained with the color and size of his strokes. The autumnal trees and the cascade are some of the most noticeable parts of the painting. Yet despite the heightened color of the dab and the extended length of the scrape, these elements never appear grossly out of place, nor do they upset the balance of the picture.

However, it was undoubtedly the third kind of mark, the deposit, that most impressed Claudet. This is because, of the three, it is the most conducive to the use of a palette knife. Looking, for instance, at the rocky overhang, we see that Courbet has applied paint evenly across the entire length of a stroke, from the initial contact to the final lifting of the tool. The stiffness of the knife-blade helps the painter maintain the consistent pressure that a flat, uniform application requires. While this is most evident in the uppermost layers of opaque gray, where the deposits are almost constant in thickness and almost totally smooth in texture, it is also true of many of the darker underlayers. Had the artist used a brush, it would have been difficult to achieve the peel-like paint marks that we witness above the cave. For, no matter how hard a painter tries to eliminate them, brushstrokes, at a certain size, often produce curved ridges, toothed grooves, and stray wisps, effects that disrupt a smooth surface (a self-styled modern such as Courbet would have avoided on principle the alternative course, the academic route of applying fine glazes, free of accidents of the brush). Courbet's attraction to the palette knife thus inverted normal preference; it was precisely the flexibility of the brush that had traditionally recommended it to artists, which had made possible painting's seemingly infinite variety of textures and effects. Yet, for Courbet, the opposite was true: the inflexibility of the knife was its greatest strength and the pliability of the brush its major weakness, at least when it came to depicting landscape.

The three categories of dab, scrape, and deposit are not mutually exclusive. The last two often complement one another. It is clear, for instance, that the artist has, in the rocky volute, varied the pressure of the knife while making certain deposits, causing otherwise flat and even marks to become scraped or edged. The reverse has occurred in the rocky outcrop on the right with the brown trees. Here the scrapes are so broad and paint-laden that they are comparable to deposits in terms of surface covered, however broken in appearance. Instead of an absolute distinction between the two or three kinds of mark-making, then, what we find in Courbet's landscapes is something more like a continuum ranging from the "pure," unbroken deposit to the extreme, almost intangible scrape. If we can classify them at all, it is because certain strokes seem particularly suited to rendering certain types of things, deposits for rocks, scrapes for water and grass, dabs for trees and bushes.

At this point, it is instructive to return briefly to what had been said in the preceding chapter about the *ca.* 1862 Saintonge picture *Stream in the Forest* (see fig. 10). There Courbet had combined the tonal painting of Corot with the delicate mark-making of still life. The result is an exercise in visual deprivation. The main features of the painting have tightly restricted landscape's familiar tropes: chroma is reduced to an austere palette of mostly close-valued greens; spatially, there is no obvious means of egress; and, except for a strangely incongruous deer, the landscape itself is devoid of incident. Without the usual focal points, the viewer's attention inevitably gravitates to the only visual elements that *do* seem to provide animation: the touches of paint, particularly at the central impasse, that we can now identify as examples of the dab and the scrape.

Source of the Lison emphasizes, expands, and adds to forces already at work in *Stream in the Forest.* Its palette now comprises colors beyond a narrow range of greens, moving into grays, rusty browns, and light blues. The dab and the scrape are boosted in size and have been supplemented with the knifed deposit. Perhaps most dramatically, *Source of the Lison* amplifies an effect that was only beginning to be explored in the earlier work: the illusion of great physical mass, almost as if in relief, built from the accumulation of thin, flattened paint layers (usually three at most). Even more so than in *Stream in the Forest*—and once again contrary to all expectation—surfaces that appear to resemble masonry are not too much thicker than those found in more conventional painting. Courbet realized this effect without depending on a drawing or an ébauche as a preconceived template for his painting. Instead, the size, shape, and substance of individual landscape forms were determined in the act of painting them. His strokes did not follow drawn contours; they formed their own patterns. Courbet compared this process to the way that sunlight strikes an object's salient points as it slowly emerges from obscurity. In *Stream in the Forest*, this act of "illumination" led to a four-way collision of embankment, river, reflection, and background at the heart of the painting. By contrast, the center of *Source of the Lison* remains shrouded in mystery; the illumination is only partial; there are still more layered forms to see. Poor lighting alone is not responsible for this effect, nor is the choice of a subterranean motif. What is necessary above all to maintain the illusion of an unceasing birth is the strategic use of the dark ground as an unknowable point of origin from which all form is seen to rise gradually yet visibly.

This rare achievement should not be underestimated. For this kind of temporal dilation is utterly foreign to our usual experience of landscape painting. Traditionally, our sense of the passage of time is a function of the time it takes the eye to travel from one point to another within a pictorial field. Color gradients, markers of scale, atmospheric perspective, and the organization of receding planes were the classic means by which artists turned a flat canvas into an illusory world. However, it is precisely the ways in which Courbet whittled away at such conventions that distinguish his landscapes from those of his contemporaries. For example, in *Source of the Lison*, expected pathways are largely absent, space is compressed, and viewers are made to feel as if they had stumbled upon a scene caught in a state of suspended animation. As the eye begins to resolve the various dabs, scrapes, and deposits emerging from the darkness, the landscape is seemingly reactivated, and time begins to elapse again, now at a deliberate, almost plodding pace. The kind of temporality we have here is not the linear time of movement from point A to point B. Rather, it is the distended time required to bring things into the light of day. Whereas most landscape painting presumes locomotion between *places*, *Source of the Lison* is a voyage into the substance of *things*.

Buchon, who owned one example of *Source of the Lison*, would have been able to embark on such an imagined journey almost every day. His forays into linguistics and geology had taught him that all objects—a word, a rock, a place—are subject to deep historical forces, even—or especially—when they appear to be ahistoric. It is up to the observer to detect within each thing the traces of the past buried deep within it, even if that means excavating those traces at the level of the least detail, be it a grammatical root or the slimmest stratum. For Buchon and his circle, Courbet's 1864 landscapes were almost "excavations" of nature performed in the field of painting. Starting with the most outfacing points and working backwards toward the ground, the viewer acts as a kind of visual archeologist, identifying each constituent layer. Just as the study of patois uncovered forgotten parts of a language, so did the study of landscape reveal an entire hidden chronology of form.

Yet doesn't the close analysis of *any* painting yield similar results? The impressive finds of modern conservation, with its stunning ability to break down even the most well-blended passages of paint into stratified cross-sections, would seem to suggest so. However, to gain such a level of detail often requires an examination so near to the canvas that the observed area is scarcely recognizable as part of a larger whole, as if the intimate view existed in an alternative reality. By contrast, Courbet's best landscapes do not break down when viewed up close, the movement from the far view to the near view can be compared to a smooth and continuous zoom rather than an abrupt jump-cut from the telescopic to the microscopic. It takes a relatively long time to realize that what appears to be a patch of rock, or a patch of moss is a patch of paint, that the moist surfaces and dense textures before us belong to our own world and not to the depicted one. A Courbet landscape forestalls like no other painting up until this point in the post-Renaissance pictorial tradition the inevitable moment when the image finally devolves in the viewer's eye into pure paint. The collapse of the image into matter arrives only after a long, temporally extended period of looking, in which every forward step, far from initiating a complete breakdown of illusionism, seems on the contrary to have triggered another part of the scene to come into focus from the darkness. Getting close to the painting, rather than making everything dissolve straightaway into a formless mass, instead hints that there might be even more forms to be discovered as we approach a still-unseen point of origination.

Yet the plunge into the depths of a Courbet landscape is a journey that, crucially, never arrives at the origin, if by "origin" we mean a unique point in time and space that fixates the birthplace of form. Instead, the voyage through substance that his landscape painting proposes is like traveling along a mathematical asymptote; just as an asymptotic line is continually approached by a given curve but does not meet it within a finite distance, so does the act of peeling back the layers of a Courbet landscape bring us tantalizingly close to the point at which its first forms must have come into being, without however completely delivering us there. The impenetrable dark ground, seemingly the most inconsequential and most technically conservative aspect of Courbet's painting, thus acquires an altogether different epistemological status. For in Courbet's landscapes, the ground is no longer a blank slate or neutral staging area against which finished forms are set. It is no longer an idealized, timeless, and empty space of nonfiguration, of what is merely not form. The ground is reconceived instead as a kind of unseen and unknowable matrix of origination, a temporal threshold beyond which it is impossible to trace any further the emergence of form. Far from being a priori a backdrop for what we see, the ground marks the limits of what vision itself can apprehend.

The approximating, asymptotic approach to the origin is such an insistent feature of Courbet's 1864 landscapes that it is likely *this* process of excavating form, rather than the discovery of its birthplace, is the ultimate subject of his painting. These works reveal what viewing landscape is at the most basic level: a process of uncovering. A Courbet source painting may indeed depict a specific primordial site and therefore be considered a "landscape of an origin." But at his best Courbet invented something much more significant, what could be called the "landscape of origin." This is where his work is linked with the linguistic and geological interests of his Salinois cohort. By Courbet's time, both the study of language and the study of the earth had reconceived the notion of origins; linguists no longer sought the first words, and geologists no longer pondered the first stages of creation, or at least they no longer made it their top priority. They did not dismiss such questions completely. But they acknowledged that further knowledge of more recent linguistic and geological history was necessary before any determination of origins could be made. As the sheer scale and complexity of their task became more and more evident over the course of the century, scientists realized that identifying the first object was secondary to discovering the fundamental laws guiding the process of that object's historical formation. Quite simply, the histori-comparative sciences of the nineteenth century were concerned with the internal historicity of their objects, the hidden forces that shaped their formation, and not with the external point of their origin, the moment when those forces came into being and thus a point that, strictly speaking, lay outside their sphere of influence (for how could the rules of inflection in grammar, or horizontal accumulation in stratigraphy, pertain to something that did not yet have grammar or strata?).

Like nineteenth-century linguistics and geology, Courbet's landscape painting approached but refused to designate an exact origin. His painting intersected with these two fields, however, in slightly different ways. Painting and language are both means of representation. Just as linguistics for the purposes of analysis divides what at first glance appears to be language's smallest unit, the word, into even smaller units known as roots, so Courbet divides basic forms such as rock faces, trees, and water into even smaller representational units, his various brushstrokes and knife-marks, for the purposes of his own pictorial analysis. However, unlike language, terrestrial formations are not explicitly representational. Even though we can break single rocks into multiple strata, echoing the division of words into roots and landscapes into brushstrokes, the individual layers in combination do not point to an absent referent, as do words and painted forms. Rocks are what they appear to be, physical manifestations of the earth. The link between Courbet's painted forms and geological ones therefore comes from their shared sense of a vastly extended duration of time, what could be called a *deep time*, and less so from the visible division into representational units. Of course, nineteenth-century linguistics *did* realize that languages had a deep history. But the history of linguistic roots and their inflections could only extend as far back as the moment human beings first spoke—and not before. Contrariwise, in geology, time surveys the world *before* the existence of human forms of representation, be they verbal or visual. Geology includes in its compass the prehistoric era in which the earth produced *its own* forms. And in this sense the geological world is not unlike that self-formative world whose unfolding processes are made open to examination in Courbet's unpeopled landscapes.

One of the first observers, and certainly the most historically important, to have noticed the geological temporality of Courbet's landscapes was a fellow painter, Paul Cézanne, who supposedly saw in one of Courbet's later paintings a "tide [which] comes from the depth of the ages."[62] Whether or not Cézanne uttered these words, they capture what it is like to look at Courbet's best landscapes. But, curiously enough, the Courbet painting triggering Cézanne's reflection is not one of the 1864 source paintings, but a Salon-scale painting of a large crashing wave, *The Stormy Sea* (1870; Musée d'Orsay, Paris). The impact of Courbet's 1864 landscapes of origin extended far beyond his close group of friends and patrons in Franche-Comté. They proved instructive for Courbet's later painting outside the region, in places with such different kinds of landscape as the Normandy coast; they also left a lasting impression on ambitious artists of the next generation, the Impressionists, and thus on the future of modern art.

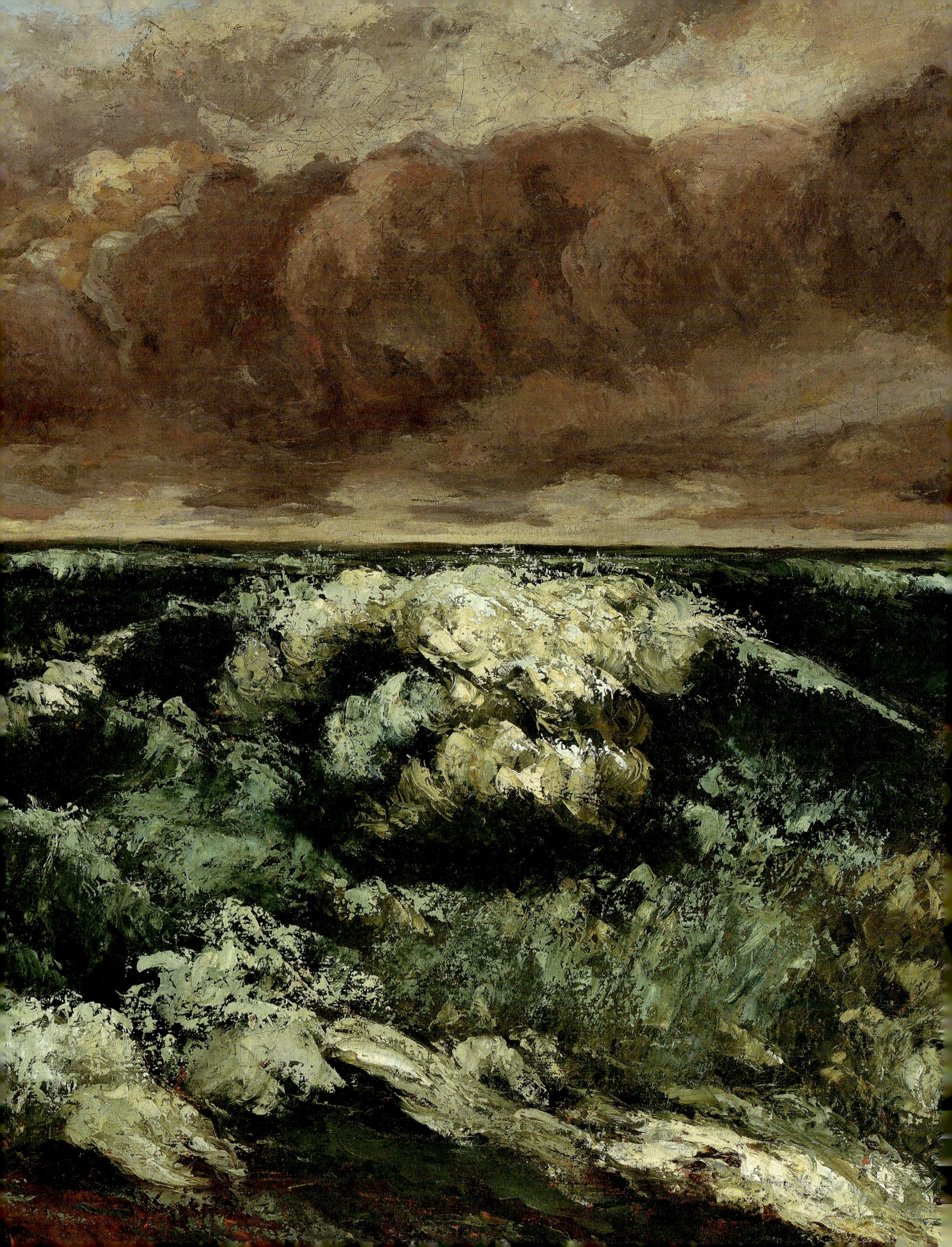

Chapter 3

MILK OF THE SEA

By the time Courbet made the return journey from Salins to Ornans with Castagnary in January 1865, the painting of substantive, local landscapes of origin had been occupying the artist for over a year. However, within weeks of his arrival, something happened that would alter his immediate plans. The death of Proudhon on 19 January 1865 led Courbet to submit a portrait of the philosopher, *Pierre Joseph-Proudhon and His Children in 1853*, painted in about five weeks, to the Salon in the same year. Although a portrayal of the socialist thinker could never be considered a neutral act in the political climate of the Second Empire (in 1866 the government would censor *La Rue* before the journal could publish a drawing by Courbet of Proudhon on his deathbed), the tone of Courbet's portrait was more commemorative than controversial, at least in comparison with the artist's two most recent submissions, *Return from the Conference* and *Study of Women*, both of which the artist knew would be rejected.

Courbet paired the Proudhon portrait with a landscape from the *Puits noir* series, *The Stream of the Puits noir* (fig. 32).[1] Of the two, the portrait, understandably, drew the lion's share of attention. Courbet was nonetheless puzzled about the landscape's more muted reception, for the same composition had received widespread acclaim when he had showed a similar work in Besançon with the Société des Beaux-Arts. Perhaps the artist's recent immersion in the provincial landscape had blinded him to the fact that, on the cramped walls of the Salon, the evocation of an unknown origin in his landscape might have been lost on those with no firsthand experience of such places. Thus, despite Courbet's insistence (for once without too much exaggeration) that the *Puits noir* painting and its variants were some of his most accomplished paintings, he seemed ready to abandon, or at least to scale back, the 1864 project if it was not going to translate into sales.[2]

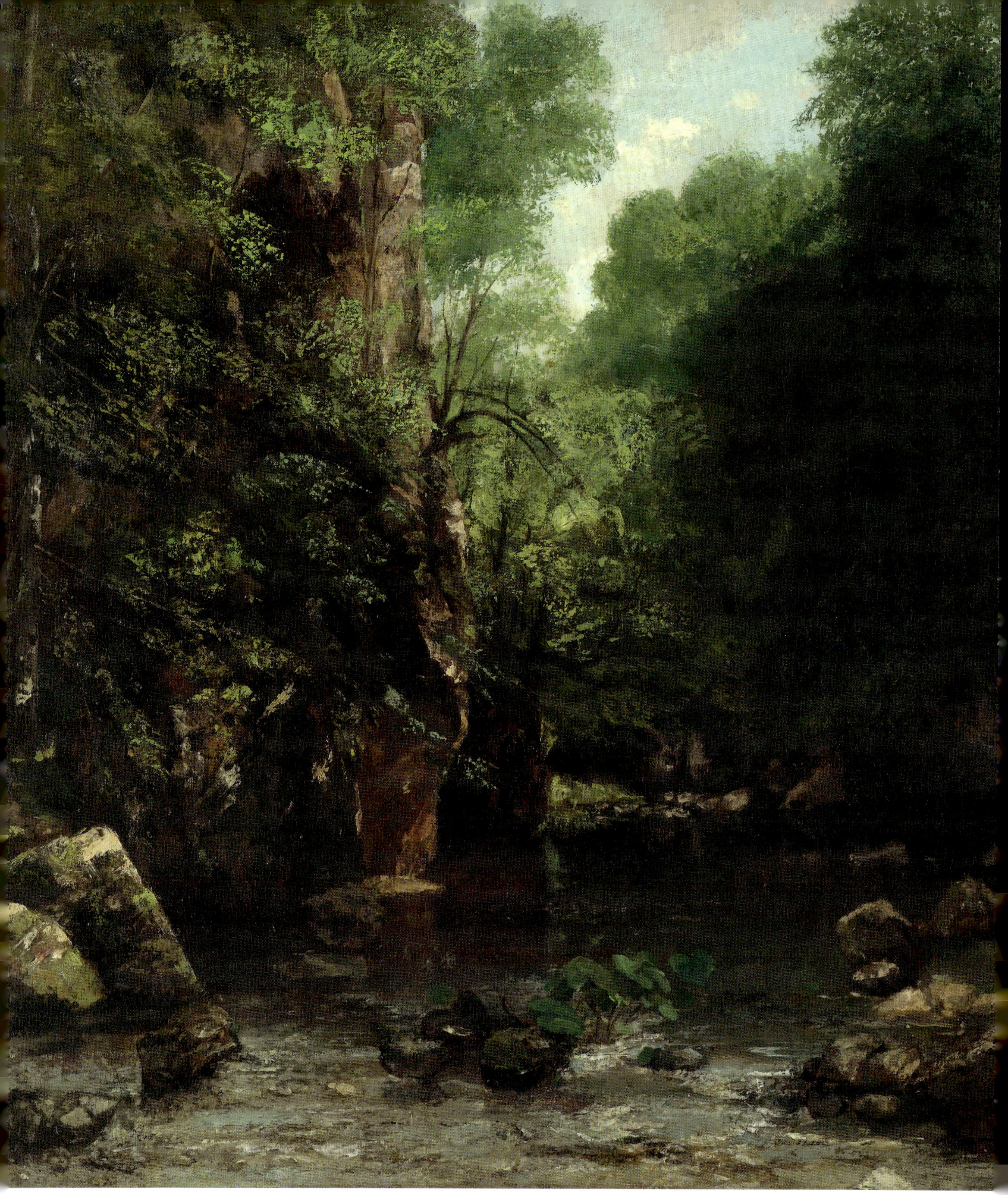

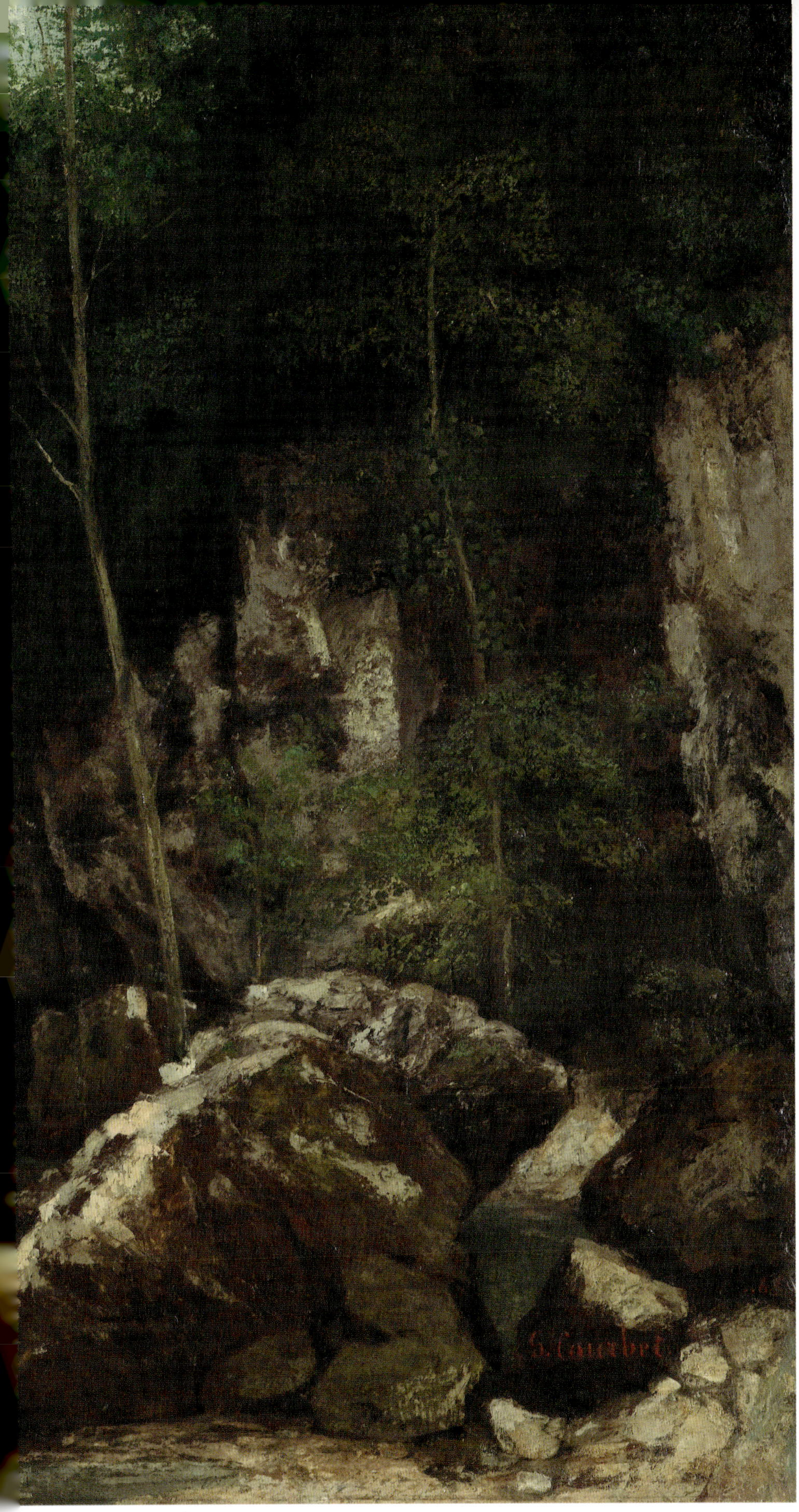

32 | *The Stream of the Puits noir*, 1865. Oil on canvas, 94 × 135 cm. Musée d'Orsay, Paris

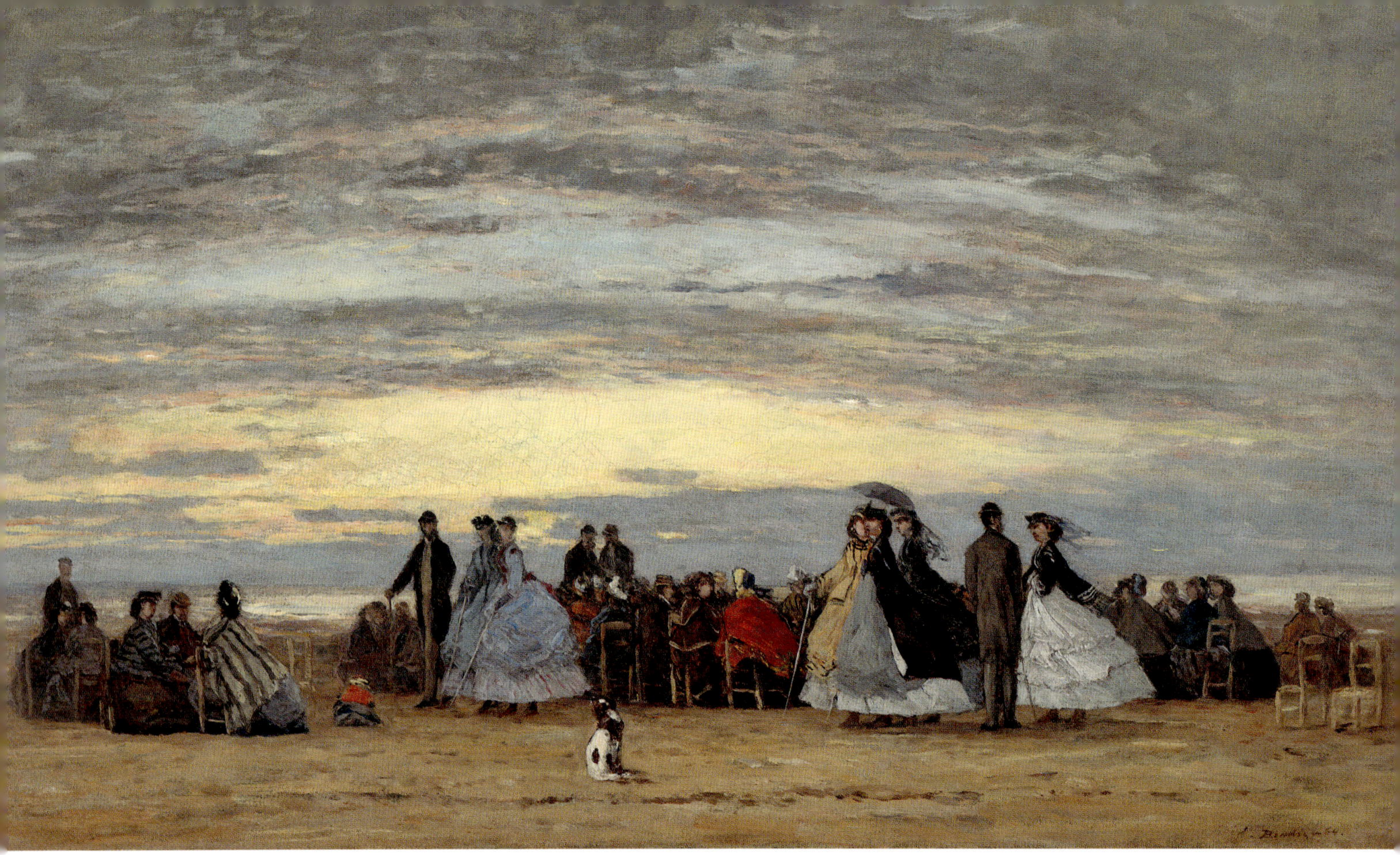

33 | Eugène Boudin, *The Beach at Villerville*, 1864. Oil on canvas, 45.7 × 76.3 cm. National Gallery of Art, Washington, D.C.

As it turns out, he need not have worried. *The Stream of the Puits noir* was acquired by Comte Alfred Émilien de Nieuwerkerke, Superintendent of Beaux-Arts and the man responsible for state patronage of the arts, including acquisitions for the civil list, and different versions made their way into private collections.[3] Eventually Courbet would brag that the *Puits noir* series had earned him 20,000 to 22,000 francs (for comparison's sake, a small Saintonge landscape would have gone for about 300 francs, while the Salon version was sold for 2,000).[4] This public acceptance contributed to Courbet's decision to spend September to November 1865 in the fashionable coastal town of Trouville in Normandy, which in the 1860s was growing rapidly. The Old Normandy character of the region, with its medieval towns and enduring peasant farming methods, had been irrevocably transformed over the course of the nineteenth century by increasing numbers of out-of-town visitors. The coast's proximity to England and Paris, the vogue for hydrotherapeutic bathing, and, most of all, an expanding railroad network turned the coast on either side of the Seine estuary into one of France's most popular vacation spots.[5] Courbet enjoyed his time in Trouville so much that he would return to the coast on two further occasions: in September 1866, at the invitation of the Comte de Choiseul, to Deauville, the newly constructed and even more fashionable town next to Trouville (whose rapid development in the 1860s had been supported by the emperor's own half-brother, the Duc de Morny); and from August to September 1869 to Étretat, the popular fishing village turned summer resort that would later appear in the writings of its most famous son, Guy de Maupassant. (Courbet would paint one of its most popular landmarks, the rocky cliff known as the Porte d'Aval for the Salon of 1870.)[6]

Traditional marine painting, burdened as it was with the weight of eighteenth- and nineteenth-century depictions of ship and harbor as symbols of the nation-state, was ill equipped to represent the new mondain society. That historical task would fall not to the painters of the ports of France but to artists from individual regions who had themselves witnessed the modernization of the seaside. The painter Eugène Boudin, for instance, would represent the urbane tourist with a mixture of fascination and wariness (fig. 33). His beach views, showing clusters of fashionable figures across a low horizon, were seen from the standpoint of a detached local observer, close enough to take in the spectacle of umbrellas, crinolines, and bathing costumes, while far enough to maintain some distance from the crowd. They thus perfectly encapsulated the artist's own social position, as Boudin worked in the provinces while nonetheless relying on Parisians for sales and commissions.

Given the genre's popularity then and now, it is easy to forget that in the 1860s such "modern" seascapes were a relatively new phenomenon. When Courbet turned his attention to painting the sea in 1865, he was entering a field every bit as novel as the society it catered to (and indeed often represented). If Boudin's beach scenes depict the viewpoint of a curious observer of new tourist promenades, Courbet's comparatively unpopulated compositions turn away to escape such social perambulations. Courbet's *paysages de mer* (landscapes of the sea), as he liked to call them, are generally uninterrupted views of the horizon, from the vantage point of someone standing on the shore looking out toward the sea, where the beach, the waves, and the sky (sometimes punctuated with boats or rocks) each occupy their own quasi-distinct horizontal band stretching unbroken across the whole canvas.

He had first experimented with the formula during the 1850s in a few paintings of the Mediterranean coast, while visiting his patron Alfred Bruyas in the south of France.[7] Almost a decade later, in Trouville, he would claim to have painted 25 seascapes and the same number of "autumn skies" in three months.[8] A published account of his 1866 work reported that he had painted a seascape a day for 30 straight days, presumedly to capture the same motif under varying conditions of light and weather, anticipating Impressionist practice.[9] The simplicity of the seascapes—most are composed of pastose bands of shore, sea, and sky and nothing more—has almost no precedent in the history of European painting. It is not until early nineteenth-century Romanticism that anything vaguely comparable is created. And even then, highly reductive painting of the sort Courbet practiced was undertaken mostly outside France and usually involved extreme situations, cataclysmic floods, otherworldly maelstroms, ascetic isolation at the end of the earth. With Courbet, the sea view becomes for the first time a de-dramatized, somatic experience of an apparently self-contained, yet nonetheless accessible "world." At first glance seemingly the antithesis of the analytic 1864 landscapes of origin, the seascapes reveal Courbet's commitment to the pictorial representation of matter. Indeed, they would ultimately exceed the stream and grotto paintings in their ability to immerse the viewer in a hypersubstantial, paint-like universe.

The Trouville marine paintings were first shown publicly at Cadart & Luquet in March 1866. Charles Beauquier, a Franc-comtois music critic (and future stalwart for the preservation of the source of the Loue River), reviewed the exhibition as part of his Parisian chronicle for Max Buchon's *Revue littéraire de la Franche-Comté*.[10] The critic had begun his account of cultural events in the capital with a review of another work about the sea, Victor Hugo's *Les Travailleurs de la mer* (1866), in which the reviewer also mentioned Jules Michelet's natural history *La Mer* (1861). For someone in the artist's milieu, one of the main reference points on the subject of the sea would have been contemporary literature, specifically entire books on the topic by two of France's most popular authors. As the numerous epigraphs and quotations plucked from their pages in the Courbet literature attest, Hugo's novel and Michelet's natural history are rife with memorable passages about the sea and its substances. For Hugo, the unfathomable sea was the greatest metaphor for the limits of language; the watery depths signified that part of reality that words were powerless to describe, that was inaccessible to humankind. For Michelet, the sea was a material plenum, a world seething with organic matter, the supreme image for the universality of the body whose substances were detectable not only throughout nature but also throughout human history, as the historian's attentiveness to blood, food, sex, and other corporeal aspects of life demonstrated. Courbet, too, saw the sea as the ultimate way to experience matter in all its multiple states and movements. This chapter elucidates how Courbet constructed his substantive worldview in his paintings of the sea and compares his approach to that of Hugo and Michelet. The argument is that Courbet's attitude towards matter came closest to Michelet's. The material sumptuousness of the world for both was not limited to the ocean but was a universal quality that could be unearthed to varying degrees everywhere. Courbet discovered ways to declare the presence of matter not only in the genres most obviously suited to the task, landscape and still life, but also in the Salon compositions and Realist canvases, in which the human figure and its place in society were paramount. Seascape was thus to both artist and historian the purest realization of a more general impulse: to luxuriate in the substance of the world.

IN THE WAVE'S WAKE

"These splendid marines are like incrustations of marble and metal, the waves like rearing horses, and the advancing foam like falling fragments of hammer-struck stone," wrote the Belgian writer Camille Lemonnier in 1878, the year after Courbet's death.[11] Before comparing Courbet's marine paintings with the writings of literary counterparts, we must first determine why the seascapes *as painting* elicited primal, tactile sensations of a hypersubstantial world when other contemporaneous works did not. There is nothing unusual about depicting water as having paint-like properties. The history of painting is not lacking in rivers whose surfaces mimic transparent glaze; maelstroms in the past have been rendered as impenetrable as lead paint; swirling seawater has come to resemble color applied wet-on-wet several times over. According to this line of reasoning, far from being an innovator, Courbet is simply doing what landscape painters have been doing for centuries. This would be true were it not for two things: first, no painter prior to Courbet (with the exception of Joseph Mallord William Turner) made their seas so viscous at such intimate scale. True, untamed frothy areas often erupt into the foreground of many large early nineteenth-century marine paintings when observed closely. But by and large the waves in these paintings were meant to coalesce at a distance, to eventually harmonize with the rest of the otherwise relatively flat picture. When depicting rivers, bays, and oceans, marine painters generally sought to emphasize the paint's fluidity and transparency, not its density and creaminess. Second, Courbet did not limit this special kind of material coincidence to aqueous areas. In his seascapes, it is not

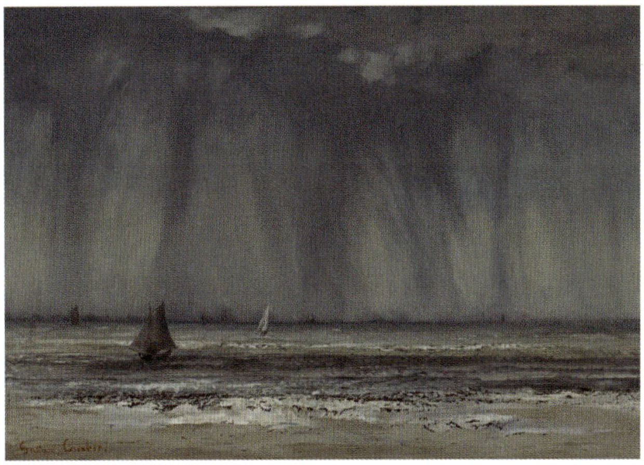

34 | *Marine*, 1866. Oil on canvas, mounted on cardboard, 43.2 × 65.7 cm. Philadelphia Museum of Art

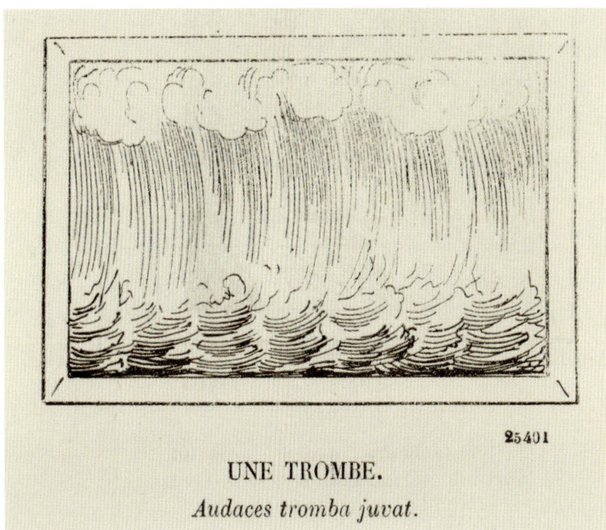

35 | Gustave Randon, "The Waterspout," *Le Journal amusant*, 1867

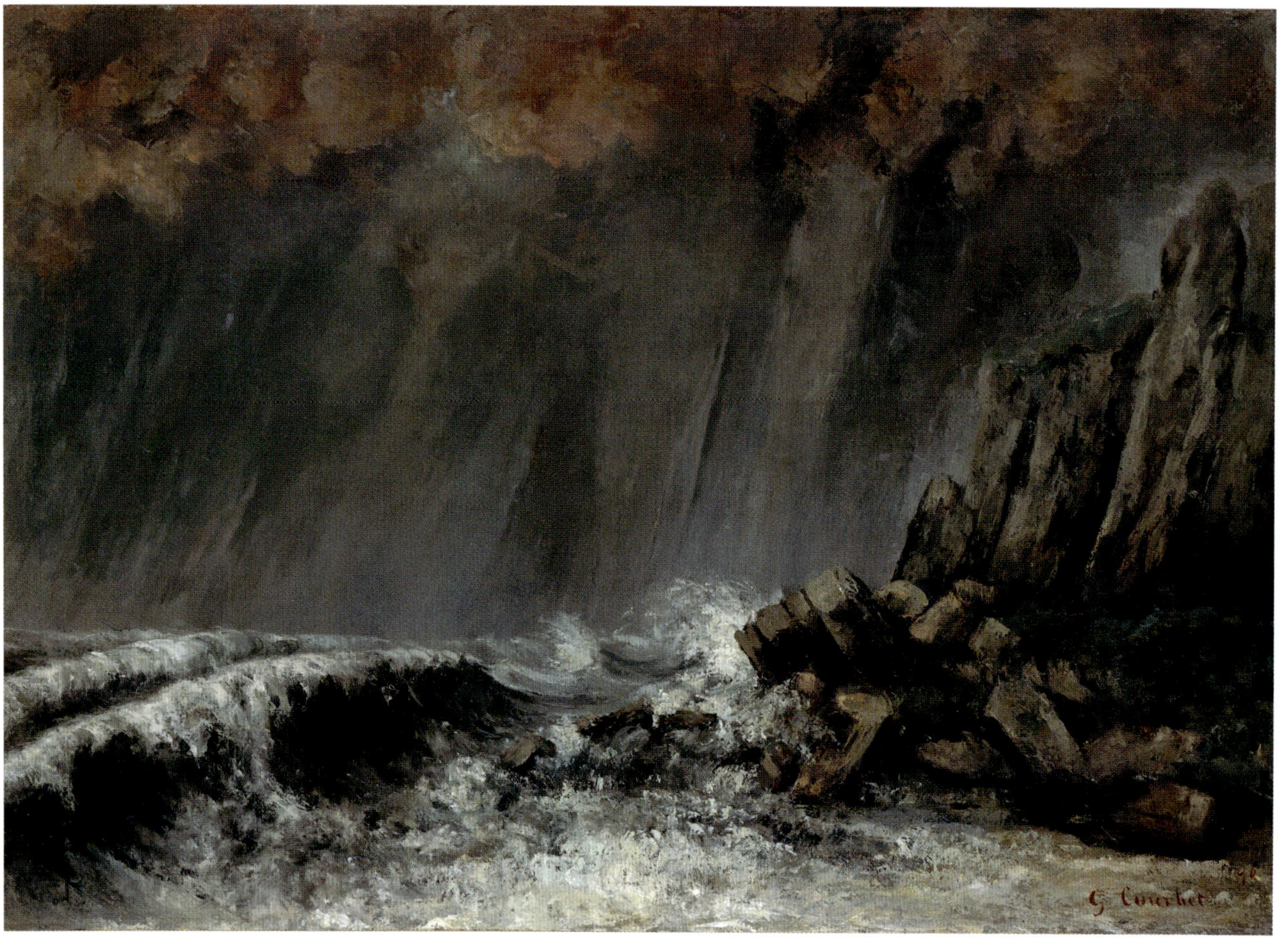

36 | *Marine: The Waterspout*, 1870. Oil on canvas, 68.9 × 99.7 cm. The Metropolitan Museum of Art, New York

just a single wave, nor even the entire sea that is palpable. It is also the sky and, when visible, the beach. Everything is of rich consistency: clouds are waterlogged; breakers have saturated the sands; and the ocean is full of froth. By contrast, step onto land or rise into the sky in a marine painting by another artist and the co-substantiality of landscape and paint is lost. (However ominous, a stormy sky by Claude-Joseph Vernet, the model French marine painter of the eighteenth and early nineteenth centuries, is never pasty.)

Courbet surpasses almost all his predecessors in the genre in the way he applies paint thickly to every part of the composition: his seascapes are relatively thick, and they are thick all over. There is no shortage of remarks about this: "It's as if it was carved from a piece of basalt. Courbet's technique makes one very much aware that one is looking at something as solid as marble."[12] But Klaus Herding was the first to link surface solidity to all-overness: "[The palette knife] was indeed decisive in producing the material quality of his *peinture* and in equalizing compositional emphases. The quality of the late seascapes ... consists precisely in an exact materialization of the atmosphere, and in a transition from one object to another produced by broad paint application."[13]

Using Herding's insight as a guide, we can trace the various ways Courbet pursued this principle of general material equivalence. Sometimes the dispersal of matter is the work's explicit subject. It is often noted that Courbet was fond of painting the meteorological phenomena of waterspouts, which are essentially oceanic tornadoes whose ferocious circling winds suck seawater

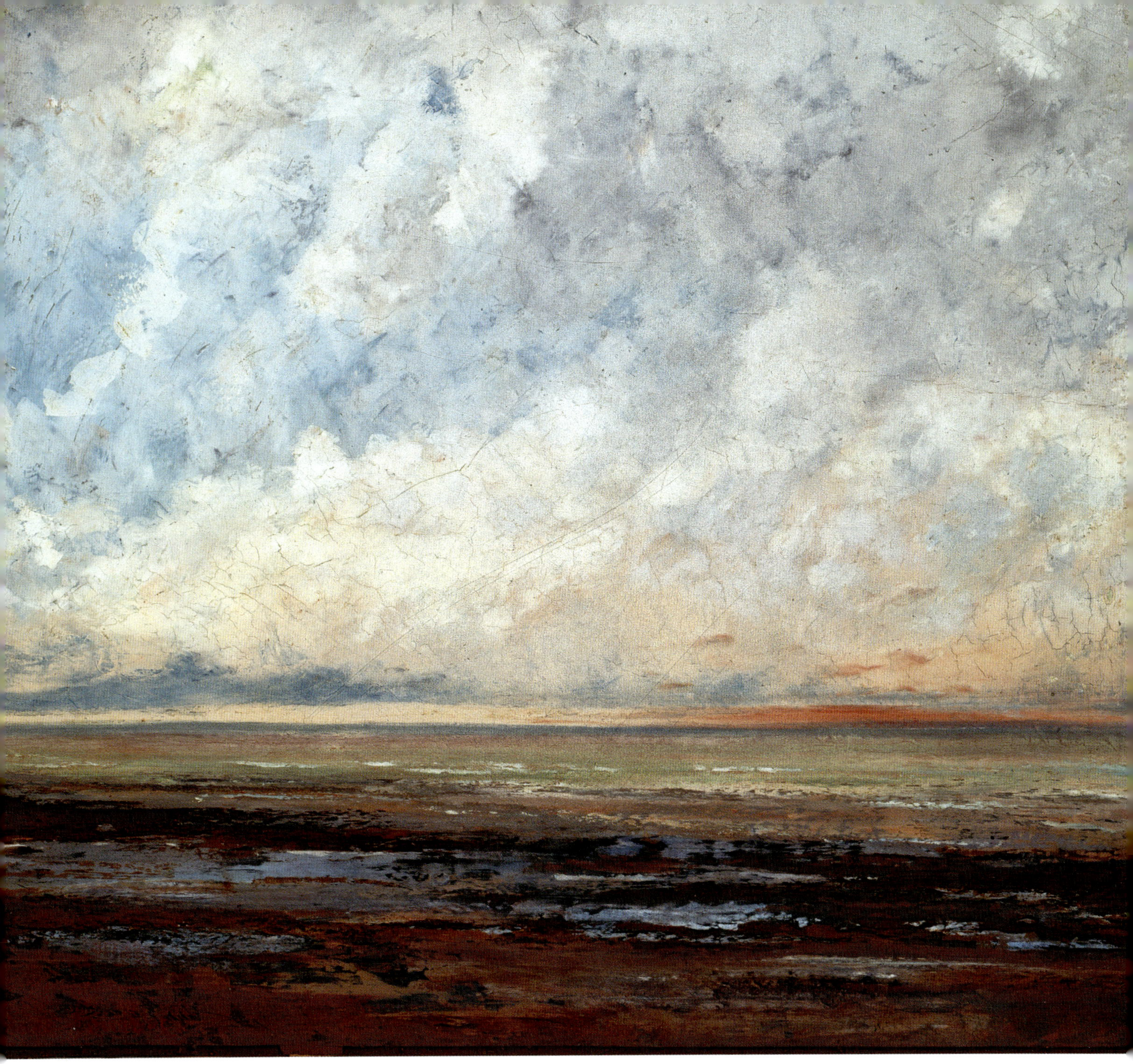

up into the atmosphere. From afar, they resemble pillars supporting the sky. One contemporaneous caricaturist intimated as much by rendering the background of the waterspout painting, now in the Philadelphia Museum of Art (fig. 34), as a set of vertical lines (fig. 35). Other examples are two canvases now in Musée des Beaux-Arts, Dijon, and the Metropolitan Museum of Art, New York (fig. 36). But whereas the waterspout is the primary spectacle of the Philadelphia painting, it is secondary to

37 | *Marine*, *ca.*1865–66. Oil on canvas, 50.2 × 61 cm. Norton Simon Museum, Pasadena

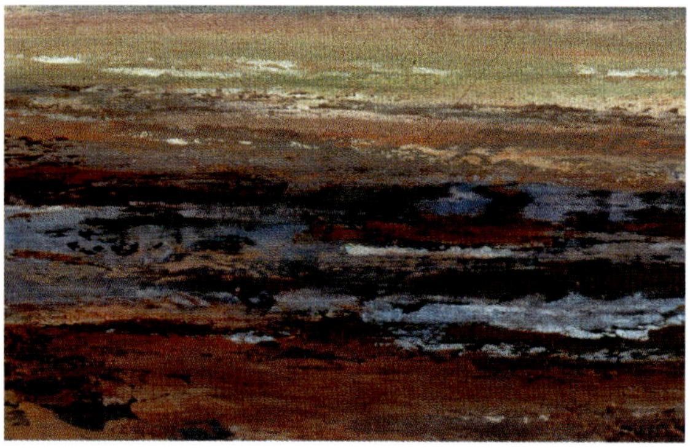

38 | *Marine* (detail), *ca.*1865–66. Oil on canvas, 50.2 × 61 cm. Norton Simon Museum, Pasadena

crashing waves in the last two canvases (a result, perhaps, of the artist wanting to parade his skill at combining within a single composition a Normandy sea and sky with a Franc-comtois landmass).

Because they are about the exchange of matter, the waterspout paintings are inevitably cited in discussions of Courbet's depiction of substance in the seascapes. But, and this is crucial, substance is ubiquitous in Courbet's marines even when there is no obvious agitation. Owing to technical limitations of illustrations, a painting such as the *Marine* in the Norton Simon Museum, Pasadena, appears somewhat empty and dull when featured in a book, for reproductions stunt our appreciation of the painting's most stunning feature: the solidity and consistency of paint accumulation across the entire pictorial field (fig. 37). In the actual painting, Courbet uses the technique he had been developing since at least his trip to the Saintonge in 1862, which involved deploying the knife and the brush to impress onto the canvas a carefully calibrated patchwork of flattened paint deposits (in the case of the seascapes, usually some combination of white, gray, blue, and pink). The result is that, instead of a topographic impasto in high relief, we find something closer to a thin layer of adhesive patches. As we saw in previous chapters, this touch-by-touch approach creates the illusion of great mass from a relatively small amount of paint. Rather than canceling out or competing with each other every mark builds upon the other, contributing to a collective mass that the viewer thinks is an agglomeration of matter when it is composed of at most three layers of discrete touches.

For the principle of general equivalence to hold, what lies below the horizon must be as sensuous as what lies above it. If, for instance, we move from the foreground to the horizon in the lower third of the Norton Simon picture (fig. 38), the eye traverses a series of thin horizontal bands. If not for the chromatic shift from brown to green, we would be hard-pressed to say where the shore ends and the ocean begins. Courbet takes advantage of something many a beach-walker has experienced: that when a wave breaks, it can feel like wet particles of sand on the feet. Is the "ground" here mostly saturated sand or agitated seawater? Instead of a clear demarcation, we have deliberate intermingling.

The Courbetian seascape is a homogenized field of substance comprising zones of natural pastes that behave in many ways like the artificial paste that is paint. Courbet activates areas that for other artists are "empty" background—clear skies, green fields, open water, etc. Space itself has become a thing.[14] And while it would be going too far to say that this activation of space is *exactly* even across the picture—after all, we can distinguish areas of accumulation such as individual tide pools and sandbanks or the edges of hovering cumuli—matter is certainly more equally dispersed than in most seascapes.

The magnificent series of crashing waves from Courbet's trip to Étretat in 1869 is undoubtedly the pinnacle of his achievement in seascape. If it only enters our discussion here after a description of the Norton Simon marine painting, it is to stress that, despite obvious Romantic overtones, the 1869 waves are not a break with, but an extension of—in a different key—the underlying principle of general equivalence already at work in the 1865–66 Trouville–Deauville shore views. In the starkly split Étretat seascapes, as is often noted, bulbous storm clouds and cresting waves mirror each other across the horizon. In a contemporaneous illustration, it is as if Courbet carried his treatment of the wave, with its panoply of opaque, foam-imitating marks, over to the depiction of cloud form, where similar strokes congeal into solidified vapor (fig. 39).[15] This is an obvious exaggeration for comic effect. In the actual canvas from the Salon (1870; Musée d'Orsay, Paris), the distribution of substance is more asymmetrical. The paint layers are thicker in the wave than in the sky, and this inevitably adds weight to the picture's lower half.

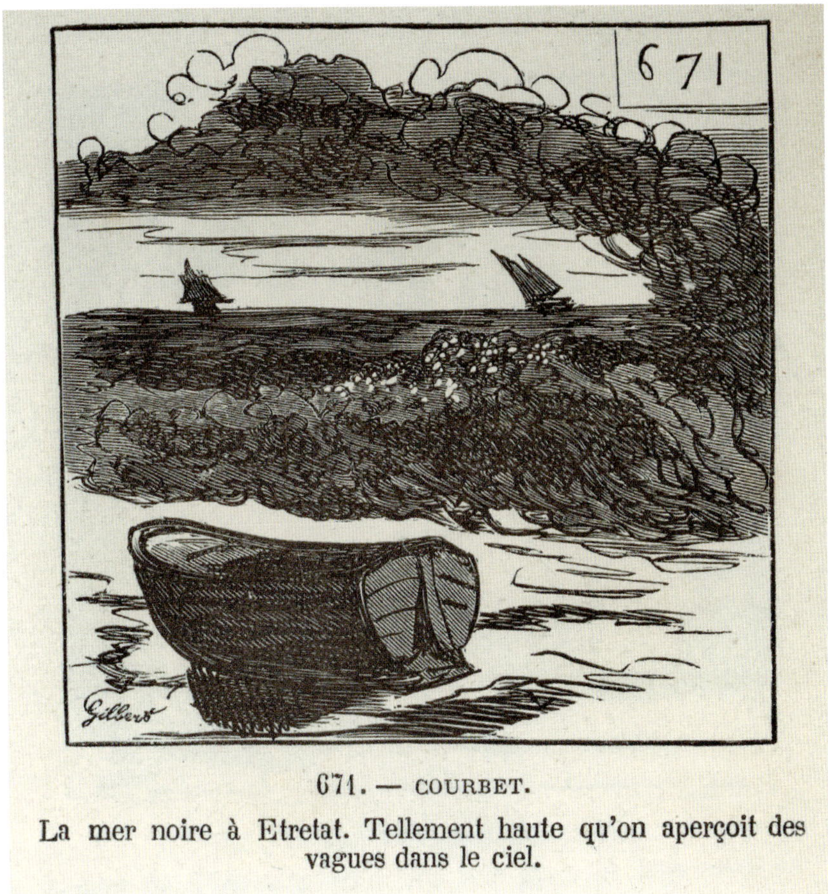

39 | Cham, "La Falaise d'Étretat, après l'orage," *Cham at the Salon of 1870*, 1870

But the caricaturist's general intuition is correct. Though in the Étretat wave series Courbet's skies are often not as thick as his waves, it is hard nevertheless to name another painter who makes theirs as emulsified and wave-like.

Courbet's interpenetrative triad of cloud, wave, and beach produces a world of plenitude without void. This illusion came at considerable cost. To make the emptiest of scenes pulsate with matter, nothing could be allowed to detract from nature's material continuity. Anything requiring isolation—the boats, locals, and tourists that populate seascapes by contemporaries such as Eugène Boudin and the Dutchman Johan Barthold Jongkind, to name only two of the most talented—had to be minimized or excised (fig. 40). When Courbet did paint people at the seaside, he opted for other genres, usually portraiture.

How could an artist so instrumental in making the heroism of contemporary life an appropriate and even necessary subject matter for art so thoroughly reject it just at the moment it was irrecoverably transforming his immediate surroundings? We know from his letters that Courbet enjoyed many aspects of modern leisure resorts by the sea, from the beachfront houses with their opulent interiors to public bathing and the new casinos.[16] In this, he was no different from the aristocratic de Mornys and de Choiseuls of the world, plus all the Parisian tourists taking advantage of new rail connections to visit the coast. He did not ignore recent social developments in his paintings therefore out of a sense of repugnance to them. He seems to have decided to suppress them because of his overriding commitment to the representation of matter. If narratives of human activity, and even narrative altogether, had to be sacrificed for such a commitment, so be it.

40 Johan Barthold Jongkind, *Honfleur*, 1865. Oil on canvas, 52.1 × 81.6 cm. The Metropolitan Museum of Art, New York

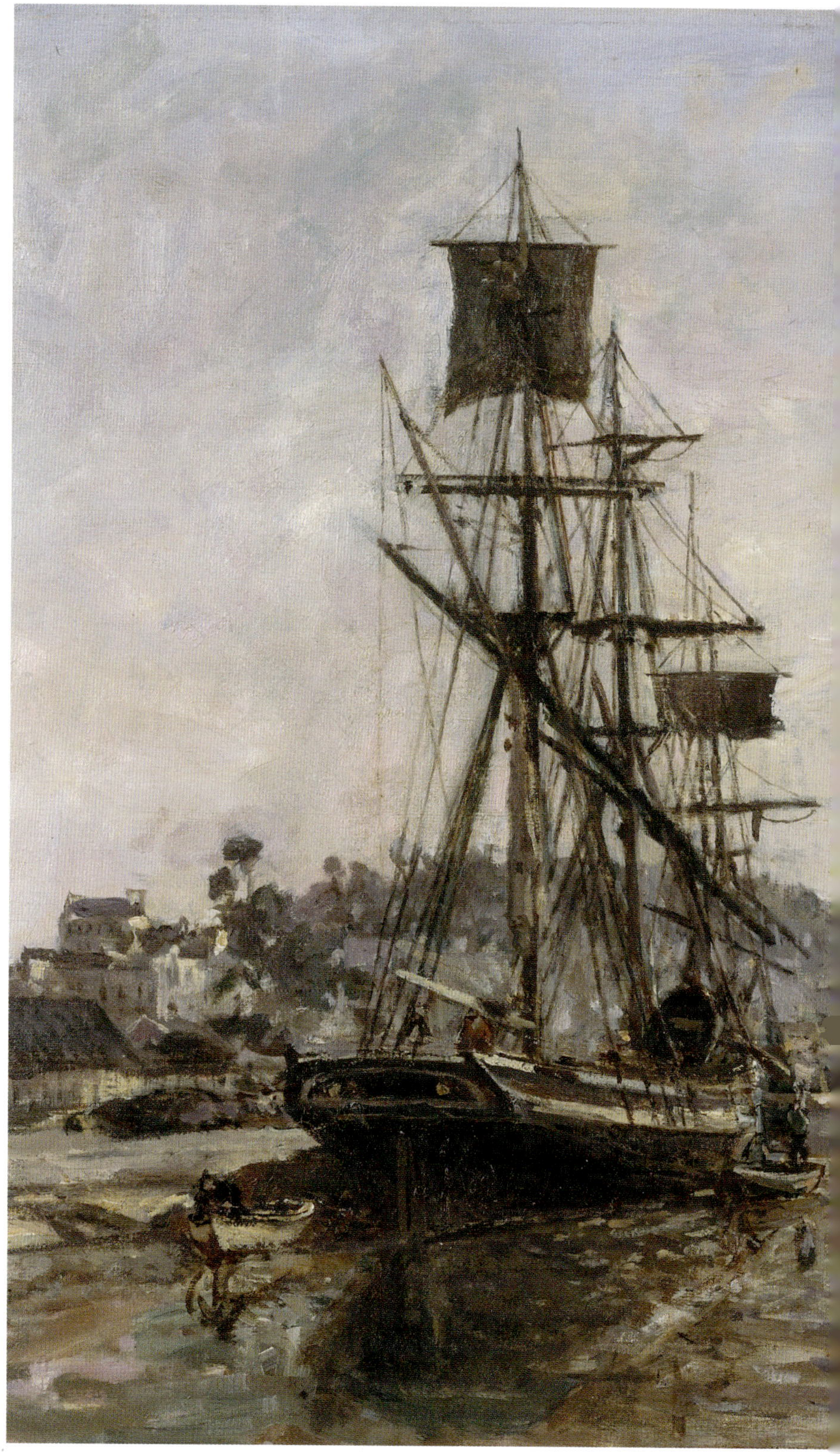

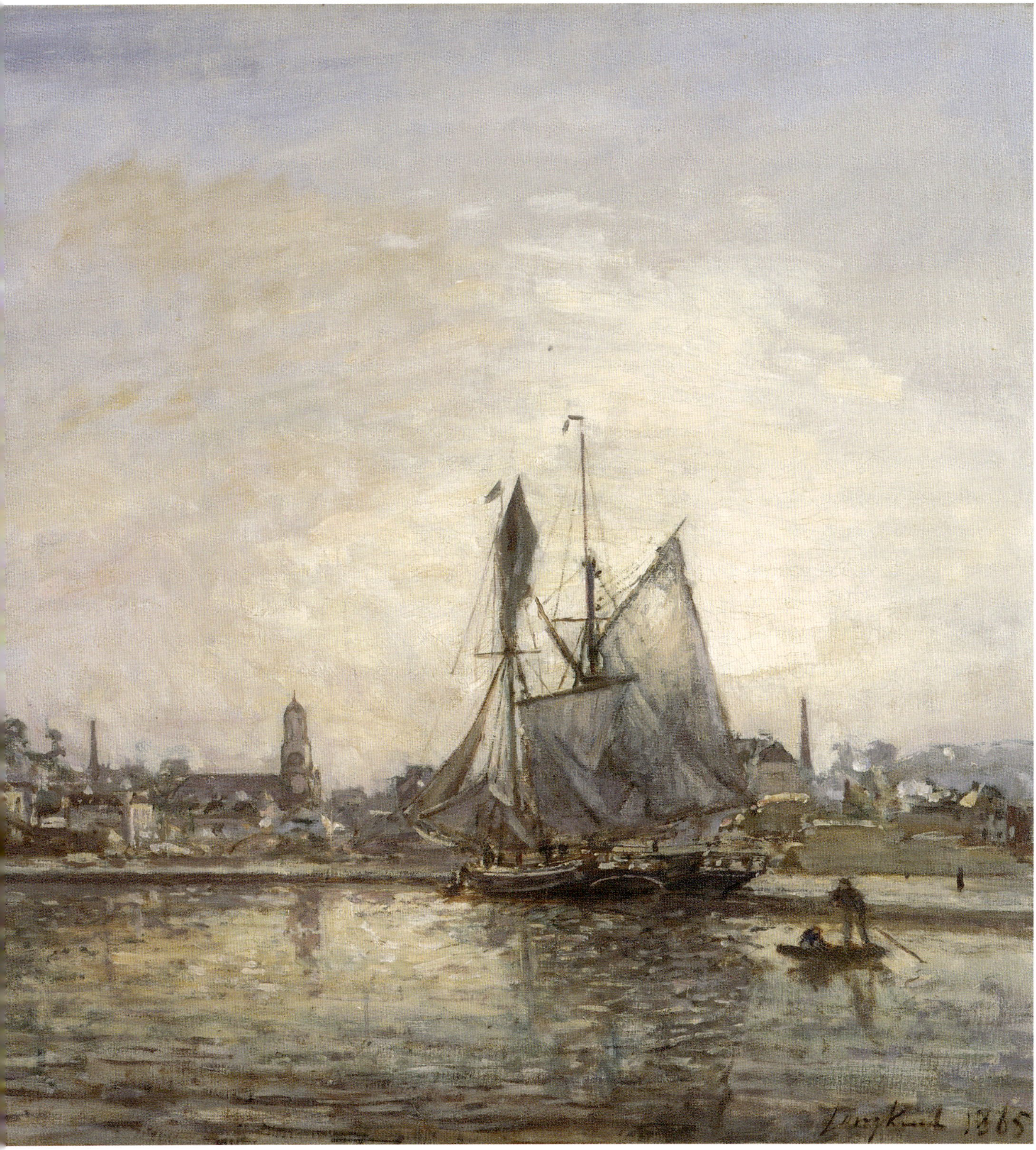
Jongkind 1865

FROM ANOTHER POINT OF VIEW

Yet the biggest obstacle to Courbet's painting of a material, tactile nature was neither the people impinging upon it nor what they brought with them. Tourists in their fine holiday attire, boating paraphernalia, hard-at-work fishermen: all these could be easily removed from a composition. It was much less easy to sidestep the distancing effect of the horizon. The innate human tendency to perceive horizontal lines as far horizons, as divisions of pictorial space into, on the one hand, a ground extending outward from below our feet, the realm of bodily movement, and, on the other hand, the atmosphere above accessible through sight alone worked against the painter. As we saw in previous chapters, Courbet's 1864 landscapes counteracted the horizon by blocking out the sky with trees and cliffs. But at land's limit the horizon is almost impossible to avoid, unless perhaps a large ship or jetty were to eclipse the view, in which case it would no longer be pure seascape (Édouard Manet's 1868 paintings of Boulogne harbor come to mind).

Courbet's strategies to combat the horizon's distancing effect were ingenious. As others have addressed these elsewhere with great insight, we can summarize them here (with qualifications).[17] Extreme frontality was one of the preferred options. Courbet's seascapes tend to address the viewer head-on, or nearly so. There are a few exceptions to this rule, such as the waterspout pictures (see fig. 36). An oblique view, what we would see if we turned toward the right, has the effect of shifting the orientation of the entire scene: though seemingly innocuous, this rotation acts to insert space between the nearby shore and the sky on the far side of the land mass. Clouds and sea, thus separated, are less likely to engage physically with each other (or if they do, they do so out of view). To avoid creating such rifts in space, Courbet made frequent recourse to the frontal approach. True, waves sometimes do roll obliquely in a single direction. But never so far as to make our necks pivot, because doing so would introduce a coastline—and thus the illusion of receding distance—into the field of vision.

Perhaps Courbet put too much faith in this stratagem, for the frontal view, even at its most head-on, still leaves us with a distant horizon. Indeed, our sense of infinite distance may only be exacerbated by this most basic of world-dividing pictorial conceits. Herding sharply observed that "in an attempt to disguise this artificial limit, Courbet often was led to repaint the horizon."[18] This overpainting muddied the juncture of sea and sky, making it difficult to determine distance. Courbet also let his clouds burst forward, often so that the largest among them would rest right on top of the horizon, as if touching it. As we look at the picture, we cannot help but compare cloud and wave—and in the process take notice of their material similarity.[19]

Another solution was to deliberately destabilize points of view. According to Charles Léger, one of the artist's early biographers, Courbet told his friend Cherubino Pata that he had once chided Baudelaire for showing him a particular view overlooking the sea: "Was he ever bourgeois! What are viewpoints? Do viewpoints exist?"[20] Real or fabricated, the scenario raises a point germane to Courbet's seascapes. Herding has given us the most succinct formulation of the artist's subterfuge: "The central peak surmounts the horizon; we

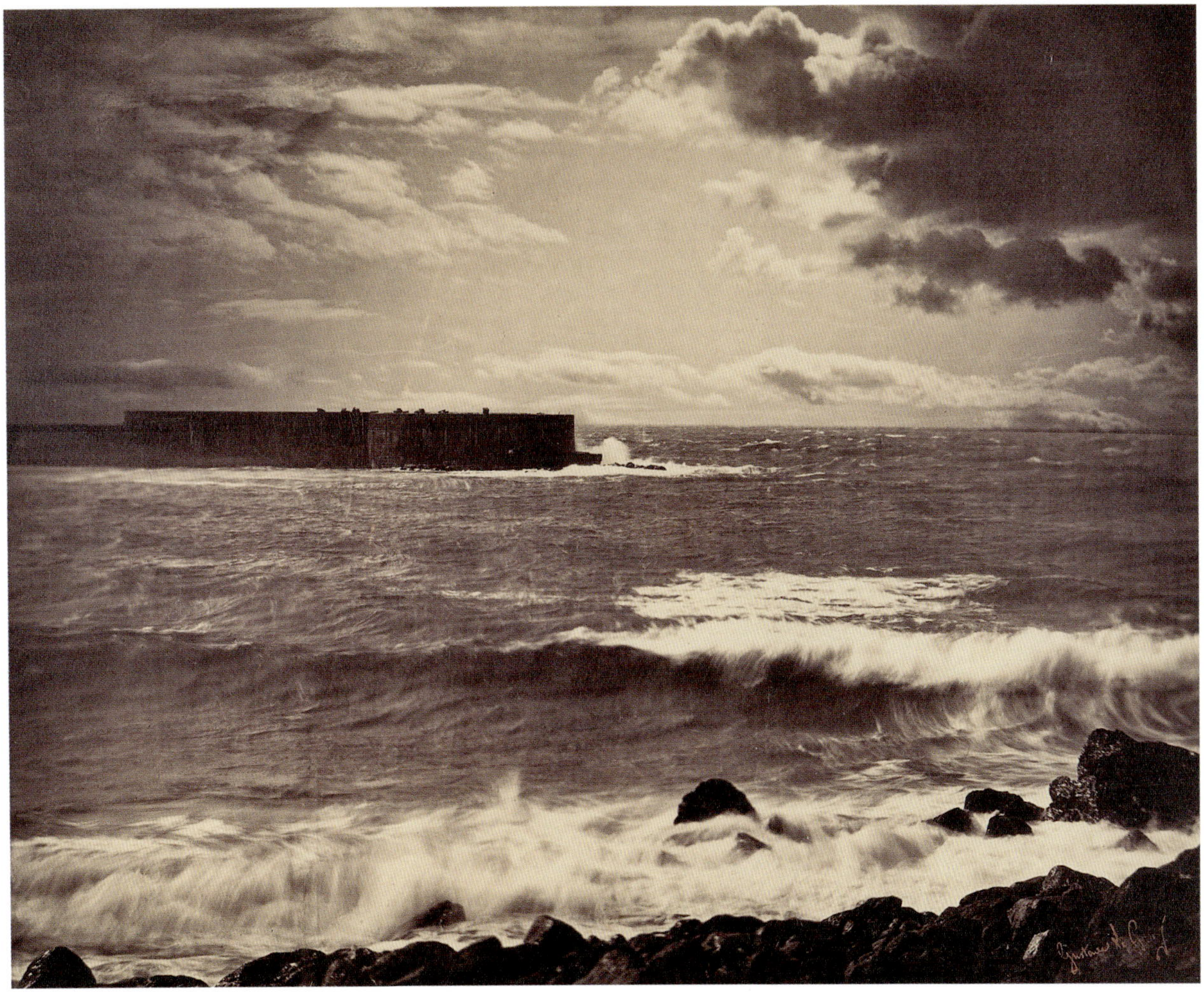

41 | Gustave Le Gray, *The Great Wave, Sète*, 1857. Albumen silver print from glass negative, 33.7 × 41.4 cm. The Metropolitan Museum of Art, New York

find ourselves underneath it. However, we also visually survey the entire surface of the open sea; the spectator is thus located above the horizon line—a strange ambiguity resulting from the fact that a traditionally fixed point of view has been abandoned."[21] A Courbet wave is experienced from above and below simultaneously. To illustrate this, it helps to compare Courbet's wave to a contemporaneous image often cited in the literature. Gustave Le Gray's photograph *The Great Wave, Sète*, like Hugo's and Michelet's writings and Courbet's paintings, provides another example of the artistic reimagining of the sea around midcentury (fig. 41). Much has already been written about whether or not Courbet knew of Le Gray's photographs (he probably did, but there's no ironclad proof).[22] Even more has been said about the relationship of Courbet's landscapes to photography and thus about the relationship of Realist painting to photography in general.[23] Setting aside for the moment

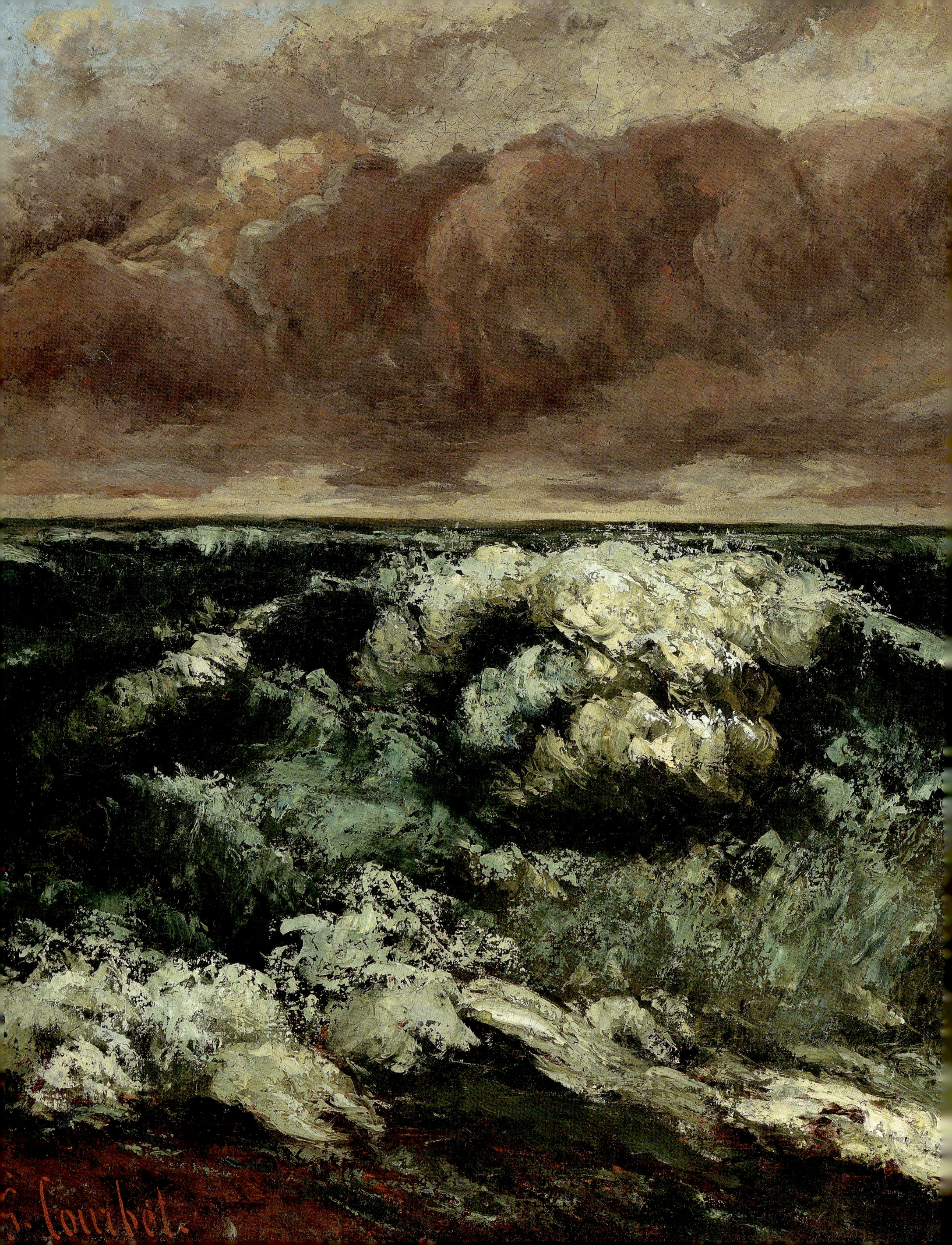
G. Courbet.

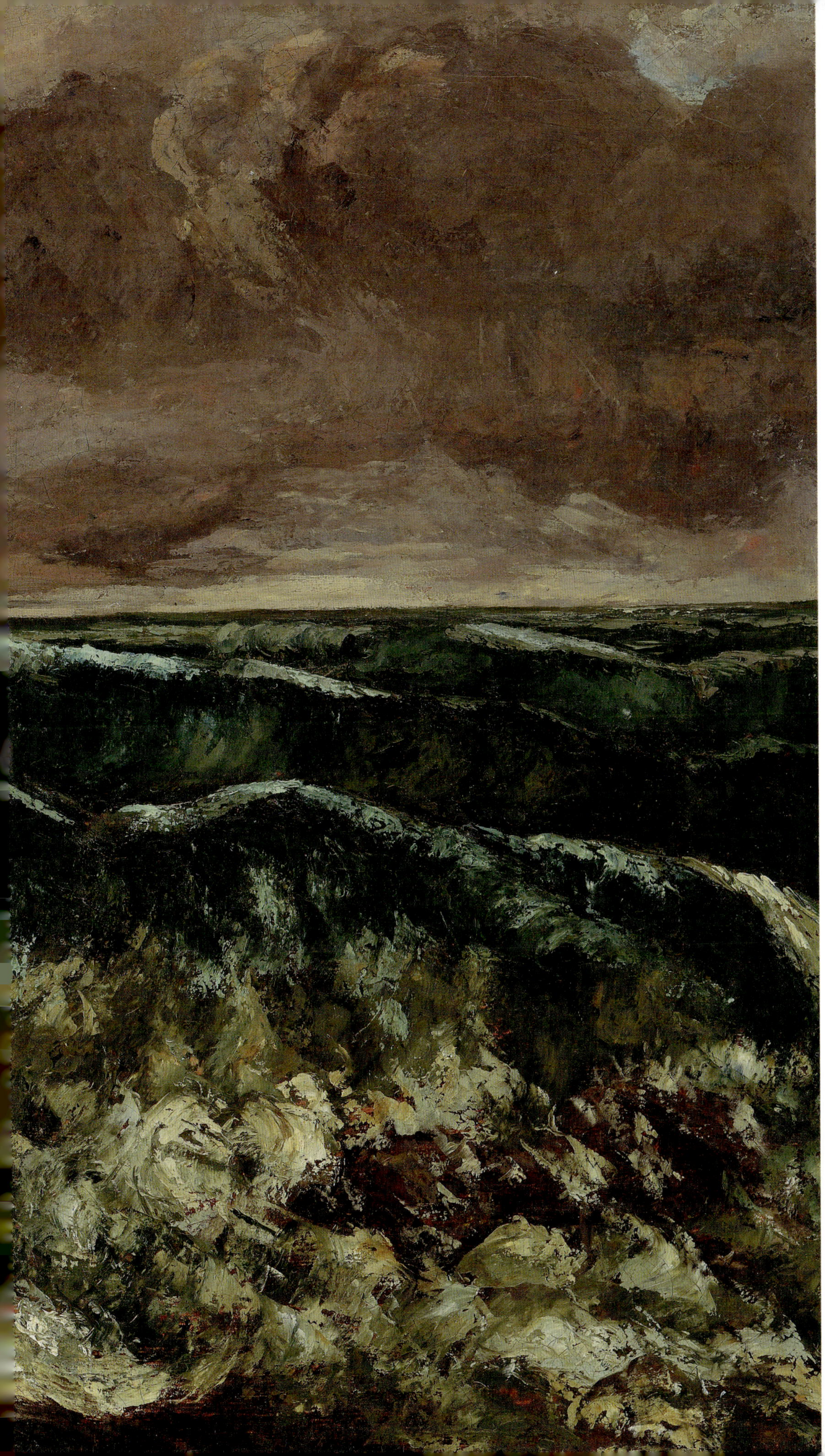

42 *Wave*, 1869. Oil on canvas, 65.8 × 90.5 cm. Musée des Beaux-Arts, Lyons

the question of the waves' "photographic" quality, we can consider the Le Gray and the Courbet at the most basic level of composition and scale. It is often remarked that *The Great Wave* is also a combination of multiple views. To overcome one of the great difficulties then confronting the photographer of the ocean, namely that the long exposure times necessary to capture foreground details such as waves and boats inevitably led to overexposed skies, Le Gray resourcefully shot the sea and sky on separate negatives. By printing them together on the same sheet, he was able to produce a single, convincing, extraordinarily detailed photograph.[24]

However, contrary to what is often implied in the Courbet–Le Gray comparison, the painter combined the different views in an alternative way. For, as Herding observed, Courbet joins not just two views (one of wave and one of sky) but two entirely different viewpoints *within the same object*. As the world viewed through the camera lens becomes translated, via monocular perspective, into a system of legible spatial coordinates, the viewer has no doubt when looking at Le Gray's photograph of where things stand in the water; waves are breaking at a distance halfway between where we are standing and the barrier on the horizon, the measurable space in between them harbors no irregularities of scale.[25]

The same cannot be said of Courbet's various waves. Whereas Le Gray merges technically incongruous parts to create the illusion of a unified whole, Courbet takes an already given unity and stealthily inserts into it a disturbing incongruity. To take perhaps the most extreme case, the ocean rising in the *Wave* in the Musée des Beaux-Arts, Lyons, consumes almost the entire continuum between beach and horizon (fig. 42). The verticality of the wave, suggesting great height, and the physicality of the foam, expressing great proximity, can mean only that we are standing somewhere below it, staring a tsunami in the face. The breaking bank in the middle ground of Le Gray's *Great Wave*, in comparison, is a modest ripple. It is tempting to read the Lyons wave as a tidal wave or a close-up. But each reading comes with its own set of problems. If it is a tidal wave, a sea wall at such close quarters would in principle be so high that it would block everything behind it from view, including the horizon. It would simply be impossible to look up into the wave while at the same time looking over it. Yet we nonetheless see smaller waves on the other side of the main one in the Lyons picture. If it is a close-up, that is, a view of a smaller wave just about to hit us in the face, why do we still see both the horizon and the shore? If it were that close, we should be taking in water and spray, and nothing else. At best, the only way to understand the paradoxical positions in which Courbet's painting puts us is to imagine ourselves suspended in front of the onrushing wave, not so far from it that the wave shrinks or that the splashes of foam coalesce into a single white spray (as happens in the *Great Wave*), but not so close that we lose sight of the horizon. Perhaps the closest experience to this state of suspension would be to place ourselves in the path of a medium-sized wave just as it is about to collapse. That we are rarely in such a situation makes Courbet's re-creation of it all the more daring. Cézanne stated that "[it] hits you right in the stomach.... The whole room feels the spray." Or as the Spanish painter Joan Miró observed, "one is drawn to [it] as by an undertow."[26] Courbet's wave does indeed make us "feel the spray" as it rolls toward us; but we can add, following Miró, that this is because Courbet makes sure that we also roll toward it.

No one reviewing the literature on Courbet's waves will fail to notice that it contains many photographic metaphors: cropping, enlargement, and, most of all, instantaneity. Paul Mantz wrote, skeptically, that "the enormous tidal wave, crowned with spattering white foam, towers like an advancing wall. I repeat that we can't be sure if painting is capable of rendering the changing silhouettes of such flowing and fleeting sights. Courbet has tried the impossible."[27] What Mantz considered impossible was for others a fait accompli; at the time of Mantz's statement, the Impressionists had already staged three group exhibitions full of "flowing and fleeting sights." Going a step further, the German literary critic Walter Benjamin claimed that Courbet even anticipated photographers in developing such effects as the close-up and the snapshot:

> "In his famous painting *La Vague*, a photographic subject is discovered through painting. In Courbet's time, both the enlarged photo and the snapshot were unknown. His painting showed them the way. It equipped an expedition to explore a world of forms and structures which were not captured on the photographic plate until a decade later."[28]

Practically everyone who has written about Courbet's waves concurs that they are remarkably still, even solidified, as if frozen in time, like a photograph: "You can study in Courbet the wonderful techniques of a worker or master artisan. He uses and abuses the palette knife ... applied to the representation of a living wave that heaves, rises, and falls, this process leads to a kind of petrification."[29] The most subtle interpretations distinguish a moment of initial shock from a subsequent feeling of permanent duration: "It is precisely this technique of crystallization that transforms the fugitive moment into an eternal monument."[30]

What is less commented upon is what happens after this feeling of utter stillness abates. For, despite the general sense that the world has been permanently frozen, our eyes are still remarkably free to roam around it. Far from holding the viewer forever hostage to a single instant, the seascape generously offers multiple glimpses into its inner workings. We begin to luxuriate in the build-up of the wave's body, to marvel at the creation of bright foam from dark water, to take pleasure in the stormy sky that is as materially rich as the stormy sea, and to imagine the densification of both to infinity. As the eye gradually circulates, the entire scene is reanimated. The slightest details—a ripple here, an aureole there—become departure points for different voyages into substance. As a result, time becomes increasingly dilated, as it had in a different manner in his originary landscapes of 1864. The wave appears no longer arrested so much as moving forward at a snail's pace.

The strategies discussed so far have led to this moment. The general equivalence of the pictorial field, the touch-by-touch technique, the abolishment of figuration and narrative, extreme frontality, the multiplicity of viewpoints—all these conspire within the seascapes to generate a pronounced deceleration of the gaze in service of the appreciation of substance. Within the general template, there is variation. The horizons are generally low in the Normandy pictures, high in the Étretat waves, where they rise anywhere from a third to a little over half the height of the canvas. Chromatically, colors used below, especially the blues and grays of the sea, are often repeated in the upper reaches of the painting. This is particularly striking with lighter hues, as in the Norton Simon painting (see fig. 37) and *Low Tide at Trouville* (*ca.*1865; Walker Art Gallery, Liverpool).[31] Conversely, the much darker waves at times contain more colors than would be expected (hints of green and light blue in addition to blue and brown). As for texture, some parts of the wave, particularly its concave interior, can be silky smooth like in the Bremen version, *The Wave* (1869; Kunsthalle, Bremen), while other parts are ragged and rough.[32] When the contrast between the wave's inner roll and its breaking crest is at its most dramatic, as in the example now in Edinburgh, *The Wave* (*ca.*1869; Scottish National Gallery, Edinburgh), the wave can cut a solitary "figure."[33] Sometimes there are steady rows behind the main wave (Lyons; see fig. 42). And sometimes these rows, despite the scene's overall frontality, tilt one way or the other, usually toward whichever side of the picture contains the most foreground rocks or beach. In a few cases, such as *The Wave* (1870; Phoenix Art Museum), Courbet experimented with making these breakers, rather than a single dominant wave, the real subject of the seascape.[34] Sometimes rocks and boats on the shore or in the distance give a sense of scale (although usually never enough to offset the overall spatial ambiguity—this is true even in the case of the 1870 Salon picture, with its prominently grounded pair of boats). Sometimes the wind seems to blow the clouds in a single direction, rightward in the case of *The Beach* (1865; Wallraf-Richartz-Museum, Cologne) and *Seacoast and Sailboat in the Face of an Approaching Storm* (*ca.*1869; Staatsgalerie Stuttgart), for example.[35]

FELLOW TRAVELERS

It is at this point that we can briefly consider some of Courbet's contemporaries in the genre. Although Johan Barthold Jongkind, Eugène Boudin, and the American-born painter James Abbott McNeill Whistler would each employ one or more of these devices—nonhierarchy, lack of narrative, visibility of touch, head-on confrontation, destabilized viewpoints—almost none used them all, nor in such an unsettling manner.[36] Jongkind's painting, for example, could sometimes match Courbet's in terms of all-over thickness but tended not to collapse distance in the same way. Instead, in his harbors and seas, Jongkind is generally respectful of perspective, his docks, buildings, and boats arrayed legibly in space, as they are in the seventeenth-century Dutch prototypes to which his marines pay homage (see fig. 40).[37]

The two also diverge at the level of mark-making. Jongkind tracked nature's fleeting movements with equally dynamic brushwork (perhaps one reason why his friend Claude Monet would later call him one of the fathers of Impressionism).[38] This is the exact opposite of Courbet, whose flat, padded strokes work to siphon off nervous energy. A congealed area of water or sky makes the difference between the work of both artists obvious. Whereas in a Jongkind it seems as though it is a luminous accident or optical trick, when sunlight bounces off water or pierces a cloud, in a Courbet it usually signals an actual thickening of things on view, a place where foam or vapor have semi-solidified.

And what of Boudin, whose pastel cloud studies Baudelaire had famously rhapsodized in his "Salon of 1859" as "firmaments of black or purple satin, crumpled, rolled or torn; these horizons in mourning, or streaming with molten metal"?[39] These were so drained of content, so spatially untethered, that there was no choice in front of them but to take in the build-up of form. Even someone as notoriously skeptical of landscape as Baudelaire was forced to admit that "never once while examining these liquid or aerial enchantments, did I think to complain of the absence of man."[40] Courbet is said to have shared Baudelaire's enthusiasm for Boudin's studies. But, interestingly, he harbored reservations about the finished pictures: "[Courbet] found my tone rather lacking in strength, and that, strictly speaking, is perhaps true."[41] Apparently, the visitor felt that the brio and physicality of the pastel studies had become lost in the transition to oil painting. Boudin was unsure what to do in response: "There is in [Courbet's] work a broad principle that one can appropriate but whose details are not fully worked out. He uses it rather freely. There is a truer and surer way to paint."[42] Had Boudin taken up Courbet's challenge by upping the "tone" of his seascapes, and thereby bringing them more in line with his cloud studies, he might have anticipated the "strength" of Courbet's *paysages de mer*. But when Boudin embarked upon a "truer and surer way" in 1862, the year that he started painting the scenes of fashionably dressed tourists congregating on the beach for which he is most famous, he ended up putting considerable distance between his own practice and the "coarse approach" of Courbet. While Boudin's painted skies did indeed begin to have a real material presence, whatever depth and richness they possessed became secondary to the attention-grabbing figures along the low horizons of his "marines." And though it is true that Boudin's frieze-like

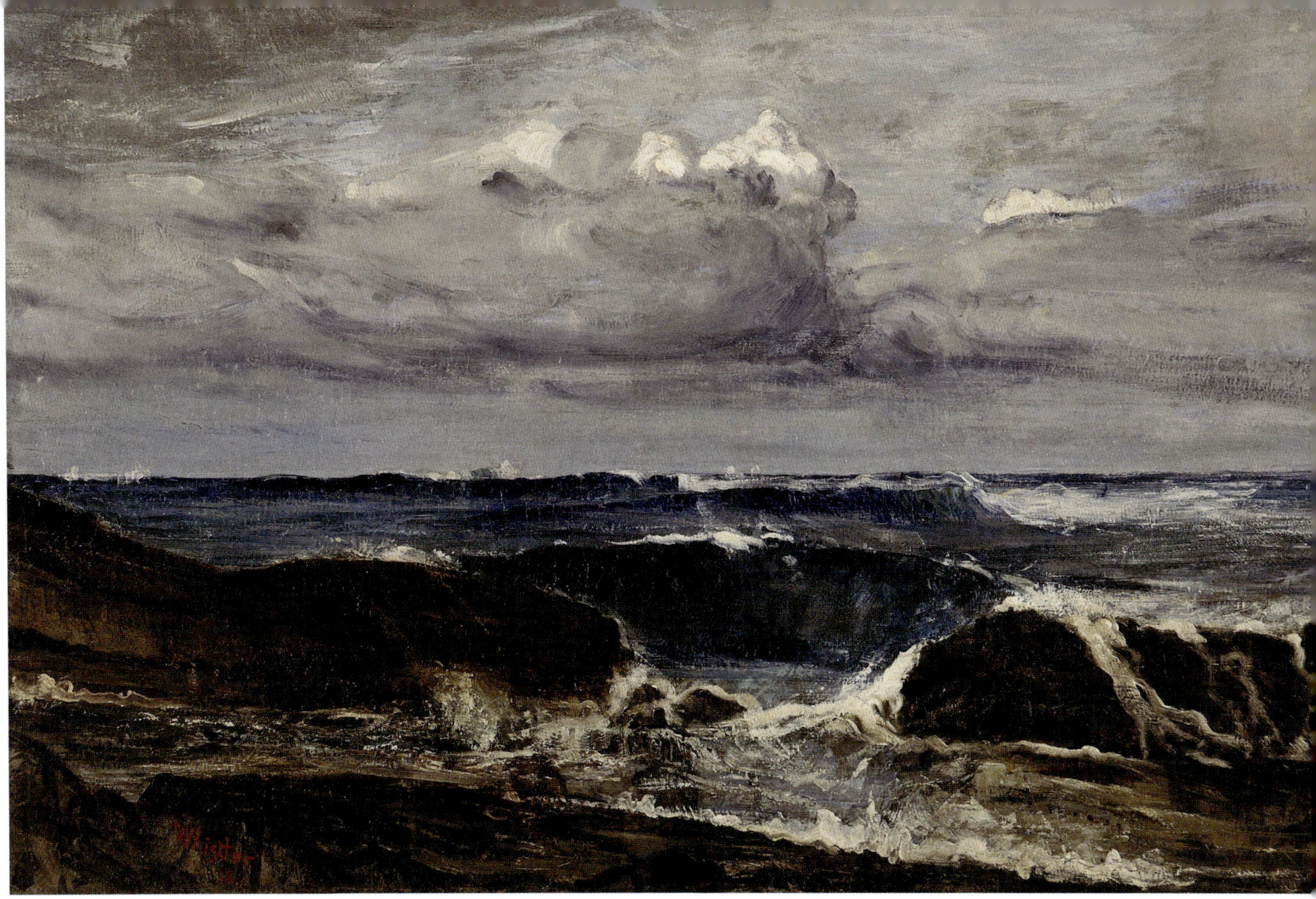

43 | James Abbott McNeil Whistler, *The Blue Wave, Biarritz*, 1862. Oil on canvas, 65.3 × 88.8 cm. Hill-Stead Museum, Farmington, Connecticut

scenes are much shallower than Jongkind's perspectives, and in this sense more Courbetian, they never disorient in the way that Courbet's seascapes do. This is not simply attributable to the presence of figures—a work such as Manet's *On the Beach, Boulogne-sur-Mer* (1868; Virginia Museum of Fine Arts) shows that a populated beach can be just as spatially perplexing. Rather, the line-up of strollers and bathers serves to stabilize the composition by clearly demarcating a foreground zone from a background one. Depth is thus reintroduced into the picture, not as a Jongkindian vista, but in much more abbreviated form: that of a stage set or décor. The tourists divide the picture into two large blocks; the beach is a natural proscenium, and the ocean and sky a scenic backdrop.

Of all the contemporaries, Whistler came closest to Courbet's manner of painting the sea. As with Boudin, the historical connection is direct, and even more well known.[43] Courbet and Whistler both painted in Trouville in 1865. The handful of sea paintings by the latter are illuminating. Like Courbet, Whistler arrived in Trouville with some experience of painting the ocean. *The Blue Wave, Biarritz* is an image of an oncoming wave crashing against nearby rocks (fig. 43). Its imposing Courbetian qualities were not lost upon one of its later owners, Alfred Pope, who astutely likened it to the *Stormy Sea* at the Louvre: "in style it's very like a Courbet—which used to be at Luxembourg (now at the Louvre) the color is different—blue instead of green—the waves more natural, not suggesting tapestry and yet far from the photographic sea of Henry Moore—There is the big feeling of the ocean similar to Courbet."[44] For Pope, Whistler's wave was positioned between two extremes: on the one hand, an unnaturalistic physicality that "suggested tapestry" and, on the other hand, the seamless illusionism of a "photographic sea."

The Blue Wave, Biarritz bears out this assessment. There are aspects in common with the "big feeling" of Courbet—the centrality and imposing nature of the wave, the spattering of foam at close quarters, and the

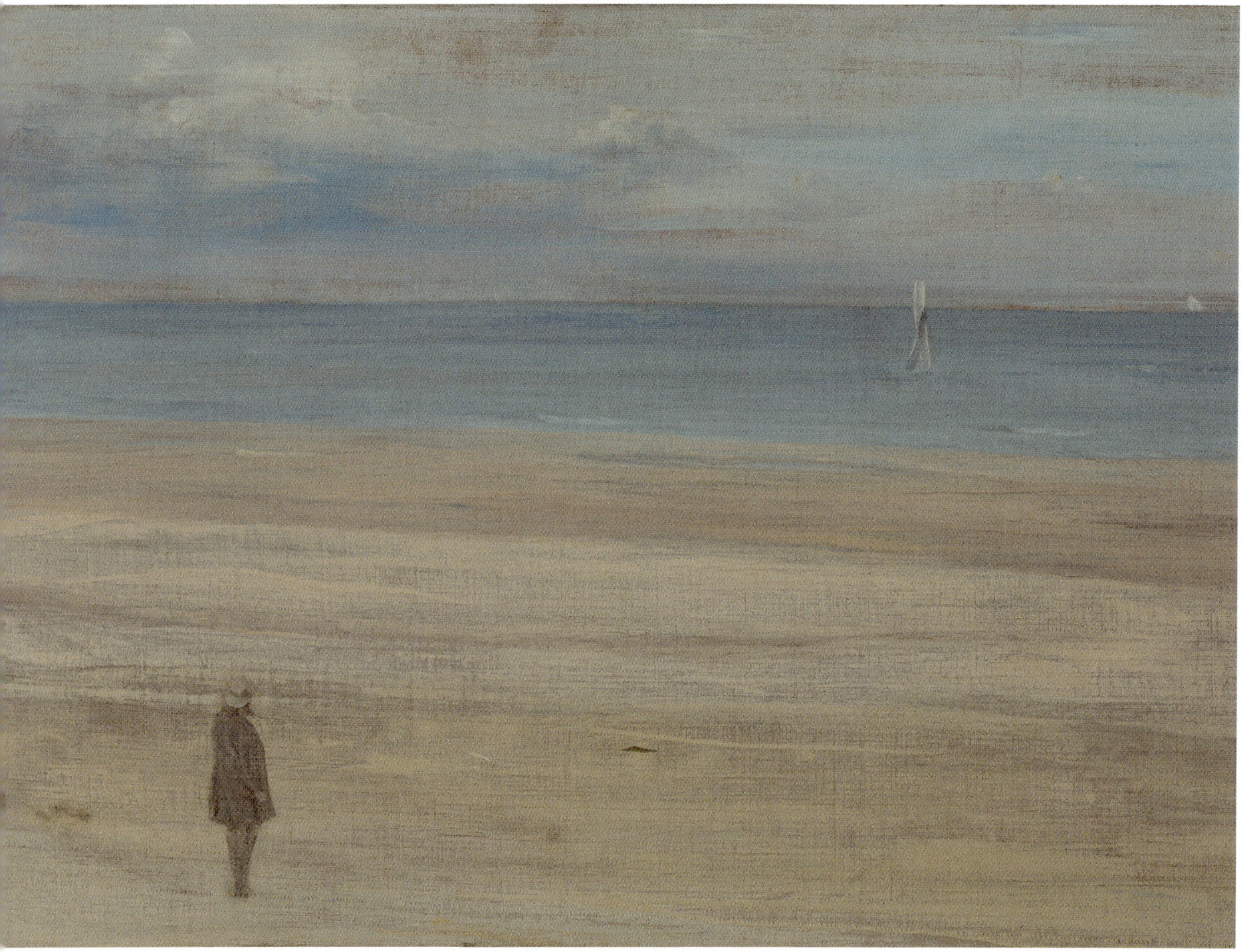

44 James Abbott McNeil Whistler, *Harmony in Blue and Silver: Trouville*, 1865. Oil on canvas, 51 × 76.7 cm. Isabelle Stewart Gardner Museum, Boston

utter lack of narrative or anecdote. But there are also significant differences. Whereas Courbet's skies are blocky, Whistler's are transparent and wispy, more mist than solid, and therefore closer to our usual expectations. Whistler also treats depth in a more a conventional manner. Unlike Courbet's disorienting wave wall, Whistler's wave is set unambiguously at a distance. As if to underscore this point, Whistler has positioned rocks on either side of the wave and made them practically level with it, an arrangement that sets up a horizontal barrier that allows us to gauge where we stand physically in relationship to the wave.

In Pope's eyes, Whistler prefigured Courbet. However, Courbet thought the influence ran in the other direction, and it is hard to disagree.[45] Nothing in Whistler's work prior to this moment (apart from the one-off 1862 wave painting [see fig. 43]) portends the empty, horizontal bands of his Trouville paintings. Courbet had already used this tripartite division in a small painting, *The Seaside at Palavas* (1854; Musée Fabre, Montpellier), to which Whistler would later pay homage in his own *Harmony in Blue and Silver: Trouville* (fig. 44), in which he repeated the figure of Courbet in the left foreground. Furthermore, the consistency of paint in Whistler's Trouville canvases (creamier than usual for him) and their lighter palette are also consistent with Courbet's practice.

Where Whistler diverges most prominently from the master of Ornans is in matters of technique. Billowing sails and streaking clouds—elements rarely encountered in Courbet's seascapes—figure prominently in the Montclair and Chicago paintings, *The Sea* (1865; Montclair Art Museum), *Trouville (Grey and Green, the Silver Sea)* (1865; Art Institute of Chicago), for example. Whistler treated them with translucent brushstrokes in which individual hairs are clearly visible, even in reproduction. This method could not be further from Courbet's steady accumulation of paint deposits, and, overall, it works to partially offset the weight of thickened paint.

However, the biggest difference concerns another aspect of his technique. In his Trouville pictures, Whistler would often drag his brush across the entire width of the canvas to create a certain translucency with economy of means. Courbet himself was not averse now and then to using the brush in this way. But when he did so, it was usually in small spurts, never in complete transversals, and was limited primarily to shore areas, as opposed to the open sea or sky. Whistler essentially takes one of Courbet's techniques for painting the beach and applies it to the entire composition, end to end, top to bottom. Just as this procedure produced in the foreground of Courbet's seascapes a certain porosity between land and sea, now the same sort of permeability is extended to the whole scene. Whistler's approach does result in a certain egalitarian material treatment of the picture surface. But it is different from that which we addressed earlier (following Herding's suggestion of "equalizing compositional emphases"). For while we generally sense a universal material that binds together land, sea, and air (since all are by-products of the same substance), its all-over translucency encourages us to read that physical substance as an omnipresent fog rather than as an accumulation of much more concentrated—yet still equally distributed—pockets of paste. In the form of striated, edge-to-edge brushstrokes, the unifying substance no longer appears to coalesce into different landscape masses, such as clouds, sandbanks, or waves, as it does in Courbet. It has become an unfixed entity, and instead of a build-up or condensation of matter, what we witness is matter's partial atomization. No longer constituting the landscape's material essence, which was the *modus vivendi* of Courbet's *paysages de mer*, Whistler's paint layers instead function as a scrim or mystifying veil.

After 1865, the two fell out. Whistler's biographers have given several hypotheses for this: it may have been a matter of aesthetics, a dissatisfaction with Realism, as he would later complain in acerbic terms to the French artist Henri Fantin-Latour. He may have been jealous that his muse, the Irishwoman Jo Heffernan, had had an affair with Courbet. His ambition may simply have led him to want to disassociate himself from such a controversial figure. Whatever the case, the increasing distance he put between himself and Courbet can clearly also be measured in his art. As his banded paint layers became more transparent, his forms more dissolute, his compositions more monochromatic and ethereal, he moved further and further away from the solidity and density of Courbet's seascapes, and, for the rest of the century, toward the symphonies and nocturnes for which he became best known.

INK AS ABYSS

We can now return to Charles Beauquier's 1866 chronicle for *Revue littéraire de la Franche-Comté* that was introduced at the beginning of this chapter. Beauquier reported on Courbet's March exhibition at Cadart & Luquet, a diverse show including among other exhibits some of the marines from the artist's recent Trouville excursion.[46] Given Courbet's landscape production prior to the Normandy trip, Beauquier and others might have expected the *paysages de mer* to be pictures of shoreline grottoes and caves, not unlike the various river sources of 1864. Instead, the sea paintings were expansive vistas stretching from beach to horizon, with not a shelter or shady enclosure to be seen. In comparison to his landlocked Franc-comtois landscapes, they must have struck viewers as paintings from another universe, let alone another part of France. According to Beauquier, two other towering figures of the time, Victor Hugo and Jules Michelet, had also dealt with the subject. Their contemporaneous works, each of which belonged to a larger system of thought spread across several books, reiterated, and also departed from, Courbet's seascapes in such crucial ways that they warrant deeper analysis here.

Hugo's novel *Les Travailleurs de la mer* was published during the run of Courbet's show on 12 March. Beauquier called the story "only a frame that the poet uses to join pictures of the sea: warm watercolors, blurred drawings, setting suns, storms, calms and terrors."[47] His summary in pictorial terms was incredibly perceptive. Although the critic probably had not been aware of it at the time, Hugo *did* execute a series of "blurred" ink drawings, including some of "storms, calms, and terrors," both during and after the preparation of *Les Travailleurs de la mer*.

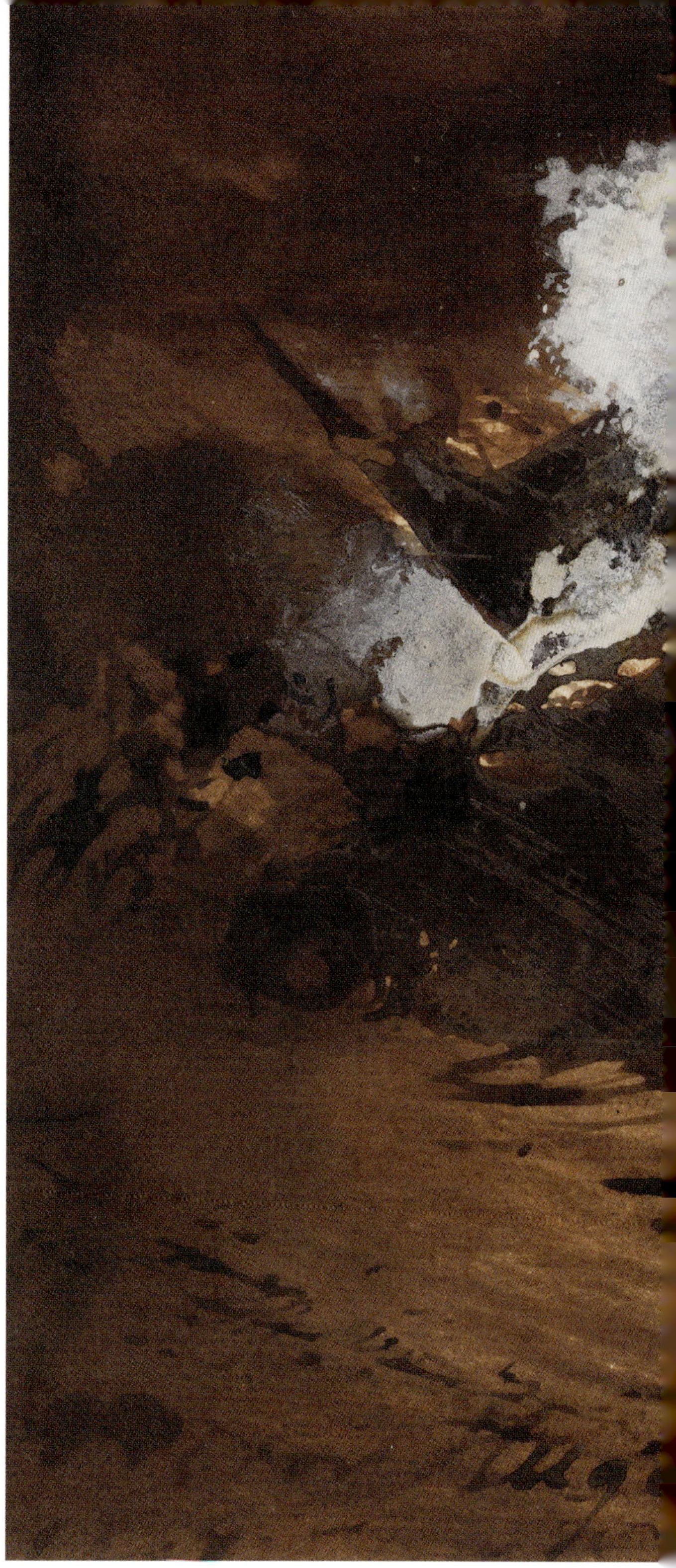

45 | Victor Hugo, *Ma Destinée*, 1867. Ink and gouache on paper, 17.2 × 26.4 cm. Maison Victor Hugo, Paris

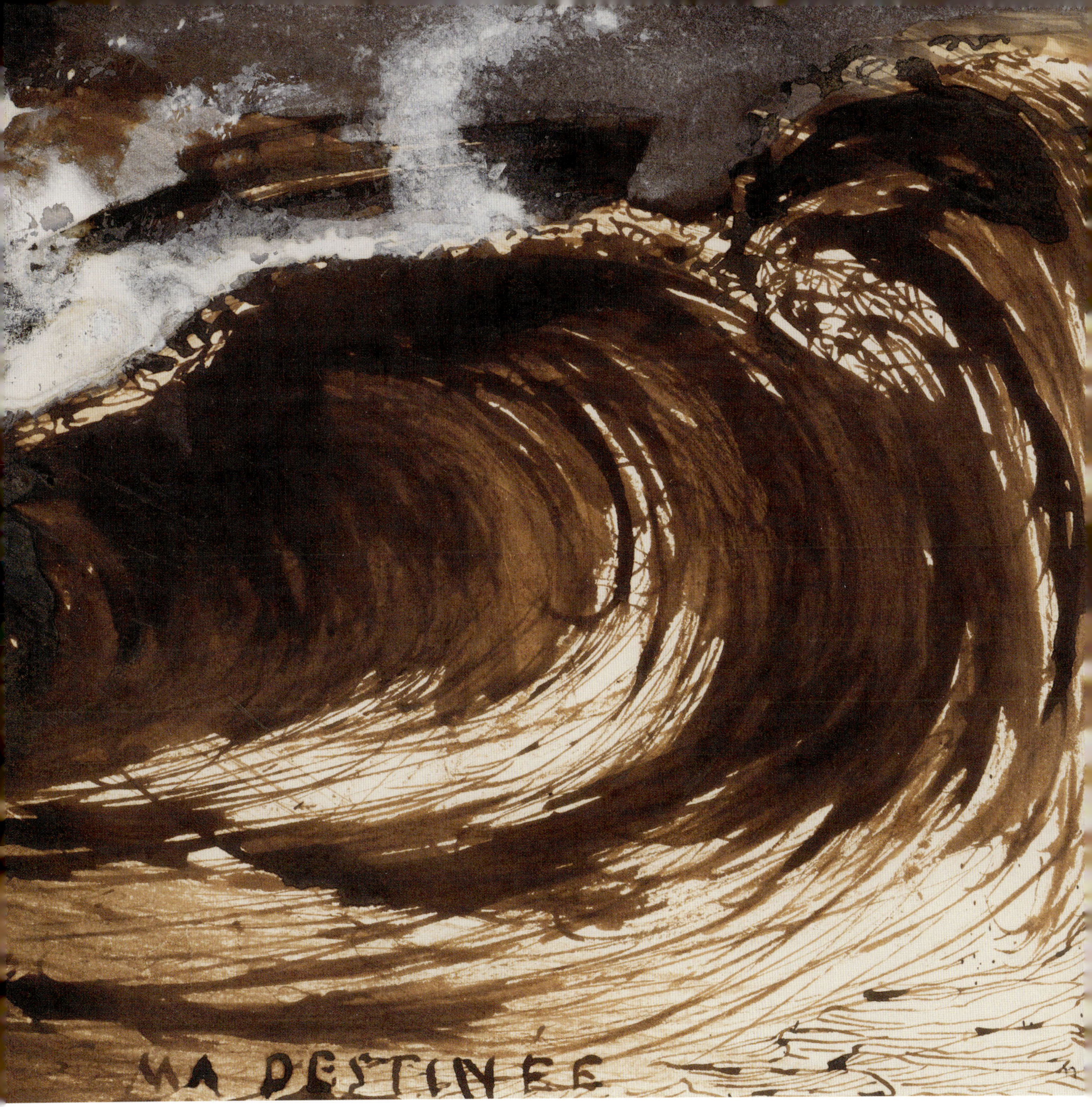
MA DESTINÉE

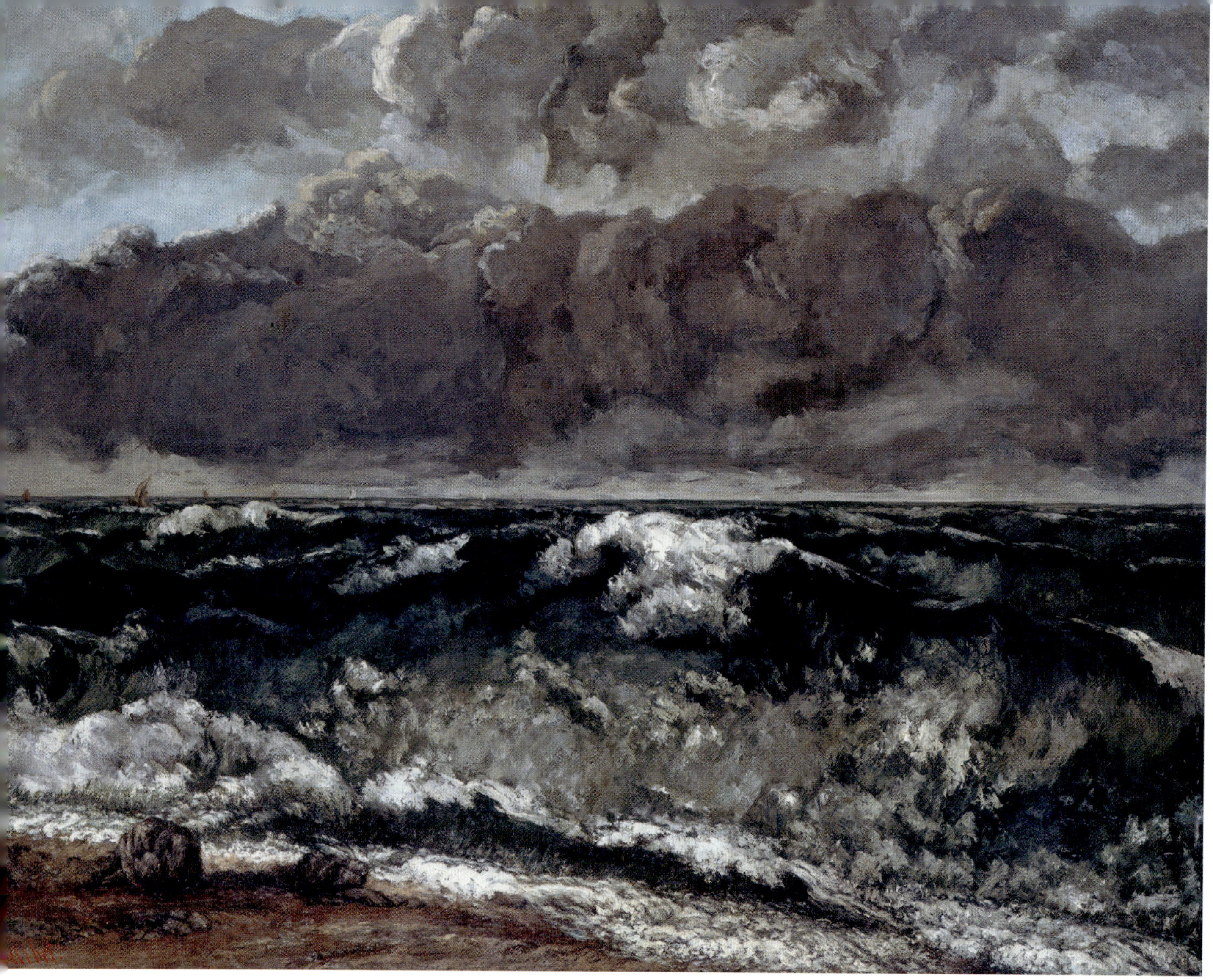

46 | *Wave*, 1869–70. Oil on canvas, 112 × 144 cm. Staatliche Museen zu Berlin, Nationalgalerie

The Hugo drawing usually associated with Courbet's seascapes is a slightly later work, one of the most impressive to arise in the wake of *Les Travailleurs de la mer*, a large wave drawing dubbed, in typically enigmatic Hugolian fashion, *Ma Destinée* (fig. 45).[48] Because of its subject matter, date, and innovative use of materials, it is often compared with Courbet's *Stormy Sea* exhibited at the Salon of 1870 and the similar version now in the Nationalgalerie, Berlin (fig. 46). Both waves dramatize a coincidence of image and matter in which the imagined substance (water) and the actual one (ink or paint) approximate each other. In each case, the medium physically behaves like the thing it represents; ink runs like dark splashes of seawater in the Hugo, and dense paint accumulates like wave foam in the Courbet. However, the works are notably different in other respects, for example, in the context of production and exhibition. On the one hand, we have the exiled Romantic writer churning out ink drawings in private for his friends and himself, and, on the other hand, the Realist artist creating large oil paintings for the Salon.[49] The opposition could be taken even further, pitting Hugo's drawing practice against Courbet's painterly method, which sets up an even more jarring clash of worldviews, and particularly of the role of substance within them. In Hugo's case, that worldview was largely spelled out in various philosophical fragments written while working on his major works of the early 1860s, *Les Misérables* (1862), *William Shakespeare* (1864), and *Les Travailleurs de la mer*.[50]

A fragmentary text originally conceived for *Les Travailleurs de la mer*, "La Mer et le vent," summarizes one of Hugo's central themes, the sea, as a dark, amorphous, and impenetrable realm of the imagination. Oceanic blackness was for Hugo the ultimate source of artistic inspiration, and he liked to compare the various literary creations emerging from it to monsters arising from the deep:

> The possible is a formidable matrix. Mystery concretizes into monsters. Pieces of shadow come forth from this block of immanence. They separate, detach, roll, float, condense, borrow from the ambient blackness, undergo unknown divisions, come alive, compose for themselves some unknown form out of the obscurity, an unknown soul from the miasma, and wander off, like larvae, through the vitality. It is something like darkness made into beasts.[51]

The secretion of monsters from a "formidable matrix" of nothingness is thematized in the drawing *Head of a Devil* (fig. 47). Here a pair of eyes and horns hint at a mysterious beast lurking in the shadows. Taking advantage of the indeterminate nature of ink drawing, of the chance accidents that occur when fluid permeates paper, Hugo initiates "unknown divisions" on the sheet that gives birth to an "unknown soul."[52]

Head of a Devil does not simply illustrate Hugo's philosophy; it physically *enacts* it. As pools of ink are also, materially, areas of "ambient blackness," and as ink drawing literally extracts forms from it, the draftsman is also a sort of inspired poet. In both artistic and literary creation, a monster is born from an initial black blot. It is as both writer *and* artist that Hugo makes darkness create beasts. Hugo does not limit the literalization of metaphor to monsters. The ocean itself is given the same treatment. In one passage from *Les Travailleurs de la mer*, for example, the sea is described as "supple" and "incompressible" and as something that "slides away under pressure."[53] Hugo's language evokes ink drawing. Indeed, in a sheet depicting a shipwreck, *Mast Floating at Sea* (fig. 48), the dark liquid medium performs exactly the kind of movement Hugo attributes to the sea. To visualize the ocean's suppleness and incompressibility, the writer physically pushes ink around, making it "slide away under pressure," in order to produce the image of a ship bobbing on the waves.

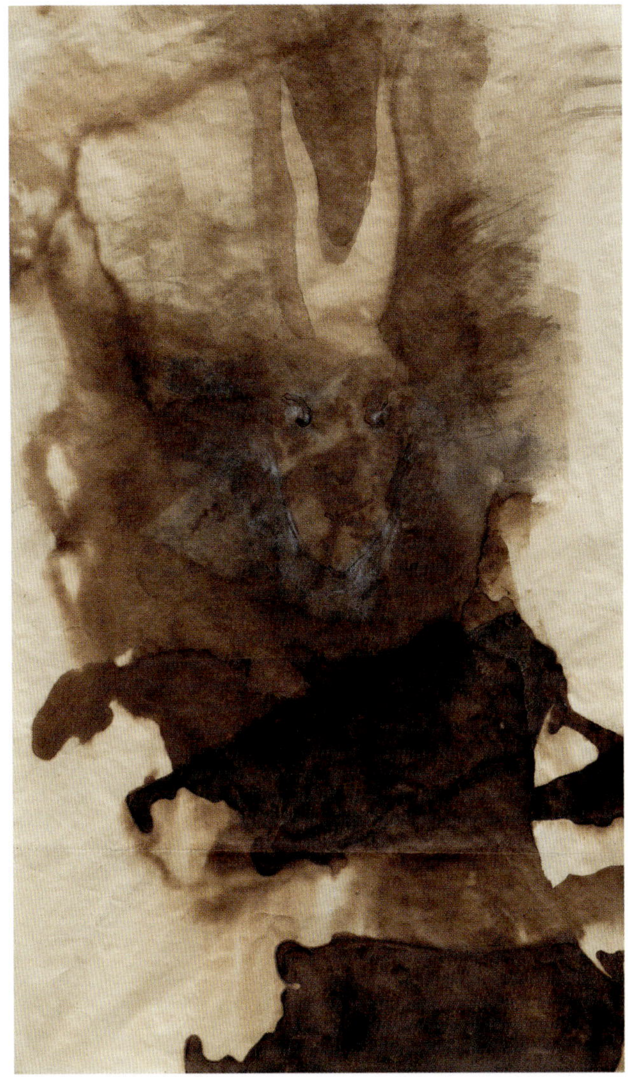

47 | Victor Hugo, *Head of a Devil*, *ca.*1864–69. Brown ink and wash with white gouache on paper, 38.5 × 23.5 cm. Fundación Almine y Bernard Ruiz-Picasso para el Arte, Brussels

Head of a Devil and *Mast Floating at Sea* are two of many examples in Hugo's work where metaphors of substance are realized as art. Anything that separates, detaches, rolls, floats, condenses, or borrows from the "immanent block" that is the sea (or from surrogates such as the abyss, the void, the night, etc.) is potentially a subject for ink drawing, because, in Hugo's practice, figures *do* separate, detach, roll, float, condense, and borrow from the obscure darkness that is the ink blot.

The drawing *Le Pieuvre* provides perhaps the most stunning example of a mysterious shadow "concretizing into a monster" (fig. 49). Taking its name from the

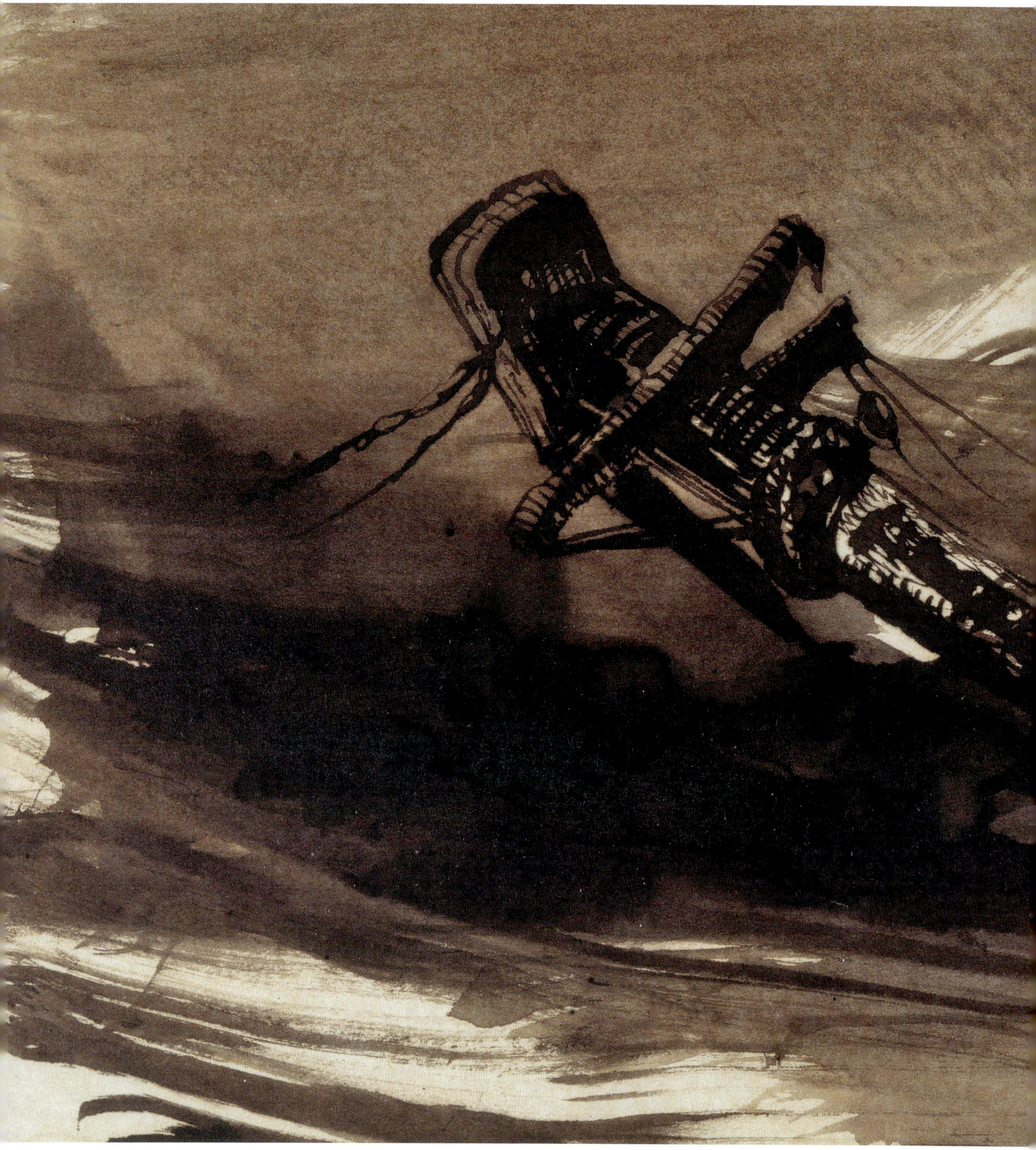

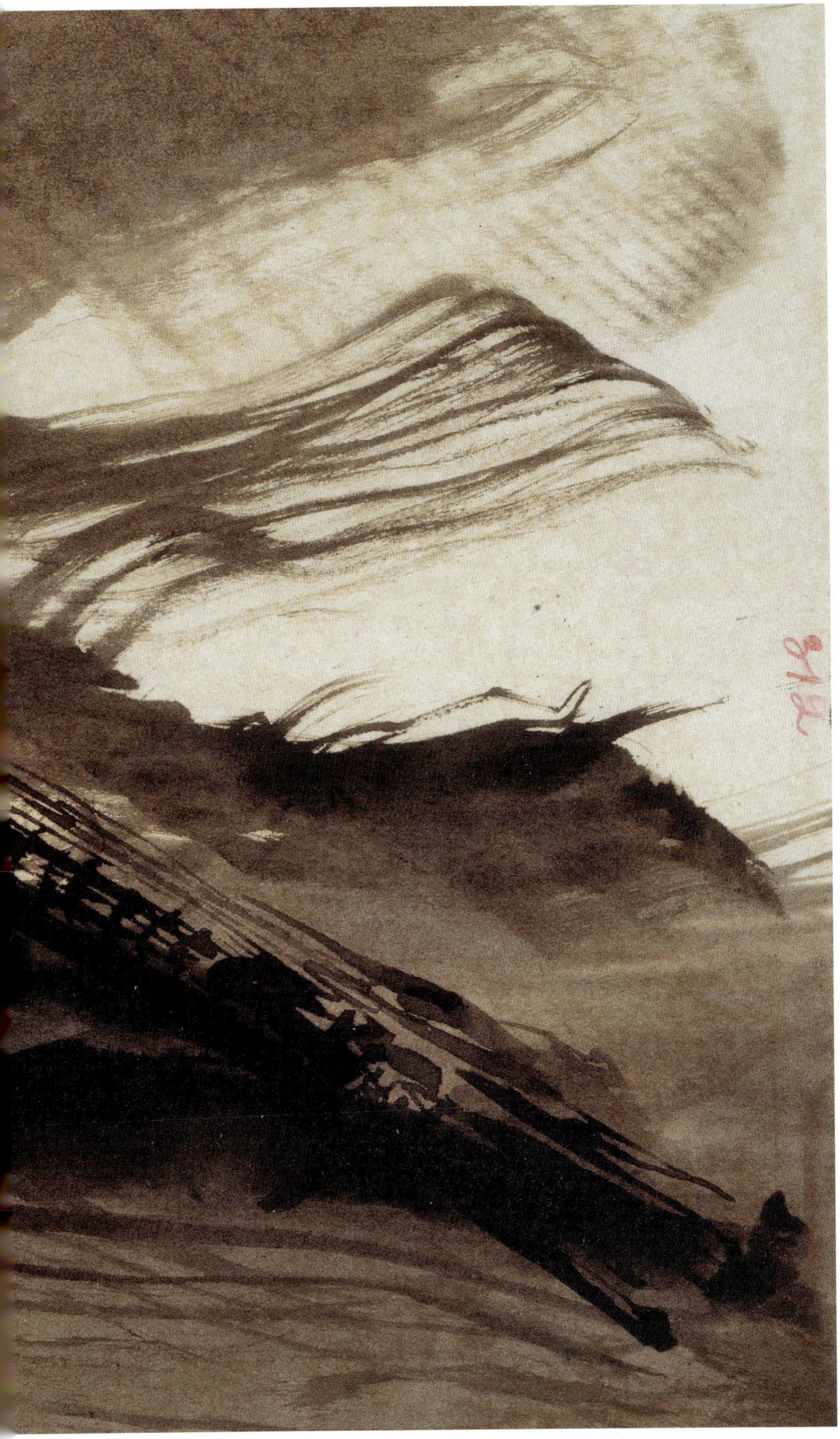

48 Victor Hugo, *Mast Floating at Sea*, *ca.*1866. Brown ink and wash on paper, 19.2 × 24.6 cm. Bibliothèque nationale de France, Paris

49 | Victor Hugo, *Le Pieuvre*, 1865–66. Brown ink and wash on paper, 35.8 × 25.8 cm. Bibliothèque nationale de France, Paris

Norman word *pieuvre* (octopus in local dialect), the deadly creature succumbs to the hero Gilliat in one of the novel's most thrilling chapters. But Hugo did not depict this epic battle in his drawing. Instead, the octopus appears less like a character from the novel than an apotropaic symbol or talisman. At first glance, it seems to float freely, tentacles splayed like spokes of a wheel or solar rays (to use Hugo's metaphors). Yet, on closer inspection, almost half of its eight limbs are still tethered to the fathomless pit at the bottom of the sheet. Is this area a hidden underwater mooring, a deep trench, or an area untouched by sunlight? Whatever the case, it cannot be doubted that it, too, is an amorphous blackness emitting a monster. We see this emission taking place in the drawing, for the creature's very body is made from the same dark fluid as the abyss where dried ink is so thick that it is visibly in relief.[54]

Hugo's conception of drawing, defined by a startling congruence of the literal and the referential, was rare in his time, an era dominated by an illusionism in which the work of art was admired precisely to the extent to which it hid or downplayed its material. We must go all the way back to the medieval period to find comparable works in significant numbers. Before the rise of Renaissance naturalism, in a world dominated by Christian theology, matter was often considered divine.[55] Medieval culture revered certain objects because they were thought to be at once holy and earthly; they represented God while also representing themselves. Hugo's ink drawings of the sea are a kind of secularized version of holy matter. Instead of embodying the divine, his waves literalize the power of the imagination (always for Hugo its own kind of divinity). What makes this possible is the elemental bond between seawater and ink. A wave in greasy charcoal or crumbly pastel would not possess the same co-substantiality (unless the sea was meant to be as sticky as grease or as powdery as chalk). With ink, Hugo discovered a medium that allowed him not only to picture individual monsters but also to dramatize the mysterious nature of the visionary, that "formidable matrix" of the possible.

Unique among nineteenth-century artists and writers, Hugo showed sensitivity in applying literary metaphors and images to the actual materials he was working with and in turning physical actions performed on the sheet into the fictional acts taking place in his writing. This was reflected in his work habits. Hugo often used the same tools for writing and drawing.[56] We can imagine him, for instance, writing about a "black sun" and then quickly creating a planet-like inkblot in response. Or, conversely, he could sketch different versions of the *pieuvre* and then choose characteristics from one or all the drawings to include in a written description of the beast.[57]

The interrelationship of writing and drawing is also often thematized *within* the Hugolian text itself. It is particularly important, as Jean-Pierre Montier makes clear, in *Les Travailleurs de la mer*.[58] The first chapter, "A Word Written on a Blank Page," refers to the moment in the novel when the reader first encounters Gilliat's name. Instead of revealing the hero's identity right away, Hugo waits until Déruchette, the object of his affection, traces the word "GILLIAT" into the snow to introduce the character's name. The first appearance of the name on the actual page of the book therefore coincides exactly with its first appearance in the story, on the blank "page" of the snowbank.

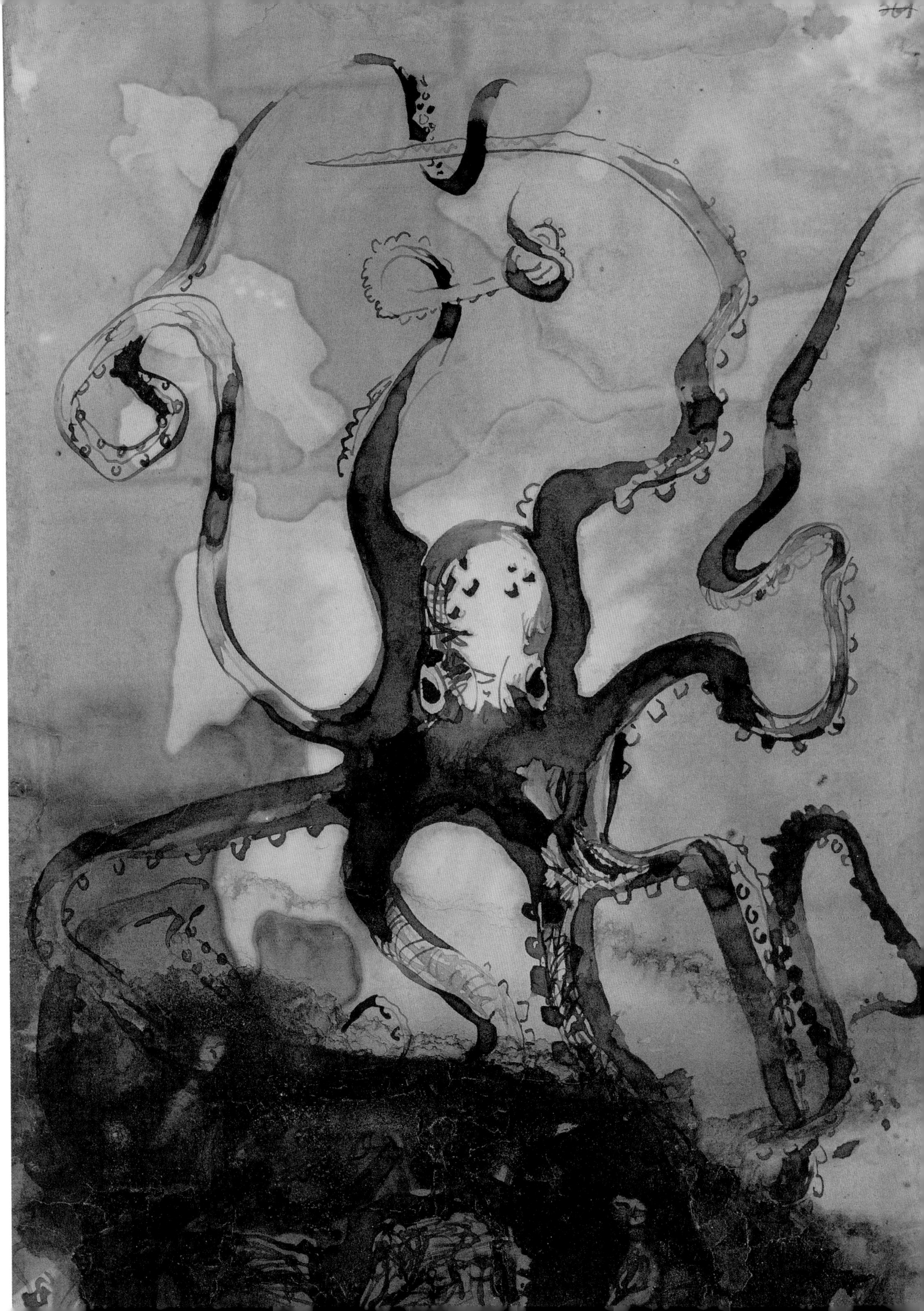

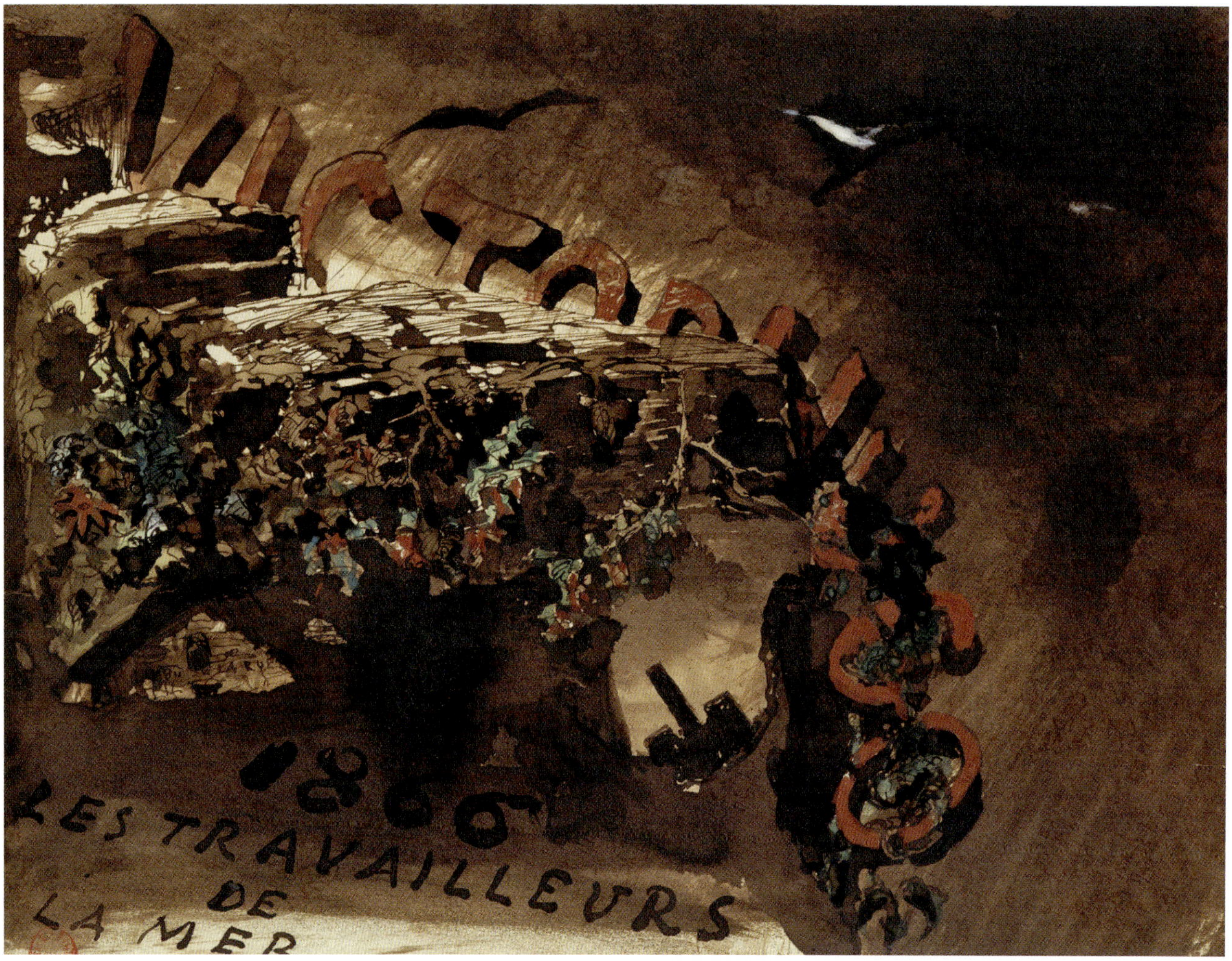

50 | Victor Hugo, frontispiece for *Les Travailleurs de la mer*, 1866. Brown ink, wash, gouache, and watercolor on paper, 19.2 × 25.4 cm. Bibliothèque nationale de France, Paris

Later, in the central event of the novel, Gilliat recovers the steam engine of a boat owned by Déruchette's uncle that had become wedged between two towering Channel rocks known as the Douvres. Gilliat uses his considerable nautical prowess and skill to complete the nearly impossible mission, only to discover upon his return that Déruchette and a visiting pastor have in the meantime fallen in love. In an act of extraordinary self-sacrifice, Gilliat facilitates their marriage, helps them off the island, and, perched high on a rocky promontory and watching the lovers' boat disappear over the horizon, lets the rising waves claim his life.

The novel's final sentences revisit the initial image of the blank sheet. Gilliat disappears underwater as Déruchette vanishes on the horizon as a fading *tache* (blot). There is an obvious parallel between the white blankness at the novel's beginning and the pitch blackness at its end. If inscribing a blank surface is the narrative's initiatory gesture, disappearing into liquid darkness is its concluding one. The entire novel in a sense is the passage from being written in to being drawn (drowned) out.

This novelistic trajectory is prefigured in Hugo's proposed frontispiece, in which the author's name falls into the sea, anticipating Gilliat's own disappearance into the abyss (fig. 50). The frontispiece also hints at another correlation between writing and drawing. For Hugo did not simply inscribe his name as if signing a letter in cursive; the letters are blocky and intertwined with a vine. This visualization of his name is but one of several pieces of evidence showing that Hugo thought of writing as a way of "drawing" letters; that is, of treating written text as its own kind of image. Many of his drawings and handmade greeting cards turn his initials or sometimes his entire name into a pictorial device. His monogram could be a filigreed ornament interlacing his own initials with those of his lover Juliette Drouet.[59] Or, just as easily, he could embed them in architecture, as he did in his designs for his chimney at Hauteville House. In the drawing *Ruins of a Castle* (fig. 51), the red three-dimensional letters of "VICTOR" snake around an architectural structure whose double-towered form mimics the *H* (from "HUGO") positioned directly below it. The *H* as both letter and image seems to have obsessed Hugo since his early days. For example, when Hugo characterizes the twin peaks of the Douvres in *Les Travailleurs de la mer* as a giant letter *H*, he is revisiting his own earlier description of the twice-turreted cathedral in *Notre Dame de Paris* as the same letter.[60] The image-letter even appears in the *pieuvre* drawing, in which the monster's upper tentacles undulate into the shape of the letters *V* and *H*. If Hugo's inventive monograms and literary descriptions had turned letters into images, his tentacular initials did the opposite; he turned an image into letters, alphabetizing the *pieuvre*.

The parallels between his writing and drawing practices reveal that Hugo's scene of writing was equally his scene of drawing. Put another way, Hugo's practice reduced writing and drawing to the common denominator of ink on paper. Beauquier's comments in the pages of *Revue littéraire de la Franche-Comté* provided indirect evidence of this. The critic saw the novel as a series of pictures because the author himself imagined situations in terms that were easily translatable into art. Beauquier found multiple "blurred drawings" because Hugo never missed the opportunity to talk about the sea as if he were talking about a formless pool of ink.

Returning to our initial comparison between *Ma Destinée* and *Stormy Sea*, nothing would seem more out of place in Hugo's liquified universe than Courbet's clotted, creamy seascapes.[61] No darkness, no mystery, no inaccessible places beyond. Hugo's visionary ocean presented a world coming into view, whereas in a Courbetian world, everything is visible, even palpable, within arm's reach, concrete. To which literary worldview, then, did Courbet's seascapes correspond? Beauquier's observations, again, provide a clue. In addition to noting the pictorial qualities of *Les Travailleurs de la mer*, the critic also remarked that Hugo's novel would probably have been called *La Mer* had the historian Jules Michelet not already used the title for his own book on the sea published five years earlier. In *La Mer*, in contrast to Hugo's publication, the sea is almost never imagined as a bottomless well of poetic inspiration, nor is the reaction to waves primarily one of awe. On the contrary, for Michelet the destiny of waves, and of the world in general, was to be partly solidified, rich in substance—caught in a state of matter not unlike the one encountered in Courbet's seascapes.

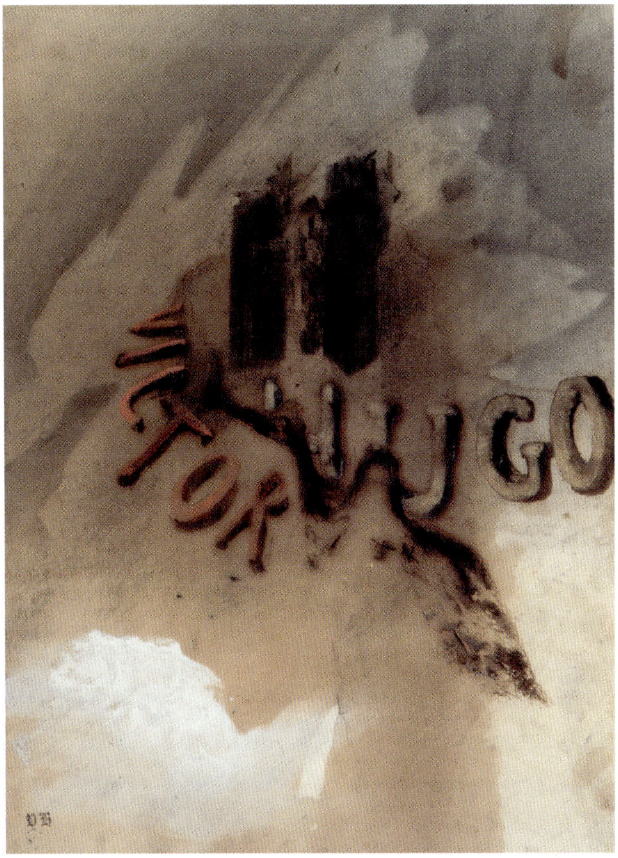

51 | Victor Hugo, *Ruins of a Castle*, 1854–55. Brown and black ink and wash, pastel, and graphite on paper, 34 × 25 cm. Maison Victor Hugo, Paris

THE FLOWERING OF BLOOD

As far as we know, Courbet did not correspond with the eminent historian turned natural historian. But the chances are that he at least knew of him. In his lifetime, Michelet's lectures on history at the Collège de France in Paris were so popular that they were stopped, first in 1848 on the eve of the French Revolution and then again (after reinstatement under the Second Republic) in 1851, as they had become the scene of antigovernment demonstrations. His firing, the result of a longstanding enmity in academic circles between Jesuits and liberals, inevitably cast a shadow over his future prospects. In 1852, he resigned from a post at the National Archives after refusing the obligatory pledge of allegiance to the state.[62]

During the Second Empire, Michelet published a series of seemingly apolitical natural histories—*L'Oiseau* (1856), *L'Insecte* (1858), *La Mer* (1861), and *La Montagne* (1868). Not everyone took kindly to his naturalist turn. A critic for the short-lived journal *Le Réalisme*, for instance, lambasted *L'Oiseau* for romanticizing nature in a similar way to Hugo.[63] Eventually, the natural histories, their factual content outdated, became historical curiosities themselves, relics of an earlier age of scientific popularization. However, opinion began to change after the Second World War.[64] What was once considered the books' greatest weakness—their literariness—came to be seen as their greatest strength. Michelet's writings began to be treated as literature. Readers started to notice, for instance, the striking recurrence of certain images, often signaled by the same word or phrase, no matter the date or subject of the text, that formed a sort of substructure of leitmotifs. As Roland Barthes, the pioneer of this kind of thematic criticism within Michelet studies, put it: "We must read Michelet as a polyphony," since the theme is lodged in the text "the way a musical theme is lodged in every part of a symphony.... The theme's iterative character is effective only because there is in Michelet a verbal fixity of themes: they always indicate their presence by the same word or the same image."[65]

Foremost among these themes was that of substance. Certain kinds of material had personal, psychological, and even moral value in Michelet's writing: anything hot, wet, and fluid suggested health, fertility, and soundness of mind; cold, drought, or brittleness indicated malady, defect, or evil. Consider, for instance, blood. What connected Michelet's heroes and heroines was the bodily substance pulsating through their veins, warm and rich, nourishing and fecund, circulating and mobile. By contrast, the villains of history had blood that was desiccated and sterile or were royal inbreds with sealed-off bloodlines. Whatever his subject and no matter what effects contemporary history had wrought upon his thinking—the way socialism changed his views on religion or the way the violent 1848 Revolution influenced his attitude toward the masses—the sanguine opposition endured essentially unchanged throughout his career.

The blood theme appears in his work even in the absence of human beings. For instance, in the chapter of *La Mer* called "La Mer de lait" ("The Sea of Milk"),

52 | *After the Hunt*, ca.1859. Oil on canvas, 236.2 × 186.1 cm. The Metropolitan Museum of Art, New York

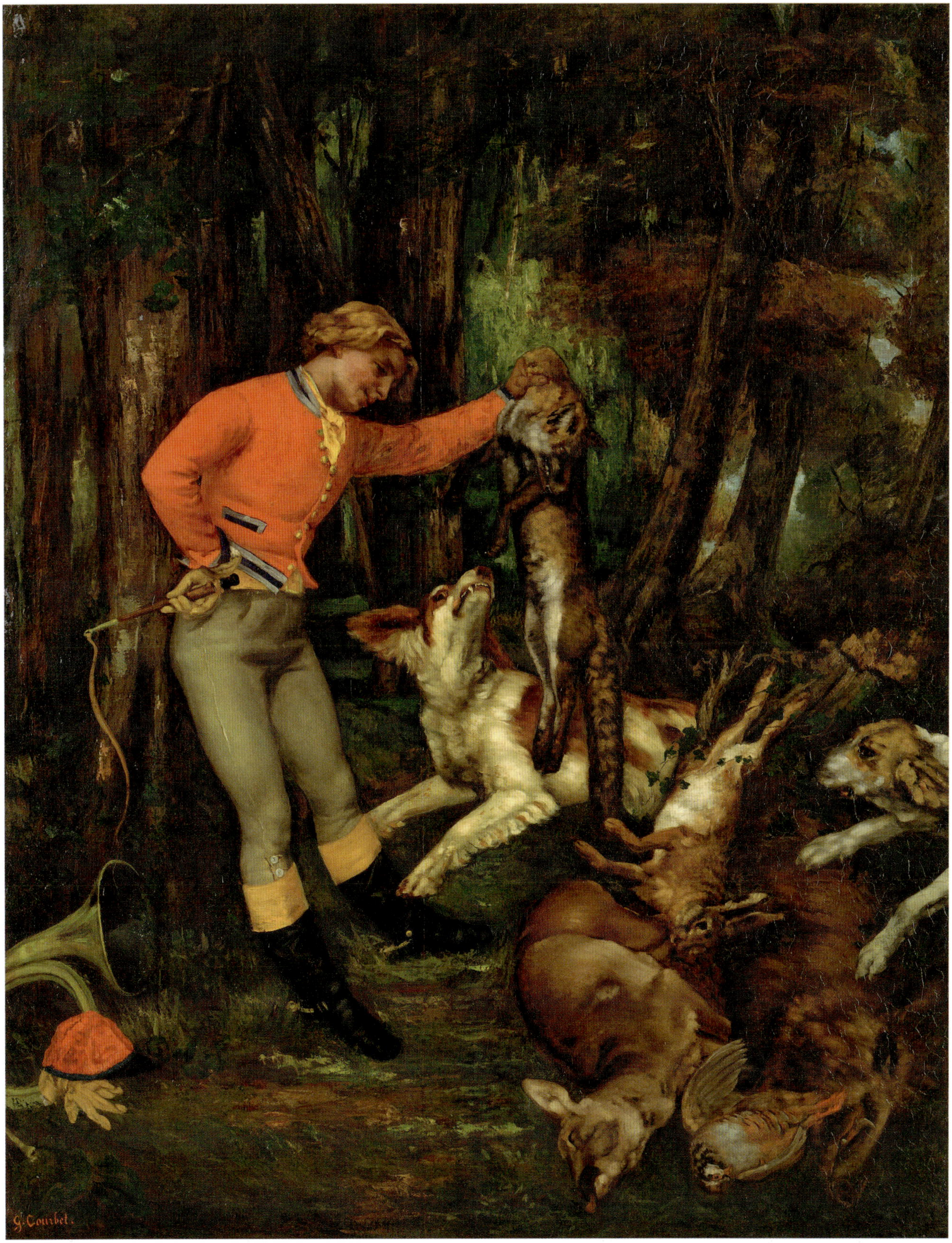
G. Courbet.

Michelet presents the ocean as blood's purest form. According to Barthes,

> this is because, for Michelet, blood is not at all a sealed biological element, strictly belonging to this or that person who possesses blood as he might possess eyes or legs. It is a cosmic element, a unique and homogeneous substance, which traverses all bodies, without losing, in this accidental individuation, anything of its universality. Itself a transformation of the earth (of bread and of the fruits that we eat), it has the immensity of an element. Hence, the superlative form of blood is finally the sea.[66]

Bodily metaphors appear in *La Mer* even more than usual. An entire chapter is devoted to a coral species known as *fleur de sang* (flower of blood) which is not only blood-colored but also indistinguishable to the touch from human skin.[67] Phrase after phrase recalls the pastose consistency of Courbet's painted seas. The sea is alternatively viscous, gelatinous, mucus-like, and milky, recalling criticisms of the artist's seascapes as creamy, solidified, and wall-like. However, what connects Michelet's writing to Courbet's painting goes beyond their mutual appreciation for the physical make-up of the sea.

For a history organized around a theme as it is in Michelet's histories is different from a history based on documents and texts. It has the power to portray key historical figures and events from an unorthodox point of view, accentuating seemingly trivial details at the expense of vital information. What often takes on supreme importance in Michelet's writing are the unspoken and often-overlooked aspects of bodies, not what is officially said or written. As a result, the reader experiences the past in unlikely places: in weather, food, the land (and sea and air), and the body. Thus, embedded into the usual lives of kings and saints is an internal connective tissue of substances, "a way of apprehending the dead men of the past, not in a chronology or a Rationality, but in a network of carnal practices in a system of ailments, of garments, of everyday customs, of mythic representations, of amorous actions. Michelet reveals what we might call the sensual side of History."[68]

If oil painting since the Renaissance has been traditionally thought of as a means of historical narration, of visually "apprehending the dead men of the past," then might the unleashing of substance in Courbet's pictures not reveal, following Barthes, the sensual side of painting? Just as Michelet's blood theme infuses his writing with a sensuous subtext, do not Courbet's painted substances constitute a kind of underlying "texture" coursing throughout his work? We can imagine the pictorial representation of matter in Courbet functioning like a Micheletian theme. An omnipresent leitmotif, the depiction of substance, is particularly emphasized in his landscapes. And just as the sea for Michelet was the purest form of blood, seascape for Courbet is perhaps the ultimate realization of matter.

Courbet's subterranean theme of pictured substance lends coherence to certain puzzling and at first glance unrelated features of his work. For example, Courbet's idiosyncratic use of still life outside the genre appears less arbitrary. He devoted much attention to nature in several canvases. The flowers in *Trellis* (see fig. 12) and the dead quarry in *After the Hunt* (fig. 52) are not only as richly painted as their human partners; they also seem to orient themselves outward, as if they, and not the woman at the trellis or the hunting valet, are the true subject of the picture. Foregrounding still-life elements within a large figure painting was a sign of the ongoing collapse of the genres. But rarely are inanimate things so exaggerated, so compositionally prominent and out of scale, so daringly brushed, as to subvert the overall cohesion of the picture.[69]

The spatial discord between figures and the landscapes they occupy is another consequence of Courbet's accentuation of matter. Courbet's thickly painted backgrounds often do not abate at a figure's edge. In such cases, figure and ground abruptly clash; no softening of landscape or dissolving of contour mediates their encounter. This feature is particularly apparent in his nudes in a landscape such as *The Spring* (fig. 53). Whereas in more conventional painting a carefully gradated series of tones eases the naked body into its surroundings, in Courbet's hands the two confront each other awkwardly. The vigorously painted background foliage in the unfinished *Bather* (ca. 1866–68; Private collection) brushes right up against the seated

53 | *The Spring*, 1868. Oil on canvas, 128 × 97 cm. Musée d'Orsay, Paris

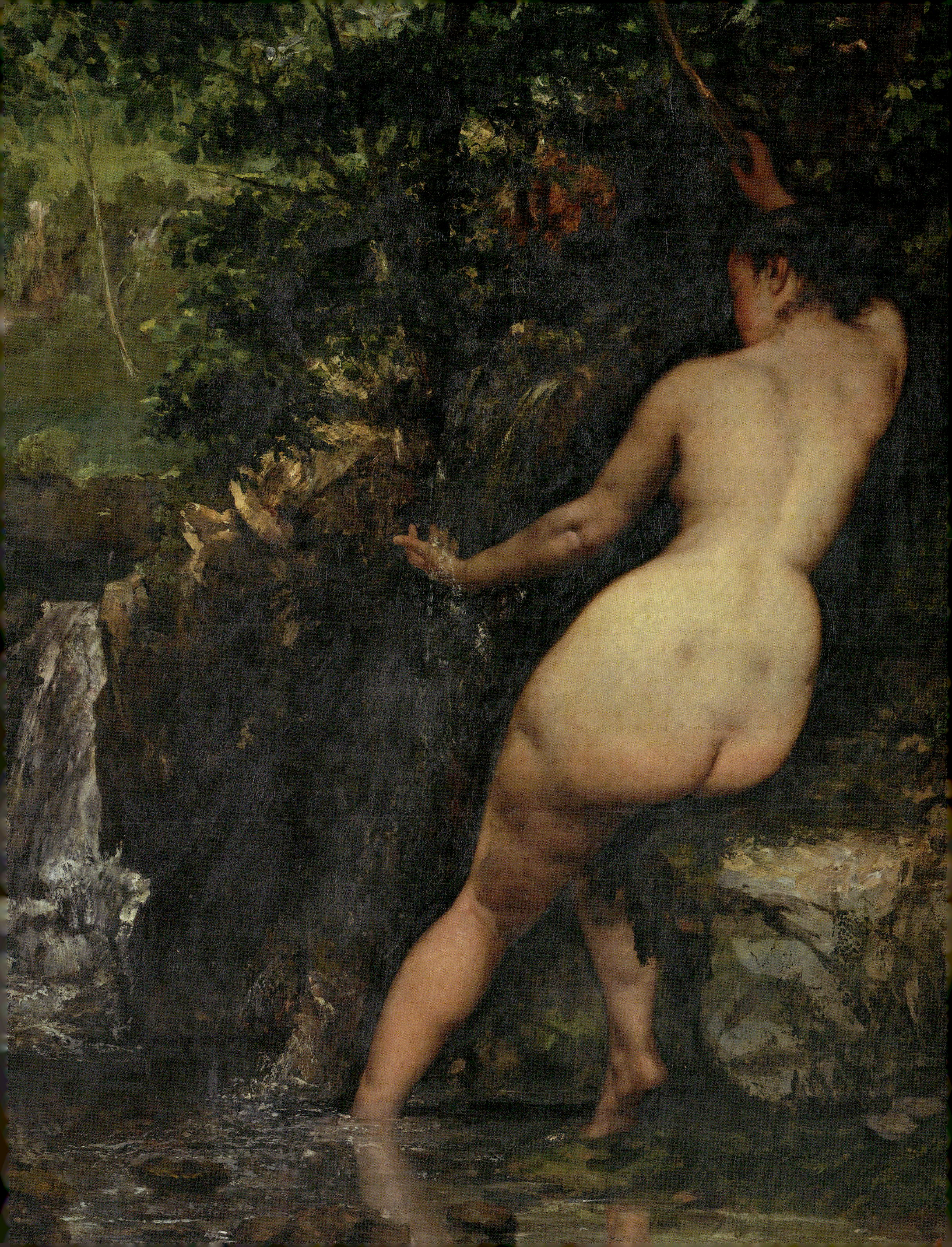

nude's right breast, torso, and arms.[70] Some discarded clothes do likewise for the figure's posterior. Only a small sliver of dark-brown ground, visible in reproduction, halts the imminent grinding together of flesh with fabric and landscape. A corollary to this phenomenon in *Bather* (and many other works) is an apparent lack of interest in the anatomically correct depiction of bodies as they come into contact with the physical world. Feet, hands, arms, and legs that should be tensed and flexed as they press the ground or against a tree or rock often appear weirdly detached and disconnected from their surroundings, as if the body to which they belong had been extracted from another composition entirely.[71] It is obvious why caricaturists liked to compare his figures to stiff dolls. In visual terms, the juxtaposition of a fleshed-out figure and its landscape setting sometimes jars so much that the two appear for all intents and purposes to inhabit different worlds, forced into uncomfortable proximity.

With the independent landscapes, it is easy to notice the foregrounding of matter, as nothing else competes for attention. In this regard, landscape has an advantage over still life because it can represent matter even in the absence of discrete, bounded objects. Fog, clouds, oceans, flatlands, and rock faces can all be highly material without being isolated as "figures"; in effect, they function as fields (with a geographic scope that no pelt or crinoline can rival). Examples include the oversized tree trunks and Franc-comtois settings of Courbet's early self-portraits, the somber forests and snow-covered clearings in his hunting pictures of the late 1850s and 1860s, and Lac Léman and its environs in his later Swiss works, to name just a few notable examples not addressed in this book. Even the great Realist masterpieces of the period from 1848 to 1855 that for some critics represent everything the "pure" landscapes do not, such as *A Burial at Ornans* and *The Peasants of Flagey Returning from the Fair*, are indelibly marked by nature's presence. Of the so-called highway series, including *Stonebreakers*, *Young Ladies of the Village* and *The Wrestlers* (1853; Museum of Fine Arts, Budapest), all feature unusual, thickly painted landscape settings, while in *The Artist's Studio*, most famously of all, we see Courbet making landscape his primary endeavor.[72]

Before going any further, one caveat. The mere appearance of elements from nature, however repetitive, cannot alone be an iteration of the substance-theme. The primacy of landscape was not unique to Courbet (the Barbizon painters are the most obvious examples). To be a theme in a Micheletian sense, nature must not only be omnipresent, but its substance must also somehow be declared. Courbet's most obvious means of accomplishing this task was to paint landscape backgrounds and foregrounds as thickly as his human or animal subjects, especially in those areas of the composition that tradition dictated be more subdued. The foreground with the black hole of the grave staring the viewer in the face at the lower edge of *A Burial at Ornans* is one example. The rock-enclosed valley dwarfing Courbet's sisters in *Young Ladies of the Village* is another.

Art historians have produced several explanations for the prominence of landscape in Courbet's work: the artist's attachment to his native terroir; the land's link with the people and the popular (in the nineteenth-century sense of the word); Realism's rejection of classical subject matter; the equation of landscape with democratic principles; the idealization of Nature; and the rise of tourism. No doubt all of the above played a role. Yet underneath it all was an almost unconscious predilection for substance, one so all-pervasive that it had practically become a general condition of the work.

With this in mind, let us return to some of the Normandy paintings, which illustrate in microcosm the broader developments outlined above. Focusing on the 1865 Trouville campaign, we discover seascape backgrounds in many of the portraits—*Three English Girls at a Window* (1865; Ny Carlsberg Glyptotek, Copenhagen) and *Portrait of M. Nodler the Elder* (1865; Smith College Museum of Art, Northampton, Massachusetts)—genre scenes, *Girl with Seagulls, Trouville* (fig. 54), and even in one unfinished attempt at a Salon painting, *Woman in a Podoscaphe* (1865; Murauchi Art Museum, Tokyo).[73] If we look closely enough, the background is sometimes as briskly painted as the *paysages de mer* themselves (without, it must be said, the same interplay of sea, sky, and shore). This near equivalence of figure and ground dramatizes the world's heft, especially when incompatible textures, such as flesh and landscape, clash. So too, again, does still life maintain an outsized presence, particularly in the way that hair rivals the body. This is evident in *Girl with Seagulls, Trouville*. A gentle turn of the body is sufficient to integrate her blond hair with the seagulls' feathers to produce a single mass. Much the same occurs in *Three English Girls at a Window*, minus the birds, in the form of the middle sister's tumbling coiffure.

Once seascape is viewed as contributing to a thematic system, it is no longer sufficient to think of a marine painting as a work created to appeal to middlebrow taste. Or at least doing so would reduce these seascapes to this one aspect, blinding us to arguably their outstanding feature: their substantiality. We might question here the necessity of bringing Michelet into the discussion. It seems perfectly reasonable to acknowledge that Courbet preferred a particularly thick manner of paint application and that he liked to show it off in his paintings, regardless of genre, and leave it at that. Yet there are several things to be gained from reading Courbet's seascapes through the lens of Michelet's *La Mer*. Such an approach subjects what is sometimes casually called "style" and, more recently, "technique" to much more rigorous interrogation. Under these familiar rubrics, how Courbet painted is treated largely as an issue of personal idiosyncrasy, aesthetic taste, or practical preference. In this way, it is separated from broader considerations. A side-by-side analysis of Michelet and Courbet historicizes what at face value looks like a simple love of Nature but is in reality a by-product of a thematics of matter in dialectical relationship with more narrative forms of history.

This helps us to be more precise about what we mean when talking about "matter" in painting. It is not simply the representation of stuffs here and there, devoid of any guiding logic. If this were true, the abundance of fabric in Jean-Auguste-Dominique Ingres's portraits or the plethora of horsehair in Delacroix's North African pictures would be enough to qualify their makers as painters of matter, although the surfaces painted by them are much thinner (and thus, from our point of view, less substantive) than Courbet's. Nor is Courbet's approach to substance allegorical. He does not need someone touching or caressing a rich surface or material in order to declare its substance. To act as a subtext, the substance-theme must sometimes *not* be the work's higher "idea" or "meaning." For only as an iterative phenomenon cutting across all topics, subjects, and genres, high and low, can the thematics of substance operate as history's undercurrent, rising to the surface at times, remaining in the background (but nonetheless present) at others. In addition to the allegorical impulse, there is also a great temptation to make the depiction of substance signify "paint itself." How often have we heard that Courbet's thick surfaces are statements about the medium of painting? The material emphasis in Courbet, however, is never about paint itself, painting as such, or painterly self-reflexivity (nor even mostly). On the contrary, it is essential that paint *not* be itself. To disseminate as a theme, it must be elastic in its identity within a given range (but not so malleable that it becomes something totally different, like a transparent gas or an obdurate solid, as in an alchemical operation). Instead of paint being self-referential, it is understood as one species in a genus of viscous or coagulated substances—blood, slime, mucus, milk, mud, and foam—whose rich consistency Courbet liked to find everywhere he looked.

One of the aims of this study has been to show how the representation of matter in landscape operates at different points in Courbet's career. Sometimes landscape *is* just background or merely symbolic, in a conventional sense. Sometimes it is just picturesque cliché or an umpteenth representation of the sublime. But elsewhere more specific and unique aspects of the material world are explored: a Saintonge picture reinterprets a scene of romantic travel as a sensuous yet disconcerting immersion into the thick of things; the 1864 series of riverbeds and grottoes analyze nature as if it were linguistic or geological material formed by layers of deep history. The differences between the seascapes and these slightly earlier series are therefore revealing. Unlike the Saintonge landscapes of 1862–63, plunging into the oceanic world of the seascapes does not terminate, unsettlingly, at a visual impasse. Remarkably, we experience the same sense of being bathed in matter, but this time ad infinitum, as if in a nonclaustrophobic womb. The key to this achievement was to adopt the lighter palette of marine painting while simultaneously negating the distancing effects

54 | *Girl with Seagulls, Trouville*, 1865. Oil on canvas, 81 × 65 cm. Phillips Art Holdings LLC

of atmospheric perspective that the presence of a far horizon in a composition traditionally demanded. And unlike the sources of 1864, the slow acclimatization to the world's sumptuousness that transpires in the seascapes is not one way; it is not about peeling back layers of the landscape as a way of moving backward in time to the world's origin. On the contrary, the seascapes put the viewer in the paradoxical position of constantly circulating while nonetheless staying still, of following the movements of wind and wave, only to return to where we began, as if we were tracking a molecule of water passing through all its various states (brackish water, sea foam, cloud vapor, fog, rain, etc.). Seascape is thus the ultimate form of landscape because it gives free rein to our experience of matter—arrest as well as motion, deep time as well as contemporaneity, the contingent as well as the universal, the proximate as well as the infinite. Painting, by virtue of a viscosity unique among the arts, is well suited to achieve this condition.

There is no doubt that in *La Mer* Michelet posits this kind of bodily pleasure as an antidote to modern leisure. An account of summer tourists in Normandy was so damning that it received the highest praise from none other than that great chronicler of bourgeois stupidity, Gustave Flaubert, who admitted to Michelet that it reminded him of Trouville.[74] Yet unlike the novelist, whose skepticism would have kept him from putting too much stock in the idea that something as simple as bathing could solve the ills of modern life, Michelet still entertained the possibility of rebirth and restoration through bodily communion with nature, especially at the sea. Perhaps because he himself was a fun-loving out-of-town visitor, Courbet did not recoil from coastal vacation society as Michelet and Flaubert did. Indeed, he embraced the art form that arose from it, the modern seascape. Because he also shared Michelet's receptiveness to the visceral and the corporal dimensions of lived experience (both were avid bathers), he was still able to carve out from within the genre a space, however temporary, for the pleasures of pure substance in opposition to those of social entertainment.[75] Courbet's seascapes, being neither wholly traditional nor ultra-mondain, thus stand on their own as a unique response to two basic competing pressures within modernity: to be part of—or not part of—the seaside crowd.

The last word belongs to Flaubert: "*la mer de lait*, what a chapter! especially that last exquisite phrase, 'attentive caresses ... the *tenderness* of a woman's breast *made visible* [*tendresse visible*].'"[76] At the end of "La Mer de lait", Michelet imagines the world's coastlines as a series of life-producing "maternal contours," their most recognizable shape that of the female breast, their most outstanding quality a *tendresse visible*. Neither Flaubert nor Michelet could have known Courbet's *Woman in the Waves* (it was painted seven years later, in 1868; fig. 55). In the painting, a "maternal contour" is inserted where there would normally be a shoreline running to the horizon. Courbet even highlights the maneuver by positioning one nipple just below the horizon, pointing toward it, and making the other jut out toward the viewer. At one level, the white froth, worthy rival to any in his oeuvre, is a logical result of the sea's caress. But it also seems to gather deliberately around the breasts, and from no direction in particular, making the association

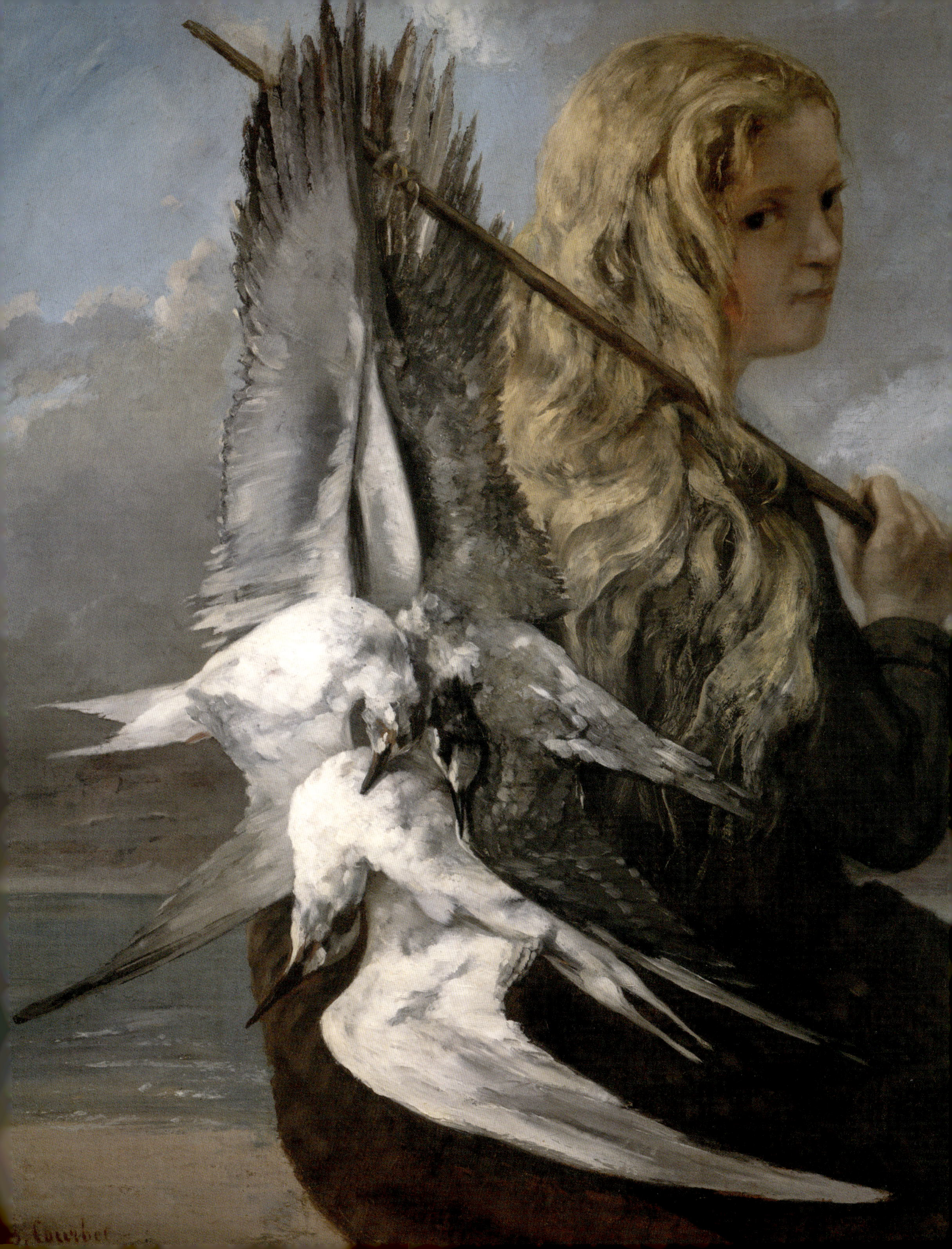
G. Courbet

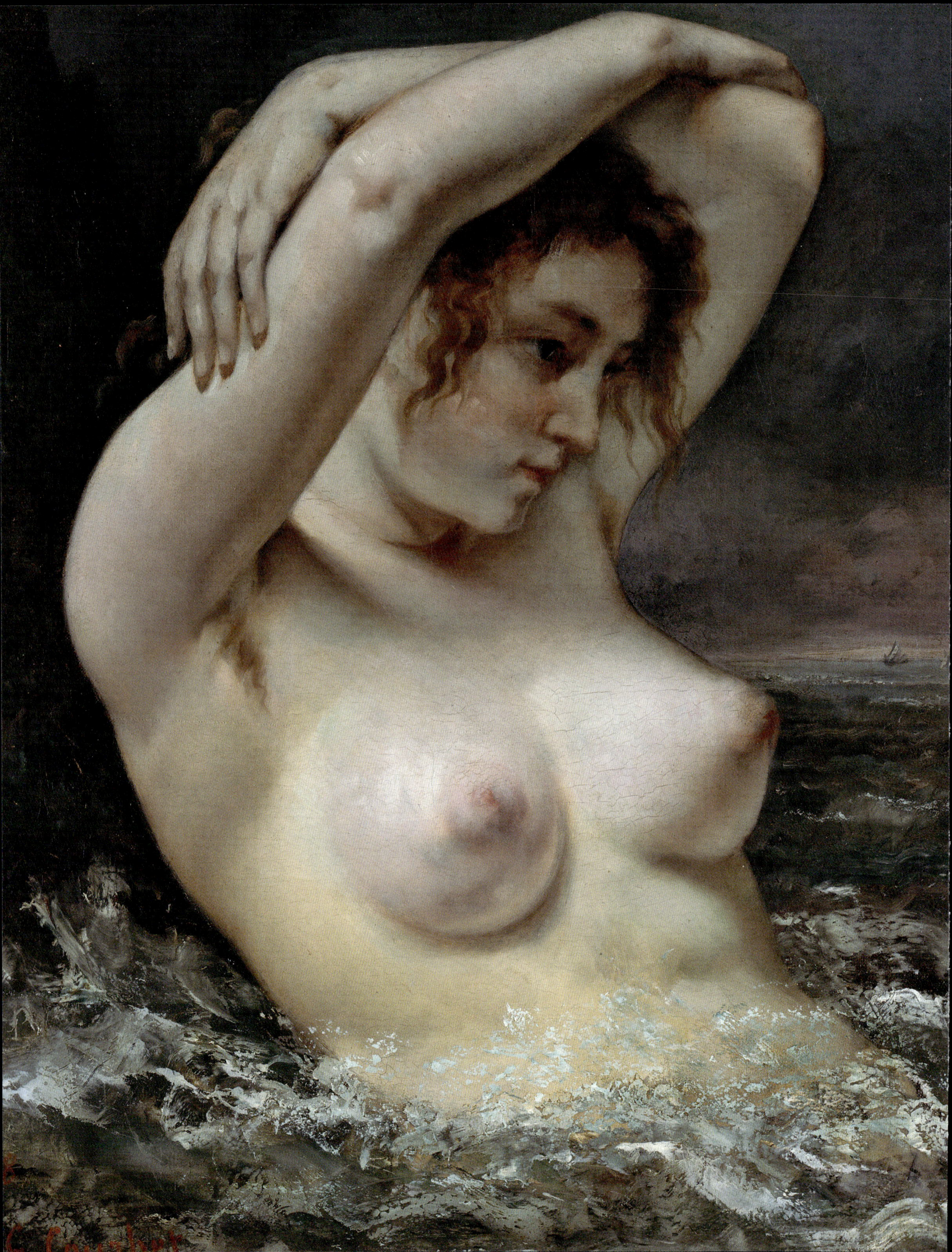

55 | *The Woman in the Waves*, 1868. Oil on canvas, 65.4 × 54 cm. The Metropolitan Museum of Art, New York

with maternal nourishment difficult to ignore. The waves thus constitute metaphorically a milk of the sea. By performing these substitutions in painting, Courbet makes visible a tactile sensibility, a *tendresse*, that Michelet himself could only pursue in words. There is nothing special about personifying *la terre* (earth) or *la mer* (sea) as *la mère* (mother)—Venus, after all, came from the ocean (the Salon of 1863 was infamously nicknamed the "Salon of Venus" because of the subject's popularity). But few artists, if any, did it quite like Courbet. For he was perhaps the only painter of his era truly committed to not just the picturing but also the re-presentation of substance.

This is the closest Courbet came to allegorizing the physicality of the sea. And it is perhaps for the best that the occasions were infrequent, for figured in human form, matter loses something of its immediacy. The more we watch the waves hit someone else, the less directly we experience their force ourselves. With Courbet, our sense of matter is most intense and most palpable when that classic figure of desire, the nude, is not there. *Woman in the Waves* stands in a category apart; it differs from the other marine paintings in that it all too easily satisfies our instinctual desire to understand the world in human terms, which means in this case to reduce the irreducible experience of matter to some sort of symbol or figure easily grasped. The desire for figurative content is repeated at the level of critical interpretation. In the art-historical literature, bodies, whole or in parts, are constantly identified in Courbet's landscapes or, as in the case of the grotto paintings, *as* landscape. This anthropomorphism tames the unruliness of matter through recourse to a more comfortable mode of figurative reading. However, what distinguishes Courbet's landscapes is that they make possible the strangest of feelings: a corporeality in the absence of any body.

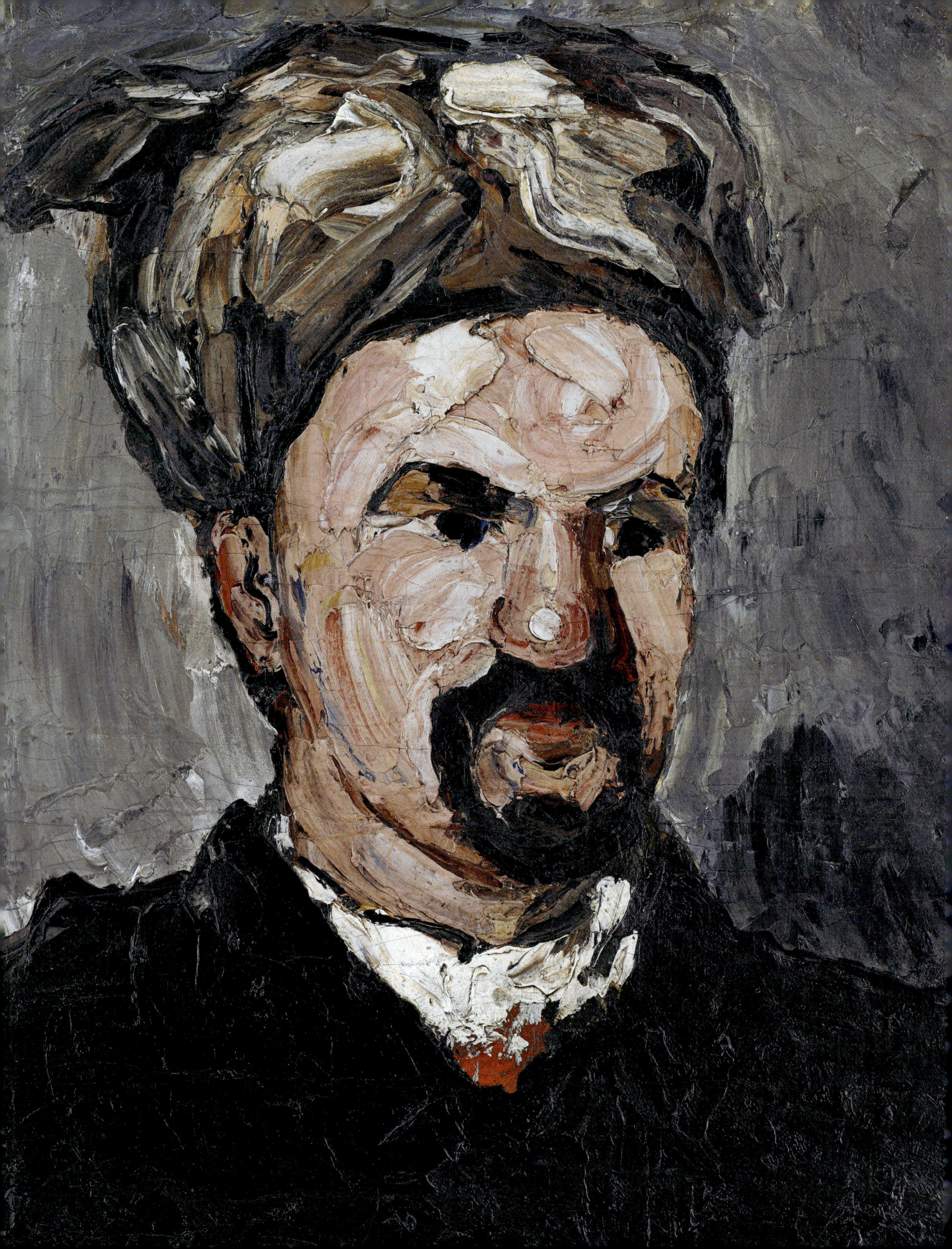

Chapter 4

CUT WITH A PALETTE KNIFE

By several measures 1866 was a good year for Courbet. Despite acrimony between Courbet and the administration, the artist's *Woman with a Parrot* (fig. 56) and *Covert of Roe-Deer by the Stream of Plaisir-Fontaine* (see fig. 20) were hung in a place of honor at the Salon and received significant press coverage. His paintings were also selling well, with several prominent collectors, including officials at the highest levels of government, bidding for them.[1] Well before the opening of the 1866 Salon, Nieuwekerke, who had acquired *The Stream of the Puits noir* (see fig. 32) the previous year, was already in discussions with Courbet to buy *Woman with a Parrot*. The banker Louis Lepel-Cointet had also coveted that painting of a nude, but he settled for the landscape *Covert of Roe-Deer by the Stream of Plaisir-Fontaine*, purchasing it before Philippe de Chevennières, curator and influential administrator, could acquire it for the Empress. The March exhibition at Cadart & Luquet had introduced the public to Courbet's seascapes, and there were the plans for another private pavilion outside the 1867 Universal Exhibition. All this activity would keep Courbet's name on everyone's lips throughout the year and into the next.

Yet not all the talk was positive. Although the young Realist painter Frédéric Bazille thought Courbet one of the highlights of the Salon, he deemed the master's efforts inferior to those of previous years;[2] Théophile Thoré put his disappointment more colorfully in his Salon review: "*Voilà*! You are accepted, medaled, decorated, glorified, embalmed."[3] And Émile Zola, comparing Courbet's Salon pictures to earlier ones he had seen on a recent studio visit, warned that "the more you are admired and understood, the more ordinary you are."[4]

In the case of Courbet's landscapes, it is hard not to concur with these negative assessments. After 1866, his

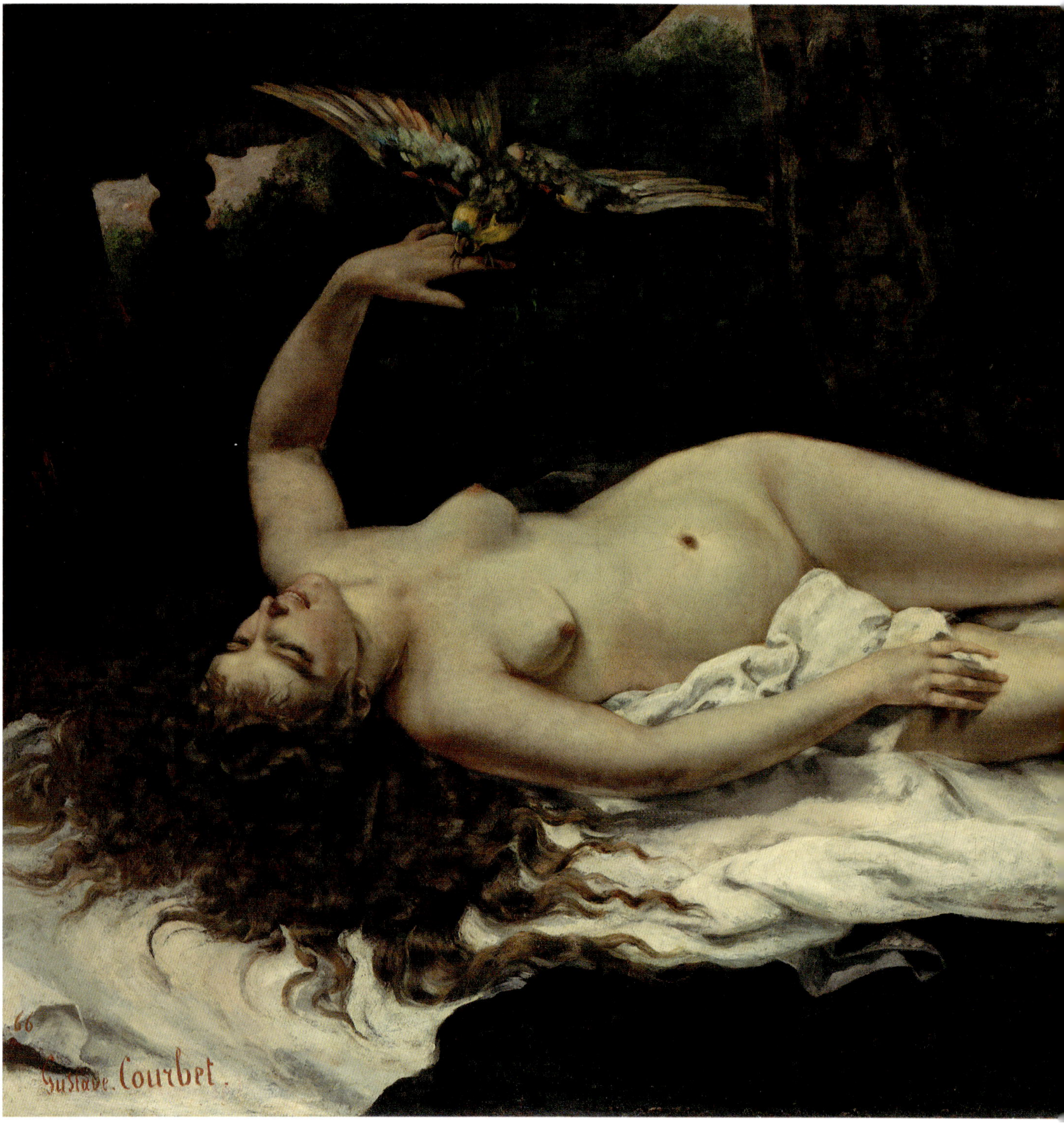

56 | *Woman with a Parrot*, 1866. Oil on canvas, 129.5 × 195.6 cm. The Metropolitan Museum of Art, New York

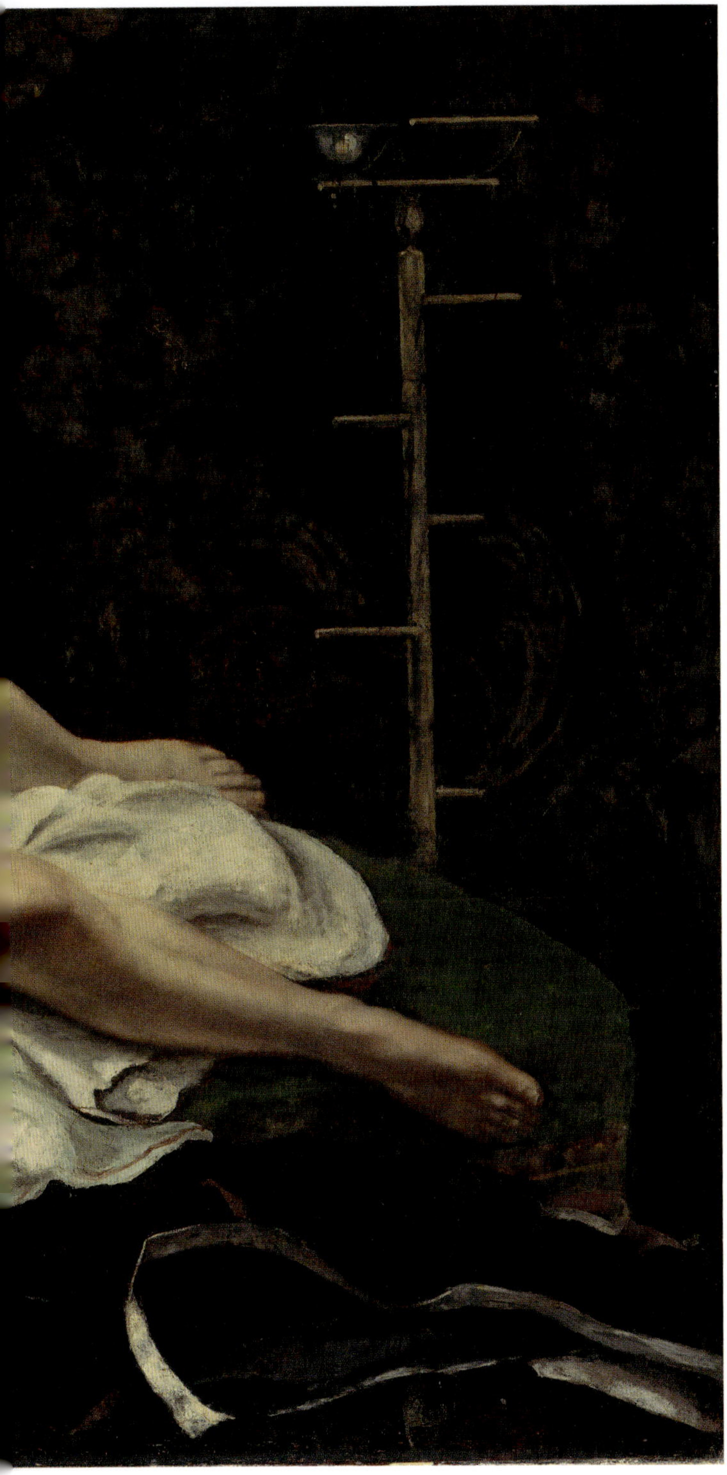

creativity in the genre stagnates. Except for a striking group of Franc-comtois snow-scenes and his waves from 1869 to 1870, he invents nothing new in terms of landscape for the rest of the decade. The sumptuous background of *Covert of Roe-Deer by the Stream of Plaisir-Fontaine*, a popular success, had been executed in 1864, at the same time as his grotto and riverbed series. It is not until his Swiss exile that new subjects, Lac Léman and the Alps, emerge in his art (and by then landscapes of lesser accomplishment, if not questionable authorship, had begun to dominate his oeuvre).[5]

However, Courbet's sheer public presence made him impossible to ignore. Some among the younger generation envied his success, others identified with his rebellious persona, and still others were struck by his unusual ability to court and simultaneously insult the public. The history of Courbet's reception by younger artists, in all its multiple facets and it all its many locales, is still—and perhaps always will be—a work in progress and is certainly beyond the scope of any one book, let alone one focused on his landscapes.[6]

However, no study of Courbet's landscapes would be complete without discussing to a certain extent the influence of his work on the Impressionists. For it is within their circle that Courbet's efforts in the genre find their most fertile reception. Fortunately, scholarship on nineteenth-century art has provided a well-developed picture of the movement's history, its group dynamics, and the diverse critical reaction, as well as an extensive bibliography of its major participants. This chapter's focus on the palette-knife technique and its adoption (and nonadoption) by Édouard Manet, Pierre-Auguste Renoir, Edgar Degas, Camille Pissarro, and Paul Cézanne around 1866–67 draws connections between seemingly unrelated works in the hope of adding further nuance to our understanding of Courbet's reception.[7]

THE COURBET EFFECT

There were four main reactions to Courbet's palette-knife technique in the wake of the Salons of 1865 and 1866: First, to ignore or reject his use of the tool; second, to repurpose it for figure painting; third, to quote or ironize it; and, fourth, to accentuate its crudeness.

MANET'S INDIFFERENCE

The first option, the default response, is only of interest to us here because at this time it is the path followed by Édouard Manet, who adopted many of Courbet's artistic strategies but avoided similar use of the palette knife. After seeing Courbet's Salon painting, Manet painted his own woman with a parrot, *Young Lady in 1866* (fig. 57), in which Courbet's splayed figure is replaced by the standing, pink-clothed painter and model Victorine Meurent. Not for the first time, Manet took up a pictorial model and utterly transformed it.

While no correspondence between Courbet and Manet survives, part of their interaction in the 1860s is clearly expressed in their Salon paintings. Courbet had already exhibited canvases depicting contemporary nudes in 1853, with *The Bathers* (1853; Musée Fabre, Montpellier) at the Salon, and, in 1855, with *The Artist's Studio* in the private exhibition outside the Universal Exhibition. Courbet must have realized that Manet's *Déjeuner sur l'herbe* (1863; Musée d'Orsay, Paris), exhibited at the 1863 Salon des Réfusés, encroached upon his terrain. Over the next two years, Courbet planned (but failed to complete) an allegorical painting featuring a nude Parisian model for the Salon of 1864 (*Hippocrene Spring*), had a painting of two nudes rejected from the same Salon (*Study of Women*, also known as *Venus in Jealous Pursuit of Psyche*), and worked on a "modern Amphitrite"[8] (*Woman in a Podoscaphe*) for the Salon of 1866. The last of these was painted in the wake of the scandal surrounding Manet's *Olympia* (1863; Musée d'Orsay, Paris) at the Salon of 1865.

The nude Courbet eventually submitted to the Salon of 1866 (see fig. 56) was thus a long time coming. It is highly likely that Manet noticed how it traded off *Olympia*'s notoriety while simultaneously subverting his original subversion. Courbet redirected Olympia's confrontational gaze, relocated the scene to a place evocative of Renaissance Italy, and rendered Manet's transactional encounter between courtesan and client as once again a titillating interaction between male voyeur and female nude (and parrot). The scandalous Realist nude had been partially tamed.

Rather than continue the one-upmanship, Manet cannily recast the contest in a new light. *Young Lady in 1866* is a pointed reinterpretation of *Woman with a Parrot*. Meurent's hair is carefully parted and neatly tied, no longer a medusa-like sprawl. The model is now standing, wearing a robe, a garment that was criticized at the time for drawing too much attention away from the face. That was Manet's point; he made sure that any residual sensuousness would be displaced from flesh to fabric. Finally, Courbet's macaw has become a large gray parrot on a perch. More of a pet than a symbol of desire, it blends into the neutral background. In relation to

57 | Édouard Manet, *Young Lady in 1866*, 1866. Oil on canvas, 185.1 × 128.6 cm. The Metropolitan Museum of Art, New York

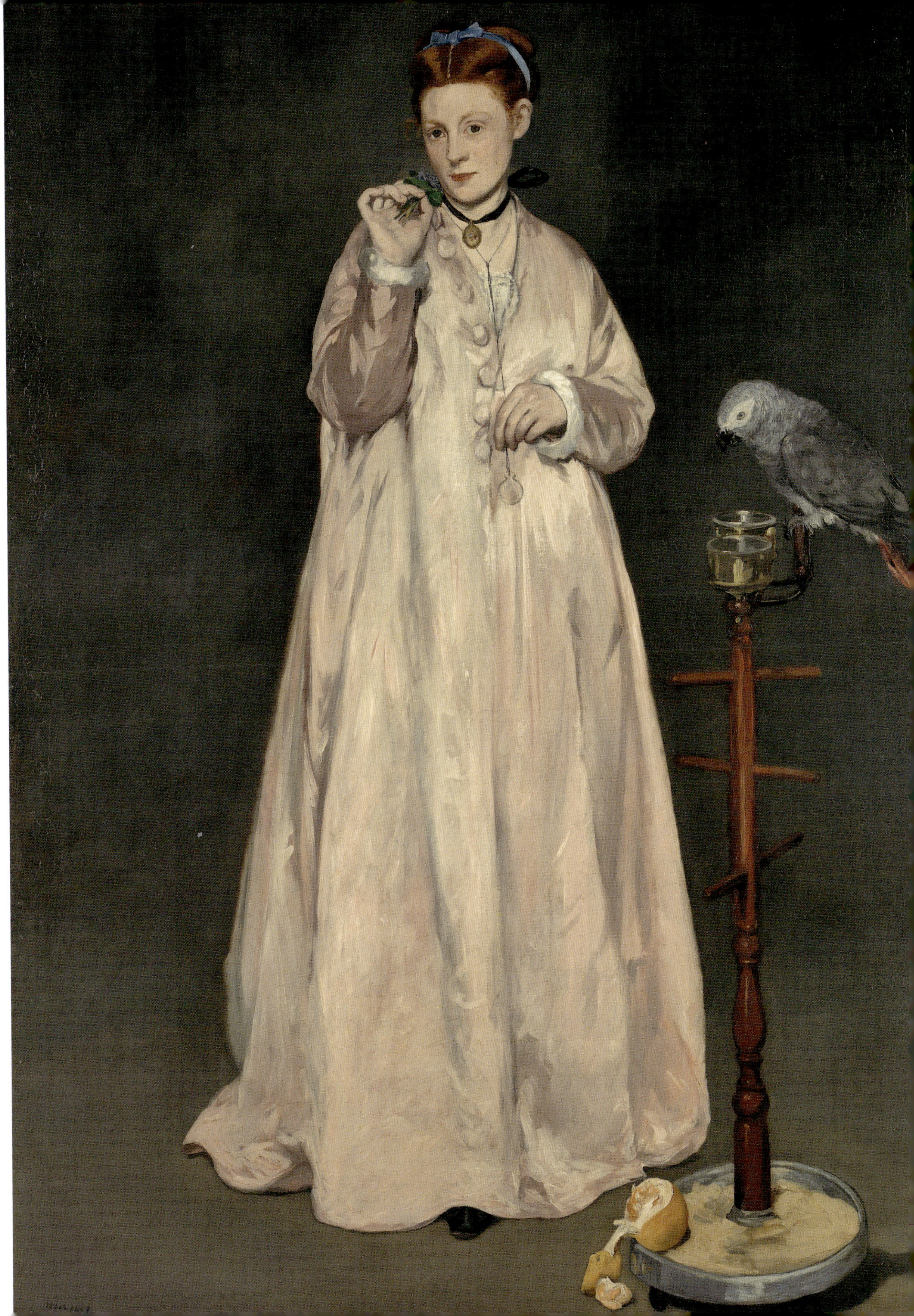

Woman with a Parrot, the eroticism of *Young Lady in 1866* is deliberately muted and displaced, suggested by details such as the hair ribbon, necklace, a glimpse of lace, monocle, pointed shoe, and peeled lemon. With typical wit and economy, Manet transposed Courbet's wild, flamboyant nude into a different key—the full-length, socially restrained painting of modern life.

While Manet takes up the gauntlet thrown down by Courbet's *Woman with a Parrot*, he paints nothing in response to the landscape. Indeed, landscape was so low on Manet's list of priorities that he would rarely paint an example in its own right. When he did incorporate nature in his painting, he dramatized its urbanity or artificiality. The background of *Déjeuner sur l'herbe* has more in common with the Rubensian landscape of Manet's *Fishing* (*ca.*1862–63; The Metropolitan Museum of Art, New York) than it does with a local bathing site. When nature is identifiable as a specific place, it is often full of Parisians—the Tuileries Garden, the Universal Exhibition, the Longchamp Racecourse—or is being re-made by them, as in suburban Argenteuil. The garden in *Laundry* (1875; Barnes Foundation, Pennsylvania) and conservatory of *In the Conservatory* (1878–79; Staatliche Museen zu Berlin, Nationalgalerie) are by definition built, not natural structures.

Manet gave free rein to nature when he painted the sea. But even in the pictures of Boulogne-sur-Mer, jetties, docks, ships, and beachgoers inevitably take center stage. Manet had always aspired to success at the Salon and for him that meant prioritizing the higher genres of history painting and portraiture over landscape and still life. Despite his republican sympathies, the dandy-artist largely avoided landscape, a genre at the time strongly associated with democratic ideals. In the end, like his friend Baudelaire, he found scenes of nature too "herbivorous"[9] (ironically, one of the works most given over to landscape was an image of the poet's funeral procession). There can be no questioning that Manet's finely attuned sense of how to manage the art world owed much to Courbet's example. He would stage his own private exhibition during the 1867 Universal Exhibition, just as Courbet had in 1855 and 1867. But equally undeniable is the younger artist's indifference to the physicality of landscape and to Courbet's special means of depicting it.

RENOIR'S BLOCKAGE

Neither Courbet nor Manet used the knife to paint the human figure.[10] Indeed, around 1866 there were no immediate models in the work of Realism's foremost practitioners for adapting the technique to anything other than landscape. To succeed in this endeavor—to attempt to translate the palette-knife technique to the representation of people—was the task of artists in our second category of reaction to Courbet's technique. One of the most intriguing of these adaptations was Pierre-Auguste Renoir's submission to the Salon of 1867, *Diana* (fig. 58).[11]

By the time he undertook *Diana*, Renoir had already been accepted to the Salons of 1864 and 1865. In 1866, emboldened to make even more ambitious works, Renoir painted three canvases that each in their own way responded to Courbet. *Jules Le Coeur in the Forest of Fontainebleau* (1866; Museu de Arte de São Paulo) depicts Renoir's wealthy friend Jules Le Coeur, the amateur architect turned painter, walking his dogs in the Forest of Fontainebleau (Renoir would often stay at Le Coeur's house in Marlotte at the edge of the forest).[12] Nominally a portrait, the work was a demonstration of Renoir's skills as a landscapist. Although its composition owes more to the woodland scenes of Narcisse-Virgilio Diaz de la Peña than to Courbet's *sous-bois* paintings, Renoir executed it largely in palette knife. Renoir's *Figures in a Landscape* (1866; destroyed), portraying two contemporary ladies, one in fashionable dress, the other nude, also produced for the 1866 Salon, pays homage to Courbet's much-discussed *Bathers* (1853). Like its predecessor, *Figures in a Landscape* presents the awkward juxtaposition of a seated, fully dressed woman and a naked companion.[13] The favorable opinion of Corot and Charles-François Daubigny (a contemporary who was a strong advocate for open-air painting and whose example would inspire many an ambitious landscapist of the next generation) on that year's jury did not prevent its rejection. In retrospect, it was perhaps entirely predictable because the artist failed to justify the painting of such a socially unacceptable encounter. *At the Inn of Mother Anthony* (1866; Nationalmuseum, Stockholm) reimagined a convivial tavern scene along the lines of Courbet's *After Dinner in Ornans* (1849; Palais des Beaux-Arts, Lille) by inserting Renoir's own friends (including Le Coeur) in place of Courbet's.

As a group, the trio of 1866 paintings were modern interpretations of familiar genres: the portrait, the nude, and the genre picture. They also ranged widely in terms of technique, from the Courbet-like daubs of green and brown in the Le Coeur portrait to the more restrained facture of *At the Inn of Mother Anthony*. For the Salon of 1867, Renoir again took up the nude as a subject (perhaps encouraged by the success of Courbet's *Woman with a Parrot*). *Diana* depicts Renoir's lover Lise Tréhot thinly disguised as a hunting goddess. She is perched lopsidedly on a sloping rock, her outstretched arms grasping a ridiculously oversized bow. The dead deer is awkwardly inclined, as is often the case in animal pictures by Courbet, Renoir's reference point. Renoir hoped his more classical approach to the academic nude would find favor with the Salon jury where *Figures in a Landscape* had not. The goddess of the hunt was an ideal choice, as Renoir had studied Diana's natural habitat during visits to the Forest of Fontainebleau with Le Coeur. After making the necessary adjustments to the subject matter, Renoir seems to have allowed himself a calculated risk in terms of technique—he would paint *Diana* with liberal use of the palette knife.[14]

Much of the picture, from the foreground to the deer's fur to the sky, has traces of the knife (or of large brushwork resembling the latter's flat application).[15] Renoir's logic seems to have been this: if Courbet's particular kind of knifework rendered nature as thick as paint, then even more use of the knife and in even more parts of the canvas, would produce something even more substantial and "real." The rocks below the goddess, as we would expect, display the patch-like quality and coloring of Courbet's landscapes. But something unusual occurs in other parts of the composition. In broadly

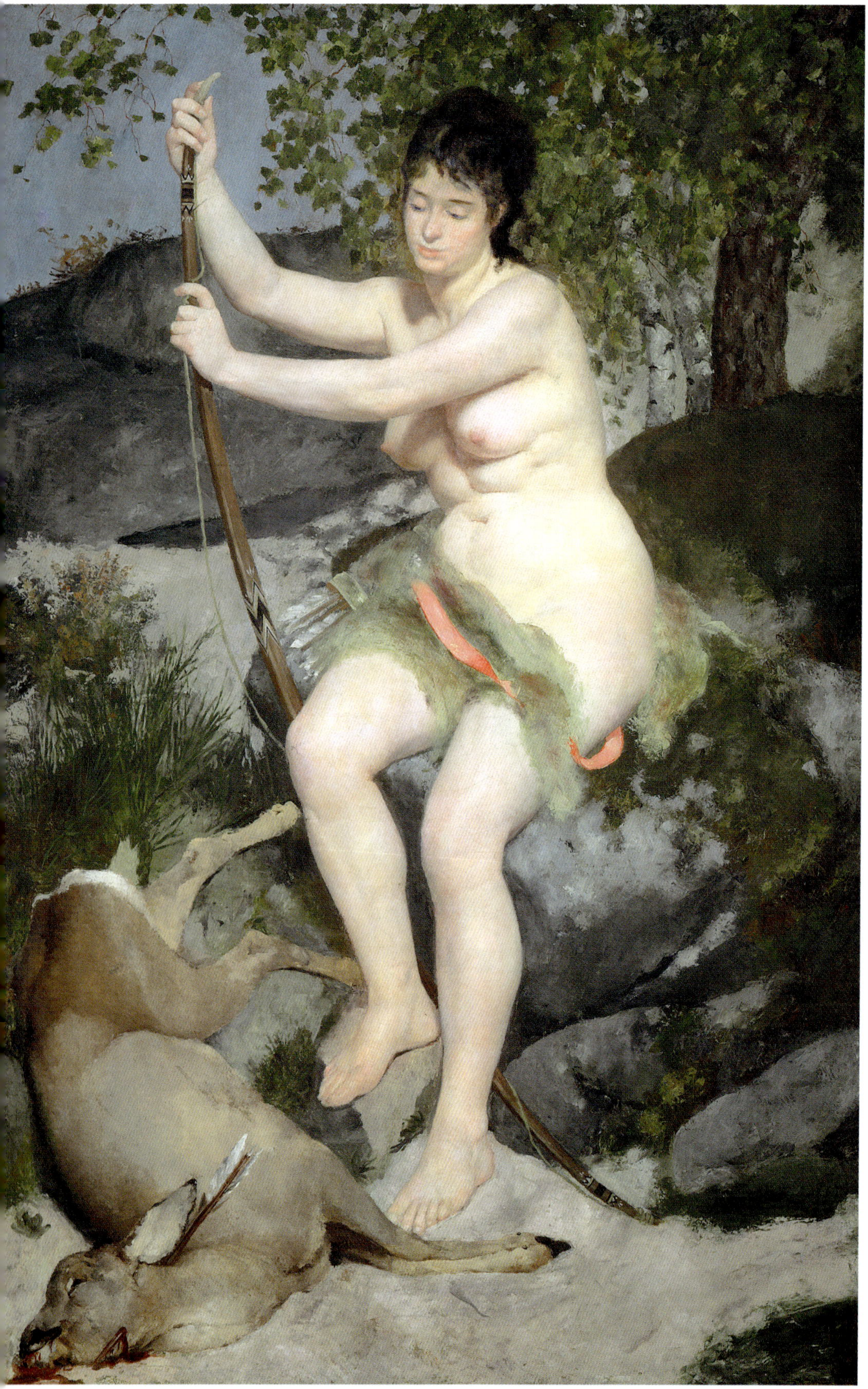

58 | Pierre-Auguste Renoir, *Diana*, 1867. Oil on canvas, 199.5 × 129.5 cm. National Gallery of Art, Washington, D.C.

painted areas such as the beige foreground and the blue-gray sky, elements appear absorbed or subsumed into a single pastose plane. There is no trace of the slow emergence of form that we have come to associate with Courbet's touch-by-touch technique. Instead, Renoir's objects end up looking flatter, not more volumetric (an effect further exacerbated by his use of relatively unmodulated hues and crisp contours). The net effect is a painting of disconcerting uniformity, as if bathed in a layer of encaustic.[16] The waxy, almost homogeneous surface of Renoir's *Diana* cannot be visually peeled back or progressively mined, as was possible in the multilayered world of Courbet's landscapes. Its oddly unified texture operates against the work's conventional representation of pictorial space, which conceives the painting as a window onto the world receding into depth, and this makes it feel, at a visceral level, like a barrier to vision, as if that traditional window had been clogged with paste. After the rejection of *Diana*, Renoir never attempted such all-over use of the palette knife again. He decided around 1867–68 that Courbet's technique was not conducive to the contemporary figure painting to which he found himself increasingly drawn. Looking at his *Diana*, he must have realized that the gravity of Courbet's palette-knife painting could not be achieved through the mere accumulation of pictorial matter. Renoir's touches, melded into a single homogeneous stratum, would never produce the effect of plunging into layers of substance, of investigating material origins, that characterizes the "thickness" of Courbet's landscapes.

DEGAS'S ARTIFICE

For our third type of reaction to Courbet's technique, to quote or ironize the technique, we turn to an artist, Edgar Degas, for whom the palette knife ostensibly held little appeal. Although Degas would always recognize the older artist's importance to the Realist movement and would even admit later in life that the economy of Courbet's painting made his own seem overworked in comparison, Courbet's painting made him feel "as if he were being stroked by the sticky muzzle of a calf."[17] For instance, in the artist's otherwise Courbetian *Dead Fox in the Undergrowth* (1861–64; Musée des Beaux-Arts, Rouen)—the vertical format, pinched cropping, and forest background evoke Courbet's *The Quarry* (1856; Museum of Fine Arts, Boston), while the dead animal recalls the subject of Courbet's 1861 Salon painting *Fox in the Snow* (1860; Dallas Museum of Art)—Degas's unfinished sylvan landscape is almost transparent, seemingly barely painted on.[18] Uncharacteristically, Degas never returned to the painting. Henri Loyrette argues persuasively that Degas feared more paint would render the finished work too Courbetian.[19] And, indeed, Degas would revert to type in one of the major paintings done in its aftermath, *Scene from the Steeplechase: The Fallen Jockey* (1866, reworked 1880–81 and *ca.*1897; National Gallery of Art, Washington, D.C.) from the Salon of 1866, where the landscape is noticeably more color field than solid ground.

As portraiture and images of contemporary life began to replace historical subjects at the heart of Degas's oeuvre over the course of the decade, he continued to avoid thickly painted nature. This makes the one Degas canvas of the 1860s that *does* include a dense, Courbet-like passage of landscape painting even more intriguing. At first glance, *Portrait of Mlle. Fiocre in the Ballet "La Source"* (fig. 59) seems to have little to do with the painter from Ornans. Begun in 1867 and first exhibited at the Salon of 1868, it depicts the celebrated dancer Eugénie Fiocre in the role of Princess Nouredda from *La Source* (The Spring), a ballet that had opened on 12 November 1866 at Le Peletier, one of the buildings where the Paris Opéra performed.[20] The painting depicts the moment in the first act when Fiocre's Nouredda comes to rest at a magical spring, just before performing the thrilling dance called the *pas de la guzla* (the guzla is a musical instrument). The spring and its surrounding rocks possess a solidity unusual in set painting. But, as Degas scholars have noted, we *do* associate it with the landscape painting of Courbet.

Why would Degas, who had seemingly rejected Courbet's painting of substance in the earlier *Dead Fox in the Undergrowth*, suddenly turn to it around 1867 in, of all things, a ballet picture? As many commentators have pointed out, what is unusual about Degas's representation of the dance is how hard it tries to disguise its theatricality. Fiocre is not dancing the *pas de la guzla* or otherwise showcasing her virtuosity or celebrity. The picture displays no signs that we are inside a theater; no stage flats, architecture, lights, audience. It is a dance scene with no dancing on a stage with no signs of stagecraft. Were it not for the Salon title referencing the ballet and its star by name, a viewer from the period might have easily mistaken the work for an exotic genre painting. Degas was struggling with competing demands in the Fiocre portrait. He was trying to visualize modern spectacle in fully Realist terms while at the same time holding on to certain elements of traditional painting.

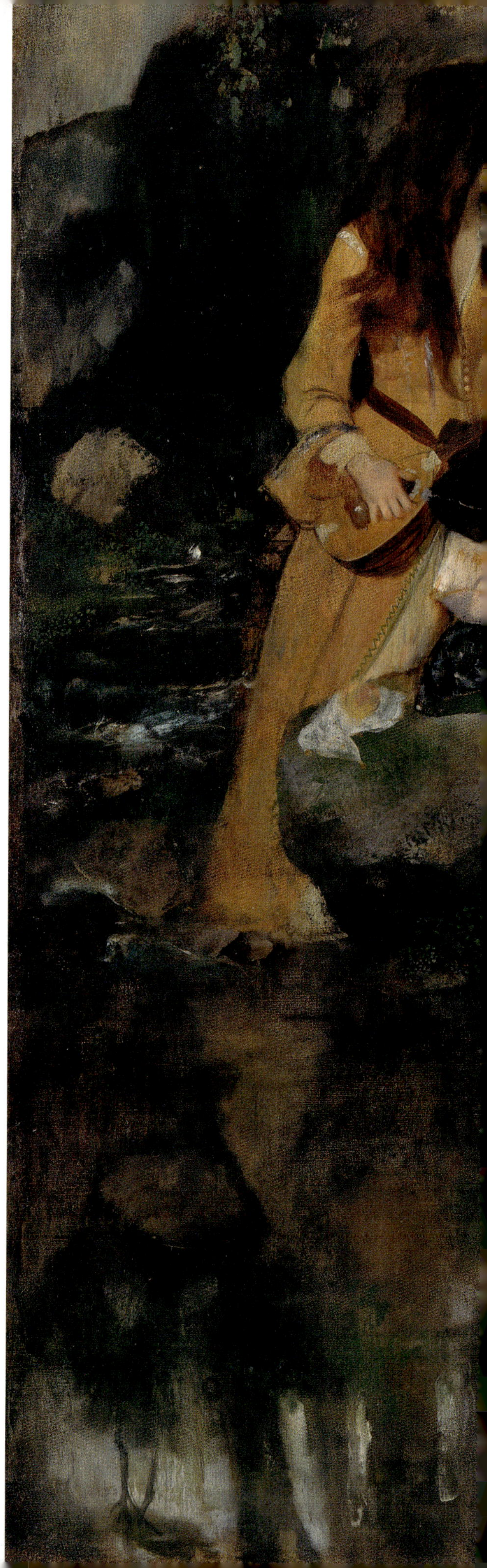

59 | Edgar Degas, *Portrait of Mlle. Fiocre in the Ballet "La Source," ca.*1867–68. Oil on canvas, 130.8 × 145.1 cm. Brooklyn Museum of Art, New York

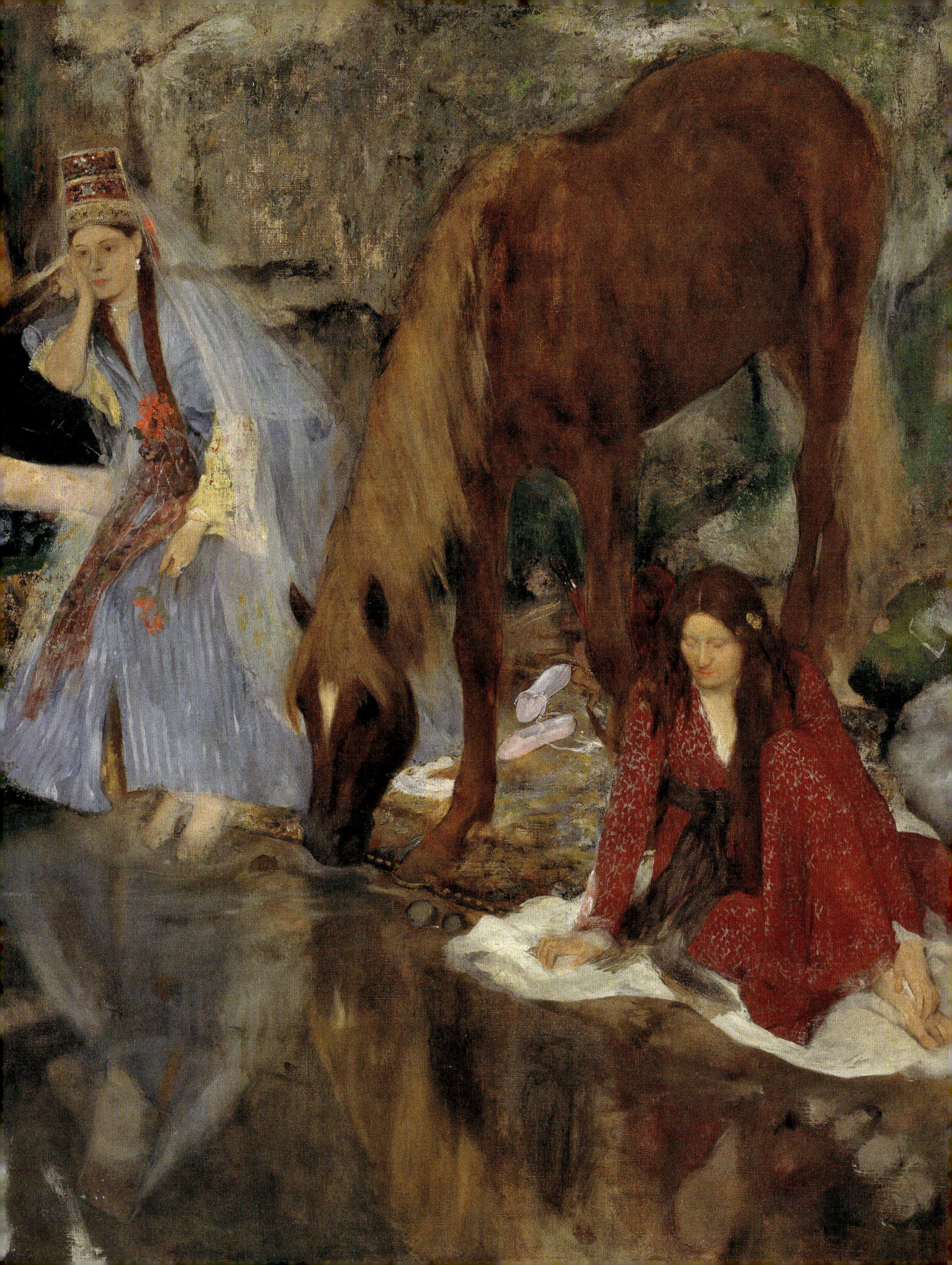

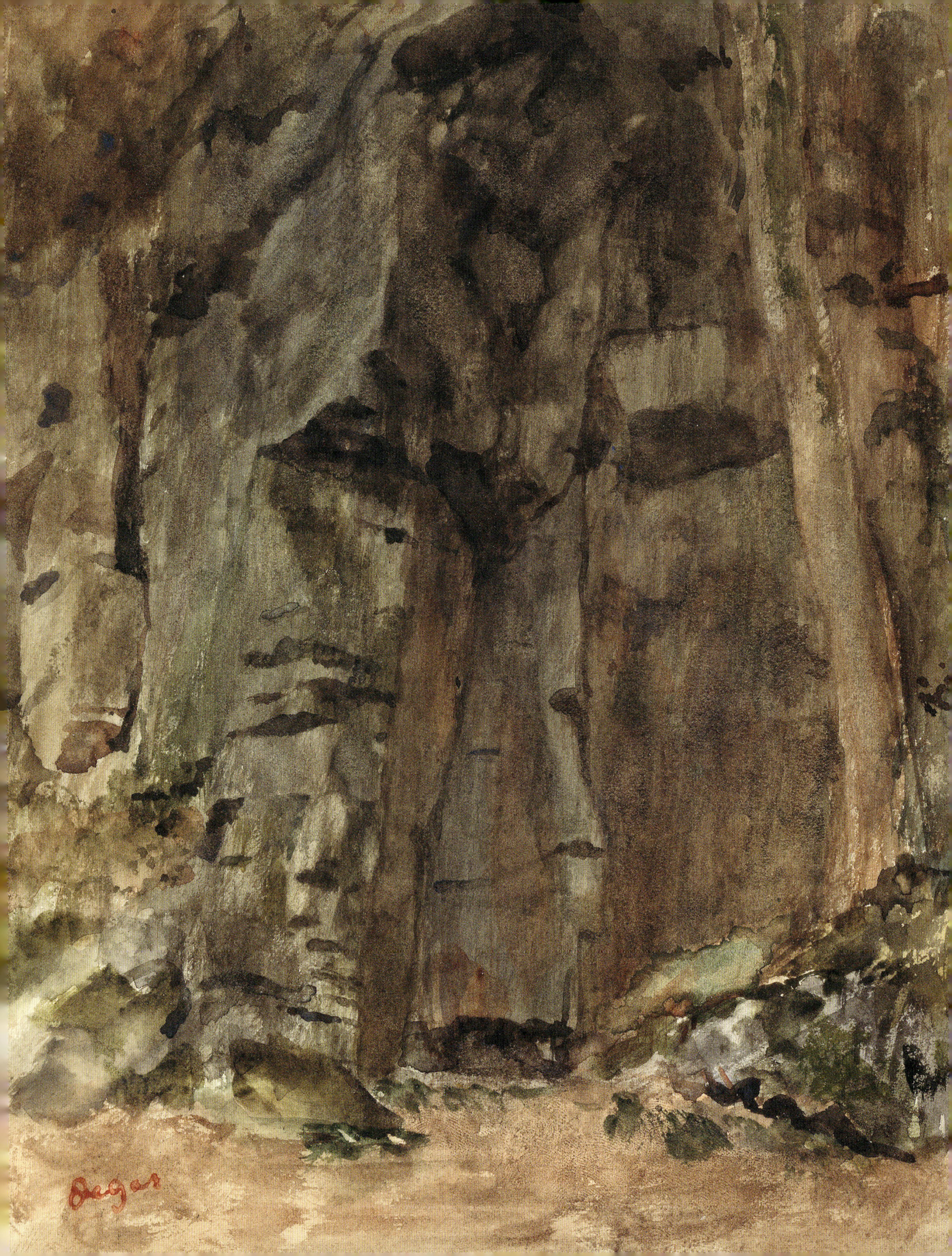
Degas

60 | Edgar Degas, *Rocks at Bagnoles-de-l'Orne*, *ca.*1867. Watercolor, 25.5 × 20 cm. The Fitzwilliam Museum, Cambridge, England

61 | *(overleaf)* Camille Pissarro, *The Marne at Chennevières*, *ca.*1864–65. Oil on canvas, 91.5 × 145.5 cm. National Galleries of Scotland, Edinburgh

The horse, fabrics, and rocks in the Fiocre portrait would not have looked out of place in the era's most forward-looking images of the racetrack, fashion, and landscape. But the exotic costumes, magical setting, and the dancers' physical and psychological disposition all harkened back to earlier Romantic and Orientalist depictions of fantasy and stage.

By replacing scenic backdrops with a Courbetian landscape in *Portrait of Mlle. Fiocre in the Ballet "La Source"*, Degas allowed viewers to envision the spring somewhere other than in a Parisian opera house. The realism of the landscape was so important to Degas that he experimented with the Franc-comtois painter's landscape technique in studies executed at Bagnoles-de-l'Orne in Normandy around this time (fig. 60). Two existing watercolors contain layers in which dilute pigment was laid in a distinctly Courbetian manner—patches of green, brown, and gray were superimposed to produce the illusion of a massive cliff.[21] Translated into oil in the Fiocre portrait, the stratified touches generate a materially sumptuous background seemingly humidified by the spring. Degas's quoting of Courbet's landscape painting thus ended up transforming the model altogether. Far from bringing us to the brink of some unknown origin, Degas's own technique of overlaid patches, originally developed by Courbet for the depiction of nature's deepest untouched recesses, is in *Portrait of Mlle. Fiocre in the Ballet "La Source"* refashioned for a competing, even opposing, purpose: to participate as one among many modes of representation in the play of fantasy and reality occasioned by the contemporary Parisian stage.[22]

The experiments with Courbet's technique in Renoir's *Diana* and Degas's *Portrait of Mlle. Fiocre in the Ballet "La Source"* taught both artists important lessons. Renoir would henceforth avoid highly compressed surfaces, finding them antithetical to the lightness and sketch-like quality of the open-air painting he was increasingly pursuing. Degas realized that it was not necessary to copy Courbet when painting a landscape, and he subsequently followed his own path in this regard.

PISSARRO'S AND CÉZANNE'S INSURRECTION

Whereas Renoir's and Degas's use of the palette knife was relatively fleeting, it was much more sustained in the work of artists in our fourth category, the painters whose reaction to Courbet's technique was to emphasize its rawness. Camille Pissarro and Paul Cézanne, its two main representatives, painted many more palette-knife pictures than either Renoir or Degas did and over a longer period. For them, knife-painting was more than a practical solution to the immediate needs of a particular work. It was almost an ethical choice. As their mutual friend, the landscape painter Antoine Guillemet, put it: "Let's seize our weapons, and, with a feverish hand, get hold of the insurrection *knife*.... Let's all build up paint with full impasto and dance on the bellies of those horrified bourgeois."[23] To be antibourgeois was to wield, like a weapon, the palette knife, and to use that particular tool brought Courbet to mind. Echoing this sentiment, though in less belligerent terms, was Cézanne's friend Zola, who declared around the same time that landscape was "the proper domain—I no longer say of the paintbrush—but of the palette knife."[24]

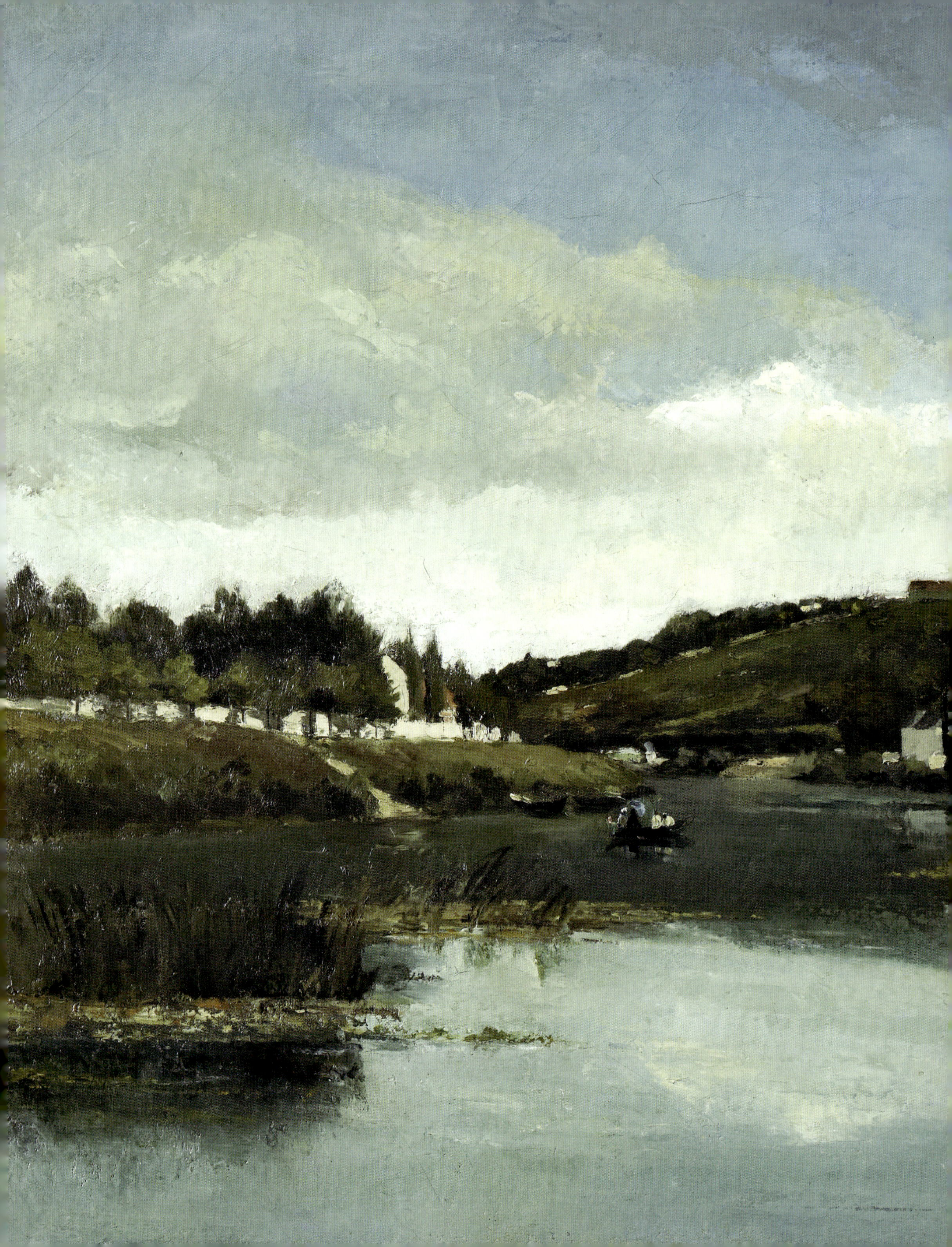

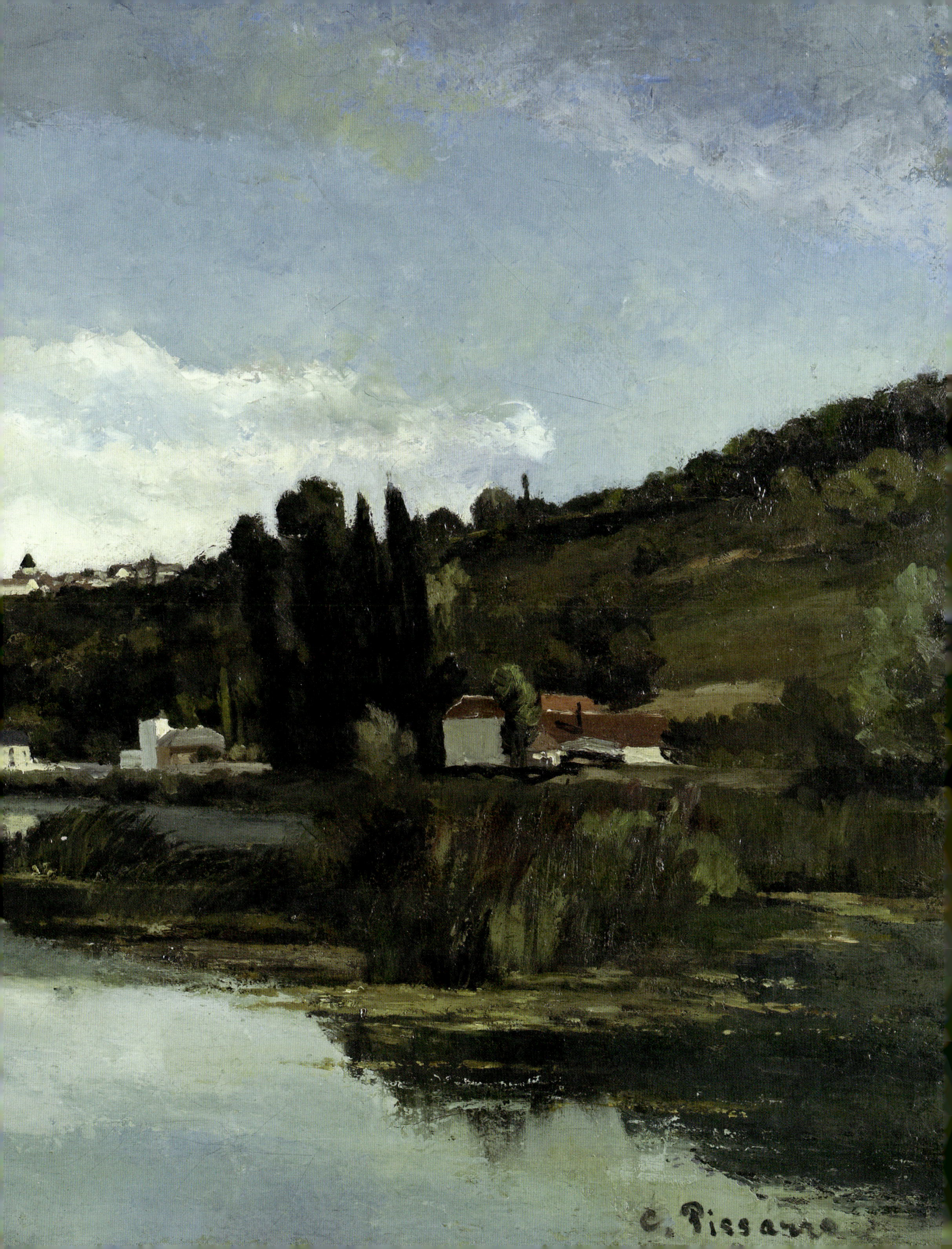
C. Pissarro

In Guillemet's and Zola's reckoning, Courbet's knifed painting, which they could have seen at the Salons of 1865 and 1866 and at Cadart & Luquet in 1866, set the tone for future art. And even had they not seen the actual works, they could have heard about them from Pissarro, an acquaintance of Zola through Cézanne. By this time Pissarro had already taken Guillemet's call to arms deeply to heart. In three Salons between 1864 and 1866, he exhibited landscapes marked by heavy use of the palette knife, each more ambitious than the next.[25] Whereas the task confronting artists such as Renoir and Degas had been to translate the palette-knife technique from one genre to another, Pissarro was essentially trying to outdo Courbet in his own area of expertise. He broke with Courbet's model, for example, in *The Marne at Chennevières* (fig. 61), exhibited at the Salon in 1865, the same year as one of Courbet's *Puits noir* (see fig. 32).

Like Courbet in his Franche-Comté landscapes, Pissarro knew his chosen surroundings well. Chennevières was located to the southeast of Paris across the Marne River from the village of La Varenne-Saint-Hilaire, where Pissarro resided between 1863 and 1865. *The Marne at Chennevières* depicts an unassuming everyday scene, the kind that anyone familiar with rural Île-de-France would have had immediately recognized. Here Pissarro altered the Courbetian template by adding elements derived from the work of Corot and Daubigny. Rejecting Courbet's enclosed primeval undergrowths, Pissarro opted in *The Marne at Chennevières* for the wide horizontal format dear to Daubigny. The panoramic view admirably conveyed the calm scene of an embanked village sandwiched between bands of sky and river. From Corot (whom, along with the Danish marine painter Anton Melbye, Pissarro credited as a teacher in the Salon catalogues of 1864 and 1865), the artist borrowed a lighter palette and an almost architectonic way of placing buildings in the landscape. Pissarro succeeded in combining both Daubigny's and Corot's compositional order and the latter's bright colors with Courbet's touch. Corot and Daubigny often sat on the Salon jury in those years, and these elements might have served to blunt any objection to Pissarro's aggressive technique. Pissarro demonstrated in *The Marne at Chennevières* that painting with the palette knife need not produce pictures as gloomy as Courbet's, and, just as importantly, that it could still achieve works of daring technical expertise, as long as certain compromises were made with the original model.

Viewers today are so familiar with highly worked-up canvases that it is difficult to recapture just how odd a landscape built out of thick dollops and scrapes of bright paste would have appeared to an audience in the 1860s. In his Salon landscapes, Pissarro had partially softened the visual impact of knife-painting. His younger colleague Cézanne, whom he had known since 1861 from the Académie Suisse, Paris, was not so constrained. Indeed, of the artists in our fourth group, Cézanne is the one whose painting would most deserve the epithet "insurrectionist."[26] If Pissarro's Salon landscapes, however strongly knifed, were within the bounds of respectability, a work such as Cézanne's *River Bend* (fig. 62), one of a series of palette-knife paintings dated from 1865 to 1866, defies almost all convention.[27] Even taking into account its sketch-like size and thus allowing for a certain looseness of technique, few, if any, painters in the 1860s would have constructed a landscape on a foundation of gooey black. Indeed, the work resembles more the encrusted corpse of an abandoned palette than a structured composition.[28] Perhaps only the water in the foreground, in which the ripples are stacked like bricks, appears to have followed some preconceived design. Yet if this is an attempt to impose order, then it is a deliberately clumsy, almost laughable one; the quasi-grid of these rather unconvincing constructive strokes seems only to put the abject formlessness of the rest of the picture into even starker relief.[29] After 1867, Pissarro and Cézanne put the predominantly knifed landscape on hold for several years.[30] Pissarro would move toward the large landscape painting that is the summit of his work in the 1860s. At the same time, Cézanne went in an altogether different direction through portraiture, an event so momentous, at least in terms of its transformation of Courbet's palette-knife technique, that it will occupy us for the rest of the chapter.

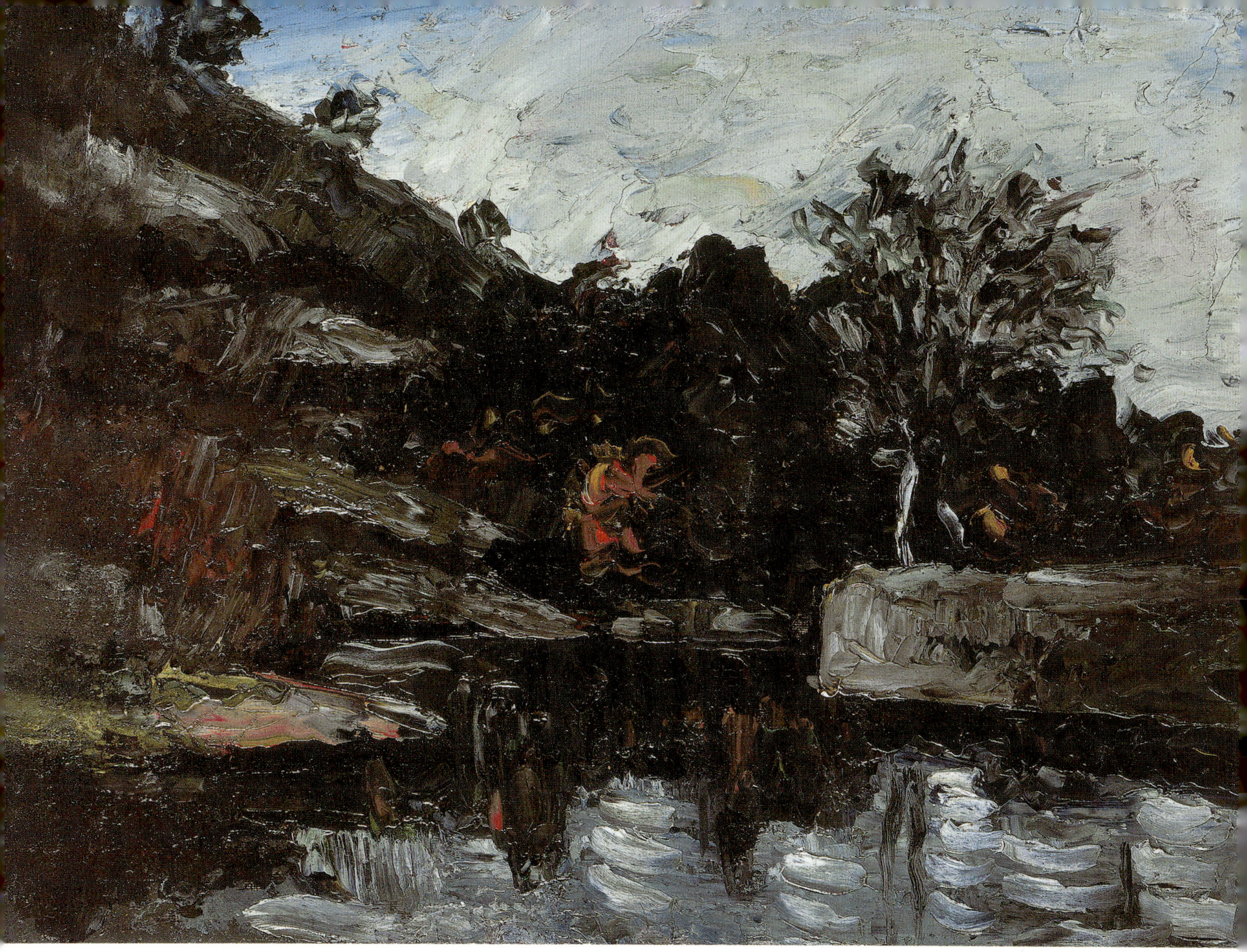

62 | Paul Cézanne, *River Bend*, *ca.*1865. Oil on canvas, 35.2 × 44 cm. The Israel Museum, Jerusalem

MON ONCLE

It has been argued in previous chapters that Courbet's landscape painting was not the troweled masonry of legend. On the contrary, Courbet often disguised or minimized overt traces of the tool. But the cliché *does* apply to the palette-knife painting of Cézanne. Between spring 1866 and February 1867, Cézanne painted several portraits of family members and friends, beginning with the large, three-quarter-length *Antony Valabrègue* (fig. 63) for the Salon of 1866 and culminating in the full-length *The Artist's Father, Reading "L'Événement"* (1866; National Gallery of Art, Washington, D.C.) that would radically transform Courbet's palette-knife technique. Several of the family portraits have survived to the present day: two large full-length portraits of his father; nine of his maternal uncle, Dominique Aubert (see figs. 64, 65, and 66), comprising six small head studies and three larger portraits; one of his sister, Marie Cézanne; and another of his mother (on the verso of this painting).[31]

Unlike Courbet, who had largely suppressed sharp visible knife-edges, Cézanne in the 1866 portraits pressed his overloaded tool with such force that excess paint oozed out at the blade's edges, creating elevated ridges along the tool's path. In one and the same gesture, paint was flattened *and* raised, with both indentations and excrescences contributing to the final appearance.

For out-and-out surface relief, Cézanne's 1866 palette-knife portraits in what Gowing called his "slab-like style" are unprecedented in the history of European painting.[32] Such thickly applied paint would not appear again in modern art for almost two decades (notably in the art of Vincent van Gogh). In these paintings, Cézanne is extraordinary not only in terms of how much material he added to the canvas, but also in the manner in which he applied it. Antony Valabrègue, a poet and art historian close to the artist, compared them to acts of vengeance: "Every time he paints one of his friends, it seems as though he were revenging himself on him for some hidden injury."[33]

Such violent manipulation of the paint also occurs when the painter smears different colors together with knife or spatula on the palette. Thus, Cézanne did more than invent a particularly vigorous form of palette-knife painting; he painted his portraits almost as if he were working on a palette, that is, doing "palette-painting." Valabrègue hinted at this unusual way of working while recounting his own experience of sitting for Cézanne:

> Paul made me sit yesterday for the study of a head. Flesh: Fire-red with scrapings of white; the painting of a mason. I am colored so strongly that I am reminded of the statue of the curé of Champfleury when it was coated with crushed blackberries. Fortunately, I only posed for it one day. The uncle is more often the model.[34]

63 Paul Cézanne, *Antony Valabrègue*, 1866. Oil on canvas, 116.3 × 98.4 cm. National Gallery of Art, Washington, D.C.

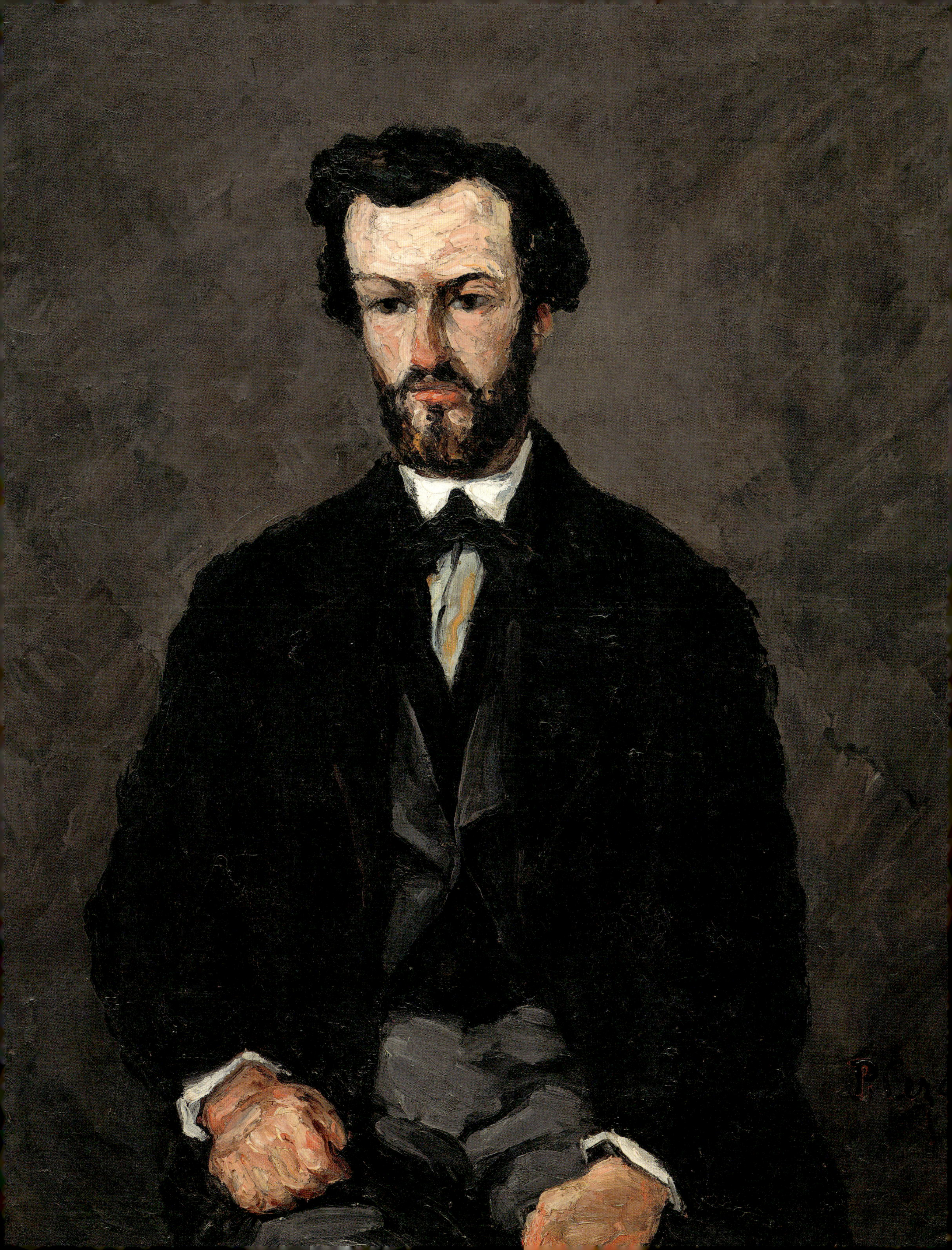

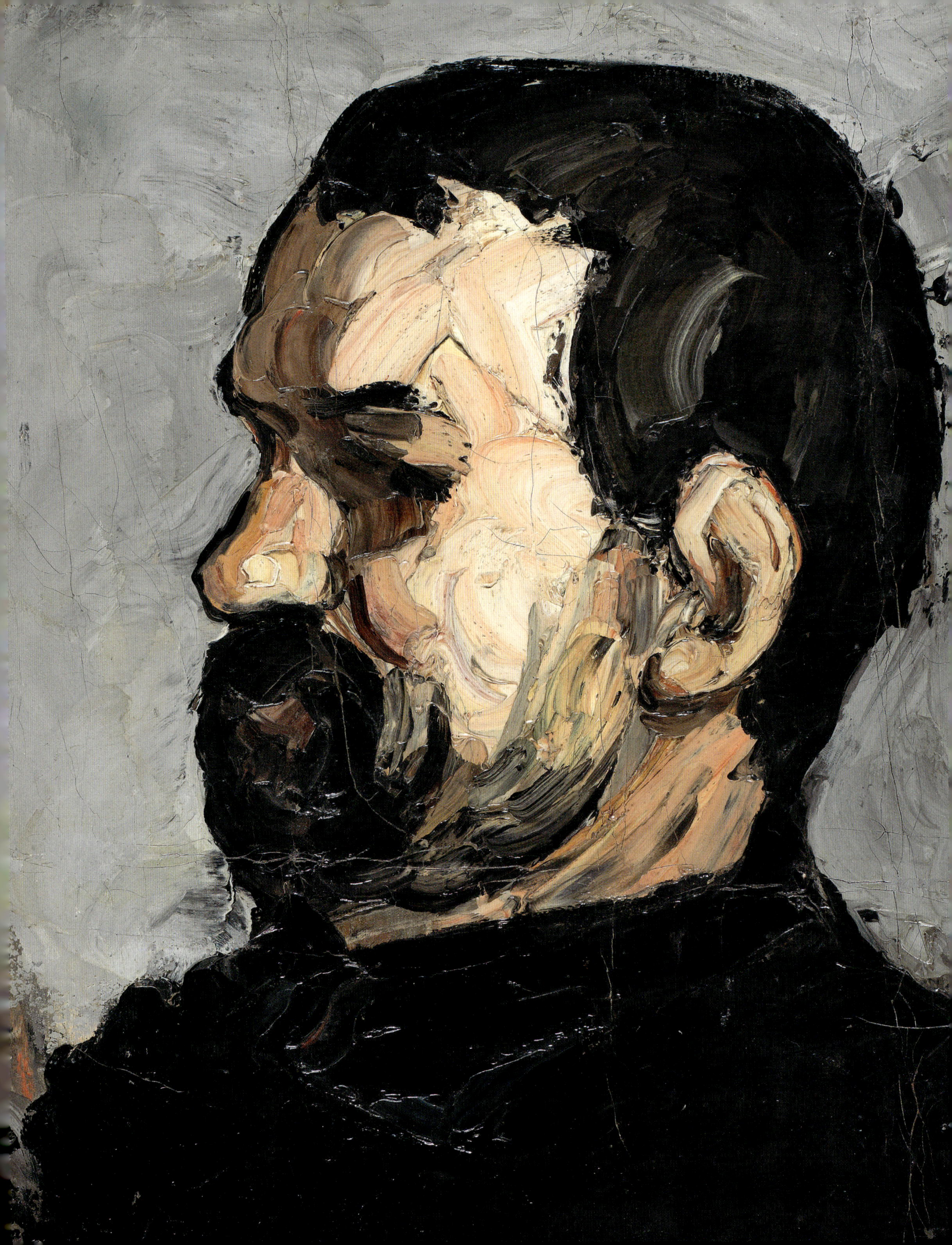

65 | Paul Cézanne, *Uncle Dominique with a Turban*, 1866–67. Oil on canvas, 44 × 37 cm. Private collection

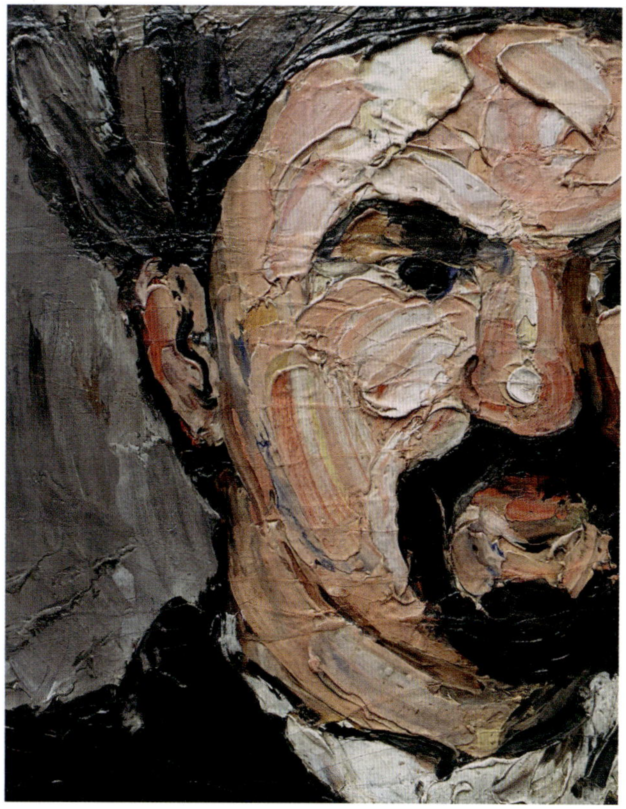

66 | Paul Cézanne, *Uncle Dominique with a Turban* (detail), 1866–67. Oil on canvas, 44 × 37 cm. Private collection

Unfortunately, the portrait in question has not survived (or is lost).[35] But Valabrègue's description recalls contemporaneous portraits such as *Uncle Dominique with a Turban* (figs. 65 and 66). In this painting, the headgear of Dominique Aubert, the younger brother of Cézanne's mother and a bailiff in the law courts of Aix, does resemble "crushed blackberries."[36] In comparison with the earliest significant example of Cézanne's "masonry" technique, the earlier Salon-bound *Antony Valabrègue*, which had still made slight concessions to pictorial convention (pockets of shadow under the eyebrows and on the left side of his nose and cheek hinted at traditional modeling, however cursorily), *Uncle Dominique*, one-third the Salon portrait's dimensions but with marks of roughly the same size, pushed "mason painting" to the limit, taking the most gouged parts of the Valabrègue portrait, the lumpen fists closest to the viewer, and making them the model for *all* of Uncle Dominique's flesh.[37]

64 | Paul Cézanne, *Uncle Dominique*, 1866. Oil on canvas, 39 × 30.5 cm. The Fitzwilliam Museum, Cambridge, England

In the portraits of Uncle Dominique, Cézanne frequently left streaks of "fire"—red and white visible within his knife-strokes depicting skin. Assuming that these were the same colors mixed on the palette to create the overall pinkish skin color in the first place, then Cézanne was doing something curious: he was letting the most basic color mixing that occurs on the palette infiltrate the final paint application. The palette knife takes its name, after all, from the handheld board that artists use to mix colors. The blade, which is stiffer than the pliant brush, makes it easier to pick up and deposit large quantities of paint. At the time, the taboo of letting this preliminary mixing stage contaminate the final work meant that artists usually did not even refer to it in their own self-portraits (the palette Courbet holds in *The Artist's Studio*, for example, is neat and tidy).

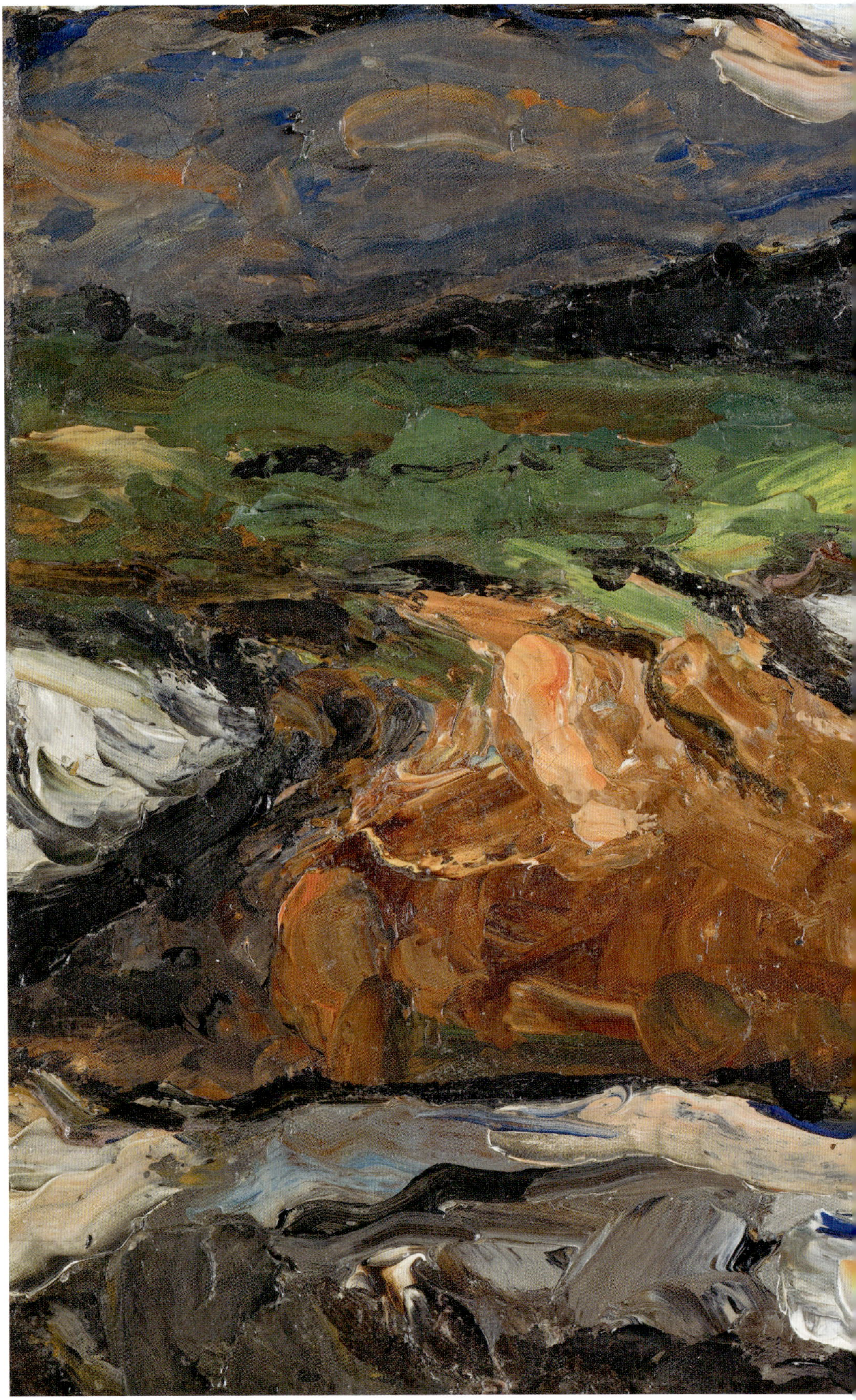

67 Paul Cézanne, *Rocks at the Seashore*, 1865–66. Oil, possibly on board, mounted on canvas, 22.8 × 33 cm. Carnegie Museum of Art, Pittsburgh, Pennsylvania

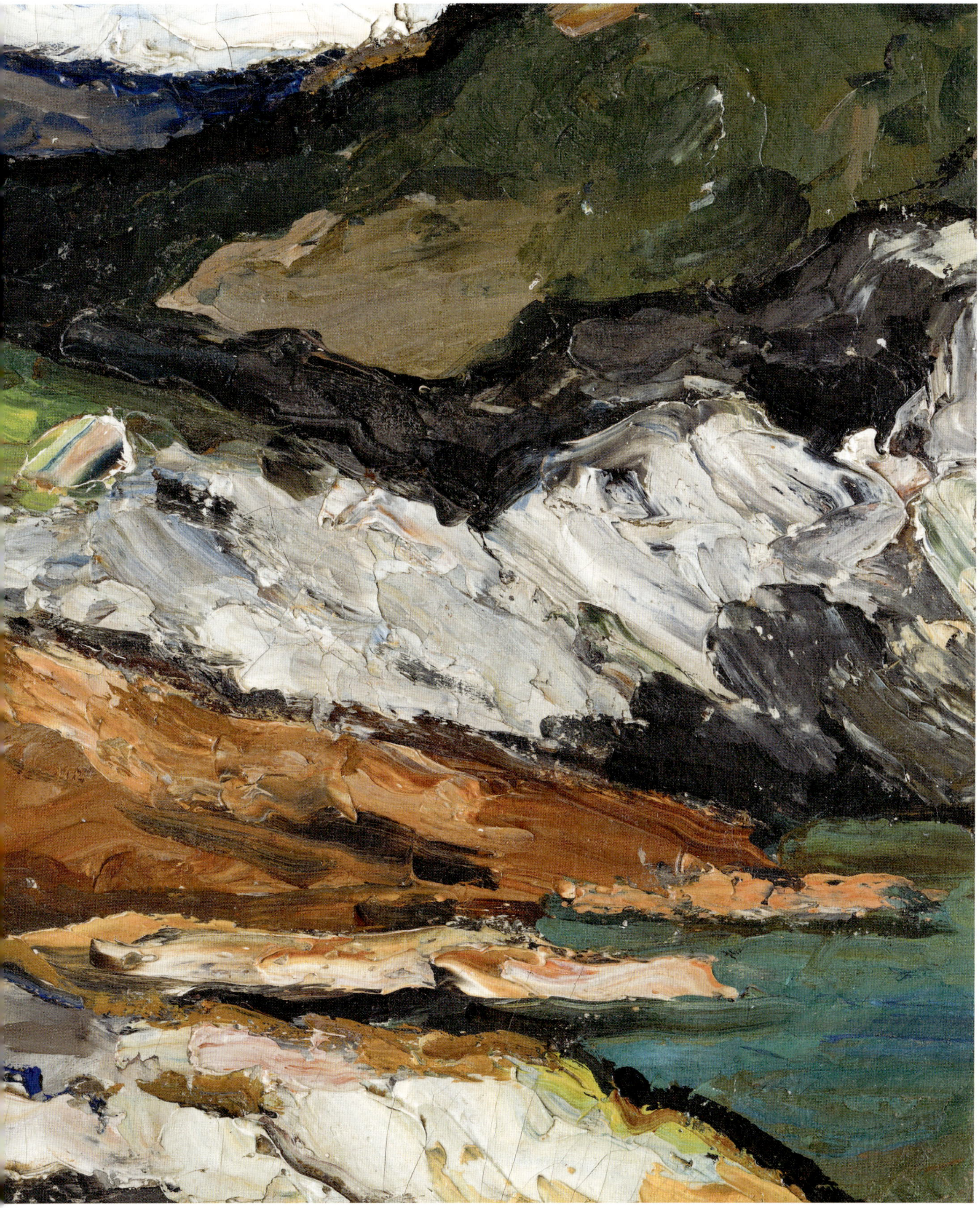

It must be emphasized that these "scrapings" were highly unusual (even Courbet at his roughest hardly ever used them). When a brushstroke is meant to be visible, it is normal practice for an artist to apply one color per stroke. We perceive a multitude of colors through layers of individual marks. The marks intermingle visually, sometimes even physically when the artist mixes colors by putting one above, around, and through another. But it is rare for the one-color-per-stroke rule to be broken, even in areas of paint applied in a slapdash way. A painter seldom applies two or more colors with the same tool and in one and the same stroke to produce a multicolored streak, although this is the essence of Cézanne's technique. In the portraits, he does not apply a fully premixed skin tone (or set of tones) in single-colored touches; instead, the streaks that normally occur on the palette whenever two colors are swirled together now appear on the canvas itself, and they are achieved, most importantly and most radically, *within a single stroke*.

It is important to note that these visible colors are not just extra flourishes, such as those in some of the artist's knifed or roughly brushed landscapes of 1865–66—for example, the blue accent along the shore of *Rocks at the Seashore* (fig. 67). In the portraits of his uncle, the colors red and white are an essential part of the chosen skin color; they are integral, not supplementary to it. It might seem that our argument is not valid in cases such as the right cheek in *Uncle Dominique with a Turban*, where blue and yellow invade the usual combination of red, white, and pink. But following the logic outlined here, Cézanne is not violating protocol. On the contrary, it is likely that the artist incorporated *all* three primary colors into the overall flesh tone, which is why they are so visible.

The 1866 portraits were part of the artist's multipronged assault in the 1860s on almost all existing artistic conventions. Cézanne targeted everything from the Old Masters he copied in the Louvre to the newest forms of Realism to subvert narrative and compositional formulae, introducing "low" forms of print culture, caricature, and fashion imagery into high art, and dismantling the most basic chromatic and gestural norms.[38] Yet even among this diverse output, his portrayals of his uncle stand out. In the various portrayals of Cézanne's uncle, aggression operates at the level of the pictorial mark, not at the level of subject or story. Even more importantly, that aggression is also a kind of regression. Every swipe of the knife that obliterates matter beneath its blade and every "pure" color that is sullied by "impure" streaks evokes an earlier stage of the painting process in which material is handled on the palette prior to its application onto canvas. There are no parallels in the visual art of Cézanne's time for this kind of abject mark-making. Courbet's epidermal patches of paint are tame in comparison. But the idea that the artistic desire to create is sometimes intertwined with an urge to destroy was current in the writings of Cézanne's friends, especially in those of Zola. In the latter's work, we find the model for a violent and conflicted form of picture-making, one completely at odds with the organic and incremental approach taken in Courbet's landscapes.

CRIME AND PUNISHMENT

As Cézanne was painting his portraits, Zola published a short story in *Le Figaro*, "Un Mariage d'amour," which would be developed into the novel *Thérèse Raquin* (1868). The book features a group of pictures strikingly similar to Cézanne's contemporaneous portraits:

> There were five studies, two female heads, and three male heads, painted with incredible energy; oily and solid, they were alluring, each morsel with its magnificent patches against a light-grey ground ... certainly these studies were rough, but they had a strangeness to them.[39]

These studies have formal similarities with Cézanne's heads, most of which are also on a light-gray ground and certainly all roughly rendered. As a group, their thick encrusted surfaces are so "strange" that it is hard to think of another series of portraits from the period, in art or literature, with the same obsessive quality and physical intensity. It is striking that such similar practices of portraiture appeared in both Cézanne's and Zola's work within a couple of months. Indeed, there is evidence that Zola might have seen the portraits first hand, as he wanted Cézanne to bring his latest work with him to Paris, where Zola was completing his novel (Cézanne was there by February 1867).[40] Yet not much has been made of this coincidence, despite the importance of Zola's writings to Cézanne studies.[41] What might have inspired Zola to incorporate such works into *Thérèse Raquin*? And can their description shed light on Cézanne's exaggerated palette-knife technique and its debt to Courbet? To fully address these issues, we must now turn to the role that the portraits play within the novel itself.

Zola conveys the essential plot of *Thérèse Raquin* to the publisher Albert Lacroix in the following terms:

> A young couple, Camille and Thérèse, let Laurent into their home. Laurent becomes Thérèse's lover. Driven by their passion, the two murder Camille by drowning him, hoping to thus lead a happy, lawfully married life. The novel is a study of a union achieved through murder. The lovers experience fright, hate, madness. They each dream of getting rid of their accomplice. In the end, they commit suicide together.[42]

During the "fright" stage of their doomed relationship, Thérèse and Laurent hallucinate that Camille's corpse has come back to haunt them. Later, a visitor to the studio of Laurent (an amateur painter) expects works of an "ignoble mason," but is instead dumbfounded to come across an extraordinary ensemble of small head studies: "so strange, so powerful that they revealed a highly developed artistic sense. It looked like lived painting [*peinture vécue*]."[43] However, there is one problem: each study seems "alive" because they all resemble Camille.

Laurent is horrified by this unconscious repetition. He produces more work, but the image of Camille haunts everything he creates. In a rage, he punches his canvases but suddenly loses control of his hand. Dispossessing Laurent of his hand is a symbolic way of cutting him off from the source of his strength and masculinity. It becomes the latest in a string of violent blows and counterblows: Laurent kills Camille, Camille's corpse haunts Laurent, Laurent paints to avoid Camille,

68 Édouard Manet, *Monk in Prayer*, 1865. Oil on canvas, 146.4 × 115 cm. Museum of Fine Arts, Boston

Camille infiltrates Laurent's painting, Laurent destroys his paintings, Camille "amputates" Laurent's hand. The more Laurent tries to evade or combat the image of Camille, the more powerfully the image attacks in turn. And it does so, cruelly and perversely, by repossessing or repurposing Laurent's means of resistance.[44]

The image of the artist as an individual terrorized by violent, internal conflict is completely at odds with the one Zola so famously champions in his art criticism. Manet, for Zola always the exemplary artist of modernity, paints in clear and simple color masses because his analytic temperament or personality predisposes him to the objective study of contemporary reality in all its aspects, however sordid and indecent.[45] Cézanne is no murderer, and he is painting his uncle consciously, not recalling him unconsciously through surrogates. Yet there is a certain duality to his painting at the level of the pictorial mark that pushes his practice closer to the fractious inner world of Laurent than to the analytical mindset of Zola's Manet (or indeed that of the writer himself).

In Zola's writings on art, the patch of paint was privileged as a category of critical analysis primarily for its styleless-ness and its crudity. Historically, a fundamental directive of picture-making has been to make something of this "pure," unmotivated substance, usually by creating the illusion that it has no substance. Even in those extreme cases when thickly slathered paint has a certain formlessness, it still functions additively to build up a formal illusion. Rough marks either cover underlayers with varying degrees of impasto or are made to blend into those underlayers. Only in exceptional cases do we perceive a certain backtracking in the essentially constructive process, where the decision is openly made to dig into what has been

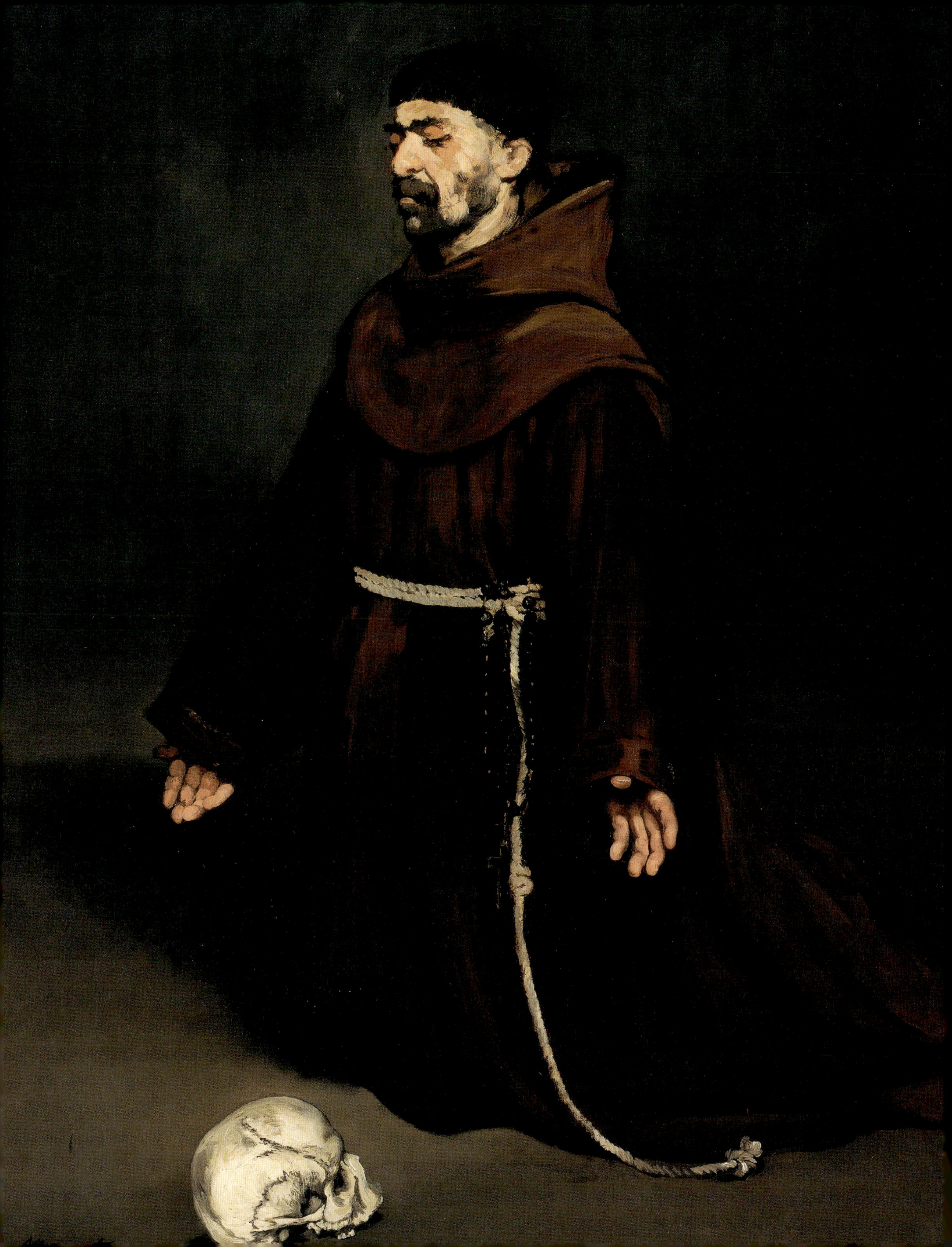

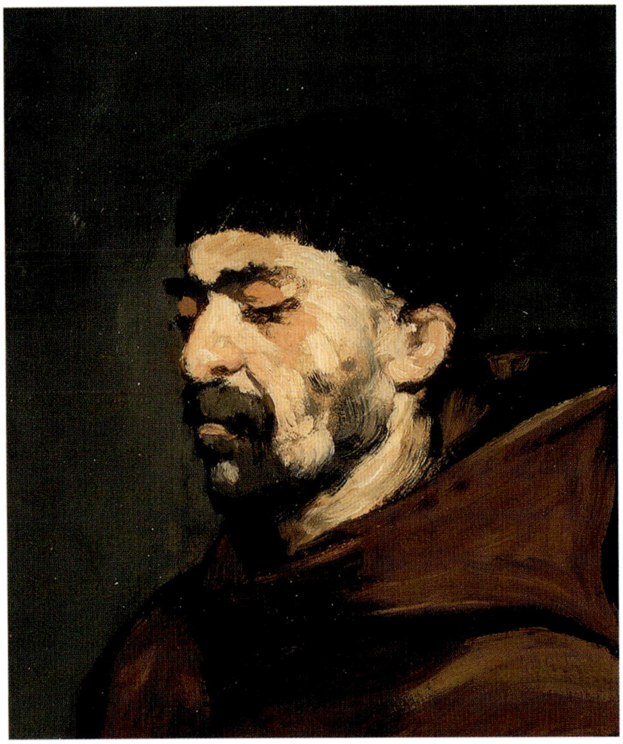

69 | Édouard Manet, *Monk in Prayer* (detail), 1865. Oil on canvas, 146.4 × 115 cm. Museum of Fine Arts, Boston

accumulated. The palette knife, when it is used to apply paint evenly and in large swaths, follows this broader pictorial tendency toward construction, as was the case in Courbet's landscapes.

However, when the knife deposits paint excessively and with sufficient force, the tool can just as easily obliterate what it deposits, and thus act as an instrument of destruction. When this happens, the raised traces of the knife-edge are simultaneously visible residues of an annihilation and eruptions of physical relief; each swipe of the knife both razes and raises the surface, energetically remapping the picture's topography. Cézanne's portraits are built up like no other paintings of their time; but they are also carved into like no others. A portrait eventually is "finished," meaning that construction in the end still prevails over destruction—but not without pushing the limits of what it means in painting to construct and to destroy.

As within each stroke equally powerful yet opposing forces collide, the gestural violence of Cézanne's early portraits is inherently double-natured. His palette-knife technique differs from Courbet's not only in its degree of impasto but also in its fundamental identity. In his choice of tool, in the impurity of his color, and in his self-conflicting touch, Cézanne has regressed to an earlier stage of the process of painting: the spreading, smearing, and mixing of paint on the palette. Cézanne does not wholly emerge from this preparatory phase, thus allowing its contradictory forces to seep into the "mature," adult stage of the final work. In this he is even more daring than artists who limited their deliberate "infantilism" to aspects of sketching or drawing (e.g., using unmodulated color, cursive stroke-making). However regressive, these acts are still beholden to the creation of pictorial form. Cézanne's regression, by contrast, involves an almost infantile relationship to substance *before* it has even taken form—the fingerprint visible in the collar of *Uncle Dominique with a Turban* being perhaps the ultimate sign of painting's devolution from art to be looked at to stuff to be played with.

Given the parallel being drawn here between pictorial and psychological development—or the stunted nature of that development—does it matter that the subject of Cézanne's knifing is so often an older male member of his family? It is striking that Cézanne's most sustained investigation of the palette-knife technique during the 1860s should take place at the same time as he painted a large portrait of his father, one of his most ambitious works to date. The artist's problematic relationship with his father is well known.[46] In the winter of 1866, the difficulties seem to be even more intense than usual.[47] A psychobiographical approach might interpret the violence of the Uncle Dominique portraits as a displacement of the artist's mixed feelings toward his father. Such a reading would indicate that Dominique Aubert, the only person willing to sit day after day for his nephew, was a substitute for an absent father (for whose grand portrait the smaller uncle portraits could have perhaps served as studies). Furthermore, painting his uncle close-up and often head-on would have entailed a physical proximity and psychological intimacy that might have been awkward had the sitter been his father (who, tellingly, is portrayed in his two portraits reading the newspaper, with his head down, avoiding eye contact and confrontation). In this view, a pictorial conflict between the desire to depict and the desire to destroy would be an expression of the love-hate relationship sons have with their fathers, whom they want to both emulate (as figures of power) and eliminate (as rivals for that power).

But we do not have to delve into the depths of Cézanne's psyche—even if that were possible—to see that his work during this period is marked by an ambivalent attitude toward authority, especially *artistic* authority.[48] For the two painters who performed the parental role for Cézanne in 1866 are men whose infamy he craved, Courbet and Manet. Indeed, in the same letter celebrating the palette knife as an instrument of insurrection, Guillemet set out Cézanne's artistic family tree: "Courbet is becoming classical. He had done superb things, but next to Manet he is traditional and Manet next to Cézanne will become traditional in turn."[49]

If we compare Manet's *Monk in Prayer* (figs. 68 and 69) with Cézanne's portraits of Uncle Dominique facing to the side (see figs. 64, 65, and 66), we notice how Cézanne adopts the former's confident stroke-making and stark light-dark contrast only to exaggerate it to the point of breakdown.[50] Like a vengeful child, Cézanne takes what he considers his father's strength and turns it against him. When Cézanne wields the palette knife, it is not to create the illusion of an eternally pleasurable world of substance that we witness so often in Courbet's landscapes. On the contrary, in Cézanne's hands the somatic dream is revealed to be a materialist nightmare, where substance does not gently coalesce into sensuous natural forms so much as buckle under the stress of competing pressures. That this struggle for survival is now played out in portraiture rather than in landscape gives an all-too-human face, and thus a deeply psychological aspect, to what in Courbet only takes place in nature.

THE REVENGE OF THE REAL

By 1866 Zola was dismissive of Courbet. Zola's 1865 article "Proudhon and Courbet" coins the celebrated phrase, art is "a corner of nature viewed by a temperament."[51] One year later he repeats the same phrase, but this time in defense of an artist not even in the exhibition, Manet (in the same series of Salon reviews, Courbet, the former hero, is now relegated to the category of the "fallen" Realist).[52] Later, in a review of the 1868 Salon, Zola dismisses Courbet's *paysages de mer* as "a little light for such a rough and magisterial hand."[53] His stance is thus seemingly at odds with the argument, presented in the previous chapter, that Courbet's best marine paintings generate for their viewers the sensation of being immersed in matter, and so, if anything, should be "heavyweight." However, when he wrote on the seascapes, Zola's aesthetic position had become as hostile to Michelet's substantive materialism, a close parallel to Courbet's own, as it had been earlier to literary Romanticism. Realist writers in his view now had to be coldhearted, even surgical, in their approach to nature, even if it meant treating topics as unpleasant as murder and sexual taboos ("when one wants to study universal history, one has to become an assassin in order to have subjects to dissect").[54] So if, by 1868, Zola is complaining that Courbet's *paysages de mer* are lightweight even though they approach the "heaviness" of the new painting, it is because at a deeper level they have been cleansed of violence and death. To represent a highly pleasurable, sumptuous, and fluid world in paint—or, better, to represent that world as paint-like—was the great achievement of Courbet's seascapes. What would the world look and feel like if matter did not intermingle and metamorphose as happily as it does in Courbet's seascapes? How to picture a world in which the forces of death and destruction are at least equal, if not superior, to the forces of life and reproduction? The obvious candidate is the palette painting of Cézanne.

Reading the painterly mark as riven by internal conflict helps shed light on one of Cézanne's most curious works. The painting known today as *Bather and Rocks* (fig. 70) had originally been part of a large mural in the salon of the Jas de Bouffan mansion. The mural itself was painted in two stages, several years apart: the background rocks and greenery, in the style of an eighteenth-century pastoral landscape, were done just after Cézanne's father's acquisition of the property near Aix-en-Provence; the bather, on a nebulous dark ground and framed on the left by what looks like flowing water and on the lower part by what seems to be creased clothing, was painted directly over the first mural sometime in the late 1860s.[55] There is an undeniable contrast between the flat, generic treatment of the original landscape and the much more vigorous style of the nude. The bather is often compared to the standing nude in Courbet's 1853 *Bathers*, which Cézanne may have seen.[56] There are striking similarities between the two bathers: corpulent bodies, posed with their backs turned, and strange hand gestures, although Cézanne's bather appears to be male, at least based on the

70 Paul Cézanne, *Bather and Rocks*, *ca.*1860–66. Oil on canvas, transferred from plaster, 167.6 × 105.4 cm. Chrysler Museum of Art, Norfolk, Virginia

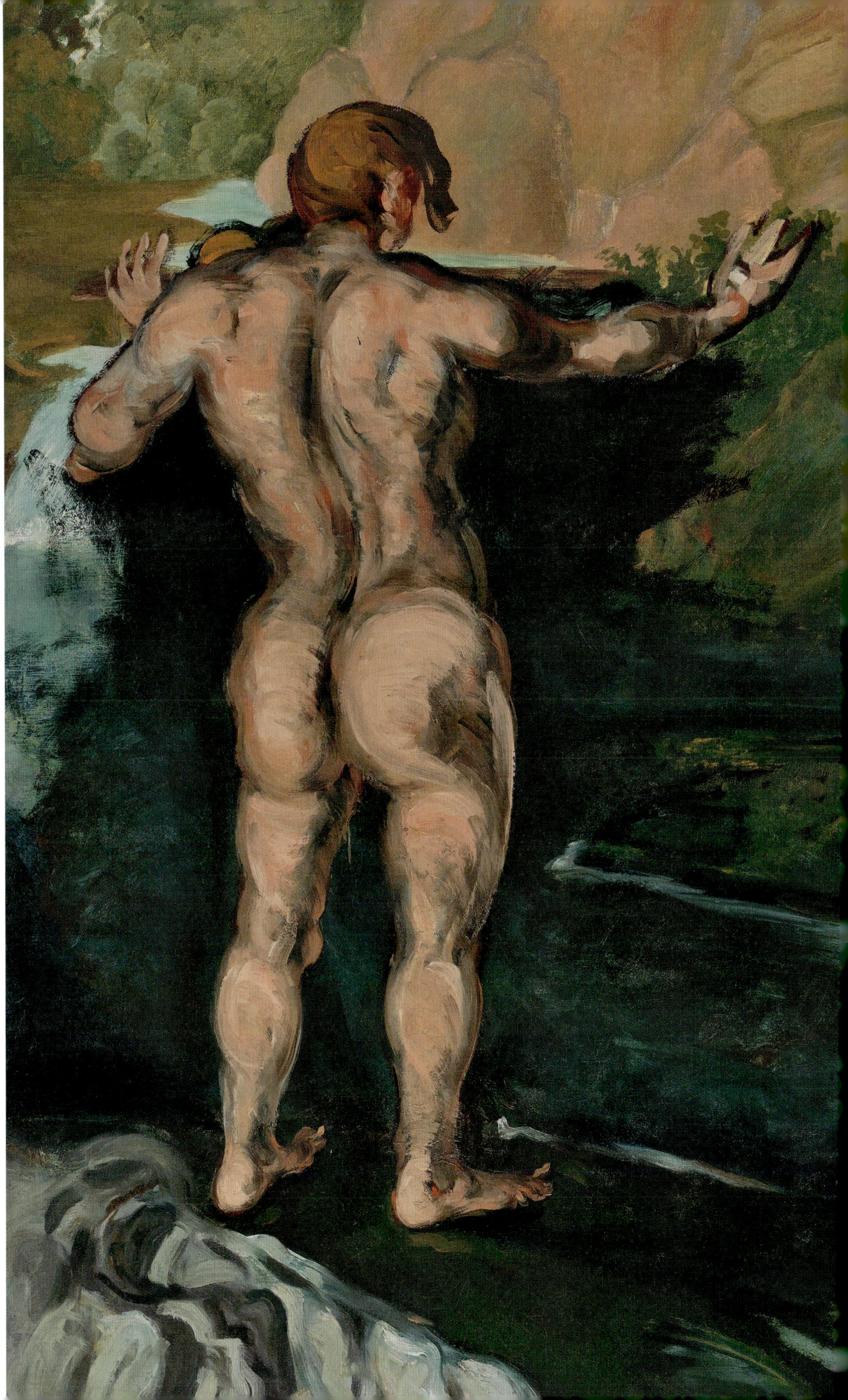

broadness of the shoulders and knotty musculature. Yet this still leaves the question of why Cézanne would paint one *on a wall* in the first place.

For a possible answer, let us look at *Bathers and Rocks* side by side with the last of Courbet's large-scale nudes, *The Spring* of 1868 (see fig. 53). *The Spring*, another bathing picture, is in many ways an allegory of touch. Each extremity is in some sort of contact with nature: one foot ankle-deep in the water, another balancing on land, one hand gripping a branch, and, most conspicuously of all, at the heart of the painting, the other hand tickling a glistening cascade. Courbet takes from his obvious model, Ingres, not only his title and subject—*The Spring* (1820–56; Musée d'Orsay, Paris)—but also the recently deceased artist's signature *profil perdu* (backturned profile). In this way, Courbet exposes the serpentine, full-length female body for which the arch-classicist was so famous. Also offered is the possibility of full physical immersion in nature, a sensation that the painting tantalizingly proposes by surrounding the nude with some of the artist's most vivid passages of paint. Yet this invitation to enter the promised land is at the same time a denial of that promise. For the figure that beckons us also blocks our entry. The painting offers in equal parts temptation and frustration. While our gaze may gravitate in the first instance to the naked human form, it does not remain there, because the way in which the nude is turned away from us suggests that there is more to see—or, better yet, feel—on the other side of the body.

Cézanne viewed reality not as a sensuous union but a battlefield of conflicting forces. In the portraits, this takes the form of a regression to an earlier stage in the painting process, where the creative and destructive instincts collide. With *Bather and Rocks*, a similar dynamic is at work. But this time it plays itself out, not on the easel canvas, but on a wall. We will probably never know if Cézanne intended one day to finish what he started in the salon of the Jas du Bouffan mansion. But the more we look at the painting, the more it appears that, whatever the final goal, it was already haunted by a sense of incompletion from the start. The bather and the dark ground rudely blot out entire swaths of the original mural's foreground, seemingly with no concern for what lay underneath. This indiscriminate treatment of the "ground" might suggest that Cézanne could not have cared less about it and would have continued overpainting had he had the time or the desire to do so. But other aspects show that in some cases he paused to consider what he was doing in relation to the previous scene. For example, the freshly painted water on the left, far from ignoring the original composition, vaguely follows the path of an existing stream. Why did Cézanne even bother, given that he could have just as easily painted a whole new spring, just as he painted a new bather from scratch?

On closer inspection, the artist seems to be undecided about what to keep and what to paint over in the mural. The bather's strange hand motions are another case in point. The left hand could be trying to feel the newly applied spring. But it could also be seen as bracing itself against the old terrain, thus acknowledging the previous landscape in its original condition, before it had been painted over. The right hand, for its part, reaches out, leading the charge to create a new scene atop the old one. But the same gesture could also be read as an attempt to block or keep something from the existing landscape at bay (perhaps the rocks directly in front of the bather?). What compounds the ambiguity is the fact that the hand—nothing more than a three-pronged, manhandled stump—is kept anatomically illegible. The ambiguity sums up a work that appears to be of two minds, undecided as to whether to work with the previous composition (by incorporating some of its elements) or against it (by completely covering it over).

Executed on the walls of a house that had belonged to his father (Cézanne's first portrait of his father hung prominently in an alcove in the same room), Cézanne's overpainting has even deeper implications.[57] For the mural is a memory of his own artistic "childhood," one that the artist in principle should have left behind after going to Paris in pursuit of modern art. But his return to, and reactivation of, it can mean only that for some reason Cézanne felt that he still had work to do and the mural needed to be revisited. The artist alternates between wanting to hold on to the image and wanting to destroy it, to work with it or to cover it over, to keep it consciously alive or to bury it. Torn in two different directions, the artist is stuck in a situation not unlike that of the bather itself.

Like the portraits of Uncle Dominique, *Bather and Rocks* marks a return of sorts. In both cases, something that should have been left behind, processed, and then superseded is allowed to come back and reassert itself in the present: in the portraits, an earlier stage in the painterly process is revisited; in the mural, it is an earlier state of execution that resurfaces; the former entails a regression to a previous configuration of matter, the latter the reworking of a past event; raw, unrefined substance erupts into the portraits, the old wall mural disrupts the new composition. Things that are traditionally repressed in painting—the material reality of pictorial substance and the material reality of the physical support—make their presence known. In other words, in both instances the real world exacts its revenge on the illusionistic sphere from which it had been all but banished. Cézanne never undertook palette painting (as opposed to *knife*-painting, which he picks up again in the 1870s) or wall-painting ever again. But it could be argued that his later "unfinished" paintings are caught between the two poles established by the Uncle Dominique portraits and *Bather and Rocks*. On the one hand, paint as pure substance, an aspect of the real world intruding into the imaginary space of illusion, and, on the other, the ground itself as its own kind of pictorial material, where it no longer functions as a blank canvas but actively participates in the act of illusion-making itself. In Cézanne's late work we reach not only the material limits of his own practice but the threshold of what is possible in modern painting. He revisited and reinterpreted a dynamic between image and matter first broached in Courbet's landscapes of origin. But whereas in a Courbet seascape wave and paint coexist in a state of suspended animation, in Cézanne's account of the same scenario we cannot witness an image of a wave originating from the depths of the picture without also feeling its spray strike us in the face. If Courbet's wave shows us what happens when image and matter most fully coincide, Cézanne by contrast reveals what happens when the wave finally breaks: image and matter, reference and substance are once again opposed but this time as bitter enemies on a much more even battlefield of representation.

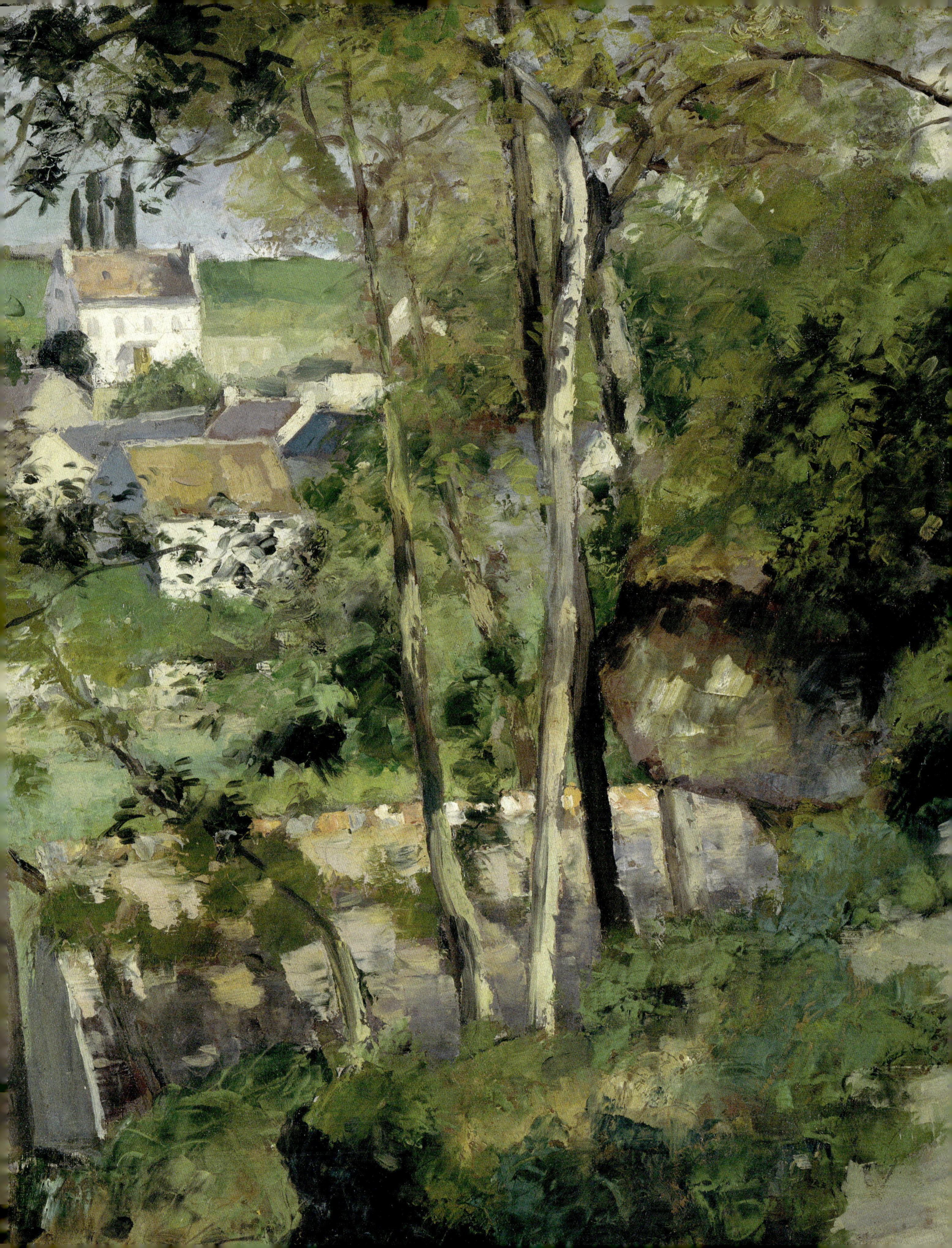

CODA: ANTI-IMPRESSIONISM

Throughout his career, Courbet's painting could be highly palpable, no matter what the subject. But it is particularly the case when he turns his attention in the mid-1860s to a specific kind of landscape—the landscape of origin. It was then that Courbet applied his palette-knife technique in earnest to depict dark, cavernous or enclosed sites untouched by human hands. In works such as *The Stream of the Puits noir* (see fig. 1) and *Source of the Lison* (see fig. 17), each patch of color is carefully overlaid from dark to light, as if sunlight had slowly illuminated the scene, to create the illusion of a world composed of substances as dense as paint.

Courbet came as close as any painter to realizing in pictorial terms the atomistic world theorized by the materialist philosophers. He reached this point around 1864 through intense engagement with the sciences of linguistics, archeology, and geology. By laying bare the various stages of landscape's material creation, his practice linked with nineteenth-century discourses that likewise sought to uncover, by means of an extended analysis of their objects of study, the hidden forces shaping the past. Seemingly ahistorical at first glance, the artist's landscapes were deeply committed to their own kind of historical investigation, the revelation of material process. Thus, the historicizing approach to visual form taken in this book, in which the multiple layers of meaning in Courbet's landscapes are analyzed to unearth their art-historical origins, is already prefigured in the artworks themselves.

In the case of the seascapes, Courbet was less concerned with the historical search for distant origins than with the immanent experience of matter. The waves and beach scenes are images of substances in various states of suspended animation, in which the materials pictured (vapor, foam, sand) and the actual substance used to depict them (dabs, scrapes, and deposits of paint) are practically equivalent in physical terms. In such situations, paint's sheer presence does not disrupt or negate the illusion. Instead, its substantiveness makes the world represented on canvas appear even more tangible and "real." For this reason, Courbet's seascapes are one of the most dramatic instances of the co-substantiality of image and matter in the history of post-Renaissance European painting. They bring out into the open what centuries of artistic tradition had repressed, namely, painting's material continuity with the real world. Yet this occurs, admittedly, only under the most extreme pictorial circumstances, that of a panoramic, starkly depopulated view where the sea meets the land.

Such a setting was so restrictive that future modern painters who wanted to address the full range of contemporary subject matter would be obliged to find other ways of registering the real in their work. The ways in which they did so are by now familiar, such as the painting of modern life, the aesthetics of the sketch, the pictorial recording of sensations. As an alternative to these artistic responses to modernity, Courbet proposed a deeply somatic experience in which matter on the canvas appeared, momentarily, to belong to both the depicted world and our own. From one point of view, the greater the lengths Courbet took to materialize substance in this fashion, the more he seemed to disavow the new realities of the day. But from a different perspective, Courbet had discovered a subject, the landscape of origin, capable of accommodating a large amount of raw paint by making it co-substantial with what it represented. Once Courbet had destabilized the traditional hierarchy of image over matter in this manner—that is, by foregrounding the latter without totally usurping the former—and brought them to near parity, modern painting in its most developed forms would have to acknowledge to at least some degree painting's nonsignifying, material component, no matter what reality it was trying to depict. Art would continue to be primarily referential until the end of the century. But its practitioners would increasingly attend to how pictorial matter escaped—or resisted—illusionism. As a result, the art of painting would continue to maintain a foothold in the real world long after its imitative function had for all intents and purposes been usurped by the image-making technologies of photography and film.

EXILE

At the Salon of 1870, Courbet exhibited two Étretat seascapes: A popular view of the coast, *The Étretat Cliffs after the Storm*, updated for the modern tourist; and *The Stormy Sea*, an imposing wave painting that plunged the viewer into a world of originary substances. The pair epitomized the two poles navigated by his landscape painting, the manufactured image of nature (the picturesque cliff) and the corporeal experience of matter (the engulfing wave). However, the events of what Victor Hugo called *l'année terrible*, France's defeat in the Franco-Prussian War (1870–71) and the downfall of the Paris Commune in 1871, put an end to this productive tension in Courbet's art.[1] His official appointments, first as president of the Arts Committee under the Government of National Defense and later as elected member of the Commune and president of the Federation of Artists, kept him from painting much. After his arrest for his part in the Paris uprising, his subsequent trial, conviction, and periods of ill health between 1871 and 1872 limited his best efforts in painting mainly to still life and portraiture.

The ultimate indignity came on 30 May 1873 when the National Assembly voted to proceed with the reconstruction of the toppled column in the Place Vendôme at the artist's expense. A symbol of militarism and imperial power since its erection under Napoleon I, the column had long been a target of republican ire and Courbet had penned a letter proposing its dismantling in 1870. The demolition of the column took place in May 1871. Although he did not give the official order (which was issued just before Courbet's election to the Commune), Courbet was implicated because of his earlier proposal and he became a scapegoat for the monument's fall. A new conservative government began seizing his property, including artworks. In July 1873, Courbet, who had been in Franche-Comté for barely a year, publicly ostracized and now fearing imprisonment, went into exile in Switzerland. There, he could paint Lac Léman and the Alps only for so long before the necessity of selling work to pay off his debts began to stifle the inventiveness of his landscape painting. At some point, he came to an arrangement with his fellow painters Cherubino Pata and Marcel Ordinaire to facilitate the production and distribution of works. For Courbet, being cut off from friends, family, and the capital was lethal, and, alcoholic and depressed, he died, on 31 December 1877.

AFTERLIFE

Though Courbet was physically absent from the art world after 1873, his impact was felt in other ways. In the years following the 1867 Universal Exhibition, a group of younger artists inspired by Courbet's private pavilion began thinking about staging their own independent exhibition. In 1874, they finally realized their plans in the photographer Nadar's old studio in the Boulevard des Capucines, Paris. Months prior to the First Impressionist Exhibition, Pissarro, one of its principal organizers, painted in his Pontoise studio a portrait of Cézanne with a caricature of Courbet conspicuously tacked onto the back wall (fig. 71). This singular portrait boldly aligned Pissarro and Cézanne with the ex-Communard just as Courbet went into exile. It was an unusual move for Pissarro (who rarely painted portraits of nonfamily members) as well as for Cézanne (who usually sat for himself). The work not only positioned the two artists politically to the left of their confrères, but it also pitted their image of the provincial, insurgent artist against the portrayal of the sophisticated dandy and connoisseur of modern life, such as the figure of Zola in Manet's *Portrait of Zola* (1868; Musée d'Orsay, Paris), their obvious reference point.[2]

In Pissarro's *Portrait of Cézanne*, Courbet's intransigeance takes the form of an image, a printed caricature. Yet the portrait is the only work by either Pissarro or Cézanne during this period making explicit reference to Courbet or the controversies surrounding him. The exiled artist's impact was in general much more highly mediated. Take, for instance, the sudden reappearance of the palette knife in Cézanne's and Pissarro's landscapes of the 1870s. From 1872 to 1874, Pissarro lived in Pontoise. Cézanne joined him temporarily in 1872, before moving to nearby (and even more rural) Auvers-sur-Oise, where he stayed until 1874. The evident closeness in style between some works by Cézanne and others by Pissarro that are securely dated to this period makes it highly likely that the two artists painted together again in 1875, although there is no documentation to corroborate this.[3] Once Cézanne "learns" Impressionism in 1872 after copying Pissarro's *Louveciennes* (1871; Private collection) in the former's painting of the same name (*ca.*1872; Private collection), the brushstrokes in both oeuvres become progressively patchier (although not without twists and turns along the way), climaxing, in Pissarro's case, with his knife-and-brush pictures of 1875. It is difficult to pinpoint exactly when either artist first starts revisiting Courbet's palette-knife technique. However, it is clear that several works by Cézanne and Pissarro, made between 1872 and 1875 and inspired by Courbet, constitute a radical break with the paintings that Monet, Renoir, and Manet were creating at the same time in Argenteuil.

There is no need to rehearse at length here what was achieved at Argenteuil, a well-documented episode in the history of modern art. The Impressionists explored the possibilities of open-air painting, combining signs of modernity (such as railroads, boating events, factories) to create a new image of Nature that was no longer the sentimental landscape of the past but a modern scene fashioned by and for city dwellers visiting the countryside.[4] For our purposes, such an achievement seems to consign Cézanne's and Pissarro's village landscapes to the dustbin of history, designating them

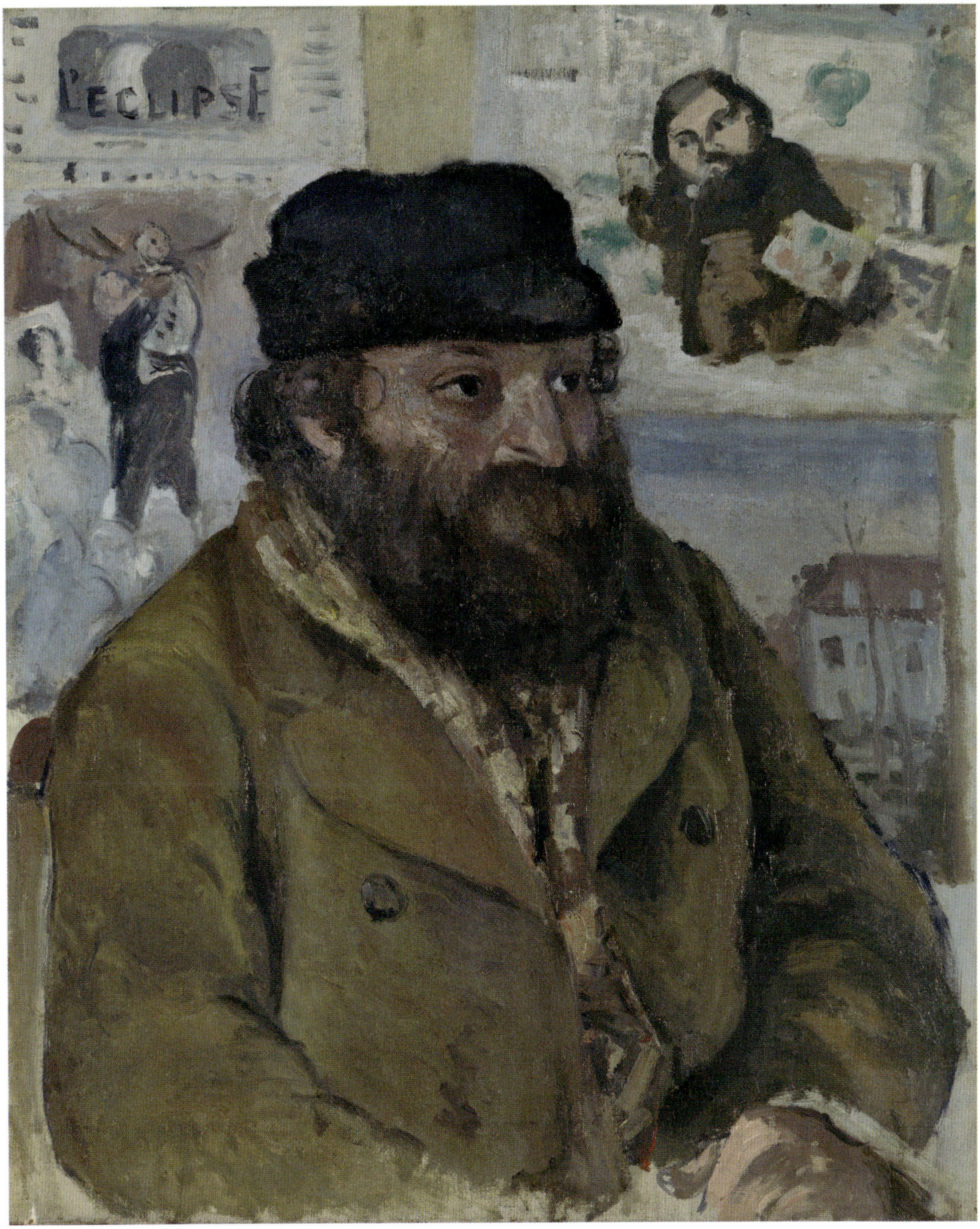

as quaint relics of a time when the small communal town could still function as a viable model for public life. Certainly, Cézanne and Pissarro paid a heavy price for choosing the rural enclave over the modernizing suburb. It cut their work off from the representation of some of the most vital subject matter of their era. But what did they gain from such a choice? What, exactly, were Pissarro and Cézanne walking away from?

71 Camille Pissarro, *Portrait of Cézanne*, 1874. Oil on canvas, 73 × 59.7 cm. The National Gallery, London, on loan from the collection of Laurence Graff OBE

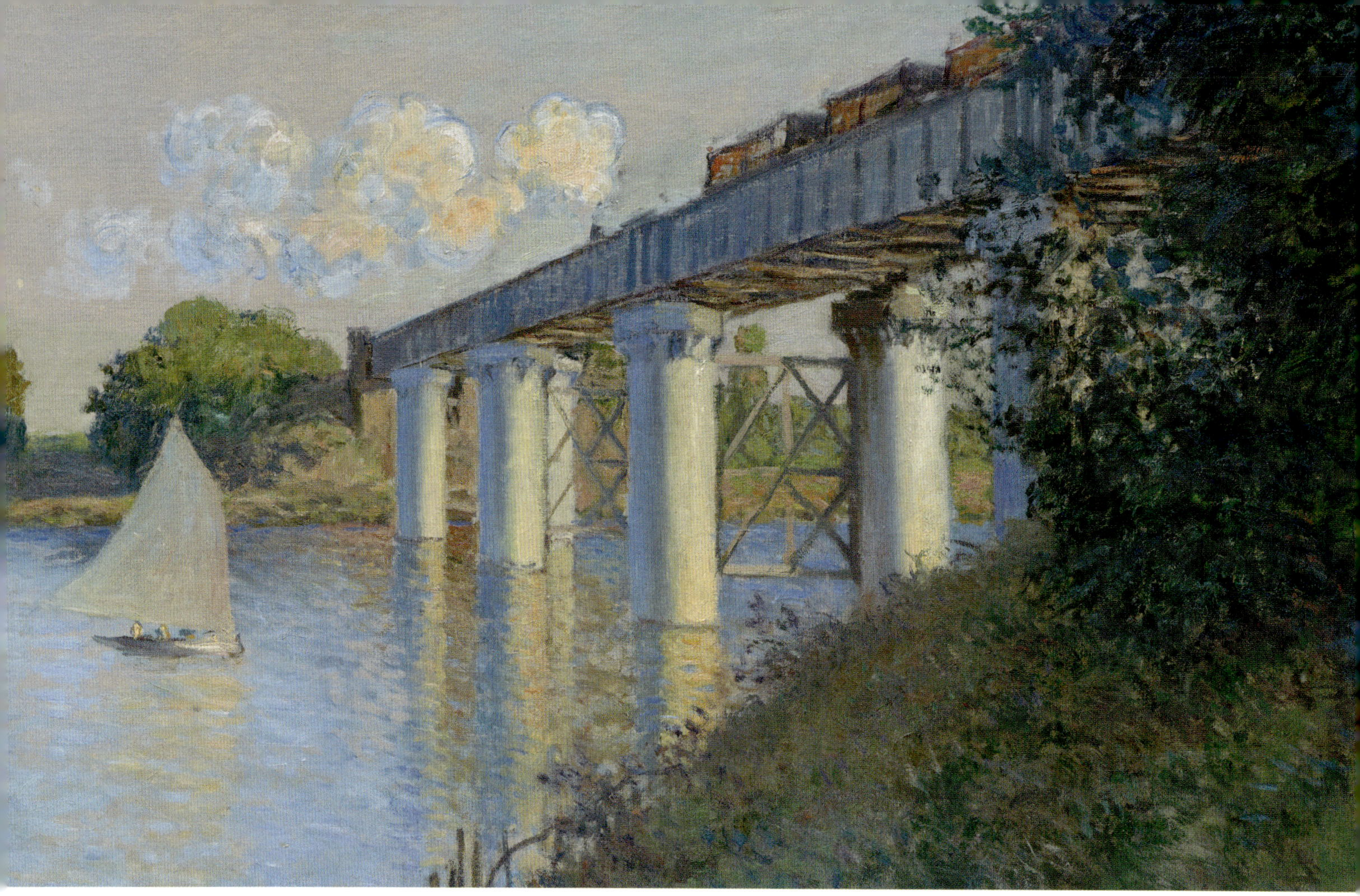

72 Claude Monet, *Railroad Bridge, Argenteuil*, 1873. Oil on canvas, 54.3 × 73.3 cm. Philadelphia Museum of Art

DISUNITY

The Philadelphia version of Monet's *Railroad Bridge, Argenteuil* (fig. 72) is typical of the Impressionist rewriting of Nature at this historical moment. Monet restabilizes the destabilizing effects of modernity by incorporating the natural and the built into a unified visual field of "spontaneously" rendered atmospheric effects, with certain passages being almost nonillustionstic (for example, the wisps in the clouds). To impose on this loose web of gestures a strong sense of overall coherence, Monet erects a rectilinear geometry of riverbanks, bridges, and boats partitioning space into distinct zones. Though lacking sharp outlines, these zones nevertheless impose a spatial order and establish boundaries between different sections. In the Philadelphia painting, for example, with its strong sense of perspective, the feathery, light-green grass of the riverbank, the dark-green leaves overlooking it, and the river broadly keep to the space allotted to them.

Monet's strokes also tend to be consistent within a given zone: the river is largely formed from parallel striations; the embankment from ministreaks bending toward the river; the dark-green foliage from an accumulation of dabs. The overall effect is that landscape elements are locked into their positions, their constituent marks restrained within their confined areas. (Incidentally, it is for this reason that Monet's brushwork is often at its most dynamic in water—a river can plausibly contain the ripples and reflections.) There are still moments when the artist overaccentuates a mark when he applies color in an extreme way. But these disruptions tend to occur *within* zones, not at their intersection. As a result, and despite at times the undisciplined technique, the viewer is always provided with enough information to unify the disparate sectors into a harmonious whole.[5]

It is precisely this visual intelligibility that Cézanne and Pissarro work hard to undermine. Perceptive viewers have identified many of the weapons in their arsenal: bends in the road that lead nowhere or terminate abruptly; receding pathways that pop up vertically to block the gaze; plunging viewpoints that bring the near and the far into uncomfortable proximity; houses with impossibly angled walls and rooftops.[6] The painters from Pontoise and Auvers, unlike their peers in Argenteuil, take full advantage of, and even relish in, spatial disruption. How often does the eye, just as it is about to determine where one part of the landscape ends and another begins, pause at a dense accumulation of out-of-scale grass or leaves? Foliage and shrubbery are constantly used to inject ambiguity into the scene. The touches at these junctures often clash with nearby strokes in size and direction (especially when the artist uses different tools).

For example, in Cézanne's *Quartier Four, Auvers-sur-Oise* (also known as *Landscape, Auvers*; fig. 73), we are made to overlook a group of buildings set against a backdrop of sloping fields. The skinny, rigid silhouette of the seemingly innocuous tree trunk just left of center uncannily rhymes with the vertical walls of the town's buildings, as if it were part of the architecture. Its crown of leaves is equally unsettling. The dark-green right half adheres to the roofline of the house behind it, while the left side becomes entangled in a web of light greens. At times, the leaves on that side almost merge with the fields

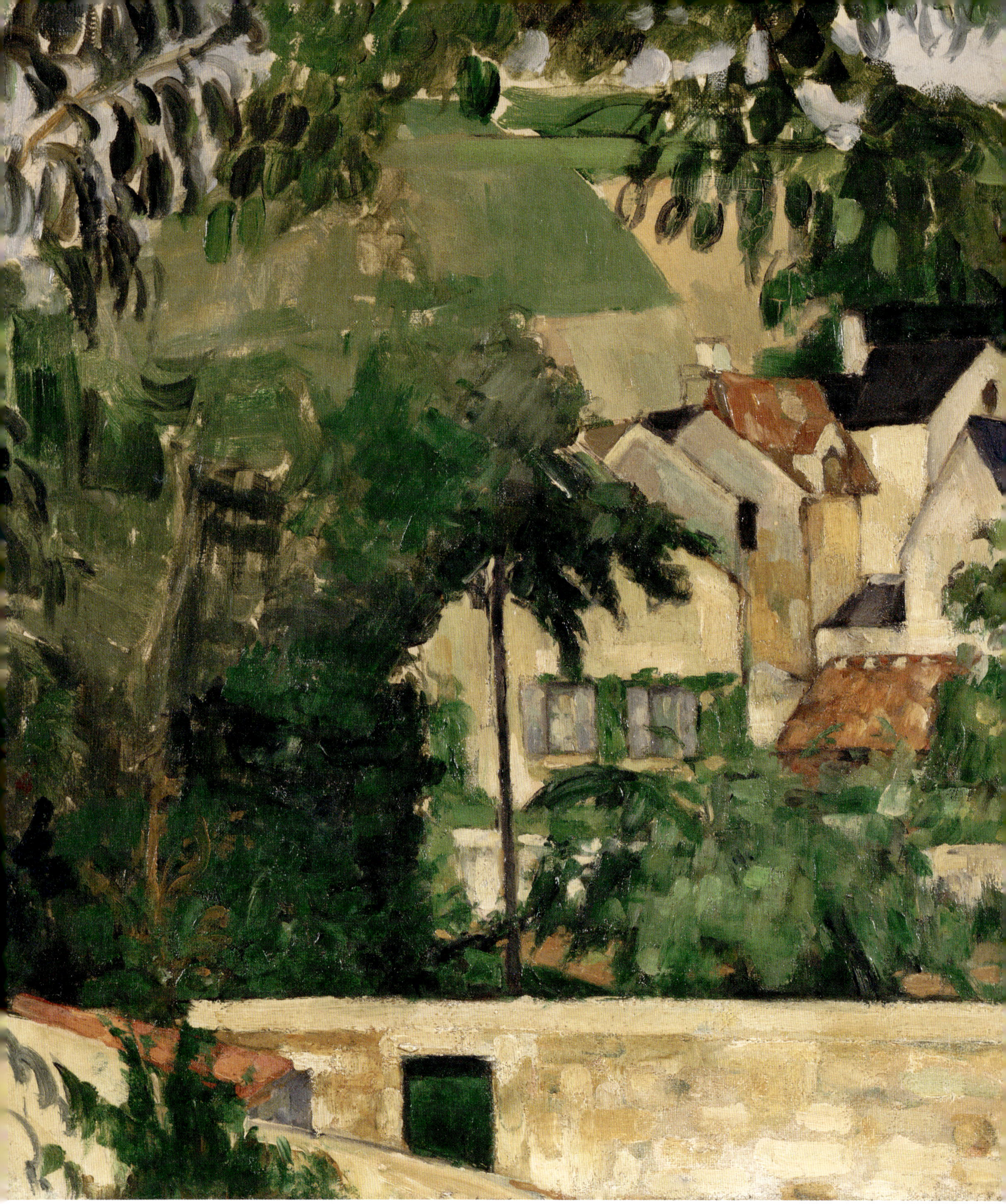

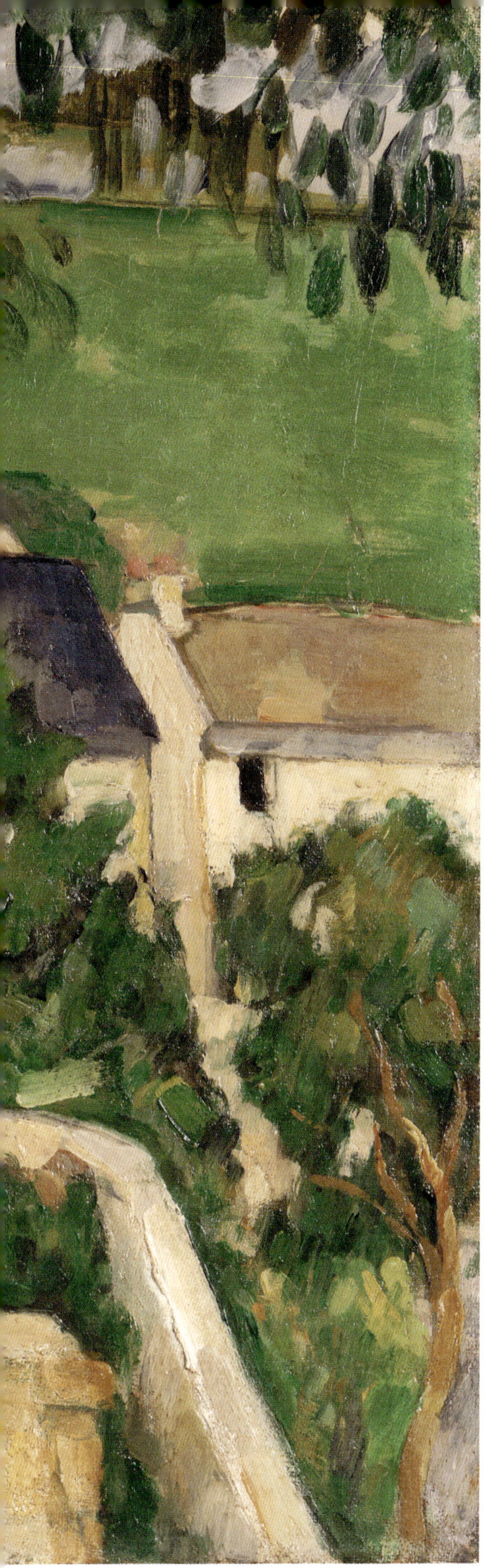

73 | Paul Cézanne, *Quartier Four, Auvers-sur-Oise* (also known as *Landscape, Auvers*), *ca.*1873. Oil on canvas, 46.4 × 55.2 cm. Philadelphia Museum of Art

in the distance; at other moments, they seem to belong to a curtain wall of textured brushstrokes. Making sense of this amorphous conglomeration of marks is difficult. The brushstrokes themselves are too large and too crude to serve as a reliable gauge of distance and scale. Practically *all* the leaves in the painting are oversized, as if they existed in a separate universe. This is just one small section of the painting; a description considering color, thickness, and perspective across the whole visual field could go on seemingly forever—which is exactly Cézanne's point.[7]

The redeployment of the palette knife in Cézanne and Pissarro's work of the 1870s did not simply resurrect Courbet's landscape painting (in either its analytic or immersive mode). The two artists were at this point too committed to luminous open-air painting to ever return to the dark, originary matrices of Courbet's Franc-comtois landscapes or the coequivalence of image and paint in the seascapes. Rather, the knife-painting of the two younger artists looks back to Cézanne's reinterpretation of Courbet's technique in works such as the portraits of Uncle Dominique (see figs. 64, 65, and 66), where the pictorial mark simultaneously constructs and destroys form. Cézanne does not go so far as to re-create his carved surfaces of the 1860s. But by violently throwing the Impressionist landscape into disarray, the Auvers and Pontoise painting of Cézanne and Pissarro performed a similar operation; it disfigured form in the act of trying to create it.

TACTILITY

Third Republic art criticism took note of the disturbing and invasive quality of knife-painting but now went beyond the common refrain linking it to the working class and manual labor. As Impressionist brushwork increasingly became linked with the registering of optical phenomena, the contrasting use of the palette knife came to symbolize the sense of touch. It is clear that the palette-knife technique was now understood in distinctly antioptical terms. For instance, in an 1878 monograph on Courbet published shortly after the artist's death, Camille Lemonnier pits the paintbrush as the instrument of the serious, conscientious mind against the palette knife as the simple, dumb tool of the artisan.[8] But onto this opposition was overlaid another equally fundamental difference between sight and touch. The brush, according to the critic, "vibrates, resonates, colors, softens, contributes to sensations," whereas the knife is "unconscious, irresponsible, mechanical" and "materializes all that it touches."[9] Lemonnier's denunciation of Courbet's palette knife reads almost as if it had been written in response to Cézanne. Certainly, the idea that the knife manifests irrationality, lack of conscious control, and psychological obsession pertains more to Cézanne's disruptive, destructive use of the instrument than it does to Courbet's more measured one. Indeed, when the critic complains that "there is no example of a beautiful head painted in knife," one imagines him railing against one of Cézanne's portraits of his uncle.[10]

The contrast between the Impressionist painting completed at Argenteuil and Cézanne's and Pissarro's contemporaneous knifed landscapes executed at Auvers and Pontoise heralded the binary opposition of vision to touch that would become the critical mainstream by the end of the decade. Jules Laforgue gave "optical" Impressionism perhaps its most succinct formulation in 1883, when he asserted that "the impressionist sees and renders nature as it is, that is to say uniquely with colored vibrations."[11] Laforgue maintained that, on the one hand, there was the world as perceived solely through the eye, and, on the other, the world as it came to be known through the sense of touch. To illustrate their relationship, Laforgue used the example of a primordial chaos of color, in which it had yet to be determined if, say, a spot of blue in the visual field was located on the horizon or at one's fingertips. In such a world, coming into physical contact with the blue spot would help determine its position in space. The longer it took to touch the visual point, the further away from one's body that point was. Over time, as tactile knowledge accumulated, spatial perception sharpened, and the world came to be known in its full depth.

Essentially, Laforgue's argument updated the Molyneux problem for the late nineteenth century: Impressionist painting came closest to what a blind man would see were he to miraculously gain sight.[12] For the critic, modern painting's objective was to re-create this original condition. To do so, painters had to avoid artificial conventions such as drawn outlines and studio light. Monet's achievement was to have registered the ex-blindman's view with the least amount of interpretation or tampering. Yet, for Cézanne and Pissarro, Laforgue's Impressionist was too quick to claim victory. The process of undoing pictorial falsehoods, their landscapes suggested, was more complicated, and more protracted than the critic thought. Laforgue hinted at this, in his celebration of the "natural eye" with a parenthetical aside about what he called the "refined eye": "Thus the natural eye (or a refined eye, for in order to function as such this organ *must shed tactile illusions* to become primitive again) forgets the dead language of tactile illusions [my emphasis]."[13] In Laforgue's system, tactility had a negative effect. In other words, our understanding of depth was based on false tactile illusions that hindered pure visual perception. Laforgue admitted that it was difficult to return to the "natural" or "primitive" optical state. It required effort. For some, the act of forgetting was sufficient, but, for most, a more active dismantling, a "shedding of the tactile illusions," was necessary.

The dichotomy that Laforgue sets up between two modes of knowledge—the visual and the tactile—thus helps us be more precise about what it means in painting for the artist's tool to "materialize all that it touches." It is not accurate to say that Cézanne and Pissarro are trying to depict the world as grasped by the sense of touch. This would assume that it is possible for the artist to re-create the experience of the first touch, just as the Impressionist eye works under the assumption that it is possible to re-create the experience of first sight. But to be visualized, tactile experience must eventually be translated in pictorial terms, meaning that some sort of coordination with visual experience is unavoidable, and therefore that the representation of pure tactility, strictly speaking, is unattainable. Instead, Cézanne and Pissarro analyze all the conventions for picturing depth—what was presented earlier in respect to Cézanne's Auvers landscape is a small sample—in order to try to "unlearn" them. Monet's defenders thought that by stripping spatial devices to their core, the artist could finally arrive at the unmediated registration of reality theorized by Laforgue. But his Argenteuil paintings still relied on the "tactile illusions" of linear perspective and bounded shape.

Cézanne and Pissarro, by contrast, are much more skeptical of the possibility of ever attaining the optical ideal. Their doubt culminates in landscapes in which so many habitual "tactile illusions" have been unpacked and interrogated that it is difficult to distinguish between what has already been broken down into primary impressions and what has begun to take shape from them. This is most evident in landscapes such as Pissarro's *The Climb, Rue de la Côte-du-Jalet, Pontoise* (fig. 74). Does the yellow "path" dominating the right-hand side appear vertical because Pissarro has stripped it of the "tactile illusion" of spatial recession, rendering it a golden haze? Or is a highly luminous, sun-lit portion of the visual field—perhaps one that was once as formless as the dense greenery brushing against it—coalescing, by means of a growing parallelism of stroke, into something that is about recognizable as a path? Or to take the opposite case—that is, the most resolved rather than the least resolved area of the canvas—is the group of buildings nestling in the top-left corner the last vestige of illusionism in an otherwise disintegrated visual field, an element destined to dissolve into the verdant surrounding area? Or has Pissarro already put his tactile knowledge to good use, to catalyze the transformation of light-blue and warm-colored patches at the upper

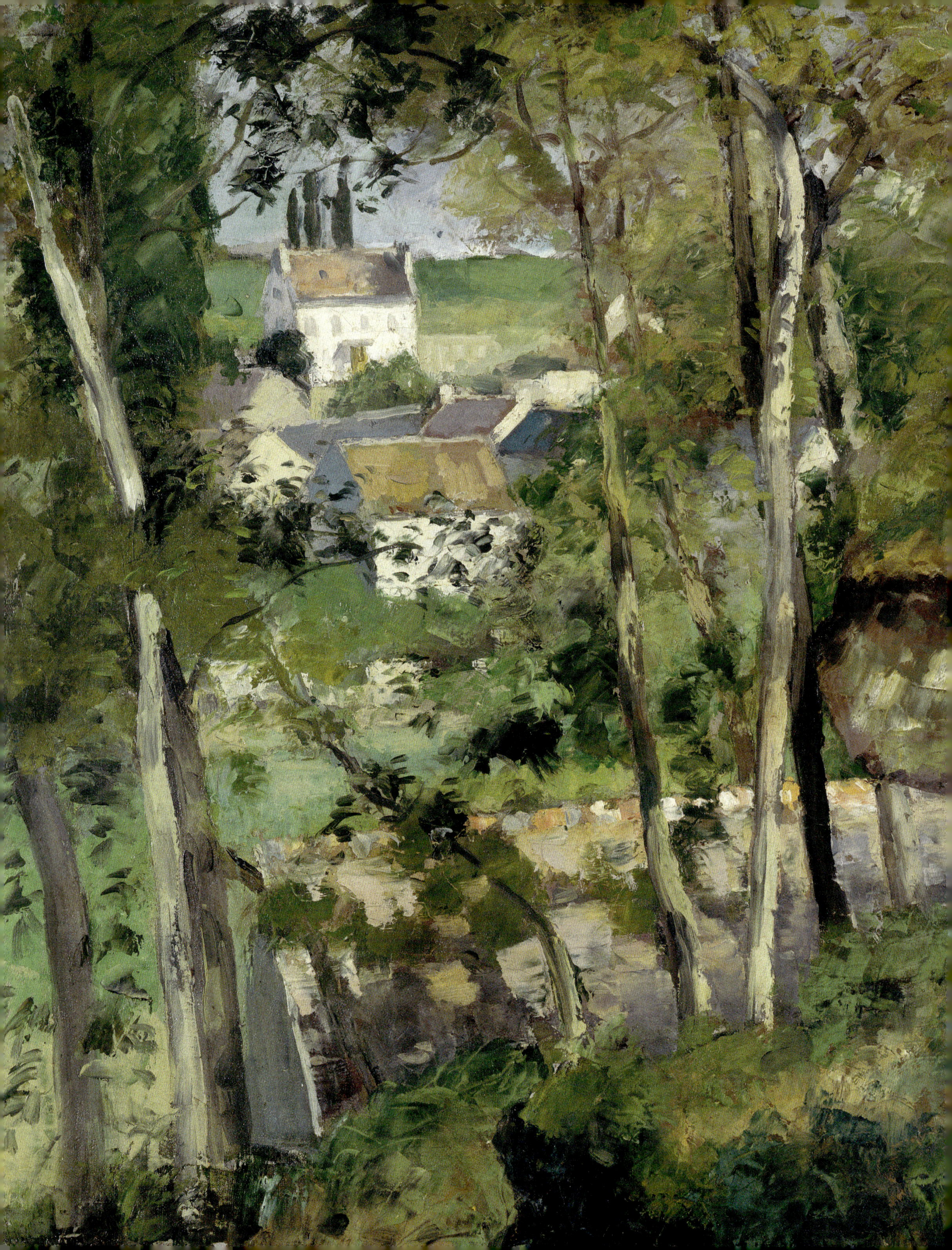

reaches of his optical sensorium into a minimally altered image of rooftops and distant sky? As old "tactile illusions" disintegrate and new, "purer" ones begin to take hold, the line between undoing and remaking becomes blurred.

Tactility in Cézanne's and Pissarro's 1870s landscapes is therefore less a sublimation of the sense of touch than a subversion of vision, mediated by the knifed or roughly brushed patch of paint. What the schism between Monet at Argenteuil and Pissarro and Cézanne in Pontoise and Auvers bequeathed to future painting, the kind undertaken later by Cézanne in Provence and by Pablo Picasso at Horta de Ebro in southern Spain, is a story for another day. But looking back, we can trace the origins of their anti-Impressionism all the way to Courbet's *The Stream of the Puits noir* (see fig. 1). In certain versions, the juncture at the center of the painting where rock wall, stream, and undergrowth collide is for a split second subject to a figure-ground reversal where a background element—the forest, a riverbank—suddenly appears to lie in front of the protruding rock face. The origin is momentarily no longer localizable as a point beyond perception, there in the depths of the landscape. Instead, in these moments the origin's location can be determined only in the act of trying to resolve the ambiguity by reading one side or the other as "background." For a brief period between 1872 and 1875, Pissarro and Cézanne take what in Courbet's landscapes is still only a fleeting condition—a constantly shifting nonoriginary origin—and install it as the true "reality" that modern painting must trace.

74 | Camille Pissarro, *The Climb, Rue de la Côte-du-Jalet, Pontoise*, 1875. Oil on canvas, 54 × 66.7 cm. Brooklyn Museum of Art, New York

ABBREVIATIONS

AD Archives départementales, Doubs, Besançon

AJ Archives départementales, Jura, Lons-le-Saunier

AN Archives nationales, Paris

B Bonniot, Roger, *Gustave Courbet en Saintonge, 1862–1863* (Paris: C. Klincksieck), 1973

BMB Bibliothèque municipal, Besançon

C Courbet, Gustave, *Letters of Gustave Courbet*, ed. and trans. Petra ten-Doesschate Chu (Chicago: University of Chicago Press), 1992

D Danchev, Alex (ed. and trans.), *The Letters of Paul Cézanne* (Los Angeles: The J. Paul Getty Museum), 2013

F Fernier, Robert, *La Vie et l'oeuvre de Gustave Courbet. Catalogue raisonné. Volume 1: 1819–1865. Peintures*, 2 vols. (Lausanne: Wildenstein Institute), 1977

FWN Feilchenfeldt, Walter, Jayne Warman, and David Nash, *The Paintings, Watercolors and Drawings of Paul Cézanne*, <http://www.cezannecatalogue.com> (accessed 16 September 2021)

GBA *Gazette des beaux-arts*

H Hugo, Victor, *Notre-Dame de Paris; Les Travailleurs de la mer* (Paris: Gallimard), 1975

M Michelet, Jules, *La Mer* (Paris: Hachette) [1861], ed. Jean Borie (Paris: Gallimard), 1983

P Courbet Papers, Bibliothèque nationale de France, Paris, BnF Yb3-1739

RL *Revue littéraire de la Franche-Comté*, eds. Charles Thuriet et al. (Besançon: d'Outhenin Chalandre fils, Jules Roblot), 1863–68

S *Le Salinois* (newspaper)

Z Zola, Émile, *Oeuvres complètes*, eds. Henri Mitterand and Françoise Juhel, 21 vols. (Paris: Nouveau monde), 2002–10

NOTES

INTRODUCTION

1 Scholarship on the sociopolitical dimensions of Courbet's early work began to achieve greater levels of nuance and historical grounding in the work of Meyer Schapiro and T. J. Clark: Meyer Schapiro, "Courbet and Popular Imagery: An Essay on Realism and Naïveté," in Meyer Schapiro, *Modern Art, 19th and 20th Centuries: Selected Papers* (New York: George Braziller), 1978, pp. 47–85; and T. J. Clark, *Image of the People: Gustave Courbet and the 1848 Revolution*, rev. edn (Berkeley and Los Angeles: University of California Press), 1999.

2 On the co-substantiality of image and matter in Courbet's work, see Anthea Callen, *The Work of Art: Plein Air Painting and Artistic Identity in Nineteenth-Century France* (London: Reaktion Books), 2014; James D. Herbert, *Brushstroke and Emergence: Courbet, Impressionism, Picasso* (Chicago: University of Chicago Press), 2015; and James H. Rubin, "Courbet in Love and Productive Disappointment," in *Gustave Courbet* (London: Matthiesen Gallery), 2016.

3 Herbert, *Brushstroke and Emergence*, p. 24. In contrast, the present study is concerned less with the subjectivity of painterly gesture and more with the historical context of Courbet's interest in the depiction of origins and substances.

4 Jules-Antoine Castagnary, "Fragments d'un livre sur Courbet," part 3, [GBA], December 1912, pp. 19–30, 21.

5 On the term's multiple meanings in period criticism, see Frédérique Desbuissons, "Courbet's Materialism," *Oxford Art Journal*, vol. 31, no. 2, June 2008, pp. 251–60. On its importance to Courbet and his milieu more generally, see James H. Rubin, "Courbet's Materialism and Positive Metaphysics," in Ulf Küster, *Gustave Courbet*, exh. cat., Fondation Beyeler, Reihen/Basle, 2014, pp. 60–69; James H. Rubin, *Realism and Social Vision in Courbet & Proudhon* (Princeton, N.J.: Princeton University Press), 1980; Mary Morton, "To Create a Living Art: Rethinking Courbet's Landscape Painting," in Mary Morton and Charlotte Eyerman, *Courbet and the Modern Landscape*, exh. cat., The J. Paul Getty Museum, Los Angeles, Museum of Fine Arts, Houston, and The Walters Art Museum, Baltimore, 2006–07; and Roger Bruyeron's postface to *Écrits, propos, lettres et témoignages* (Paris: Hermann), 2015.

6 Friedrich Lange, *Geschichte des Materialismus und Kritik seiner Bedeutung in der Gegenwart* (Iserlohn: J. Baedeker), 1866, quoted from the English translation, *The History of Materialism and Criticism of Its Present Importance*, with an introduction by Bertrand Russell, trans. Ernest Chester Thomas, 3rd edn, 3 vols., (New York: Harcourt, Brace), 1926, p. 22. Lange's ideas figured prominently in Pierre Larousse's *Grand Dictionnaire universel du XIXe siècle. Vol. 10* (Paris: Administration du Grand Dictionnaire Universel), 1873. On the impact of materialist thought on eighteenth-century painterly practice, see Ewa Lajer-Burcharth, *The Painter's Touch: Boucher, Chardin, Fragonard* (Princeton, N.J.: Princeton University Press), 2018.

7 Letter from Courbet to the young artists of Paris, 25 December 1861, in [C], p. 204.

8 Courbet to Proudhon, July – August 1863, in [C], p. 229.

9 Gustave Courbet, *Cahiers de philosophie*, ed. Roger Bruyeron (Paris: Hermann), 2011.

10 Charles Baudelaire, "Salon of 1846," in *Art in Paris 1845–1862: Reviews of Salons & Other Exhibitions*, trans. and ed. Jonathan Mayne (London: Phaidon), 1965, p. 47.

11 Letter from Buchon to Thuriet, 8 March 1864, [BMB], MS 1876. On the intellectual pursuits of the Franc-comtois intelligentsia, see Petra ten-Doesschate Chu, "It Took a Million Years to Paint that Picture," in *Courbet Reconsidered*, eds. Sarah Faunce and Linda Nochlin, exh. cat., Brooklyn Museum and Minneapolis Institute of Arts, 1988–89, pp. 55–66; Noël Barbe, "Le Laboratoire de l'artiste. Courbet et les sciences sociales," *Gustave Courbet et la Franche-Comté* (Paris: Somogy), 2000, pp. 69–77; and Noël Barbe, "Buchon, Claudet, Courbet. Un Trio politique?" in Noël Barbe and Hervé Touboul (eds.), *Courbet, peinture et politique* (Besançon: Sekoya), 2013, pp. 167–201.

12 Thuriet, unpublished preface to *Traduction du Saint Évangile de S. Matthieu* (London), 1864, [BMB], MS 1882.

13 The term, which refers to the vastly expanded time frame needed to write the history of slowly changing systems and structures, was introduced in Fernand Braudel, "Histoire et sciences sociales: La Longue Durée," *Annales: Économies, sociétés, civilisations*, vol. 13, October – December 1958, pp. 725–53, translated as "History and the Social Sciences: The *Longue Durée*," in Fernand Braudel, *On History*, trans. Sarah Matthews (Chicago: University of Chicago Press), 1980, pp. 25–54.

14 Courbet to Hugo, 11 November, 28 November, and 19 December 1864, in [C], pp. 246–47, 248–50, 253.

15 In addition to individual texts cited in subsequent footnotes, monographs with useful overviews of the landscapes include James H. Rubin, *Courbet* (London: Phaidon), 1997; Valérie Bajou, *Courbet* (Paris: Biro), 2003; Ségolène Le Men, *Courbet* (New York: Abbeville Press), 2008. Since the 1988 Brooklyn retrospective (Sarah Faunce, *Courbet Reconsidered*, exh. cat., Brooklyn Museum and Minneapolis Institute of Art, 1988–89), most exhibition catalogs have contained chapters on landscape: Laurence des Cars and Dominique de Font-Réaulx et al., *Gustave Courbet*, exh. cat., Grand Palais, Paris, Metropolitan Museum of Art, New York, and Musée Fabre, Montpellier, 2007–08; Klaus Herding and Max Hollein (eds.), *Courbet: A Dream of Modern Art*, exh. cat., Schirn Kunsthalle, Frankfurt am Main, 2010–11; Küster, *Gustave Courbet*. Exhibitions focused primarily on the landscapes include Morton and Eyerman, *Courbet and the Modern Landscape*; and Barbara Guidi, Maria Luisa Pacelli et al., *Courbet e la natura*, exh. cat., Palazzo dei Diamanti, Ferrara, 2018–19.

16 Schapiro, "Courbet and Popular Imagery," pp. 47–85, here p. 73.

17 Clark, *Image of the People*, pp. 132–33.

18 Ibid., p. 132.

19 Klaus Herding, "Equality and Authority in Courbet's Landscape Painting," in Klaus Herding, *Courbet: To Venture Independence*, trans. John William Gabriel (New Haven and London: Yale University Press), 1991, pp. 62–98. Herding revisits his argument in "The 'Other' Courbet," in Herding and Hollein (eds.), *Courbet*, pp. 10–18, and in an interview published in *Le Réalisme comme contradiction: Visions, conflits et résistances dans l'oeuvre de Courbet*, trans. Anne-Marie Green (Besançon: Sekoya), 2013, pp. 9–35.

20 Clement Greenberg, "Review of an Exhibition of Gustave Courbet," in *The Collected Essays and Criticism*, ed. John O'Brian (Chicago: University of Chicago Press), 1987, pp. 275–79, here p. 276. On Courbet's twentieth-century reception, see Charlotte Eyerman, "Courbet's Legacy in the Twentieth Century," in Morton and Eyerman, *Courbet and the Modern Landscape*, pp. 21–38; and Klaus Herding, "Courbet in Modernist and Contemporary Art," in Herding and Hollein (eds.), *Courbet*, pp. 84–96.

21 Champfleury, "Du Rôle important des paysagistes à notre époque," *Le Courrier artistique*, 15 February 1862, pp. 65–66, here p. 66.

22 Anne M. Wagner, "Courbet's Landscapes and Their Market," *Art History*, vol. 4, no. 4, December 1981, pp. 410–31. A series of studies by Petra ten-Doesschate Chu has further refined this approach: "Courbet et la commercialization de son oeuvre," in Jorg Zütter and Petra ten-Doesschate Chu et al., *Courbet: Artiste et promoteur de son oeuvre* (Paris: Flammarion), 1998, pp. 53–82; "Packaging and Marketing Nature," in *The Most Arrogant Man in France: Gustave Courbet and the Nineteenth-Century Media Culture* (Princeton, N.J.: Princeton University Press), 2007, pp. 138–69; and "Le 'Marketing' du Château de Chillon," in Laurence Madeline, *Gustave Courbet: Les Années suisses* (Paris: Éditions Artlys), 2014, pp. 186–201.

23 On Courbet's depoliticization, see, in addition to Wagner, Linda Nochlin, "The De-Politicization of Gustave Courbet: Transformation and Rehabilitation under the Third Republic," in *Courbet* (New York and London: Thames and Hudson), 2007, pp. 116–27; Jeannene M. Przyblyski, "Courbet, the Commune, and the Meanings of Still Life in 1871," *Art Journal*, vol. 55, no. 2, summer 1996, pp. 28–37; and Ting Chang, "Rewriting Courbet: Silvestre, Courbet, and the Bruyas Collection after the Paris Commune," *Oxford Art Journal*, vol. 21, no. 1, 1998, pp. 107–20.

24 Wagner, "Courbet's Landscapes and Their Market," p. 429.

25 Ibid., p. 428.

26 According to Daniel Halévy, his father, Ludovic Halévy, had heard Léon Gambetta refer to the painting by this title at a dinner in 1882, when Gambetta was describing an even earlier meeting between Courbet and Khalil Bey that was meant to have taken place between 1866 and 1867 (at which, however, he was not present). See Ludovic Halévy, *Trois Dîners avec Gambetta*, ed. and annotated by Daniel Halévy (Paris: Edition Grasset), 1929, pp. 86–88, cited in Thierry Savatier, *L'Origine du monde: Histoire d'un tableau de Gustave Courbet* (Paris: Bartillat), 2006, pp. 74–75. For recent appraisals of the painting and bibliography, see Antoinette Le Normand-Romain et al., *Cet Obscur objet de désirs: Autour de "L'Origine du monde,"* exh. cat., Musée d'Orsay, Paris, 2014.

27 On anthropomorphism in the landscapes, see Werner Hoffmann et al., "Courbets Wirklichkeiten," in *Courbet und Deutschland*, exh. cat., Hamburger Kunsthalle, Hamburg, and Städelschen Kunstinstitut, Frankfurt, 1978–79, pp. 608–10; Michael Fried, *Courbet's Realism* (Chicago: University of Chicago Press), 1990, pp. 209–14, 238–54; Neil Hertz, *The End of the Line: Essays on Psychoanalysis and the Sublime* (New York: Columbia University Press), 1985, pp. 210–11; and Dario Gamboni, "Des grains de beauté: Anthropomorphes bei Courbet," in *Psychische Energien bildender Kunst: Festschrift Klaus Herding*, ed. Henry Keazor (Cologne: DuMont), 2002, pp. 116–37.

28 On the representation of the female body in Courbet, see Beatrice Farwell, "Courbet's 'Baigneuses' and the Rhetorical Feminine Image," in *Woman as Sex Object: Studies in Erotic Art, 1730–1970*, eds. Thomas B. Hess and Linda Nochlin (London: Allen Lane), 1973, pp. 65–79; Dorothy M. Kosinski, "Gustave Courbet's *The Sleepers*: The Lesbian Image in Nineteenth-Century French Art and Literature," *Artibus et Historiae*, vol. 9, no. 18, 1988, pp. 187–99; Petra ten-Doesschate Chu, "Gustave Courbet's *Venus and Psyche*: Uneasy Nudity in Second-Empire France," *Art Journal*, vol. 51, no. 1, 1992, pp. 38–44; Chu, *The Most Arrogant Man in France*, pp. 114–37; Fried, *Courbet's Realism*, pp. 189–222; Maura Reilly, "Le Vice à la mode: Gustave Courbet and the Vogue for Lesbianism in Second Empire France" (PhD dissertation, New York University), 2000; Michèle Haddad, "Dreaming Nudes," in Herding and Hollein (eds.), *Courbet*, pp. 31–36; and Nicole R. Myers, "Courbet and the Realist Nude" (PhD dissertation, New York University), 2015.

29 Fried, *Courbet's Realism*, p. 108. On the corporealization of vision in Courbet, see Rubin, "Courbet in Love and Productive Disappointment." On temporality in Courbet and its relationship to later Realist painting, see Marnin Young, *Realism in the Age of Impressionism: Painting and the Politics of Time* (New Haven and London: Yale University Press), 2015, pp. 1–6, 205–13.

30 Useful technical studies include Bruno Mottin, "A Complex Genesis: Courbet in the Laboratory," in des Cars and Font-Réaulx et al., *Gustave Courbet*; Bruno Mottin, "From One Picture to Another: *Les Trois Baigneuses*," in Küster, *Gustave Courbet*, pp. 106–12; and Herbert Wilhelm Rott et al., *Courbet > Daubigny: Das Rätsel der "Schleuse im Tal von Optevoz"* (Munich: Hirmer), 2014.

31 Callen, *The Work of Art*; Matthias Krüger, *Das Relief der Farbe: Pastose Malerei in der französischen Kunstkritik 1850–1890* (Munich: Deutscher Kunstverlag), 2007; and Desbuissons, "Courbet's Materialism."

32 Scholarship that has worked to correct this includes Callen, *The Work of Art*; Krüger, *Das Relief der Farbe*; Klaus Herding, "Color and Worldview," in Herding, *Courbet: To Venture Independence*, pp. 111–34; and Herbert, *Brushstroke and Emergence*, pp. 8–38.

33 Nina Maria Athanassoglou-Kallmyer, *Cézanne and Provence: The Painter in His Culture* (Chicago: University of Chicago Press), 2003; Anne Byrd, "The Brush Stroke as Catastrophe: Gasquet's 'Cézanne' and the Paintings of Bibémus Quarry," *RACAR: Revue d'art canadienne / Canadian Art Review*, vol. 34, no. 1, 2009, pp. 41–52; and John Elderfield and Faya Causey et al., *Cézanne: The Rock and Quarry Paintings* (New Haven and London: Yale University Press), 2020.

34 T. J. Clark, "Phenomenality and Materiality in Cézanne," in Tom Cohen et al. (eds.), *Material Events: Paul de Man and the Afterlife of Theory* (Minneapolis: University of Minnesota Press), 2000, pp. 93–113; T. J. Clark, "Freud's Cézanne," in *Farewell to an Idea: Episodes from a History of Modernism* (New Haven and London: Yale University Press), 1999, pp. 139–67; Kathryn A. Tuma, "Cézanne, Lucretius, and the Late Nineteenth-Century Crisis in Science" (PhD dissertation, University of California, Berkeley), 2000; and Kathryn A. Tuma, "Cézanne and Lucretius at the Red Rock," *Representations*, vol. 78, no. 1, spring 2002, pp. 56–85.

CHAPTER 1

1 Michèle Hannoosh (ed.), *Eugène Delacroix, Journal*, 2 vols. (Paris: José Corti), 2009, vol. 2, p. 929.

2 On Baudry, see Yvonne Melia-Sevrain, *Étienne Baudry: Une Vie charentaise: Châtelain, dandy et écrivain militant* (Saintes: Croît vif), 2010.

3 *Explication des ouvrages de peinture et de sculpture exposés dans les salles de la Mairie [de Saintes] au profit des pauvres. 160 Tableaux signés Corot, Courbet, Auguin, Pradelles* (Saintes: Alexandre Hus), 1863.

4 On the Saintonge trip in general, see [B]; and Gaby Scaon and Jean-Roger Soubiran, *Autour de Courbet en Saintonge*, exh. cat., Musée de l'Échivinage, Saintes, 2007. A contemporary account is Jules-Antoine Castagnary, "Chronique d'art et causerie [Saintes en Saintonge]," *Courrier du Dimanche*, 13 July 1862, pp. 5–6, reprinted in *Libres Propos* (Paris: A. Lacroix, Verboeckhoven et Cie), 1864, pp. 291–301.

5 Champfleury, "Du Rôle important des paysagistes à notre époque," p. 66. Max Buchon refers to this text in the preface to Max Buchon, *Poésies Franc-comtoises, tableaux domestiques et champêtres* (Paris: Michel Lévy), 1862, but he will ultimately come to different conclusions about the provincial landscape, as argued in Chapter 2.

6 According to Francis Wey, Courbet met Corot in the summer of 1849 while painting around Louveciennes and Marly; Francis Wey, *Nôtre Maître-peintre Gustave Courbet*, ed. Fréderique Desbuissons (La Rochelle: Rumeur des âges), 2007, p. 28. An early study on the two artists is Julius Meier-Graefe, *Corot und Courbet: Ein Beitrag zur Entwicklungsgeschichte der modernen Malerei* (Leipzig: Insel), 1905. More recent studies include Gaston Delestre, "Courbet et Corot à Saintes," *Les Amis de Gustave Courbet Bulletin*, no. 27, June 1961, pp. 4–5; and John Richardson, "Introduction," in *Corot and Courbet* (London: David Carritt), 1979, pp. 5–11. On Meier-Grafe's writing on Corot and Courbet in particular, see Kenworth Moffett, *Meier-Graefe as Art Critic* (Munich: Prestel), 1973, pp. 87–88.

7 A comparison with an earlier 1847 drawing by Léo Druyn (reproduced in Scaon and Soubiran, *Autour de Courbet en Saintonge*, p. 19) shows that Corot and Courbet were faithful to the local topography. Théodore Duret, *Courbet* (Paris: Bernheim-Jeune), 1918, pp. 59–61

8 Duret, *Courbet*, p. 61.

9 Paul Mantz, "Gustave Courbet," part 1, [GBA], vol. 17, 1878, pp. 514–27, 525.

10 See Anthea Callen's analyses of Corot and Courbet in *The Art of Impressionism: Painting Technique and the Making of Modernity* (New Haven and London: Yale University Press), 2000, p. 125. Analyses of Corot's technique include Anne Roquebert, "Quelques observations sur la technique de Corot," in Chiara Stefani et al. (eds.), *Corot, un artiste et son temps* (Paris: Klincksieck), 1996, pp. 73–97; Richard Shiff, "Natural, Personal, Pictorial: Corot and the Painter's Mark," in Andreas Burmester, Christoph Heilmann, and Michael F. Zimmermann (eds.), *Barbizon: Malerei der Natur, Natur der Malerei* (Munich: Klinkhardt & Biermann), 1999, pp. 120–38; and Sarah Herring, "Six Paintings by Corot: Methods, Materials and Sources," *National Gallery Technical Bulletin* (London: National Gallery), vol. 30, 2009, pp. 86–111.

11 On the identification of these figures, see Scaon and Soubiran, *Autour de Courbet en Saintonge*, pp. 85–86.

12 Auguin to Castagnary, January 1863, [P], Box 1. Auguin would later tell Courbet that the latter's work at the Salon of 1870 brought back fond memories of the Saintonge period. Letter from Auguin to Courbet, 13 May 1870, [P], Box 1.

13 Admittedly, at over a meter tall, Pradelles's canvas has different demands, most notably that surface texture, to be visible from afar, has to be overly emphasized. Although the painting was large, it was not huge and other artists, including Courbet himself, would be much more adept at managing size.

14 On the Saintes exhibition, see [B], pp. 209–48; and Scaon and Soubiran, *Autour de Courbet en Saintonge*, pp. 91–112.

15 Victor Gruet, *Coup d'oeil sur l'exposition de peinture de Saintes* (Bordeaux: Gounouilhou), 1863, p. 33, quoted in Cécile Le Bihan, "Hippolyte Pradelles, sur le motif," in Scaon and Soubiran, *Autour de Courbet en Saintonge*, pp. 76–89, 86.

16 Pierre Conil, *Courrier des deux Charentes*, 1 February 1863, p. 3, cited in [B], p. 223.

17 It is as if Courbet were taking seriously some remarks attributed to his father: "What would I do in your place? I would take a little green and put it there, on this bunch of hazel trees. It would be magnificent, you hear me. Just take some green, I'm telling you, put it there and there, on the trees." Émile Gros-Kost, *Courbet, souvenirs intimes* (Paris: Derveaux) [1880] (Paris: Ides et Calendes), 1994, p. 43.

18 Lawrence Gowing, "Confidence and Conscience in Two Centuries of Art," *Art News Annual*, vol. 30, 1965, reprinted in Lawrence Gowing, *Selected Writings on Art*, ed. Sarah Whitfield (London: Ridinghouse),

2015, pp. 203–14, here p. 206. Also useful is Gowing's introduction to *Painting from Nature: The Tradition of Open-Air Oil Sketching from the 17th to 19th Centuries*, exh. cat., Fitzwilliam Museum, Cambridge, and Royal Academy of Arts, London, 1980–81, pp. 3–9.

19 Some nineteenth-century accounts make note of Courbet's use of studio implements other than the brush and palette knife. On his palette, see Édouard Ordinaire, "Causerie. Sur la peinture et la palette de peintre Courbet," *L'Étudiant*, 29 June 1867, p. 2; on the use of the rag, see Alexandre Schanne, *Souvenirs de Schaunard* (Paris: G. Charpentier et Cie), 1886, p. 287; on the use of the sponge to "revive" his canvases, see Castagnary as quoted by Pierre Courthion, *Courbet: Raconté par lui-même et par ses amis. Sa Vie et ses oeuvres* (Geneva: P. Cailler), vol. 1, 1948, p. 145. The full range of tools and materials available to the nineteenth-century artist is addressed in a series of studies by Anthea Callen: *Techniques of the Impressionists* (Secaucus, N.J.: Chartwell Books), 1982; *The Art of Impressionism*; *The Work of Art*.

20 Conil, *Courrier des deux Charentes*, 19 February 1863, p. 4, cited in Bonniot, [B], p. 231.

21 Thanks to Frédéric Achille at the Muséum National d'Histoire Naturelle in Paris for help with identifying the flowers.

22 *Stock Album* 1, no. 4, 1870, p. 3. An earlier issue of the same journal lists Courbet, along with Manet and Monet, as painters of the "knife, brush, broom, and other devices." On at least two occasions, André Gill depicted Courbet holding a trowel and palette but no brushes; see *Le Petit Figaro*, 14 June 1868 and *Nouveau Panthéon charivarique*, no. 18, both reprinted in Charles Léger, *Courbet selon les caricatures et les images* (Paris: P. Rosenberg), 1920, pp. 78, 83. Gill enjoyed depicting the artist; in a third caricature from *L'Éclipse*, 2 July 1870, the painter wields the full complement – brushes, knives, palette (also reprinted in Léger, *Courbet selon les caricatures et les images*, p. 87). On the association of Courbet's technique with bodily excess, see Desbuissons, "Courbet's Materialism."

23 Krüger, *Das Relief der Farbe.*

24 Castagnary, "Fragments d'un livre sur Courbet," pp. 19–30, 29.

25 Callen, *The Work of Art*; Krüger, *Das Relief der Farbe*; David Bomford et al., *Impressionism: Art in the Making* (London: National Gallery), 1990; Bernard Dunstan, *Painting Methods of the Impressionists* (New York: Watson-Guptill), 1983; Christopher Campbell, "Pissarro and the Palette Knife: Two Pictures from 1867," *Apollo*, vol. 136, November 1992, pp. 311–14.

26 "Le tableau, en effet, était si empâté que les vessies étaient à peine écrasées sur la toile. Oh, Monsieur, s'écria-t-il, oh, Monsieur! Mais c'est crêpi la pââte!" Jean Gigoux, *Revue Franc-comtoise*, October 1884, cited in Courthion, *Courbet. Raconté par lui-même*, vol. 1, p. 86.

27 "Sa peinture tantôt rude, empâtée, recrépie comme une muraille, tantôt délicate, fine, transparente est une alchimie; tantôt les couleurs qu'il applique forment masse, tantôt au contraire elles sont disposées comme des cristaux irréguliers." Conil, *Courrier des deux Charentes*, cited in [B], p. 233.

28 "Il manie [le couteau à palette] avec une adresse incomparable et en tire des effets surprenants; le ton ainsi posé plat acquiert une transparence et une intensité sans égale.... Courbet peint en plaine pâte, mais sans scories et sans aspérités; ses tableaux, où la couleur fait corps avec la toile, ont le poli de la glace, ils ont le brilliant de l'émail, ils en ont la solidité." Castagnary, "Fragments d'un livre sur Courbet," p. 29.

29 "Le couteau à palette, Goya s'en servait.... Le ton était posé sans aucune préoccupation de bavure et ses saillies offraient l'avantage de donner à la toile quelque chose de plus vibrant. Il arrive chez Courbet que certaines surfaces trop lisses s'agatisent et donnent la sensation d'une vitrification." [P], Box 5; also cited in Courthion, *Courbet. Raconté par lui-même*, vol. 2, p. 284.

30 On the critical comparison of Courbet's painting to agate and other minerals, see Matthias Krüger, "Gespachtelter Zufall: Gustave Courbet und dei Messermalerei," in *Werkzeuge und Instrumente*, eds. Philippe Cordez and Matthias Krüger (Berlin: Akademie), 2012, pp. 116–17. Moreover, as Krüger kindly pointed out to the author, agate has also long been associated with images made by chance.

31 "Il fait grand usage du couteau qui dépose la couleur sur la toile avec une franchise éclatante et brutale, tandis que les poils du pinceau creusent de petits sillons où la lumière vient s'émousser et s'éteindre, comme dans le tissu du velours." Théophile Silvestre, *Histoires des artistes vivants: Études d'après nature* (Paris: Blanchard), 1856, p. 270.

32 Émile Zola speaks in his notes about Courbet's use of knife followed by brush: "When one has sketched roughly with the *brosse* or *pinceau*, one goes over with the *blaireau* to wrap up, according to the delicateness of the work. Thus, Courbet painted with knife, then with the *blaireau*." Zola, *Carnets d'enquêtes: Une Ethnographie inédite de la France*, ed. Henri Mitterand (Paris: Plon), 1986, p. 251.

33 This helps explain why Courbet tends to avoid long sweeping gestures in the landscapes. Abbreviated, concrete deposits make it easier to maintain a consistent, level impasto. The longer the stroke, the thinner and drier the paint, the more tired the hand, and thus the more likely the appearance of tell-tale accidents of the tool. On the aleatory quality of the artist's gestures, see Krüger, "Gespachtelter Zufall," pp. 109–27; Herbert, *Brushstroke and Emergence*; Dario Gamboni, *Potential Images: Ambiguity and Indeterminacy in Modern Art* (London: Reaktion Books), 2002.

34 "Paul Meyerheim: Adolph von Menzel Erinnerungen," in *Exzellenz lassen bitten. Erinnerungen an Adoph Menzel*, ed. Gisold Lammel (Leipzig: Reclam-Verlag), 1992, pp. 196–98, cited by Ulf Küster, *Gustave Courbet* (Ostfildern: Hatje Cantz), 2014, p. 73.

35 Walter Sickert, "French Painters of the Nineteenth Century at the Lefèvre Galleries," in Walter Sickert, *Walter Sickert: The Complete Writings on Art*, ed. Anna Gruetzner Robins (Oxford and New York: Oxford University Press), 2000, p. 462.

36 Ibid.

37 Théophile Thoré, "Salon de 1861," in *Salons de W. Bürger 1861–68*, 2 vols. (Paris: J. Renouard), 1870, vol. 1, p. 50; Alfred Sensier, *Souvenirs sur Th. Rousseau* (Paris: Leon Techener), 1872, pp. 257–58. More recent treatments include Michel Schulman and Alexandra R. Murphy, *Théodore Rousseau: The Language of Nature*, exh. cat., Salander-O'Reilly Galleries, New York, 2002, pp. 70–72; Simon Kelly, "The Mystery of the Forest: Paintings of Fontainebleau at the Salon," in Kimberly Jones et al., *In the Forest of Fontainebleau: Painters and Photographers from Corot to Monet*, exh. cat., National Gallery of Art, Washington, D.C., 2008, pp. 142–51, esp. 147–48; Amy Kurlander and Simon Kelly, *The Untamed Landscape: Théodore Rousseau and the Path to Barbizon*, exh. cat., The Morgan Library & Museum, New York, 2014–15; Scott Allan and Édouard Kopp, *Unruly Nature: The Landscapes of Théodore Rousseau*, exh. cat., The J. Paul Getty Museum, Los Angeles, and Ny Carlsberg Glyptotek, Copenhagen, 2016–17; and Simon Kelly, *Théodore Rousseau and the Rise of the Modern Art Market: An Avant-Garde Landscape Painter in Nineteenth-Century France* (New York and London: Bloomsbury), 2021. On *The Rock Oak* in particular, see Simon Kelly's entry (no. 40) in Simon Kelly and April M. Watson, *Impressionist France: Visions of Nation from Le Gray to Monet* (New Haven and London: Yale University Press), 2013, pp. 148–50.

38 Robert L. Herbert, *Barbizon Revisited: Essay and Catalogue*, exh. cat., Museum of Fine Arts, Boston, California Palace of the Legion of Honor, San Francisco, Toledo Museum of Art, Ohio, and The Cleveland Museum of Art, Ohio, 1962–63, p. 63.

39 The caricature "Mosaïque" by Galletti in *Album caricatural* (Paris), 1861, p. 45, and a Salon review by Olivier Merson comparing Rousseau's paint handling to "a tapestry with tiny stitches," are both discussed in Kelly, "'An Artist Focused on His Research': Théodore Rousseau and the Marketing of His Oil Sketches and Drawings," in Kurlander and Kelly, *The Untamed Landscape*, p. 148, and Édouard Kopp, "Facing Criticism: Rousseau and the Salon," in Allan and Kopp, *Unruly Nature*, pp. 45–57, 54–55.

40 An exception to the rule is Courbet's *Gust of Wind* (ca.1865) in The Museum of Fine Arts, Houston, a highly Romanticized, Rousseau-esque landscape that, according to Alexandra Murphy, was originally part of a larger decorative cycle depicting the four seasons, a hypothesis that, if true, would explain its outlier status in the artist's oeuvre. Murphy in Christie's, New York, 27 May 1992, lot essay (no. 9), *Barbizon, Realist and French Landscape Painting* (New York), 1996.

41 On Rousseau's youth in Franche-Comté, see Sensier, *Souvenirs sur Th. Rousseau*, pp. 15–16. On later trips, pp. 72–74, 255–56, 266, 275.

42 Heléne Toussaint, from the Musée du Louvre object file. For a discussion of the ambiguous status of drawing in *Source of the Lison* (and on drawing in Rousseau's work in general), see Scott Allan, "'A Method Matters Little,'" in Allan and Kopp, *Unruly Nature*, pp. 23–43, 34.

43 As Alfred Sensier suggests in entry no. 8, "Les Sources du Lizon," in Charles Amand-Durand, *Études et croquis de Théodore Rousseau* (Paris: Goupil), 1876, n.p.

44 Herbert, *Barbizon Revisited*, p. 66. For other instances of Rousseau's drawn substructures, usually in ébauched mid-tones, see Sensier, *Souvenirs sur Th. Rousseau*, p. 295; Greg M. Thomas, "The Working Methods of Théodore Rousseau," in Burmester, Heilmann, and Zimmermann (eds.), *Barbizon*, pp. 139–52; and Allan, "'A Method Matters Little,'" pp. 23–43.

45 The difference was not just a formal one; Rousseau, according to Sensier, found the Lison as worthy of representation as the rivers of ancient Greece, a classicizing sentiment completely at odds with Courbet's version. See Sensier, "Les Sources du Lizon." I thank Simon Kelly for pointing me to this reference.

46 "Cela vous étonne que ma toile soit noire! nous disait-il. La nature sans le soleil est noire et obscure; je fais comme la lumière, j'éclaire les points saillants, et le tableau est fait. Et il prenait avec son couteau, dans une boîte où étaient des verres remplis de couleur, du blanc, du jaune, du rouge, du bleu. Il en faisait un mélange sur sa palette; puis, avec son couteau, il l'étendait sur la toile et la râclait d'un coup ferme et sur.... Encore quelques arbres par ici, un peu d'herbe verte sur le premier plan et nous aurons bientôt fini! disait-il. Et toujours son couteau courait sur la toile. A quatre heures, le tableau était terminé, et l'on y sentait la main du maître et son souffle puissant. Nous étions stupéfaits de cette rapidité d'exécution. A peine deux heures de travail pour couvrir une toile d'un mètre!" Max Claudet, *Souvenirs* (Paris: Dubuisson), 1878, p. 10.

47 On the complicated relations between Courbet and Proudhon, see Alan Bowness, "Courbet's Proudhon," *The Burlington Magazine*, vol. 120, no. 900, March 1978, pp. 123–30; Rubin, *Realism and Social Vision in Courbet and Proudhon*; Klaus Herding, "Proudhon's *Carnets intimes* and Courbet's *Portrait of Proudhon*," in Herding, *Courbet: To Venture Independence*, pp. 99–110, and "Proudhon, Courbet, Zola: Un Étrange débat," in *Proudhon, anarchisme, art, et société: Actes du colloque de la Société P.-J. Proudhon* (Paris: Société P.-J. Proudhon), 2000, pp. 15–49; Paul B. Crapo, "Disjuncture on the Left: Proudhon, Courbet and the Antwerp Congress of 1861," *Art History*, vol. 14, no. 1, March 1991, pp. 67–91. See also Herding's review of Rubin's book, *Art Bulletin*, vol. 64, no. 3, 1984, pp. 533–35, and his introduction to the German edition of Proudhon's text, *Von den Grundlagen und der sozialen Bestimmung der Kunst*, introduced and annotated by Herding (Berlin: Spiess), 1988, pp. 13–70.

48 Courbet to Castagnary, January 1864, in [C], pp. 235–37. Max Buchon published the letter in his new literary journal and added that it had been circulated to editors in Paris. Buchon, "Varietés," [RL], vol. 1, pp. 294–308, 300–302.

49 [P], Box 4.

CHAPTER 2

1 Castagnary, "Fragments d'un livre sur Courbet," pp. 19–30, 20–21.

2 Monteil's article recounting his conversation with Courbet in 1867 is quoted (without full citation) in Georges Riat, *Gustave Courbet, peintre* (Paris: H. Floury), 1906, p. 256.

3 This chapter's discussion of Courbet's interaction with other fields is greatly indebted to the pioneering article Chu, "It Took a Million Years to Paint that Picture," pp. 55–66.

4 Charles Nodier, Justin Taylor, and Alphonse de Cailleux, *Voyages pittoresques et romantiques dans l'ancienne France (Franche-Comté)* (Paris: J. Didot l'Aîné), 1825, p. 163.

5 Max Buchon, "La Loue," *Recueil des poésies* (Arbois: Javel), 1844. Buchon inserted additional verses (including ones about Courbet's most recent painting) in the revised edition, *Poésies franc-comtoises, tableaux domestiques et champêtres* (Paris: Michel Lévy), 1862. For documentation regarding water rights, see [AD] 7S77 (Ornans).

6 Courbet to Luquet, July or August 1864, in [C], p. 243.

7 Lorenz Eitner, "La Grotte de la Loue," in *French Paintings of the Nineteenth Century: Part I: Before Impressionism* (Washington, D.C.: National Gallery of Art), 2000, pp. 118–26.

8 Fried, *Courbet's Realism*, p. 212.

9 General Director of Public Safety to the Minister of Justice, 25 April 1856, [AN] BB/30/470. On the terms of Buchon's return, see Marcel Vogne, *La Presse périodique en Franche-Comté: Des Origines à 1870*, 7 vols. (Vanves: M. Vogne), 1977, vol. 3, p. 311.

10 General Director of Public Safety to the Minister of Justice, 28 April 1856, [AN] BB/30/470.

11 Buchon, *Poésies franc-comtoises; Noëls et chants populaires de la Franche-Comté* (Salins: Billet and Duvernois), 1863; *Poésies allémaniques de J. P. Hebel* (Salins: Billet and Duvernois), 1864; *Salins-les-Bains, ses eaux minérales et ses environs* (Lons-Le-Saunier: de Gauthier frères), 1862; [S]; [RL].

12 Courbet to his father, 28 July 1863, in [C], p. 227.

13 Like Courbet, Buchon attended the Petit Séminaire of Ornans (from 1830 to 1833). The literature on the Courbet–Buchon relationship concentrates mainly on the years from 1839 to 1856, roughly the period between their first collaborative publication, Buchon, *Essais poétiques* (Besançon: Sainte-Agathe), 1839, with illustrations by Courbet, and the writer's return from exile. See Jules Troubat, *Une Amitié à la d'Arthez. Champfleury, Courbet, Max Buchon, suivi d'une conférence sur Sainte-Beuve* (Paris: Lucien Duc), 1900; Buchon, *Poésies franc-comtoises. Poésies de Hebel. Notice par Champfleury* (Paris: Sandoz and Fischbacher), 1877, pp. i–xvi; Hugo Frey, *Max Buchon et son oeuvre* (Besançon: Impr. De l'Est), 1940; T. J. Clark, "A Bourgeois Dance of Death: Max Buchon on Courbet I," *The Burlington Magazine*, vol. 111, no. 793, April 1969, pp. 208–13, and "A Bourgeois Dance of Death: Max Buchon on Courbet II," *The Burlington Magazine*, vol. 111, no. 794, May 1969, pp. 286–90; Buchon, *Scènes de la vie comtoise*, ed. Michel Vernus (Besançon: Presses du Belvédère), 2004; and Buchon, *Le réalisme. Discussions esthétiques* (La Rochelle: Rumeur des Âges), 2007. Studies of Buchon's oeuvre from 1860 tend to come from outside the field of art history: see Vogne, *La Presse périodique*, vol. 3, pp. 306–15; and Barbe, "Buchon, Claudet, Courbet. Un trio politique?"

14 Buchon to Thuriet, 8 March 1864, [BMB] MS 1876. The songbook in question is almost certainly *Noëls en patois de Besançon, imprimés pour la première fois en 1758* (Dôle: J. B. Tonnet), n.d., as the publisher and date of the unnamed rare songbook match those of another one that Thuriet on another occasion recalled belonging to Courbet's sisters (Thuriet to [Lucien Napoleon], 30 January 1876, [BMB] MS 1876). On Courbet and popular song, see Charles Léger, "Les Chansons de Courbet," *Arts*, 24 September 1947; James H. Rubin, "Courbet, Wagner and Popular Song," in Herding and Hollein (eds.), *Courbet*, pp. 52–57; and James H. Rubin, "Courbet, Wagner et Proudhon: Peinture, musique et utopie, ou Courbet et la chanson populaire," in Barbe and Touboul (eds.), *Courbet, peinture et politique*, pp. 103–17.

15 Champfleury included two Franc-comtois songs brought to his attention by Buchon and Courbet's sisters; Champfleury, *Chansons populaires des provinces de France* (Paris: Bourdilliat), 1860, pp. 81–88. On nineteenth-century attitudes to patois, see Eugen Weber, "A Wealth of Tongues," in *Peasants into Frenchmen: The Modernization of Rural France 1870–1914* (Stanford, Calif.: Stanford University Press), 1976, pp. 67–94.

16 Buchon, *Noëls et chants populaires*, p. 14. Buchon is distilling a much longer argument from Abbé Dartois, "Importance de l'étude des patois en général, coup d'oeil spécial sur ceux de la Franche-Comté," in *Mémoires et procès-verbaux de l'Académie de Besançon* (Besançon: de Sainte-Agathe Ainé), 1849, pp. 118–22.

17 Buchon, *Noëls et chants populaires*, p. 8. On the difficulties of such a project, see Buchon, "Chants populaires," [RL] 1, no. 1, 1 November 1863, pp. 14–41, 19–21.

18 Dartois, a professor in the seminary of Ornans before becoming canon and then general vicar of Besançon, mentions such a game in "Importance de l'étude des patois," p. 123.

19 On the Alesia debate, see Olivier Buchsenschutz and Alain Schnapp, "Alésia," in *Les Lieux de mémoire*, vol. 3 (Paris: Gallimard), 1997, pp. 4103–40; and Noël Barbe, "Localiser Alésia. Récit d'une clôture," *Les Nouvelles de l'archéologie*, 2003, pp. 8–11.

20 The archeologist Jules Quicherat, later director of the École des Chartres, was the most influential proponent of Alaise as the site of ancient Alesia; see "Découverte d'Alésia des commentaires de César," *Athenaeum français*, 10 May 1856, pp. 384–86; and *L'Alésia de César rendue à la Franche-Comté* (Paris: L. Hachette), 1857; *Conclusion pour Alaise, dans la question d'Alésia* (Paris: Hachette), 1858, pp. 8–9, 54.

21 On Toubin, see Jacques Bourquin, *Galerie des linguistes franc-comtois* (Besançon: Presses universitaires comtoises), 2003, pp. 203–06. In his youth, Toubin had collaborated with Baudelaire and Champfleury on the short-lived 1848 broadside *Salut publique*, for which Courbet had designed a frontispiece. Toubin's memoirs were partially published in Charles Dornier, "Un Témoin de la Bohème littéraire avec Champfleury, Baudelaire, Murger et Courbet," *La Revue de France*, vol. 5, March 1925, pp. 68–89; and "La Bohème littéraire et la Révolution de 1848," *La Revue de France*, vol. 20, October 1926, pp. 740–52. The unpublished portion is in the Fonds Toubin de Salins, [AJ] 142 J 5.

22 Charles Toubin, "Alésia. Alaise Séquane. Alise en Auxois," *Mémoires de la Société d'Émulation du Doubs ser. 3, vol. 2, 1857* (Besançon: Imp. de Dodivers, 1858), pp. 57–103.

23 Alphonse Delacroix, "Alésia. Découverte d'Alésia," *Mémoires de la Société d'Émulation du Doubs*, series 2, vol. 7 (Besançon: Imp.

D'Outhenin-Chalandre Fils), 1855, pp. 113–60. On Delacroix's pioneering effort as "a patois narrative" of the event, see Auguste Castan, "Question d'Alésia. Jules Quicherat Défenseur d'Alaise" in Jules Quicherat, *Mélanges d'archéologie et d'histoire. Antiquités celtiques, romaines et gallo-romaines* (Paris: Alphonse Picard, 1885), p. 470. Toubin refers to the Gour de Conche's Latin etymology in a scene of his short story, "Paysan d'Alaise," *Revue des deux mondes*, 15 November 1861, pp. 371–404.

24 On Courbet's and other artists' responses to the Alesia question, see Linda Nochlin, "Courbet's *Oak at Flagey*: A Landscape Motif and Its Meanings," unpublished lecture, 1978. Later edited versions include "Le Chêne de Flagey de Courbet: Un Motif de paysage et sa signification," in *48/14*, no. 1, 1989, pp. 15–25; and "Courbet and His Territory: How Landscape Means," in *Courbet* (New York and London: Thames and Hudson), 2007, pp. 186–206.

25 In 1861, Napoleon III sent a Commission de la topographie de la Gaule to Alise-Sainte-Reine in order accelerate preparations for his own multi-volume biography of Julius Caesar, only two volumes of which were ever completed. Its publication effectively ended the debate in favor of Alise. *Histoire de Jules César*, 2 vols. (Paris: Plon), 1865–66.

26 [F], no. 419.

27 Buchon, "Lettre salinoise," [S], 11 December 1864. Toubin also wrote for the newspaper, see, for instance, [S], 24 April 1864. On the publication's history, see Vogne, *La Presse périodique*, vol. 3, pp. 306–15, and vol. 4, pp. 282–98.

28 Courbet to Castagnary, in [C], p. 252.

29 Toubin later sent Castagnary some of his Alesia material as an apology for some unpleasantness on his part during the tour of Alaise. See Toubin to Castagnary, 3 February 1865, [P], Box 1.

30 [P], Box 4. On Castagnary as an art critic, see Henri Dorra, "Entre romantisme et naturalisme: Castagnary et Courbet," in *La Critique d'art en France 1850–1900*, ed. Jean-Paul Bouillon (Saint-Étienne: Centre interdisciplinaire d'études et de recherches sur l'expression contemporaine), 1989, pp. 63–80; and Viviane Alix-Leborgne, "Jules-Antoine Castagnary (1830–1888), un critique d'art républicain," Thèse du doctorat, Université Paris III, 1993. I am grateful to Alix-Leborgne for assistance in navigating the Castagnary papers.

31 The *locus classicus* on the Courbet–Marcou relationship is Chu, "It Took a Million Years to Paint that Picture," pp. 55–66. A modern biography of Marcou can be found in Richard Moreau, *Jules Marcou: Précurseur français de la géologie nord-américaine* (Paris: L'Harmattan), 2002, pp. 43–57.

32 Jules Marcou, "Notice sur les différentes formations des terrains jurassiques dans le Jura occidental," *Mémoires de la Société des Sciences Naturelles de Neuchâtel*, vol. 3 (Neuchâtel: Imp. de H. Wolfrath), 1845.

33 The paper was read to the Société Géologique de la France on 4 and 18 May 1846 and was later published as a volume of *Mémoires de la Société géologique de la France*, vol. 3, 1848.

34 In unpublished autobiographical notes, Marcou mentions that Buchon occasionally lent him books and hand-delivered letters in Switzerland for him in the 1830s and 1840s; Jules Marcou, *Notes sur ma famille et ma vie* (vols. 2 and 5). Marcou's mother kept her son informed about Buchon's imprisonment in 1849; letter from Mme. Marcou to Jules Marcou, 26 June 1849 and July 1849. All documents may be found in the Fonds Marcou [AD] sous-série 3J.

35 Buchon's biography was published under the heading "Lettre salinoise," in three installments of [S], 2, 9, and 16 July 1865, and then subsequently as an independent booklet, *Biographie salinoise. Jules Marcou* (Salins: Billet), 1865.

36 Jules Marcou, *Geological Map of the World* (Winterthur: J. Wurster), 1861.

37 [P], Box 4. See also Courbet to Buchon, January 1865, in [C], p. 254; and Dornier, "Un Témoin de la Bohème littéraire," p. 86.

38 Jules Marcou, *Lettres sur les roches du Jura et leur distribution géographique dans les deux hémisphères* (Paris: F. Klincksieck), 1857–60, p. 19. Chu was the first to recognize the direct connection of the Roche pourrie to Marcou's stratigraphy; see "It Took a Million Years to Paint that Picture," pp. 58–59.

39 Marcou, *Lettres sur les roches du jura*, pp. 29–30. Brongniart surveyed the Jura region, including the area around Salins, in August 1817; *Cahier du voyage in Jura 1817*, Fonds Alexandre Brongniart, Archives of the Muséum national d'histoire naturelle, Paris.

40 On the history of stratigraphy, see Martin J. S. Rudwick, *Earth's Deep History: How It Was Discovered and Why It Matters* (Chicago: University of Chicago Press), 2014, pp. 79–154; Martin J. S. Rudwick, *Bursting the Limits of Time: The Reconstruction of Geohistory in the Age of Revolution* (Chicago: University of Chicago Press), 2005, pp. 417–556; and Martin J. S. Rudwick, "Cuvier and Brongniart, William Smith, and the Reconstruction of Geohistory," *Earth Sciences History*, vol. 15, no. 1, 1996, pp. 25–36.

41 *Exposition des oeuvres de M. G. Courbet* (Paris: Lebigre-Duquesne Frères), 1867, no. 103.

42 Buchon, *Noëls et chants populaires*, p. 26. On Buchon's analogy between linguistic research and natural science, see Barbe, "Buchon, Claudet, Courbet," pp. 186–92.

43 Michel Bréal, "De la méthode comparative appliquée à l'étude des langues," in *Mélanges de mythologie et de linguistique* (Paris: Hachette), 1877, p. 239. On Bréal, see Marc Décimo, *Michel Bréal (1832–1915) et les linguistes de son temps. Catalogue d'exposition* (Orléans: Centre Charles Péguy), 1995; and Piet Desmet and Pierre Swiggers, *De la grammaire comparée à la sémantique* (Leuven; Paris: Peeters), 1995. In comparison, Proudhon's more eighteenth-century approach to the study of language (in a study of the Franc-comtois linguist Nicolas Bergier, whom Dartois and Buchon also cited) was already outdated by the 1830s: Nicolas Bergier and Pierre-Joseph Proudhon, *Les Élémens primitifs des langues* (Besançon: Lambert), 1837.

44 Charles Toubin, *Étude sur les champs sacrés de la Gaule et de la Grèce, et en particulier sur celui des Séquanes* (Paris: Dumoulin), 1861.

45 Buchon, *Salins-les-Bains*, 1862, p. 73. "Le Bon Roi Dagobert" was an eighteenth-century song referring to the imbecility of the Merovingian king Dagobert I (and thus to that of officialdom in general).

46 Max Buchon, *Salins-les-Bains, ses eaux minérales et ses environs*, new edn, Salins: Billet), 1866, p. 9.

47 Nodier, Taylor, and de Cailleux, *Voyages pittoresques*, pls. 116, 117 ("Grotte de la Source of the Lison"), pl. 118 ("Source de la Loue"), pp. 163–65.

48 On the transformations of the Salinois economy in the second half of the nineteenth century, see Société d'Émulation du Jura, *Enquête sur le Jura depuis cent ans. Étude sur l'évolution économique et sociale d'un département français de 1850 à 1950* (Lons-le-Saunier: Maurice Declume), 1953; and Claude-Isabelle Brelot and Jean-Luc Mayaud, *La Taillanderie de Nans-sous-Sainte-Anne (Doubs)* (Paris: Éditions Garnier Frères), 1982, pp. 17–52.

49 Buchon, *Lettres salinoises* (Salins), 1866, p. 16; and Buchon, "Les Adieux," [S], 28 August 1864.

50 On tourism in the forest of Fontainebleau, see Nicolas Green, *The Spectacle of Nature: Landscape and Bourgeois Culture in Nineteenth-Century France* (Manchester: Manchester University Press), 1990. On the case of Normandy, see Chapter 3, n. 5. On regional guidebooks, see Greg M. Thomas, "The Topographical Aesthetic in French Tourism and Landscape," *Nineteenth-Century Art Worldwide*, vol. 1, no. 1, spring 2002, http://www.l9thc-artworld-wide.org/index.php/spring02/198-the-topographical-aesthetic-in-french-tourism-and-landscape (accessed 16 September 2021).

51 [S], 22 and 29 January 1865.

52 [S], 25 September 1864.

53 Buchon, *Salins-les-Bains*, 1862: on the reservoir, p. 15; on the path, p. 50; on the baths, p. 19.

54 [S], 19 and 26 February 1865 (on bakeries); 4 December 1864 (on noise from public balls); 22 January 1865 (on the temporary committee to replace the mayor). On Buchon writing for [S], see Max Claudet to Jules-Antoine Castagnary, 20 October 1869, [P], Box 5.

55 Buchon, *Lettres salinoises* (Salins), 1866, pp. 8–11. Some of those acquisitions were listed along with their donors in the library committee proceedings published in [S], 7 and 14 May. Relations between Grimaldi and Buchon had been polite (but not effusive) during Courbet's visit. In early 1865, Grimaldi still received Buchon's public support ([S], 22 January 1865). By year's end the situation had deteriorated, thus leading to the publication of Buchon's vitriolic *Lettres*.

56 Grimaldi had been the most generous contributor to the subscription for Claudet's sculpture ([S], 31 July 1864).

57 At the Salon of 1865, Claudet's bust of Buchon was dubbed the "Homer of the Salins Baths," *Lettres salinoises*, p. 3. On Claudet, see Barbe, "Buchon, Claudet, Courbet," pp. 167–201.

58 [S], 11 December 1864.

59 Claudet, *Souvenirs*, p. 11.

60 Nodier, Taylor, and de Cailleux, *Voyages pittoresques*, n.p.

61 Claudet, *Souvenirs*, p. 10.

62 "Conversation with Joachim Gasquet," in Michael Doran, *Conversations with Cézanne*, trans. Julie Laurence (Berkeley: University of California Press), 2001, p. 144.

CHAPTER 3

1 The Salon of 1865 painting was listed under the title *Entrance of the Valley of the Puits noir (Doubs), Twilight Effect* in the catalogue for Courbet's private 1867 exhibition, *Exposition des oeuvres de M. G. Courbet. Rond-point du pont de l'Alma (Champs-Elysées)* (Paris: Lebigre-Duquesne frères), 1867, no. 26. Later titles include *Ruisseau du Puits noir* upon entering the Musée du Luxembourg, Paris, in 1881, and *Ruisseau couvert* for the artist's large retrospective the following year. See *Exposition des oeuvres de Gustave Courbet à l'École des beaux-arts* (Paris: Martinet), 1882, no. 55.

2 Courbet to Jules Luquet, May or April 1865, in [C], p. 263.

3 For instance, those of Alfred Bruyas (see the letters from Courbet to Alfred Bruyas, January 1866 and January – February 1866, in [C], pp. 272, 275) and Claude-Hélène Prospère Teste, mayor of Ornans (see Courbet to Jules Luquet, April or May 1865, in [C], p. 264).

4 Courbet to Urbain Cuenot, 6 April 1866, in [C], p. 277.

5 On the impact of these developments on the visual arts, see Robert L. Herbert, *Monet on the Normandy Coast: Tourism and Painting, 1867–1886* (New Haven and London: Yale University Press), 1994; Heather Lemonedes, Lynn Federle Orr, and David Steel, *Monet in Normandy*, exh. cat., Fine Arts Museums of San Francisco, California, North Carolina Museum of Art, and The Cleveland Museum of Art, Ohio, 2006–07; Carole McNamara, *The Lens of Impressionism: Photography and Painting along the Normandy Coast, 1850–1874* (Ann Arbor: University of Michigan Museum of Art), 2009.

6 Guy de Maupassant, "La Vie d'un paysagiste," *Gil Blas*, 28 September 1886, p. 1.

7 [F], nos. 150, 151, 152.

8 Courbet to Alfred Bruyas, January 1866, in [C], pp. 272–73.

9 Édouard Ordinaire, "Causerie," p. 2. Courbet purposefully exhibited the seascapes as a group in his 1867 private exhibition, *Exposition des oeuvres de M. G. Courbet*, 1867, nos. 57–66, p. 17.

10 Charles Beauquier, "Chronique. Paris," [RL], 1866, pp. 284–86. Compare the review by Jules Vallès in *L'Événement*, 11 March 1866. On Beauquier, see Noël Barbe (ed.), *Les Mondes de Beauquier* (Besançon: Les Éditions du Sékoya), 2014.

11 Camille Lemonnier, G. *Courbet et son oeuvre. Gustave Courbet à la Tour de Peilz (Lettre du Dr. Paul Collin)* (Paris: Alphonse Lemerre), 1878, p. 58.

12 Paul Mantz, "Gustave Courbet," [GBA], 18 December 1878, p. 381.

13 Klaus Herding, "Equality and Authority in Courbet's Landscape Painting," in Herding, *Courbet: To Venture Independence*, p. 93.

14 Castagnary discerned that Courbet "never forgot that an empty space takes up more room than filled-up space." Castagnary, "Fragments d'un livre sur Gustave Courbet," pp. 19–30, 22.

15 Cham, "La Mer noire à Étretat. Tellement haute qu'on aperçoit des vagues dans le ciel," no. 671, in *Cham au Salon de 1870* (Paris: A. de Vresse), 1870.

16 See [C], pp. 267–69, 298–300.

17 See Klaus Herding, "Gustave Courbet—La Vague," in Klaus Herding and Sabine Schulze, *Impressionisten: 6 französische Meisterwerke/Impressionnistes: 6 Chefs-d'oeuvre français*, exh. cat., Städel Museum, Frankfurt am Main, 1999, pp. 17–29; Céline Flécheux, *L'Horizon: Des Traités de perspective au land art* (Rennes: Presses universitaires de Rennes), 2009, pp. 29–36, 155–56; and Céline Flécheux, "La Vague: Courbet et la photographie," in Jackie Pigeaud (ed.), *L'Eau, les eaux: Xes Entretiens de La Garenne Lemot* (Rennes: Presses universitaires de Rennes), 2006, http://books.openedition.org/pur/32606 (accessed 16 September 2021). Young, *Realism in the Age of Impressionism*, pp. 1–4

18 Herding, "Gustave Courbet—La Vague," p. 20.

19 For art historical precedents, see Hubert Damisch, *A Theory of /Cloud/ Toward a History of Painting*, trans. Janet Lloyd (Stanford, Calif.: Stanford University Press), 2002, p. 138.

20 Charles Léger, *Courbet* (Paris: Les Editions G. Crès), 1929, p. 191.

21 Herding, "Gustave Courbet—La Vague," p. 17.

22 Barthélemy Joubert, "Au regard de la peinture," in Sylvie Aubenas, *Gustave Le Gray, 1820–1884*, exh. cat., Bibliothèque nationale de France, Paris, and The J. Paul Getty Museum, Los Angeles, 2002, pp. 233–54; Dominique de Font-Réaulx, "'Contempler le spectacle de votre mer,' quelques réflexions sur les *Vague* et *Marine* de Gustave Courbet à la lumière des photographies de son temps," in Annette Haudiquet et. al., *Vagues: Autour des paysages de mer de Gustave Courbet*, exh. cat., Musée d'art moderne André Malraux, Le Havre, 2004, pp. 30–37; and des Cars and de Font-Réaulx et al., *Gustave Courbet*, pp. 280–85.

23 Dominique de Font-Réaulx, "Courbet et la photographie: L'Exemple d'un peintre réaliste, entre vérité et réalité," in *L'Art du nu au XIXè siècle: Le Photographe et son modèle* (Paris: Bibliothèque nationale de France), 1997, pp. 84–91; Dominique de Font-Réaulx, "Reproducing Reality: Landscape Photography of the 1850s and 1860s in Relation to the Paintings of Gustave Courbet," in Morton and Eyerman, *Courbet and the Modern Landscape*, pp. 39–53; and Joël Petitjean, *Gustave Courbet et la photographie* (Lyons: Fage), 2012.

24 Aubenas, *Gustave Le Gray, 1820–1884*, p. 272.

25 On the relationship of photograph to actual site, see Marnin Young, "Photography and the Philosophy of Time: On Gustave Le Gray's *Great Wave, Sète*," nonsite.org, no. 19, 3 May 2016, https://nonsite.org/photography-and-the-philosophy-of-time/ (accessed 16 September 2021).

26 Doran, *Conversations with Cézanne*, p. 144. Miró, as quoted in Pierre Schneider, *Louvre Dialogues*, trans. Patricia Southgate (New York: Athenaeum), 1971, p. 38, first cited in Fried, *Courbet's Realism*, p. 215.

27 Mantz, "Gustave Courbet," p. 381.

28 Walter Benjamin, "Letter from Paris (2). Painting and Photography," in Howard Eiland and Michael W. Jennings (eds.), *Walter Benjamin. Selected Writings, Vol. 3: 1935–1938*, trans. Edmund Jephcott, Howard Eiland et al. (Cambridge, Mass.: Harvard University Press), 2002, pp. 236–48.

29 Mantz, "Gustave Courbet," p. 381.

30 Herding, "Gustave Courbet—La Vague," p. 19.

31 [F], no. 519.

32 Ibid., no. 679.

33 Ibid., no. 688. This in turn has led art historians to compare Courbet's waves to those depicted in Japanese prints. However, nothing could be less paste-like than a print.

34 Ibid., no. 749.

35 Ibid., nos. 498, 701.

36 John Zarobell provides a useful typology of the genre in "Marine Painting in Mid-Nineteenth-Century Nineteenth France," in Juliet Wilson-Bareau and David Degener, *Manet and the Sea*, exh. cat., Art Institute of Chicago, Philadelphia Museum of Art, and Van Gogh Museum, Amsterdam, 2003–04, pp. 17–33.

37 The references include Adolphe Stein et al., *Jongkind: Catalogue critique de l'oeuvre* (Paris: Brame and Lorenceau), 2003; Victorine Hefting, *Jongkind d'après sa correspondence* (Utrecht: Haentjens Dekker and Gumbert), 1969; Victorine Hefting, *Jongkind: Sa Vie, son oeuvre, son époque* (Paris: Arts et Métiers graphiques), 1974; and Sylvie Gache-Patin et al., *Johan Barthold Jongkind (1819–1891)*, exh. cat., Gemeentemuseum, The Hague, Wallraf-Richartz-Museum, Cologne, and Musée d'Orsay, Paris, 2003–04.

38 Letter (2348) from Monet to Gustave Geffroy, 8 May 1920, quoted in Daniel Wildenstein, *Claude Monet: Biographie et catalogue raisonné*, 5 vols. (Lausanne: Bibliothèque des arts), 1985, vol. 4, p. 405.

39 Baudelaire, "The Salon of 1859," p. 200.

40 Ibid., p. 200.

41 Georges Jean-Aubry with Robert Schmit, *Eugène Boudin*, trans. Caroline Tisdall (Neuchâtel: Éditions Ides et Calendes), 1968, p. 28. On the 1859 visit, see Jean-Aubry, *Eugène Boudin*, pp. 27–35; and Schanne, *Souvenirs de Schaunard*, pp. 229–37. Boudin mentions Courbet at several points in his correspondence with Ferdinand Martin in Isolde Pludermacher and Laurent Maneoeuvre, *Eugène Boudin: Lettres à Ferdinand Martin (1861–1870)* (Honfleur: Éditions Société des amis du musée Eugène Boudin), 2011.

42 Jean-Aubry, *Eugène Boudin*, p. 30 [translation modified].

43 See Richard Dorment, "James McNeill Whistler," in Wilson-Bareau and Degener, *Manet and the Sea*, pp. 187–93; and Alan Bowness, "Courbet, Whistler, and the Seascape," unpublished lecture, manuscript copy in the archives of the Museum of Fine Arts, Boston.

44 Pope to Harris Whittemore, 25 August 1894, from a transcription in the archives of the Hill-Stead Museum, Farmington, Connecticut.

45 Letter (65-16) from Courbet to his family, 17 November 1865, in [C], p. 269.

46 Beauquier, "Chronique. Paris," pp. 284–86.

47 Ibid., p. 285. Courbet had written to Hugo about doing a portrait. Letters from Courbet to Hugo, 11 and 28 November and 19 December 1864, in [C], pp. 246–50, 253. The correspondence between Hugo, Courbet, and Max Buchon (to whom Hugo had written separately on 7 and 17 November 1864) was publicized in Buchon's "Lettre salinoise," [S], 11 December 1864, and by Alphonse Mandrillon in consecutive issues of [RL] (November–December) 1864, pp. 148–49, and 1865, pp. 255–56.

48 The chronology followed here and throughout the chapter is from Pierre Georgel, *Les Dessins de Victor Hugo pour "Les Travailleurs de la mer"* (Paris: Herscher), 1985. On the drawings in general, see Pierre Georgel, "Histoire d'un 'peintre malgré lui,'" in Victor Hugo, *Oeuvres complètes*, vol. 18, ed. Jean Massin (Paris: Club Français du livre), 1969, pp. 13–80; and Pierre Georgel, "Le Romantisme des années 1860: Correspondance Victor Hugo-Philippe Burty," *Revue de l'art*, vol. 20, 1973, pp. 8–64. On the relationship of text to image in Hugo's work, see Madeleine Blondel and Pierre Georgel (eds.), *Victor Hugo et les images* (Ville de Dijon: Aux Amateurs de Livres), 1989; and Pierre Georgel (ed.), *L'Oeil de Victor Hugo: Actes du colloque* (Paris: Éditions des Cendres), 2004.

49 Although drawings had been published in Victor Hugo, Théophile Gautier, and Paul Chenay, *Dessins de Victor Hugo* (Paris: Castel), 1863, and circulated informally among friends, Hugo never exhibited the *Les Travailleurs de la mer* drawings, according to Georgel, "Le Romantisme des années 1860," pp. 14–15.

50 On the philosophical texts, see Jacques Seebacher's introduction to Hugo, *Oeuvres complètes*, vol. 12, 1967, pp. 3–8. On *Les Travailleurs de la mer*, see Yves Gohin's notice in Victor Hugo, *Les Travailleurs de la mer*, ed. Yves Gohin (Paris: Gallimard Collection Folio), 1980, pp. 567–73; and Gohin's contribution to [H], pp. 1257ff.

51 [H], p. 936. On the text's eventual omission from the novel, see [H], pp. 1637–40.

52 On the Hugolian trope of the unknown form emerging from darkness, see Jean-Pierre Reynaud, "Le Contour et l'infini," in Blondel and Georgel, *Victor Hugo et les images*, pp. 213–21; and Didier Philippot, *Victor Hugo et la vaste ouverture du possible: Essai sur l'ontologie romantique* (Paris: Classiques Garnier), 2017.

53 [H], p. 900. On the equivalence of sea and ink in Hugo's drawings, see Andrea Haarer, "Dark Liquids: Victor Hugo and Phosphorescent Seawater," in Marcel Finke and Friedrich Weltzien (eds.), *State of Flux: Aesthetics of Fluid Materials* (Berlin: Dietrich Reimer), 2017, pp. 59–74; and Andrea Haarer, "Zustände des Fließenden. Victor Hugo Bildermachen zu Meerwasser 1855–1877" (PhD dissertation, University of Stuttgart), 2019.

54 One of the working titles for *Les Travailleurs de la mer* was *Abîme*. See [H], pp. 1356–62.

55 On "holy matter," see Caroline Walker Bynum, *Christian Materiality: An Essay on Religion in Late Medieval Europe* (Cambridge, Mass.: MIT Press), 2011; and Herbert L. Kessler, *Seeing Medieval Art* (Ontario: University of Toronto Press), 2011, pp. 19–42.

56 On Hugo's inventive use of materials, see Hugo, Gautier, and Chenay, *Dessins de Victor Hugo*, p. 15; Hugo to Baudelaire, 29 April 1860, in Hugo, *Oeuvres complètes*, vol. 12, pp. 1097–98; Philippe Burty's reviews, "Les Dessins de Victor Hugo," *Chroniques des arts et de la curiosité*, 28 December 1862, pp. 51–53, and "Chez Victor Hugo par un passant," *Chroniques des arts et de la curiosité*, 29 November 1863; Philippe Burty, "Les Dessins de Victor Hugo," in *Maîtres et petits-maîtres* (Paris: Charpentier), 1877, pp. 310–23; Marie-Laure Prévost, "Techniques of a Poet-Draftsman," in Ann Philbin and Florian Rodari, *Shadows of a Hand: The Drawings of Victor Hugo* (New York: Drawing Center), 1988, pp. 31–33; Haarer, "Zustände des Fließenden"; and the writings of Georgel. On his attachment to his writing tools, see Marie-Laure Prévost (ed.), *Victor Hugo, l'homme océan* (Paris: Éditions Seuil), 2002, cat. 233, p. 262, and cat. 250, p. 278; and letter from Hugo to Juliette Drouet, 31 December 1859, in Jean Gaudon (ed.),*Victor Hugo: Lettres à Juliette Drouet, 1833–1882* (Paris: Jean-Jacques Pauvert), 1964, p. 138.

57 See, for example, two later "larvae-like" octopus drawings reproduced in Georgel, *Les Dessins de Victor Hugo*, pp. 118–19, and discussed in Haarer, "Zustände des Fließenden," pp. 62–85.

58 Jean-Pierre Montier, "Dessins et écriture dans le manuscrit des *Travailleurs de la mer* de Victor Hugo," *French Studies: A Quarterly Review*, vol. 60, no. 1, January 2006, pp. 15–31; and Jean-Pierre Montier, "Le 'Finale' des *Travailleurs de la mer*: Horizon et limite du texte romanesque," *Littérature*, vol. 135, September 2004, pp. 3–23.

59 Several are reproduced in Prévost, *Victor Hugo, l'homme océan*: cats. 124–125, pp. 160–61; cat. 160, p. 204; cats. 190–192, pp. 232–33.

60 [H], p. 815.

61 Although *Stormy Sea* was caricatured as splattered ink by Henry Somm in *Le Charge*, no. 91, 1870, reproduced in Hoffmann et al., *Courbet und Deutschland*, p. 508, Courbet's painting is more like oil or cream than writing fluid.

62 For Michelet's biography, see Gabriel Monod, *Jules Michelet: Études sur sa vie et ses oeuvres avec des fragments inédits* (Paris: Hachette), 1905, and *La Vie et la pensée de Jules Michelet (1798–1852)*, 2 vols. (Paris: Honoré Champion Bibliothèque de l'École des Hautes Études), 1923; Paul Viallaneix, *La Voix royale: Essai sur l'idée de peuple dans l'oeuvre de Michelet* (Paris: Delagrave), 1959; and *Michelet: Les Travaux et les jours* (Paris: Gallimard), 1998. Michelet had certainly been on Buchon's mind around this time, Max Buchon "Délibérations de la commission de la bibliothèque de Salins. Deuxième séance (4 mai 1865)," [S], 14 May 1865.

63 Jules Assézat, "Les Analogistes," *Le Réalisme*, vol. 4, 15 February 1857, pp. 71–74.

64 Roland Barthes's article "Michelet, l'histoire et la mort," *Esprit*, no. 178, April 1951, pp. 497–511, and book *Michelet par lui-même* (Paris: Éditions du Seuil), 1954, opened up several new lines of inquiry in Michelet studies, many of which were taken up with renewed vigor after the publication of Michelet's journal in 1959 and the centenary of his death in 1974. In addition to Barthes's analysis, the most useful publications for this study have been: Lionel Gossman, "Michelet and Natural History: The Alibi of Nature," *Proceedings of the American Philosophical Society*, vol. 145, no. 3, September 2001, pp. 283–333; Lionel Gossman, "The Go-Between: Jules Michelet 1798–1874," *MLN*, vol. 89, no. 4, May 1974, pp. 503–41; Linda Orr, *Jules Michelet: Nature, History, and Language* (Ithaca, N.Y.: Cornell University Press), 1976; special issues of *L'Arc*, vol. 52, February 1973, and *Revue d'histoire littéraire de la France*, vol. 5, September – October 1974; and the collection of essays edited by Paul Viallaneix, *Michelet cent ans après: Études et témoignages* (Grenoble: Presses universitaires de Grenoble), 1975. Of special note in these journals are subsequent essays by Barthes revisiting his earlier texts "Aujourd'hui, Michelet," *L'Arc*, vol. 52, February 1973, pp. 19–27, and "La Modernité de Michelet," *Revue d'Histoire littéraire de la France*, vol. 5, September – October 1974, pp. 803–09, translated into English as "Michelet, Today" and "Michelet's Modernity," respectively, in *The Rustle of Language*, trans. Richard Howard (Berkeley: University of California Press), 1989, pp. 195–211. On how his literariness was understood differently across the political spectrum, see Pierre Nora, "Troisième homme?" *L'Arc*, vol. 52, February 1973, pp. 54–58. For the immediate postwar reception, see Lucien Febvre's introduction to *Michelet 1798–1874* (Paris: Éditions des Trois Collines), 1946, pp. 5–36. A more recent appraisal is the edited volume, *Michelet: Rythme de la prose, rythme de l'histoire* (Villneuvre d'Ascq: Presses Universitaires du Septentrion), 2010. On the role of the visual arts in Michelet's writings, see Michèle Hannoosh, *Jules Michelet: Writing Art and History in Nineteenth-Century France* (University Park, PA: Pennsylvania State University Press), 2019.

65 Roland Barthes, *Michelet* (Berkeley: University of California Press), 1992, pp. 201–02.

66 Ibid., p. 128.

67 [M], pp. 133–40. Michelet states that Jacob van Ruisdael's *The Breakwater* (*ca.*1670) is his favorite painting in the Musée du Louvre because it depicts a fecund "wave of life," [M], pp. 57–58, which is not surprising given that, among seventeenth-century Dutch landscapists, Ruisdael is closest in spirit and technique to Courbet.

68 Barthes, "Michelet's Modernity," p. 208. On the opposition between "*récit*" and "*tableau*" in Barthes's early writing on Michelet, see Hannoosh, *Jules Michelet*, pp. 4–6.

69 This is also true of his still lifes, in which objects such as apples and trout are often grossly out of scale. On the trout pictures, see the interview with Brice Marden in Lucile Encrevé and Laurence des Cars, *Brice Marden, Gustave Courbet*, trans. John Lee (Paris: Argol Éditions), 2006. On the later apple still lifes, see Przyblyski, "Courbet, the Commune, and the Meanings of Still Life in 1871"; and James H. Rubin, "Courbet's Rotten Apples: Flesh and the Final Years," lecture given at the conference "Gustave Courbet and the Narratives of Modern Painting" at the Carl Friedrich von Siemens Stiftung, Munich, 27–29 March 2019

70 [F], no. 436.

71 On this point, see Clement Greenberg, "Review of an Exhibition of Gustave Courbet," in John O'Brian (ed.), *The Collected Essays and Criticism* (Chicago: University of Chicago Press), 1987, pp. 275–79; and the 1941 interview between Pierre Courthion and Henri Matisse in George Besson and Henri Matisse, *De Face, de profil, de dos: Correspondance croisée, 1913–1953*, ed. Chantal Duverget (Strasbourg: L'Atelier contemporaine), 2018, p. 148.

72 On the make-up of this series, see Courbet's letters to Francis Wey (December 1853) and Alfred Bruyas (January 1854), in [C], pp. 119, 121.

73 [F], nos. 437, 541, 449.

74 Flaubert to Michelet, 26 January 1861, in Flaubert, *Correspondance*, vol. 3, ed. Jean Bruneau (Paris: Gallimard), 1991, pp. 141–43.

75 Courbet's love of bathing was kindly pointed out to the author by Petra ten-Doesschate Chu. See also letter from Courbet to Juliette Courbet, 27 September 1866, in [C], p. 299.

76 Flaubert, *Correspondance*, vol. 3, p. 142. In contrast, Hugo tells Michelet that *La Mer* is "inexhaustible like the ocean," where "on each page, I would say almost in each wave, there are ... some reflections of the stars." Letter (8630) from Hugo to Michelet, 18 January 1861, in Jules Michelet, *Correspondance générale*, 12 vols., ed. Louis Le Guillou (Paris: Honoré Champion), 1994–2001, vol. 9, pp. 618–19.

CHAPTER 4

1 On Courbet's relationship to the government of Napoleon III, see Paul B. Crapo, "The Problematics of Artistic Patronage under the Second Empire: Gustave Courbet's Involved Relations with the Regime of Napoleon III," *Zeitschrift für Kunstgeschichte*, vol. 58, no. 2, 1995, pp. 240–61.

2 Bazille to his parents, May 1866, in Michel Schulman, *Frédéric Bazille, 1841–1870: Catalogue raisonné: Peintures, dessins, pastels, aquarelles: Sa Vie, son oeuvre, sa correspondance* (Paris: Éditions de l'Amateur), 1995, p. 351.

3 Thoré, "Salon de 1866," p. 276. In the wake of a dispute over the state's acquisition of *Woman with a Parrot*, Courbet, contra Thoré, received no official honors at the 1866 Salon.

4 Émile Zola, "Mon Salon," in [Z], vol. 2, p. 647.

5 The dating and attribution of the post-Commune landscapes remains problematic. On the question of Courbet's collaborations, see Robert Fernier, "Pata et Courbet ou Courbet empatassé," [GBA], July – August 1972, pp. 83–90; Robert Fernier, *Cherubino Pata, 1827–1899: Le Vrai Faux-Courbet*, ed. Jean-Jacques Fernier, exh. cat., Musée-Maison Natale Gustave Courbet, Ornans, 1988; Petra ten-Doesschate Chu, "Courbet, or Not Courbet, That Is the Question," *IFAR Journal*, vol. 7, no. 1, September 2004, pp. 18–26; and Bertrand Tillier, "Pour une pratique collective de la peinture," in Madeline, *Gustave Courbet*, pp. 30–35.

6 On Courbet's German reception, see Hoffmann et al., *Courbet und Deutschland*, pp. 350–474; and Mathilde Arnoux, Thomas W. Gaehtgens, and Anne Tempelaere-Panzani (eds.), *Correspondance entre Henri Fantin-Latour et Otto Scholderer: 1858–1902* (Paris: Maison des sciences de l'homme), 2011. On his impact in Belgium, see Brigitte de Patoul, *Gustave Courbet et la Belgique: Réalisme de l'art vivant à l'art libre* (Milan: Silvana Editoriale), 2013. Closer to home, several artists passed through his short-lived open studio on the Rue Notre-Dame-des-Champs in Paris, most notably Henri Fantin-Latour. See Bridget Alsdorf, *Fellow Men: Fantin-Latour and the Problem of the Group in Nineteenth-Century French Painting* (Princeton, N.J.: Princeton University Press), 2013.

7 This chapter is meant to build on the analysis of Courbet's influence expertly sketched by Callen in *The Work of Art*, pp. 105–14.

8 Courbet to Urbain Cuenot, 16 September 1865, in [C], p. 267.

9 Baudelaire, "The Salon of 1859," p. 201.

10 Callen, *The Work of Art*, p. 143. Gasquet makes a similar observation in Doran, *Conversations with Cezanne*, p. 143.

11 On Renoir's *Diana* as a response to Courbet, see Kermit Champa, *Studies in Early Impressionism* (New Haven and London: Yale University Press), 1973, pp. 44–45.

12 On the Le Coeur portrait, see Douglas Cooper, "Lise and the Le Coeur Family: A Study of Renoir's Early Development II: The Le Coeurs," *The Burlington Magazine*, vol. 101, nos. 678/679, September – October 1959, pp. 320, 322–29.

13 The painting is visible in the background of Frédéric Bazille's *Artist's Studio* (1870; Musée d'Orsay, Paris). X-ray examination of the latter has revealed a sketch related to *Diana* by either Renoir or Bazille; see *Renoir*, exh. cat., Hayward Gallery, London, Grand Palais, Paris, and Museum of Fine Arts, Boston), 1985–86, pp. 179–80.

14 In 1919, Renoir mentioned to Albert André "two or three canvases with knife following the process dear to Courbet," possibly referring to *Diana* and the Le Coeur portrait. Albert André, *Renoir* (Paris: Crès), 1919, reprinted in Augustin de Butler (ed.), *Renoir: Écrits, entretiens et lettres sur l'art* (Paris: Les Éditions de l'Amateur), 2002, pp. 18–38.

15 As Callen notes in *The Work of Art*, p. 110.

16 When Matisse visited Renoir's studio in 1918, the older artist pointed out a bathing picture that he felt "did not have enough Courbet." Matisse tells Pierre Courthion that he took Renoir's comment to mean that the painting lacked the "desired unity of paste that [Renoir] liked in Courbet." See Henri Matisse with Pierre Courthion, *Chatting with Henri Matisse: The Lost 1941 Interview*, ed. Serge Guilbaut, trans. Chris Miller (Los Angeles: Getty Research Institute), 2013, p. 91 (translation modified). Matisse had acquired between 1916 and 1919 at least four Courbet paintings, including *The Source of the Loue* at the Albright-Knox Gallery, Buffalo (see fig. 2), see Claudine Grammont (ed.), *Tout Matisse* (Paris: Robert Laffont), 2018, p. 208. Later he would admit to being haunted by the "nourishment of substance" that he found in Courbet's *Wave* (*Stormy Sea*; 1870; Musée d'Orsay, Paris) and *Covert of Roe-Deer by the Stream of Plaisir-Fontaine* (see fig. 20; then in the Musée du Louvre, Paris). See letter from Matisse to Georges Besson, 19 February 1948, in Besson and Matisse, *De Face, de profil, de dos*, p. 249.

17 Letter from Jacques-Émile Blanche to an unknown correspondent, n.d. [December 1881], Bibliothèque et Archives des Musées nationaux, Paris, quoted in Henri Loyrette, *Degas: A New Vision* (Melbourne, Victoria: National Gallery of Victoria), 2016, p. 67.

18 For an illustration of *Dead Fox in the Undergrowth*, see Paul-André Lemoisne, *Degas et son oeuvre* (New York: Garland), 1984, no. 120. Richard Kendall has identified two other paintings of the 1860s with passages of palette-knife painting (Lemoisne, nos. 285 and 286); see Kendall, *Degas Landscapes* (New Haven and London: Yale University Press), 1993, pp. 76–80.

19 Loyrette, *Degas: A New Vision*, p. 67.

20 The ballet (with a libretto by Charles Nuitter and Arthur Saint-Léon and music by Ludwig Minkus and Léo Delibes) was still in repertory when Degas started sketching Fiocre in August 1867. On the genesis and reception of the painting, see Ann Dumas, *Degas's "Mlle. Fiocre" in Context: A Study of "Portrait of Mlle. E. F...";* *à propos du ballet "La Source"* (Brooklyn: Brooklyn Museum), 1988; Jean Sutherland Boggs et al., *Degas, 1834–1917*, exh. cat., Grand Palais, Paris, National Gallery of Canada, Ottawa, and The Metropolitan Museum of Art, New York, 1988–89, pp. 133–36; Jill DeVonyar and Richard Kendall, *Degas and the Dance* (New York: Harry N. Abrams), 2002, pp. 48–54. On the production of *La Source*, see Ludwig Minkus and Léo Delibes, *La Source; Fantastic Ballet in Three Acts and Four Scenes, by Charles Nuitter and Arthur Saint-Léon: Piano Score*, ed. Robert Ignatius Letellier (Newcastle upon Tyne: Cambridge Scholars Publishing), 2010, pp. ix–xiii.

21 Though undated, Degas scholars have argued that the watercolors were most likely made in preparation for *Mlle. Fiocre*, the only other 1860s work with a similar treatment of natural texture. Lemoisne, *Degas et son oeuvre*, nos. 191 and 192. On the background of the Fiocre portrait, see Charles Stuckey, "Degas as an Artist: Revised and Still Unfinished," in *Degas: Form and Space*, ed. Maurice Guillaud (Paris: Centre Culturel du Marais), 1984, pp. 13–64, 21. According to Loyrette, *Degas: A New Vision*, subsequent damage to the painting (in the form of paint loss from varnish removal) does not alter the very Courbetian aspect of the original landscape; see cat. 77 in Boggs et al., *Degas*, p. 136.

22 *La Source* (The Spring) was also famous in its day for its novel set design, which included a live horse, electric lighting, and running water. As Paul Saint-Victor noted, "when the curtain first went up, the set was applauded on its own account, although some criticism was raised that the natural water contrasted too harshly with the painted rocks." Quoted in Robert Ignatius Letellier, *The Ballets of Ludwig Minkus* (Newcastle upon Tyne: Cambridge Scholars Publishing), 2008, pp. 79–80.

23 Letter from Antoine Guillemet to Francisco Oller, 12 September 1866, published in Réné Taylor et al., *Francisco Oller: Un realista del impresionismo*, exh. cat., Museo de Arte de Ponce, Puerto Rico, El Museo del Barrio, New York, El Museo de Arte Contemporáneo de América Latina, Washington, D.C., The Museum of Fine Arts, Springfield, Mass., and El Museo de la Universidad de Puerto Rico, 1983–84, pp. 226–27.

24 Letter from Zola to Valabrègue, 10 December 1866, Émile Zola, *Correspondance: Vol. 1: 1858–1867*, ed. B. H. Bakker (Montreal: Presses de l'Université de Montréal; Paris: Éditions du Centre national de la recherche scientifique), 1978, p. 463.

25 Joachim Pissarro and Claire Durand-Ruel Snollaerts, *Pissarro: Critical Catalogue of Paintings*, 3 vols. (New York: Wildenstein Institute Publications and Skira), 2005, nos. 90, 103, and 107.

26 On their relationship, see Joachim Pissarro, *Pioneering Modern Painting, 1865–1885: Cézanne & Pissarro, 1865–1885*, exh. cat., Museum of Modern Art, New York, Los Angeles County Museum of Art, and Musée d'Orsay, Paris, 2005–06; Theodore Reff, "Pissarro's Portrait of Cézanne," *The Burlington Magazine*, vol. 109, no. 776, 1967, pp. 627–33; and Campbell, "Pissarro and the Palette Knife," pp. 311–14.

27 For example, [FWN], nos. 23, 28, 36, 38, and 40. Are these small works (or larger ones similar to them) what Guillemet had in mind when he told Zola to expect to see "successful landscapes done with the palette knife" at the local museum were Cézanne to become its director? Letter from Guillemet to Zola, 2 November 1866, in [D], p. 129.

28 The same accusation would be leveled against Cézanne a little over a decade later: "There is no way to figure out M. Cesanne's [*sic*] impressions after nature; I took them for palettes that had not been cleaned." See Léon de Lora, "L'Exposition des impressionnistes," *Le Gaulois*, 10 April 1877, pp. 1–2, reprinted in Ruth Berson, *The New Painting: Impressionism 1874–1886: Documentation, Vol. 1: Reviews* (San Francisco: Fine Arts Museum of San Francisco), 1996, p. 163. On artists' palettes, see Matthias Krüger, "Paletten und Palettenbilder," in *Das Haptische Bild: Körperhafte Bilderfahrung in der Neuzeit*, eds. Markus Rath, Jörg Trempler, and Iris Wenderholm (Berlin: Walter de Gruyter), 2013, pp. 159–81.

29 Theodore Reff coined the term "constructive stroke" in his article "Cézanne's Constructive Stroke," *Art Quarterly*, vol. 25, no. 3, fall 1962, pp. 214–27.

30 The destruction of Pissarro's studio during the Franco-Prussian War (1870–71) makes it difficult to ascertain how many palette-knife paintings had been produced in the 1860s. On two known examples dated to 1867, a village view and a still life, and their relationship to Cézanne's own palette-knife paintings, see Campbell, "Pissarro and the Palette Knife," pp. 311–14.

31 [FWN], nos. 398, 402, 404–12, 417–18.

32 Lawrence Gowing, "The Early Work of Paul Cézanne," in *Cézanne: The Early Years 1859–1972*, Royal Academy of Arts, London, Musée d'Orsay, Paris, and National Gallery of Art, Washington, D.C., 1988–89, p. 80. On Cézanne's first decade of production, see, in addition: Mary Tompkins Lewis, *Cézanne's Early Imagery* (Berkeley: University of California Press), 1989; Robert Simon, "Cézanne and the Subject of Violence," *Art in America*, vol. 79, no. 5, May 1991, pp. 120–35, 185–86; and André Dombrowski, *Cézanne, Murder and Modern Life* (Berkeley: University of California Press), 2015. Also of interest are reviews of Gowing's 1988 exhibition: Jean-Claude Lebensztejn, "Les Couilles de Cézanne," *Critique*, vol. 44, no. 499, December 1988, pp. 1031–47; and Nina Athanassoglou-Kallmyer, *Art Journal*, vol. 49, no. 1, spring 1990, pp. 71–75.

33 Letter from Valabrègue to Zola, 2 October 1866, quoted in John Rewald, *The Paintings of Paul Cézanne: A Catalogue Raisonné, Vol. 1: The Texts* (New York: Harry N. Abrams), 1996, p. 97. In an insightful entry on Cézanne's Uncle Dominique portrait in the Norton Simon Museum (1866)—to which this section owes much—Richard Brettell and Stephen Eisenman rightly note that this much-overlooked passage foregrounds the psychologically disturbing aspect of Cézanne's portraits (and not just their physical thickness). Brettell and Eisenman, *Nineteenth-Century Art in the Norton Simon Museum, Vol. 1* (Pasadena, Calif.: Norton Simon Art Foundation), 2006, pp. 292–96. On the caricatural and quasi-photographic dimensions of Cézanne's portraits, see Nina Athanassoglou-Kallmyer, "An Artistic and Political Manifesto for Cézanne," *Art Bulletin*, vol. 72, no. 3, 1990, pp. 482–92; and Athanassoglou-Kallmyer, *Cézanne and Provence*, pp. 71–77.

34 Letter from Valabrègue to Zola, November 1866, quoted in Rewald, *The Paintings of Paul Cézanne*, pp. 97, 100; for the original French, see Coutagne et al., *Cézanne au Musée d'Aix*, p. 120.

35 Rewald notes that the large portrait *Antony Valabrègue* in the National Gallery of Art, Washington, D.C., is signed, a rarity for Cézanne, which suggests that it was submitted to the Salon, and therefore cannot be the "head study" Valabrègue is discussing here. Compare Philip Conisbee, who proposed, on the basis of coloration, the *Portrait of Anthony Valabrègue* (1869–71) in the J. Paul Getty Museum, Los Angeles, as the work under discussion; see Philip Conisbee and Denis Coutagne et al., *Cézanne in Provence*, exh. cat., National Gallery of Art, Washington, D.C., 2006, p. 327, n. 44.

36 The "curé coated with crushed blackberries" is a reference to a scene from Champfleury, *La Succession Le Camus* (Paris: Poulet Malassis et de Brosse), 1860, pp. 131–32. According to Ambroise Vollard, Cézanne also told Antoine Guillemet, "I'm painting Valabrègue's portrait; the illuminated point of the nose, it's pure vermilion!" (the nose-tips in the portraits of Uncle Dominique, however, are white, with vermilion usually reserved for the lips and inner ear). See Vollard, *Paul Cézanne* (Paris: Galerie A. Vollard), 1914, p. 22.

37 The literature often refers to Cézanne's early, thick style of painting as his "ballsy manner" or "manière couillarde," the first mention of which seems to be in Vollard's monograph, where he speaks of Cézanne wanting to realize a type of painting that was "*bien couillarde*," Vollard, *Paul Cézanne*, p. 22. Valabrègue's masonry metaphor is preferred here for its contemporaneity with the works under discussion. On paint layers in *Uncle Dominique with a Turban*, see Robert W. Ratcliffe, "Cézanne's Working Methods and Their Theoretical Background" (PhD dissertation, Courtauld Institute of Art, University of London), 1960, pp. 83–84. Ratcliffe's analysis is concerned primarily with the optical mixing of superimposed colors, whereas here we are more concerned with the *physical* mixing that occurs within single paint streaks.

38 On Cézanne and popular culture, see Simon, "Cézanne and the Subject of Violence," pp. 120–30; Athanassoglou-Kallmyer, *Cézanne and Provence*, pp. 53–99; and Dombrowski, *Cézanne, Murder and Modern Life*, pp. 189–231.

39 Émile Zola, "Un Mariage d'amour," *Le Figaro*, 24 December 1866, in [Z], vol. 2, pp. 475–78. Émile Zola, *Thérèse Raquin* (Paris: Lacroix, Verboeckhoven, 1868), reprinted in [Z], vol. 3, pp. 17-175, 135. It is tempting to speculate, although impossible to prove at this point, that the "two female heads" refer to the portraits of mother and sister, or similar works, and the "three male heads" to a selection of the Uncle Dominique studies.

40 See letter from Zola to Valabrègue, 10 December 1866, in Zola, *Correspondance*, p. 464. Two other possibilities are that Zola had seen similar portraits during earlier visits to Bennecourt, where Cézanne spent most of summer 1866, or that Cézanne had painted new portraits after arriving in Paris in 1867.

41 Studies that do connect Laurent's and Cézanne's painting styles but fail to mention the portraits of Uncle Dominique are: John C. Lapp, *Zola before the Rougon-Macquart* (Toronto: University of Toronto Press), 1964; and John Rewald, *Cézanne et Zola* (Paris: A. Sedrowski), 1936, pp. 69–70. The portraits hardly figure in Wayne Andersen, *The Youth of Cézanne and Zola: Notoriety at Its Source, Art and Literature in Paris* (Geneva: Editions Fabriart), 2003. Compare Lethbridge's identification of Laurent with Manet, Robert Lethbridge, "Zola, Manet, and *Thérèse Raquin*," *French Studies*, vol. 34, no. 3, July 1980, pp. 279–99.

42 Letter from Zola to Albert Lacroix, 13 September 1867, in Zola, *Correspondance*, p. 523. On the genesis of the novel and its major themes, see Colette Becker, "Thérèse Raquin: L'Obsession de la noyade," *Cents ans de littérature francaise, 1850–1950* (Paris: SEDES), 1987, pp. 105–11; Colette Becker, *Les Apprentissages de Zola: Du Poète romantique au romancier naturaliste, 1840–1867* (Paris: Presses universitaires de France), 1993; and Colette Becker, "*Thérèse Raquin*: La science comme projet, le fantasme comme aveu," *Études romanesques, no. 4, L'Autre du roman et de la fiction, Colloque du Centre du roman* (Picardie: Université de Picardie), 1996, pp. 191–203.

43 [Z], vol. 3, p. 136. At several points, Zola's descriptions of Laurent's portraits recall Cézanne's, [Z], vol. 3, pp. 51, 117–18.

44 For a more explicitly psychoanalytic reading of Laurent's compulsion to repeat, see Claire White, "Zola and Freud: Spent Energy in *Thérèse Raquin*," *Romanic Review*, vol. 103, nos. 3–4, 2011, pp. 349–68.

45 Émile Zola, "M. Manet," *L'Événement*, 7 May 1866, reprinted in [Z], vol. 2, pp. 636–41; and Émile Zola, "Une Nouvelle Manière en peinture: M. Édouard Manet," *Revue du XIXème siècle*, 1 January 1867, reprinted in [Z], vol. 2, pp. 657–80. On nineteenth-century ideas about artistic "temperament," see Richard Shiff, *Cézanne and the End of Impressionism: A Study of the Theory, Technique, and Critical Evaluation of Modern Art* (Chicago: University of Chicago Press), 1984, pp. 70–98; Krüger, *Das Relief der Farbe*, pp. 115–96; Dombrowski, *Cézanne, Murder and Modern Life*, pp. 74–80. On the opposition in Zola between the realism of painting and the arbitrariness of language, see Denis Hollier, "A Room with a View on the Wall," in Jean-Max Guieu and Alison Hilton (eds.), *Émile Zola and the Arts* (Washington, D.C.: Georgetown University Press), 1988, pp. 177–84.

46 On this painting and Cézanne's relationship with his father in general, see John Rewald, "Cézanne and His Father," in *Studies in Impressionism* (New York: Harry N. Abrams), 1985, pp. 69–101. Studies with a psychobiographical component include Theodore Reff, "Cézanne, Flaubert, St. Anthony, and the Queen of Sheba," *Art Bulletin*, vol. 44, no. 2, 1962, pp. 113–25; Theodore Reff, "Cézanne's *Dream of Hannibal*," *Art Bulletin*, vol. 45, no. 2, 1963, pp. 148–52; and Meyer Schapiro, "The Apples of Cézanne: An Essay on the Meaning of Still-Life" (1968), in Schapiro, *Modern Art, 19th and 20th Centuries*, pp. 1–38.

47 Letter from Cézanne to Pissarro, 23 October 1866, in [D], pp. 127–28.

48 His opposition to institutional authorities was more steadfast. See, for example, his 1866 letter criticizing the jury and calling for the re-establishment of the Salon des Réfusés, letter from Cézanne to Nieuwekerke, 19 April 1866, in [D], pp. 120–21.

49 Guillemet to Oller, 12 September 1866, in Taylor, *Francisco Oller*, pp. 226–27.

50 According to Valabrègue, Cézanne had already visited Manet by April 1866. See letter from Valabrègue to Antoine-Fortuné Marion, April 1866, cited in Rewald, *The Paintings of Paul Cézanne*, p. 88. The well-known remarks on Manet attributed to Cézanne—"Il crache le ton!" and "il manque d'harmonie et aussi de temperament"—come from Vollard, *Paul Cézanne*, p. 29. On Cezanne's complicated relationship to Manet, see Dombrowski, *Cézanne, Murder and Modern Life*, pp. 61–137.

51 Émile Zola, "Proudhon et Courbet," in *Mes Haines*, reprinted in [Z], vol. 1, pp. 732–42, here p. 734. On the importance for Cézanne of Zola's reading of Proudhon's reading of Courbet, see James H. Rubin, "Amitiés et théories: Courbet/Proudhon, Cézanne/Zola, ou comment Cézanne a connu Courbet," in *Courbet/Cézanne: La Vérité en peinture*, exh. cat., Musée Gustave Courbet, Ornans, 2013, pp. 42–61. On how the structural opposition in Zola's writing between truth and pleasure shaped the critic's view of Courbet's art, see Denis Hollier, "How to Not Take Pleasure in Talking about Sex," *Enclitic*, trans. Jean Andrews, vol. 8, spring – fall 1984, pp. 84–93.

52 Zola, "Les Réalistes au Salon," *L'Événement*, 11 May 1866, and "Les Chutes," *L'Événement*, 15 May 1866, reprinted in [Z], vol. 2, pp. 642–49.

53 Émile Zola, "Mon Salon," *L'Événement illustré*, 9 June 1868, reprinted in [Z], vol. 3, p. 661.

54 Émile Zola, "M. Jules Michelet," *Le Figaro*, 30 November 1866, reprinted in vol. 2, pp. 594–98, here p. 597. On the impact of Michelet on Zola's early novels, see Marcel Cressot, "Zola et Michelet. Essai sur la genèse de deux romans de jeunesse: 'La Confession de Claude' and 'Madeleine Férat,'" *Revue d'histoire littéraire de la France*, vol. 35, no. 3, 1928, pp. 382–89.

55 A photograph of the original work *in situ* was published in Douglas Cooper, "Au Jas du Bouffan," *L'Oeil*, vol. 2, 15 February 1955, pp. 13–16, 46.

56 For a list of photographs owned by Cézanne, including one of Courbet's *Bathers*, see Theodore Reff, "Reproductions and Books in Cézanne's Studio," [GBA], vol. 56, no. 1102, November 1960, pp. 303–09.

57 On the placement of artworks in the salon, see Rewald, *The Paintings of Paul Cézanne*, pp. 66–68, 73–76, and 94. According to Denis Coutagne, in these years Cézanne used the salon as his studio, painting the uncle portraits of Dominique there. Denis Coutagne, "The Jas du Bouffan," in Conisbee and Coutagne, *Cézanne in Provence*, p. 81.

CODA

1 In the book of poems, Victor Hugo, *L'Année terrible* (Paris: Michel Lévy Frères), 1872.

2 On the political symbolism of the portrait, see Theodore Reff, "Pissarro's Portrait of Cézanne," *The Burlington Magazine*, vol. 109, no. 776, 1967, pp. 627–33. For his part, Manet exhibited a very Courbetian portrait, *Le Bon Bock* (1873; Philadelphia Museum of Art), at the Salon of 1873.

3 On their interaction during this period, see Joachim Pissarro, *Pioneering Modern Painting*; the exhibition review by Richard Brettell, "'Pioneering Modern Painting': The Cézanne and Pissarro Exhibition," *The Burlington Magazine*, vol. 147, no. 1231, 2005, pp. 680–84; T. J. Clark, "Strange Apprentice," London Review of Books, vol. 42, no. 19, 8 October 2020; and Reff, "Pissarro's Portrait of Cézanne."

4 On the transformation of Argenteuil at this time and its impact on Monet, see T. J. Clark, *The Painting of Modern Life: Paris in the Art of Manet and His Followers*, rev. edn (Princeton, N.J.: Princeton University Press), 1999, pp. 145–204; and Paul Hayes Tucker, *The Impressionists at Argenteuil* (Washington, D.C.: National Gallery of Art), 2000. On Pontoise during the same period, see Richard Brettell, *Pissarro and Pontoise: The Painter in a Landscape* (New Haven and London: Yale University Press), 1990.

5 On Monet's use of perspective to reinforce compositional unity, see Anthea Callen's "Taking Shape: Monet's Compositional Techniques," in George Shackelford et al., *Monet: The Early Years* (New Haven and London: Yale University Press), 2016. On his use of texture for the same purpose, see Robert L. Herbert, "Method and Meaning in Monet," *Art in America*, vol. 67, no. 5, September 1979, pp. 90–108. A helpful summary of the evolution of Impressionist mark-making during the 1870s is provided by John House, *Impressionism: Paint and Politics* (New Haven and London: Yale University Press), 2004, pp. 145–86. See also Richard R. Brettell, *Impression: Painting Quickly in France, 1860–1890* (New Haven and London: Yale University Press), 2000.

6 That Pissarro was doing something different was clear to Théodore Duret, who encouraged him to continue down the path he was taking. Letter from Duret to Pissarro, 6 December 1873, in Ludovic Rodo Pissarro and Lionello Venturi, *Camille Pissarro, son art, son oeuvre*, vol. 1 (Paris: Paul Rosenberg), 1939, p. 26. I thank Richard Shiff for pointing out the highly irregular topography of the area in and around Pontoise. For another view of Pissarro's work during this period, see Rachael Ziady DeLue, "Pissarro, Landscape, Vision, and Tradition," *Art Bulletin*, vol. 80, no. 4, December 1998, pp. 718–36.

7 On the breakdown of perspective in Cézanne, see Fritz Novotny, *Cézanne und das Ende der wissenschaftlichen Perspektive* (Vienna: Schroll), 1938; selections translated in Christopher S. Wood (ed.), *The Vienna School Reader: Politics and Art Historical Method in the 1930s* (New York: Zone Books), 2000, pp. 379–433. On the deviation from linear perspective in *Quartier Four, Auvers-sur-Oise* in particular, see Paul Smith, "Cézanne's 'Primitive' Perspective, or the 'View from Everywhere,'" *Art Bulletin*, vol. 95, no. 1, March 2013, pp. 102–19.

8 On the distinction between instrument and tool in the period's art criticism, see Matthias Krüger, "Courbet's Knife—Or the Ideology of Painting Tools," paper presented at the symposium "Gustave Courbet and the Narratives of Modern Painting," Ludwig-Maximilians-Universität, Munich, March 2019.

9 Lemonnier, *G. Courbet et son oeuvre*, p. 62.

10 Ibid.

11 Jules Laforgue, "L'Impressionnisme," *Oeuvres complètes: Vol. 3: Oeuvres et fragments posthumes* (Paris: L'Age d'homme), 2000, pp. 329–36, here p. 330. On the opposition of vision to touch in Cézanne, see Richard Shiff, "Cézanne's Physicality: The Politics of Touch," in *The Language of Art History*, eds. Salim Kemal and Ivan Gaskell (Cambridge: Cambridge University Press), 1993, pp. 129–80.

12 In 1688, the Irish scientist and politician William Molyneux posed the question of whether a blind man, upon being relieved of his affliction, would be able to distinguish a cube from a globe through sight alone, after having only known them previously via touch. The "Molyneux problem" became a cause célèbre in philosophical circles, primarily through its inclusion in the second edition of John Locke's *Essay Concerning Human Understanding* (1694).

13 "Donc un oeil naturel (ou raffiné puisque, pour cet organe, avant d'aller, il faut redevenir primitif en se débarassant des illusions tactiles), un oeil naturel oublie les illusions tactiles," Laforgue, "L'Impressionnisme," p. 330.

SELECT BIBLIOGRAPHY

Abrille, Raphaël, et al., *Les Chasses de monsieur Courbet*, exh. cat., Musée Gustave Courbet, Ornans, 2012

Alix-Leborgne, Viviane, *Castagnary, un homme de la Saintonge* (Tusson, Charente: du Lérot), 2015

——, "Jules-Antoine Castagnary (1830–1888), un critique d'art républicain," Thèse du doctorat, Université Paris III, 1993

Allan, Scott, and Édouard Kopp, *Unruly Nature: The Landscapes of Théodore Rousseau*, exh. cat., The J. Paul Getty Museum, Los Angeles, and Ny Carlsberg Glyptotek, Copenhagen, 2016–17

Andersen, Wayne, *The Youth of Cézanne and Zola: Notoriety at Its Source: Art and Literature in Paris* (Geneva: Editions Fabriart), 2003

Armstrong, Carol, *Cézanne's Gravity* (New Haven and London: Yale University Press), 2018

——, *Manet Manette* (New Haven and London: Yale University Press), 2002

Arnoux, Mathilde (ed.), *Courbet à neuf!* (Paris: Maison des sciences de l'homme), 2010

Athanassoglou-Kallmyer, Nina Maria, *Cézanne and Provence: The Painter in His Culture* (Chicago: University of Chicago Press), 2003

Aubenas, Sylvie, *Gustave Le Gray, 1820–1884*, exh. cat., Bibliothèque nationale de France, Paris, and The J. Paul Getty Museum, Los Angeles, 2002

Bajou, Valérie, *Courbet* (Paris: Biro), 2003

Barbe, Noël, and Hervé Touboul (eds.), *Courbet, peinture et politique* (Besançon: Sekoya), 2013

Barbe, Noël, Hervé Touboul, and Frédérique Thomas-Maurin, *Courbet, Proudhon: L'Art et le peuple* (Besançon: Sekoya), 2010

Barthes, Roland, *Michelet par lui-même* (Paris: Éditions du Seuil) [1954]; *Michelet*, trans. Richard Howard (New York: Hill and Wang), 1987

——, *The Rustle of Language*, trans. Richard Howard (Berkeley: University of California Press), 1989

Berson, Ruth, *The New Painting: Impressionism, 1874–1886: Documentation: Volume I: Reviews; Volume II: Exhibited Works* (San Francisco: Fine Arts Museums of San Francisco), 1996

Blondel, Madeleine, and Pierre Georgel (eds.), *Victor Hugo et les images* (Ville de Dijon: Aux Amateurs de Livres), 1989

Bomford, David, et al., *Impressionism: Art in the Making* (London: National Gallery), 1990

Bonniot, Roger, *Gustave Courbet en Saintonge, 1862–1863* (Paris: C. Klincksieck), 1973

Bossi, Laura (ed.), *Les Origines du monde. L'Invention de la nature au XIXe siècle*, exh. cat. Musée d'Orsay, Paris, 2021

Bourquin, Jacques, *Galerie des linguistes franc-comtois* (Besançon: Presses universitaires comtoises), 2003

Brettell, Richard R., *Impression: Painting Quickly in France, 1860–1890* (New Haven and London: Yale University Press), 2000

——, *Pissarro and Pontoise: The Painter in a Landscape* (New Haven and London: Yale University Press), 1990

Brötje, Michael, "Das Bild als Parabel. Zur Landschaftsmalerei Gustave Courbets," *Jahrbuch der Hamburger Kunstsammlungen*, vol. 23, 1978, pp. 75–106

Bruyeron, Roger, *Écrits, propos, lettres et témoignages* (Paris: Hermann), 2015

Buchon, Max, *Biographie salinoise. Jules Marcou* (Salins: Billet), 1865

——, *Noëls et chants populaires de la Franche-Comté* (Salins: Billet et Duvernois), 1863

——, *Oeuvres choisies*, 3 vols. (Paris: Sandoz et Fischbacher), 1878

——, *Le réalisme. Discussions esthétiques* (Paris: Sandoz et Fischbacher) [1856], ed. Frédérique Desbuissons (La Rochelle: Rumeur des Âges), 2007

——, *Salins-les-Bains, ses eaux minérales et ses environs* (Lons-le-Saunier: de Gauthier frères), 1862

——, *Salins-les-Bains, ses eaux minérales et ses environs*, new edn (Salins: Billet), 1866

——, *Scènes de la vie comtoise*, ed. Michel Vernus (Besançon: Presses du Belvédère), 2004

Burmester, Andreas, Christoph Heilmann, and Michael F. Zimmermann (eds.), *Barbizon: Malerei der Natur, Natur der Malerei* (Munich: Klinkhardt & Biermann), 1999

Callen, Anthea, *The Art of Impressionism: Painting Technique & the Making of Modernity* (New Haven and London: Yale University Press), 2000

——, *Courbet* (London: Jupiter Books), 1980

——, *Techniques of the Impressionists* (Secaucus, N.J.: Chartwell Books), 1982

——, *The Work of Art: Plein Air Painting and Artistic Identity in Nineteenth-Century France* (London: Reaktion Books), 2014

Campbell, Christopher, "Pissarro and the Palette Knife: Two Pictures from 1867," *Apollo*, vol. 136, November 1992, pp. 311–14

des Cars, Laurence, *Courbet et la Commune* (Paris: Réunion des musées nationaux), 2000

des Cars, Laurence, and Dominique de Font-Réaulx et al., *Gustave Courbet*, exh. cat., Grand Palais, Paris, Metropolitan Museum of Art, New York, and Musée Fabre, Montpellier, 2007–08

Castagnary, Jules-Antoine, *Exposition des oeuvres de Gustave Courbet à l'école des Beaux-Arts (mai 1882)* (Paris: Impr. E. Martinet), 1882

——, *Gustave Courbet*, ed. Bertrand Tillier (Rezé: Séquences), 2000

——, *Gustave Courbet et la colonne Vendôme: Plaidoyer pour un ami mort* (Paris: E. Dentu) [1883] (Tusson, Charente: Du Lérot), 2000

——, *Salons*, 2 vols. (Paris: G. Charpentier et E. Fasquelle), 1892

Cézanne, Paul, and Émile Zola, *Lettres croisées: 1858–1887* (Paris: Gallimard), 2016

Champa, Kermit S., *Studies in Early Impressionism* (New Haven and London: Yale University Press), 1973

Chang, Ting, "Hats and Hierarchy in Gustave Courbet's *The Meeting*," *Art Bulletin*, vol. 86, no. 4, 2004, pp. 719–30

——, "'The Meeting': Gustave Courbet and Alfred Bruyas," *The Burlington Magazine*, vol. 138, no. 1122, 1996, pp. 586–91

——, "Rewriting Courbet: Silvestre, Courbet, and the Bruyas Collection after the Paris Commune," *Oxford Art Journal*, vol. 21, no. 1, 1998, pp. 107–20

Chu, Petra ten-Doesschate, *Courbet in Perspective* (New York: Prentice-Hall), 1977

——, "Gustave Courbet's *Venus and Psyche*: Uneasy Nudity in Second-Empire France," *Art Journal*, vol. 51, no. 1, 1992, pp. 38–44

——, "It Took a Million Years to Paint that Picture," in *Courbet Reconsidered*, eds. Sarah Faunce and Linda Nochlin, exh. cat., Brooklyn Museum, 1988–89, pp. 55–66

——, *The Most Arrogant Man in France: Gustave Courbet and the Nineteenth-Century Media Culture* (Princeton, N.J.: Princeton University Press), 2007

Chu, Petra ten-Doesschate (ed.), *Courbet, épistolier – 24 lettres inédites* (Dijon: Les Presses du réel), 2017

Clark, T. J., "A Bourgeois Dance of Death: Max Buchon on Courbet I," *The Burlington Magazine*, vol. 111, no. 793, April 1969, pp. 208–13

——, "A Bourgeois Dance of Death: Max Buchon on Courbet II," *The Burlington Magazine*, vol. 111, no. 794, May 1969, pp. 286–90

——, *Image of the People: Gustave Courbet and the 1848 Revolution*, rev. edn (Berkeley and Los Angeles: University of California Press), 1999

——, *The Painting of Modern Life: Paris in the Art of Manet and His Followers*, rev. edn (Princeton, N.J.: Princeton University Press), 1999

——, "Phenomenality and Materiality in Cézanne," in *Material Events: Paul de Man and the Afterlife of Theory*, eds. Tom Cohen et al. (Minneapolis: University of Minnesota Press), 2000, pp. 93–113

Clarke, Michael, "Courbet Peintre Des Paysages," in Jörg Zutter and Petra ten-Doesschate Chu et al., *Courbet: Artiste et promoteur de son oeuvre* (Paris: Flammarion), 1998, pp. 83–100

Claudet, Max, *Souvenirs. Gustave Courbet* (Paris: Dubuisson), 1878

Conisbee, Philip, and Denis Coutagne et al., *Cézanne in Provence*, exh. cat., National Gallery of Art, Washington, D.C., 2006

Conisbee, Philip, Sarah Faunce, and Jeremy Strick, *In the Light of Italy: Corot and Early Open-Air Painting*, exh. cat., National Gallery of Art, Washington, D.C., 1996

Corot, Jean-Baptiste-Camille, *Corot, raconté par lui-même et par ses amis* (Vésenaz, Geneva: P. Cailler), 1946

Courbet, Gustave, *Cahiers de philosophie*, ed. Roger Bruyeron (Paris: Hermann), 2011

——, *Letters of Gustave Courbet*, ed. and trans. Petra ten-Doesschate Chu (Chicago: University of Chicago Press), 1992

Courbet/Hugo: Les Peintres et les littérateurs, exh. cat., Musée Gustave Courbet, Ornans, 2002

Courthion, Pierre, *Courbet: Raconté par lui-même et par ses amis. Sa Vie et ses oeuvres*, 2 vols. (Geneva: P. Cailler), 1948

Coutagne, Denis (ed.), *Courbet/Cézanne, la vérité en peinture*, exh. cat., Musée Gustave Courbet, Ornans, 2013

Crapo, Paul B., "The Problematics of Artistic Patronage under the Second Empire: Gustave Courbet's Involved Relations with the Regime of Napoleon III," *Zeitschrift für Kunstgeschichte*, vol. 58, no. 2, 1995, pp. 240–61

Danchev, Alex (ed. and trans.), *The Letters of Paul Cézanne* (Los Angeles: The J. Paul Getty Museum), 2013

DeLue, Rachael Ziady, "Pissarro, Landscape, Vision, and Tradition," *Art Bulletin*, vol. 80, no. 4, December 1998, pp. 718–36

Desbuissons, Frédérique, "Courbet's Materialism," *Oxford Art Journal*, vol. 31, no. 2, June 2008, pp. 251–60

——, "Enigme et interpretations: L'Atelier du peintre de Gustave Courbet. Histoire d'une oeuvre inachevée, 1854–1996," Thèse du doctorat, Université Paris I, 1997

Dittmar, Gérald, *Gustave Courbet et la Commune, le politique* (Paris: Dittmar), 2007

Dombrowski, André, *Cézanne, Murder, and Modern Life* (Berkeley: University of California Press), 2013

Doran, Michael, *Conversations with Cézanne*, trans. Julie Lawrence (Berkeley: University of California Press), 2001

Dornier, Charles, "La Bohème littéraire et la Révolution de 1848," *La Revue de France*, vol. 20, October 1926, pp. 740–52

——, "Un Témoin de La Bohème littéraire avec Champfleury, Baudelaire, Murger et Courbet," *La Revue de France*, vol. 5, March 1925, pp. 68–89

Dunstan, Bernard, *Painting Methods of the Impressionists* (New York: Watson-Guptill), 1983

Elderfield, John, *Cézanne Portraits*, exh. cat., Musée d'Orsay, Paris, National Portrait Gallery, London, and National Gallery of Art, Washington, D.C., 2017–18

Elderfield, John, and Faya Causey et al., *Cézanne: The Rock and Quarry Paintings* (New Haven and London: Yale University Press), 2020

Encrevé, Lucile, *Brice Marden, Gustave Courbet*, trans. John Lee (Paris: Musée d'Orsay), 2006

Eugène Boudin: Lettres à Ferdinand Martin. Vol. 1: 1861–1870 (Honfleur: Société des Amis du Musée Eugène Boudin), 2011

Faunce, Sarah, *Courbet Reconsidered*, exh. cat., Brooklyn Museum and Minneapolis Institute of Art, 1988–89

Faunce, Sarah, and Leon Wieseltier, *Gustave Courbet*, exh. cat., Salander-O'Reilly Galleries, New York, 2003

Fernier, Robert, *La Vie et l'oeuvre de Gustave Courbet. Catalogue raisonné. Volume 1: 1819–1865. Peintures*, 2 vols. (Lausanne: Wildenstein Institute), 1977

Flécheux, Céline, *L'Horizon: Des Traités de perspective au land art* (Rennes: Presses universitaires de Rennes), 2009

Frey, Hugo, *Max Buchon et son oeuvre* (Besançon: Impr. de l'Est), 1940

Fried, Michael, *Courbet's Realism* (Chicago: University of Chicago Press), 1990

Galassi, Peter, *Corot in Italy: Open-Air Painting and the Classical-Landscape Tradition*, exh. cat., National Gallery of Art, Washington, D.C., Brooklyn Museum, and The Saint Louis Art Museum, 1991

Gallwitz, Herding, and Klaus Herding, *Malerei und Theorie: Das Courbet-Colloquium* (Frankfurt am Main: Städel), 1980

Gamboni, Dario, *Potential Images: Ambiguity and Indeterminacy in Modern Art* (London: Reaktion Books), 2002

Gautier, Théophile, *Courbet, le Watteau du laid*, ed. Christine Sagnier (Biarritz: Séguier), 2000

——, *Dessins de Victor Hugo* (Paris: Castel), 1863

Georgel, Pierre, *Les Dessins de Victor Hugo pour "Les Travailleurs de la mer"* (Paris: Herscher), 1985

Georgel, Pierre, Jean-Paul Boulanger, and Geneviève Renisio, *La Gloire de Victor Hugo*, exh. cat., Grand Palais, Paris, 1985–86

Georgel, Pierre (ed.), *L'Oeil de Victor Hugo: Actes du colloque* (Paris: Éditions des Cendres), 2004

Georgopulos, Nicole, "'The Cradle of Things': Origins and Ontogenesis in the Late Landscapes of Gustave Courbet" (MA thesis, Stony Brook University), 2016

Gohin, Yves, *Sur l'emploi des mots immanent et immanence chez Victor Hugo* (Paris: Lettres modernes), 1968

Gossman, Lionel, "The Go-Between: Jules Michelet, 1798–1874," *MLN*, vol. 89, no. 4, May 1974, pp. 503–41

——, "Jules Michelet: Histoire nationale, biographie, autobiographie," *Littérature*, vol. 102, no. 2, May 1996, pp. 29–54

——, "Michelet and Natural History: The Alibi of Nature," *Proceedings of the American Philosophical Society*, vol. 145, no. 3, September 2001, pp. 283–333

Gowing, Lawrence, *Cézanne: The Early Years 1859–1872*, Royal Academy of Arts, London, Musée d'Orsay, Paris, and National Gallery of Art, Washington, D.C., 1988–89

——, *Lawrence Gowing: Selected Writings on Art*, ed. Sarah Whitfield (London: Ridinghouse), 2015

Green, Nicholas, *The Spectacle of Nature: Landscape and Bourgeois Culture in Nineteenth-Century France* (Manchester: Manchester University Press), 1990

Gros-Kost, Émile, *Courbet, souvenirs intimes* (Paris: Derveaux) [1880] (Paris: Ides et Calendes), 1994

Güdel, Niklaus Manuel (ed.), *Gustave Courbet: Les Dessins*, exh. cat., Musée Gustave Courbet, Ornans, and Musée Jenisch Vevey, Switzerland, 2019–20

Guidi, Barbara, Maria Luisa Pacelli et al., *Courbet e la natura*, exh. cat., Palazzo dei Diamanti, Ferrara, 2018–19

Guieu, Jean-Max, and Alison Hilton (eds.), *Émile Zola and the Arts* (Washington, D.C.: Georgetown University Press), 1988

Haarer, Andrea, "Zustände des Fließenden. Victor Hugos Bildermachen zu Meerwasser 1855–1875" (PhD dissertation, University of Stuttgart), 2019

Haddad, Michèle, *Gustave Courbet: Peinture et histoire* (Sainte-Croix: Presses du Belvédère), 2007

Haudiquet, Annette, et al., *Vagues: Autour des Paysages de mer de Gustave Courbet*, exh. cat., Musée d'art moderne André Malraux, Le Havre, 2004

Heilmann, Christoph, Michael Clarke, and John Sillevis, *Corot, Courbet und die Maler von Barbizon: "Les Amis de la nature"* (Munich: Klinkhardt & Biermann), 1996

Herbert, James D., *Brushstroke and Emergence: Courbet, Impressionism, Picasso* (Chicago: University of Chicago Press), 2015

Herbert, Robert L., *Barbizon Revisited: Essay and Catalogue*, exh. cat., Museum of Fine Arts, Boston, California Palace of the Legion of Honor, San Francisco, Toledo Museum of Art, Ohio, and The Cleveland Museum of Art, Ohio, 1962–63

——, "Method and Meaning in Monet," *Art in America*, vol. 67, no. 5, September 1979, pp. 90–108

——, *Monet on the Normandy Coast: Tourism and Painting, 1867–1886* (New Haven and London: Yale University Press), 1994

Herding, Klaus, *Courbet: To Venture Independence*, trans. John William Gabriel (New Haven and London: Yale University Press), 1991

Herding, Klaus (ed.), *Realismus als Widerspruch: Die Wirklichkeit in Courbets Malerei* (Frankfurt am Main: Suhrkamp), 1978. French translation with author interview: *Le Réalisme comme contradiction: Visions, conflits et résistances dans l'oeuvre de Courbet*, trans. Anne-Marie Green (Besançon: Sekoya), 2013

Herding, Klaus, and Max Hollein (eds.), *Courbet: A Dream of Modern Art*, exh. cat., Schirn Kunsthalle, Frankfurt am Main, 2010–11

Herding, Klaus, and Sabine Schulze, *Impressionisten: 6 französische Meisterwerke/Impressionnistes: 6 Chefs-d'oeuvre français*, exh. cat., Städel Museum, Frankfurt am Main, 1999

Hofmann, Werner, et al., *Courbet und Deutschland*, exh. cat., Hamburger Kunsthalle, Hamburg, and Städelschen Kunstinstitut, Frankfurt, 1978–79

Hollier, Denis, "How to Not Take Pleasure in Talking about Sex," *Enclitic*, trans. Jean Andrews, vol. 8, spring – fall 1984, pp. 84–93

——, "A Room with a View on the Wall," in *Émile Zola and the Arts*, eds. Jean-Max Guieu and Alison Hilton (Washington, D.C.: Georgetown University Press), 1988, pp. 177–84

House, John, *Impressionism: Paint and Politics* (New Haven and London: Yale University Press), 2004

Howe, Jeffery (ed.), *Courbet: Mapping Realism: Paintings from the Royal Museums of Fine Arts of Belgium and American Collections*, exh. cat., McMullen Museum of Art, Boston College, 2013

Hugo, Victor, *Notre-Dame de Paris; Les Travailleurs de la mer* (Paris: Gallimard), 1975

——, *Oeuvres complètes*, ed. Jean Massin (Paris: Le Club français du livre), 1967

——, *Les Travailleurs de la mer* (Paris: Librairie internationale), 1866

——, *Les Travailleurs de la mer* (Paris: Garnier-Flammarion), 1980

Ideville, Henri, *Gustave Courbet: Notes et documents sur sa vie & son oeuvre* (Paris: Paris-Gravé), 1878

Jean-Aubry, Georges, *La Vie et l'oeuvre d'après les lettres et les documents inédits d'Eugène Boudin* (Neuchâtel: Idées et Calendes), 1968

Joly, Carine (ed.), *Courbet en privé: Correspondance de Gustave Courbet dans les collections de l'Institut Gustave Courbet* (Besançon: Sekoya), 2019

Jones, Kimberly, et al., *In the Forest of Fontainebleau: Painters and Photographers from Corot to Monet*, exh. cat., National Gallery of Art, Washington, D.C., 2008

Kelly, Simon, "The Landscapes of Théodore Rousseau and Their Market," in *Barbizon. Im Auftrag der Bayerischen Staatsgemäldesammlungen*, eds. Andreas Burmester, Christoph Heilmann, and Michael F. Zimmermann (Munich: Klinkhardt & Biermann), 1999, pp. 419–36

——, *Théodore Rousseau and the Rise of the Modern Art Market: An Avant-Garde Landscape Painter in Nineteenth-Century France* (New York and London: Bloomsbury), 2021

Krüger, Matthias, "Gespachtelter Zufall. Gustave Courbet und die Messermalerei," in *Werkzeuge und Instrumente*, eds. Philippe Cordez and Matthias Krüger (Berlin: Akademie), 2012, pp. 109–27

——, "Jean-Léon Gérôme, His Badger and His Studio," in *Hiding Making – Showing Creation. The Studio from Turner to Tacita Dean*, eds. Rachel Esner, Sandra Kisters, and Ann-Sophie Lehmann (Amsterdam: Amsterdam University Press), 2013, pp. 43–61

——, *Das Relief der Farbe: Pastose Malerei in der französischen Kunstkritik 1850–1890* (Munich: Deutscher Kunstverlag), 2007

Kurlander, Amy, and Simon Kelly, *The Untamed Landscape: Théodore Rousseau and the Path to Barbizon*, exh. cat., The Morgan Library & Museum, New York, 2014–15

Küster, Ulf, *Gustave Courbet* (Ostfildern: Hatje Cantz), 2014

——, *Gustave Courbet*, exh. cat., Fondation Beyeler, Reihen/Basel, 2014

Lapp, John C., *Zola before the Rougon-Macquart* (Toronto: University of Toronto Press), 1964

Lavallée, Marie-Hélène, et al., *Gustave Courbet et la Franche-Comté*, exh. cat., Musée des Beaux-Arts et d'Archéologie, Besançon, 2000

Lebel, Jean-Jacques and Marie-Laure Prévost, *Du chaos dans le pinceau: Victor Hugo, dessins*, exh. cat., Musée Thyssen-Bornemisza, Madrid, and Maison de Victor Hugo, Paris, 2000–01

Léger, Charles, *Courbet* (Paris: Éditions G. Crès & Cie), 1929

——, *Courbet et son temps: Lettres et documents inédits* (Paris: Éditions Universelles), 1948

——, *Courbet selon les caricatures et les images* (Paris: P. Rosenberg), 1920

Le Men, Ségolène, *Courbet* (New York: Abbeville Press), 2008

Lemonedes, Heather, Lynn Federle Orr, and David H. Steel, *Monet in Normandy*, exh. cat., Fine Arts Museums of San Francisco, California, North Carolina Museum of Art, and The Cleveland Museum of Art, Ohio, 2006–07

Lemonnier, Camille, *G. Courbet et son oeuvre. Gustave Courbet à la Tour de Peilz (Lettre du Dr. Paul Collin)* (Paris: Alphonse Lemerre), 1878

Le Normand-Romain, Antoinette, et al., *Cet Obscur Objet de désirs: Autour de "L'Origine du monde,"* exh. cat., Musée d'Orsay, Paris, 2014

Lewis, Mary Tompkins, *Cézanne's Early Imagery* (Berkeley: University of California Press), 1989

Lindsay, Jack, *Gustave Courbet: His Life and Art* (New York: Harper & Row), 1973

Mack, Gerstle, *Gustave Courbet* (New York: Alfred A. Knopf), 1951

McNamara, Carole, *The Lens of Impressionism: Photography and Painting along the Normandy Coast, 1850–1874* (Ann Arbor: University of Michigan Museum of Art), 2009

Madeline, Laurence, *Gustave Courbet: Les Années suisses* (Paris: Éditions Artlys), 2014

Manty, Paul, "Gustave Courbet (Part 1)," *Gazette des Beaux-Arts*, vol. 17, 1878, pp. 514–27; "Gustave Courbet (Part 2)," *Gazette des Beaux-Arts*, vol. 17, 1878, pp. 17–30; "Gustave Courbet (Part 3)," *Gazette des Beaux-Arts*, vol. 17, 1878, pp. 371–84

Marchal, Stephanie, *Gustave Courbet in seinen Selbstdarstellungen* (Munich: Wilhelm Fink), 2012

Marcou, Jules, *Lettres sur les roches du Jura et leur distribution géographique dans les deux hémisphères* (Paris: F. Klincksieck), 1857–60

Marcou, Jules, and Jakob Melchior Ziegler, *Carte géologique de la terre* (Winterthur: J. Wurster & Co.), 1861

Meier-Graefe, Julius, *Corot und Courbet; Ein Beitrag zur Entwicklungsgeschichte der modernen Malerei* (Leipzig: Insel), 1905

Michelet, Jules, *La Mer* (Paris: Hachette) [1861], ed. Jean Borie (Paris: Gallimard), 1983

——, *Oeuvres complètes* (Paris: Flammarion), 1971

Montier, Jean-Pierre, "Dessins et écriture dans le manuscrit des *Travailleurs de la mer* de Victor Hugo," *French Studies: A Quarterly Review*, vol. 60, no. 1, January 2006, pp. 15–31

——, "Le 'Finale' des *Travailleurs de la mer*: Horizon et limite du texte romanesque," *Littérature*, vol. 135, September 2004, pp. 3–23

Morton, Mary, and Charlotte Eyerman, *Courbet and the Modern Landscape*, exh. cat., The J. Paul Getty Museum, Los Angeles, Museum of Fine Arts, Houston, and The Walters Art Museum, Baltimore, 2006–07

Muther, Richard, *Courbet* (Berlin: Marquardt), 1908

Myers, Nicole R., "Courbet and the Realist Nude" (PhD dissertation, New York University), 2015

Nochlin, Linda, "Le Chêne de Flagey de Courbet: Un Motif de paysage et sa signification," *48/14*, no. 1, 1989, pp. 15–25

——, *Courbet* (New York and London: Thames & Hudson), 2007

——, *Gustave Courbet: A Study of Style and Society* (New York: Garland Publishing, Inc.), 1976

——, *Realism* (New York: Penguin Books), 1971

Nodier, Charles, Justin Taylor, and Alphonse de Cailleux, *Voyages pittoresques et romantiques dans l'ancienne France (Franche-Comté)* (Paris: J. Didot l'Aîné), 1825

Orr, Linda, *Jules Michelet: Nature, History, and Language* (Ithaca, N.Y.: Cornell University Press), 1976

Patoul, Brigitte de, *Gustave Courbet et la Belgique: Réalisme de l'art vivant à l'art libre* (Milan: Silvana Editoriale), 2013

Petitjean, Joël, *Gustave Courbet et la photographie* (Lyons: Fage), 2012

Philbin, Ann, and Florian Rodari, *Shadows of a Hand: The Drawings of Victor Hugo* (New York: Drawing Center), 1988

Pissarro, Joachim, *Pioneering Modern Painting: Cézanne & Pissarro, 1865–1885*, exh. cat., Museum of Modern Art, New York, Los Angeles County Museum of Art, and Musée d'Orsay, Paris, 2005–06

Prévost, Marie-Laure, *Victor Hugo, l'homme-océan*, exh. cat., Bibliothèque nationale de France, Paris, 2002

Proudhon, Pierre-Joseph, *Du Principe de l'art et de sa destination sociale* (Paris: Garnier frères), 1865

Rajakaruna, Chandrasiri, F. Lépine, and J. Fernier, *Gustave Courbet: L'Amour de la nature*, exh. cat., Fondation Mona Bismarck, Paris, 2011

Les Réalismes et l'histoire de l'art, special issue of *Histoire et critique des arts*, vols. 4–5, May 1978

Reff, Théodore, "Cézanne's Constructive Stroke," *Art Quarterly*, vol. 25, no. 3, fall 1962, pp. 214–17

——, "Pissarro's Portrait of Cézanne," *The Burlington Magazine*, vol. 109, no. 776, 1967, pp. 627–33

Reilly, Maura, "Le Vice à la mode: Gustave Courbet and the Vogue for Lesbianism in Second Empire France" (PhD dissertation, New York University), 2000

Rewald, John, *Cézanne et Zola* (Paris: A. Sedrowski), 1936

——, *The History of Impressionism* (New York; Greenwich, Connecticut: Museum of Modern Art: Secker and Warburg), 1973

Riat, Georges, *Gustave Courbet, peintre* (Paris: H. Floury), 1906

Robaut, Alfred, and Étienne Moreau-Nélaton, *L'Oeuvre de Corot* (Paris: Léonce Laget), 1965

Rott, Herbert Wilhelm, et al., *Courbet > Daubigny: Das Rätsel der "Schleuse im Tal von Optevoz"* (Munich: Hirmer), 2014

Rubin, James H., "Amitiés et théories: Courbet/Proudhon, Cézanne/Zola, ou comment Cézanne a connu Courbet," in *Courbet/Cézanne: La Vérité en peinture*, exh. cat. Musée Gustave Courbet, Ornans, 2013, pp. 42–61

——, *Courbet* (London: Phaidon), 1997

——, "Courbet in Love and Productive Disappointment," in *Gustave Courbet* (London: Matthiesen Gallery), 2016

——, *Realism and Social Vision in Courbet & Proudhon* (Princeton, N.J.: Princeton University Press), 1980

Sarfati, Yves (ed.), *Transferts de Courbet* (Dijon: Les Presses du réel), 2013

Sarfati, Yves, Thomas Schlesser, and Bertrand Tillier et al., *La Correspondance de Courbet: 20 ans après* (Dijon: Les Presses du réel), 2018

Savatier, Thierry, *L'Origine du monde: Histoire d'un tableau de Gustave Courbet* (Paris: Bartillat), 2006

Scaon, Gaby, and Jean-Roger Soubiran, *Autour de Courbet en Saintonge*, exh. cat., Musée de l'Échivinage, Saintes, 2007

Schanne, Alexandre, *Souvenirs de Schaunard* (Paris: G. Charpentier et Cie), 1886

Schapiro, Meyer, "Courbet and Popular Imagery: An Essay on Realism and Naïveté," in Meyer Schapiro, *Modern Art, 19th and 20th Centuries: Selected Papers* (New York: George Braziller), 1978, pp. 47–85

Schlesser, Thomas, and Bertrand Tillier, *Courbet face à la caricature: Le Chahut par l'image* (Paris: Kimé), 2007

Schulman, Michel, *Théodore Rousseau, 1812–1867: Catalogue raisonné de l'oeuvre graphique* (Paris: Éditions de l'Amateur: Éditions des Catalogues raisonnés), 1997

——, *Théodore Rousseau, 1812–1867: Catalogue raisonné de l'oeuvre peint* (Paris: Les Éditions de l'Amateur), 1999

Schulman, Michel, and Alexandra R. Murphy, *Théodore Rousseau: The Language of Nature*, exh. cat., Salander-O'Reilly Galleries, New York, 2002

Sensier, Alfred, *Souvenirs sur Th. Rousseau* (Paris: Leon Techener), 1872

Shiff, Richard, *Cézanne and the End of Impressionism: A Study of the Theory, Technique, and Critical Evaluation of Modern Art* (Chicago: University of Chicago Press), 1984

——, "Cézanne's Physicality: The Politics of Touch," in *The Language of Art History*, eds. Salim Kemal and Ivan Gaskell (Cambridge: Cambridge University Press), 1991, pp. 129–80

——, "Mark, Motif, Materiality: The Cézanne Effect in the Twentieth Century," in *Cézanne: Finished – Unfinished*, eds. Felix Baumann et al. (Stuttgart: Hatje Cantz), 2000, pp. 99–123

——, "Natural, Personal, Pictorial: Corot and the Painter's Mark," in *Barbizon: Malerei der Natur, Natur der Malerei*, eds. Andreas Burmester, Christoph Heilmann, and Michael F. Zimmermann (Munich: Klinkhardt & Biermann), 1999, pp. 120–38

Sickert, Walter, *Walter Sickert: The Complete Writings on Art*, ed. Anna Gruetzner Robins (Oxford and New York: Oxford University Press), 2000

Silvestre, Théophile, *Histoire des artistes vivants: Études d'après nature* (Paris: E. Blanchard), 1857

Simon, Robert, "Cézanne and the Subject of Violence," *Art in America*, vol. 79, no. 5, May 1991, pp. 120–35, 185–86

Smith, Paul, "Cézanne's 'Primitive' Perspective, or the 'View from Everywhere,'" *Art Bulletin*, vol. 95, no. 1, March 2013, pp. 102–19

Thomas, Greg M., *Art and Ecology in Nineteenth-Century France: The Landscapes of Théodore Rousseau* (Princeton, N.J.: Princeton University Press), 2000

Thomas-Maurin, Frédérique, Julie Delmas, and Élise Boudon, *Courbet et l'impressionnisme*, exh. cat., Musée Gustave Courbet, Ornans, 2016

Titeux, Gilbert, *Au Temps du brame: Les Représentations de la chasse dans l'oeuvre de Gustave Courbet et dans la peinture allemande du XIXe siècle (1800–1900)* (Dijon: Presses du réel), 2014

Toussaint, Hélène, *Gustave Courbet: 1819–1877*, exh. cat., Grand Palais, Paris, and Royal Academy of Arts, London, 1977–78

Tuma, Kathryn A., "Cézanne, Lucretius, and the Late Nineteenth-Century Crisis in Science" (PhD dissertation, University of California, Berkeley), 2000

——, "Cézanne and Lucretius at the Red Rock," *Representations*, vol. 78, no. 1, spring 2002, pp. 56–85

Viallaneix, Paul (ed.), *Michelet cent ans après: Études et témoignages* (Grenoble: Presses universitaires de Grenoble), 1975

Vogne, Marcel, *La Presse périodique en Franche-Comté: Des Origines à 1870*, 7 vols. (Vanves: M. Vogne), 1977

Wagner, Anne M., "Courbet's Landscapes and Their Market," *Art History*, vol. 4, no. 4, December 1981, pp. 410–31

Wey, Francis, *Notre Maître-peintre Gustave Courbet*, ed. Frédérique Desbuissons (La Rochelle: Rumeur des âges), 2007

Wilson-Bareau, Juliet, and David Degener, *Manet and the Sea*, exh. cat., Art Institute of Chicago, Philadelphia Museum of Art, and Van Gogh Museum, Amsterdam, 2003–04

Young, Marnin, *Realism in the Age of Impressionism: Painting and the Politics of Time* (New Haven and London: Yale University Press), 2015

Zola, Émile, *Le Bon Combat: De Courbet aux impressionnistes: Anthologie d'écrits sur l'art*, ed. Jean-Paul Bouillon (Paris: Hermann), 1974

——, *Carnets d'enquêtes: Une Ethnographie inédite de la France*, ed. Henri Mitterand (Paris: Plon), 1986

——, *Correspondance: Vol. I: 1858–1867*, ed. B. H. Bakker (Montreal: Presses de l'Université de Montréal; Paris: Éditions du Centre national de la recherche scientifique), 1978

——, *Oeuvres complètes*, eds. Henri Mitterand and Françoise Juhel, 21 vols. (Paris: Nouveau monde), 2002–10

——, *Thérèse Raquin* (Paris: A. Lacroix, Verboeckhoven et Cie), 1868

Zutter, Jörg, and Petra ten-Doesschate Chu et al., *Courbet: Artiste et promoteur de son oeuvre* (Paris: Flammarion), 1998

INDEX

Figures are shown by a page reference in **bold**.

A

Académie des Beaux-Arts 13
Alaise; *see* Alesia
Alesia, Battle of 66–9, 76
Auguin, Louis-Auguste 27, 33, 36
Auguin, Nelly 30, 33

B

Barbizon School 13–14, 47–8, 122
Barthes, Roland 118, 120
Baudelaire, Charles 13, 53, 98, 104, 134
Bazille, Frédéric 129
Baudry, Étienne 27, 33, 39, 53
Beauquier, Charles 90, 108, 117
Boudin, Eugène 95, 104–5
  Beach at Villerville, The **88**, 89
Bouvet, Alfred 67, 69
Brongniart, Alexandre 74–5, **75**
brushwork
  of Cézanne 152
  of the Impressionists 172–3
  interplay with knife-work 43–4
  in Saintonge paintings 38–9
  in Whistler's seascapes 107
Buchon, Max
  the *colonie réaliste* 69
  on Jules Marcou 72
  Le Salinois 14, 61, 78
  Revue littéraire de la Franche-Comté 14, 63, 90, 108, 117
  Salins-les-Bains: Ses Eaux minérales et ses environs 76–7
  study of language 14–15, 58, 63–4, 66, 72, 75, 82

C

Castagnary, Jules-Antoine 12, 27, 53, 57, 69, 72–3
Cézanne, Paul
  color mixing 149–52, 156
  Émile Zola and 23, 141, 152–3
  geological time and 83
  landscapes 166–7, 169, 172–5
  paintings: *Antony Valabrègue* 146, **147**; *Bather and Rocks* 158–61, **159**; *Quartier Four, Auverssur-Oise* 169–71, **170–1**; *River Bend* 144, **145**; *Rocks at the Seashore* **150–1**, 152; *Uncle Dominique* **148**, 149; *Uncle Dominique with a Turban* 149, **149**, 152
  palette-knife technique 23, 131, 141, 144, 146–52, 166, 169–71, 172
  Portrait of Cézanne (Pissarro) 166, **167**
  psychobiographical readings of 157, 158, 160, 172
Cham, "La Falaise d'Étretat après l'orage" **95**
Champfleury 16, 18, 28, 63
Claudet, Max 52–3, 63, 78
color
  Cézanne's use of 149–52, 156
  of the Roche pourrie 72–3
  Rock Oak, The (Rousseau) 47
  in seascapes 103, 123–4
Corot, Jean-Baptiste-Camille 27, 135, 144
  Bath of Diana, The 30–3, **34**
  Corner of the Park at Port-Berteau, near Rochemont 30–3, **31**, 38
  mark-making contrasted with Courbet 38–9
  Saintonge Landscape **28**
  side-by-side paintings with Courbet 23, 30–3
Courbet, Gustave
  caricatures of 42, **43**, **44**, **167**
  the column, Place Vendôme 165
  exile 10, 165, 166
  paintings: *After the Hunt* **119**, 120; *Artist's Studio, The* 25, 132, 149; *Bathers, The* 120–2, 132, 135, 158; *Beneath the Trees at Port-Berteau* **32**, 33, 36, 38; *Burial at Ornans, A* 10, 25, 122; *Covert of Roe-Deer by the Stream of Plaisir-Fontaine* 53, **54–5**, 129, 131;

Étretat Cliffs after the Storm, The 165; *Fort de Joux* 69; *Girl with Seagulls, Trouville* 123, **125**; *Gour de Conche, Le* 14, 66, **67**, 69, 78; *Grotto of the Giants near Saillon, Switzerland* 19; *Hippocrene Spring* 53; *Le Salinois* 14, 69, 77, 78; *Marine* (series) **91**, **93**, 94, **94**, 103; *Marine: The Waterspout* **92**, 93, 98; *Oak of Flagey* 68–9, **70–1**; *Origin of the World* 16; *paysages de mer* 89, 104, 108, 122–3, 158; *Peasants of Flagey Returning from the Fair, The* 25, 122; *Pierre-Joseph Proudhon and His Children in 1853* 53, 85; *Return from the Conference* 53, 57, 63, 85; *Roche pourrie* 72–5, **74**; *Source of the Lison* 23, **50**, 51–2, **51**, 57–8, 78–82, 163; *Source of the Loue, The* (series) **8–9**, 10, 14, 18–19, 57–8, 59–61, **60–1**, **64**, **65**; *Spring, The* **121**, 160; *Stonebreakers, The* 10, 122; *Stormy Sea, The* 83, 105, 110, 117, 165; *Stream, The* **20–1**, 25, 26; *Stream in the Forest* 23, **24**, 36–9, **37**, **38**, 47, 49, 53, 80, 81; *Stream of the Puits noir, The* **6**, 7–10, 12, 14, 16, 19, 26, 57–8, 85, **86–7**, 88, 129, 163, 175; *Study of Women (Venus in Jealous Pursuit of Psyche)* 53, 85, 132; *Trellis, The* 39–41, **40–1**, 120; *View of Saintes* 28–30, **29**; *Voyages pittoresques et romantiques dans l'ancienne France* 59, 61, **62**, 78–80, **79**; *Wave* (series) **100–1**, 102, 103, 110, **110**; *Woman in a Podoscaphe* 122, 132; *Woman in the Waves, The* 125–6, **126**; *Woman with a Parrot* 129, **130–1**, 132–3; *Wrestlers, The* 43, 122; *Young Ladies of the Village* 43, 122
at Rochemont 26, 27–8, 39, 53
side-by-side painting with Corot 30–3
sites painted *see* Franche-Comté; Salins
studio in Ornans **52**, 53, 57
Cuvier, Georges **75**

D

Daubigny, Charles-François 13, 135, 144
Deauville 15, 88, 94
Degas, Edgar
Portrait of Mlle. Fiocre in the Ballet "La Source" 138–40, **138–9**
response to Courbet 131, 137–41, 142
Rocks at Bagnoles-de-l'Orne **140**
Diaz de la Peña, Narcisse-Virgilio 13, 47, 135
Duret, Théodore 27, 30

E

Étretat 10, 15, 88, 94–5

F

Feyen, Eugène *Interior of Courbet's Studio at Ornans* **52**
figure painting
in landscapes 19, 120–2
palette-knife technique and 134
in seascapes 122–3
still life within 120
Flaubert, Gustave 124
flower paintings 39–41, 120
Fontainebleau, Forest of 30, 47, 77
Franche-Comté
Battle of Alesia 66–9
Courbet's studio in Ornans **52**, 53, 57
dialects and patois 14–15, 58, 63–4, 66, 72, 75–6, 78, 82
intellectual culture of 58, 63
Puits noir 10, 12, 25–6, 58
source of the Lison river 10, 14, 67, 78
source of the Loue river 10, 14, 58
tourism 77
see also originary landscapes; Salins

G

Gaudin, Phoedora 27, 39
geology 72–4, **75**, 76, 82, 83; *see also* history; Marcou, Jules
Germain, Claude-Marie 72
Gill, André 42, **43**, **44**
Gowing, Lawrence 38–9, 146
Grimaldi, Jean-Marie de 77
Guillemet, Antoine 141, 142, 157

H

Herbert, Robert L. 47–9, 51
Herding, Klaus 16, 92, 98–9, 102
history
  Battle of Alesia 66–9, 76
  deep time 14–15, 23, 64, 66, 82–3
  as discursive model 58, 63, 72–7
Hugo, Victor
  frontispiece for *Les Travailleurs de la mer* 116–17, **116**
  Head of a Devil 111, **111**
  Ma Destinée **108–9**, 110, 117
  Mast Floating at Sea 111, **112–13**
  Pieuvre, Le 111–14, **115**
  Ruins of a Castle 117, **117**
  Travailleurs de la mer, Les 15, 90, 108–10, 111, 114–16, 117
  writing and drawing in works of 15, 114–17

I

Impressionism 10, 131, 166–7, 169–75

J

Jongkind, Johan Barthold 95, **96–7**, 104, 105

L

Laforgue, Jules 172–3
landscapes
  anthropomorphism 16, 18–19
  art historical interpretation of 15–19, 22
  Barbizon School 13–14, 47–8, 122
  experience of Nature in 11–12, 18, 28, 122
  form-matter relationship in 10, 11, 13, 14, 16, 17–18, 22, 122, 123
  Impressionists 166–7, **168**, 169, 172–5
  mark-making 23, 38–9, 47, 49, 52, 58, 80, 81, 163
  nudes within 120–2
  as originary worlds 10, 11, 14–15, 23
  post-1866 129–31
  rise of Romanticism and 13, 14, 18, 28
  Saintonge views 27–33, 36
  schools of 13–14
  within seascapes 122–3
  still life modalities and 12
  symbolic readings of 16–17
  tactility and 172–5
  temporality of 15, 19–22
  see also Source of the Lison; *Source of the Loue, The* (series); *Stream in the Forest*; *Stream of the Puits noir, The*
Le Gray, Gustave, *The Great Wave Sète* 99, **99**, 102
Lemonnier, Camille 91, 172
linguistics 75–6, 83; *see also* Max Buchon; patois
literature
  the sea in 15, 90, 108–17
  see also Hugo, Victor; Zola, Émile

M

Manet, Édouard
  Déjeuner sur l'herbe 132, 134
  Monk in Prayer **155**, **156**, 157
  the palette-knife technique and 131, 132–4
  seascapes 98, 105
  Young Lady in 1866 132–3, **133**
Marcou, Jules 58, 69, 72–4, **73**
mark-making
  of Cézanne 23, 169–71
  molecularization 47–9
  of Monet 169
  perception of surface and thickness in 42–3, 45
  psychological parallels 153–7, 158, 160
  Rock Oak, The (Rousseau) **46**, 47–9, 51
  Rousseau vs. Courbet 49–52
  scrape/smear 80, 81, 163–4
  skin-like quality 17, 26, 44–5
  slimming of impasto 19, 22, 42–3, 44, 94
  tactility and 172–5
  in *Trellis, The* 39–41
  types of 47–9, 80, 81, 94, 163–4
  see also palette-knife technique

materialism 10–11, 12–13
matter
allegorization of 123, 127, 160
as theme across Courbet's oeuvre 15, 120–3
co-substantiality of image and 11–12, 13, 14, 91–2, 82, 94, 110, 111, 114, 163–4
in high modernism 17–18, 123
in seascapes 890, 91–2, 94–5, 110, 117, 163–4
repression in painting 11, 154, 161, 164
term 12, 13
Maupassant, Guy de 88
Menzel, Adolphe 44
Michelet, Jules
blood theme 118–20
Mer, La 117, 118–20, 123, 124
natural histories 118
theme of substance 15, 90, 108, 117, 158
Monet, Claude 17, 169
Railroad Bridge, Argenteuil **168**, 169

N

Napoleon III 22, 77
De Nieuwekerke, Comte Alfred Émilien 88, 129

O

origin 10, 11, 14, 15, 23, 57–8, 81–3, 124, 163, 175; *see also* landscapes

P

paint layering
geological metaphors for 75
of Cézanne 146, 156
of the seascapes 92, 94–5, 103, 104, 107
scientific parallels 58, 63–4, 72–7, 163
visual effects of 23, 42–5
palette-knife technique
art historical study of 42–5, 172
as masonry 26, 42, 81
association with Courbet 22–3, 42, 52–3, 156
caricatures of Courbet 42, **43**
of Cézanne 23, 131, 141, 144, 146–52, 156, 166, 171, 172
Degas's references to 131, 137–41, 142
the deposit 80–1, 94, 163–4
destructive potential of 156
figure painting and 134
historical accounts of 52–3
knife-strokes 19–22, 42, 43–4
Manet's non-adoption of 131, 132–4
of Pissarro 141, 142, 166, 171
Renoir's adaption of 134–7, 141, 142
see also mark-making
patois 14–15, 58, 63–4, 66, 72, 75–6, 78, 82
photography **52**, 99–102
Pissarro, Camille
Climb, Rue de la Côte-du-Jalet, Pontoise, The 173, **174–5**
landscapes 166–7, 169, 172–5
Marne at Chennevières, The **142–3**, 144
Portrait of Cézanne 166, **167**
use of the palette-knife technique 131, 141, 142, 166, 171
Pradelles, Hippolyte 33, 36
Moonlight Promenade by Boat 33–4, **35**, 36
Proudhon, Pierre-Joseph 13, 53, 63, 85

R

Randon, Gustave, "The Waterspout" **91**, 93
Realism
Courbet and 13, 122
photography and 99–102
Renoir, Pierre-Auguste
adaption of the palette-knife technique 131, 134–7, 141, 142
Diana 134, 135–7, **136**, 141
Figures in a Landscape 135
Jules Le Coeur in the Forest of Fontainebleau 134–5
Romanticism 13, 14, 18, 28
Rousseau, Théodore
the Barbizon School 13, 18, 47
vs. Courbet 49–52
mark-making 47–9
Rock Oak, The **46**, 47–9, 51
Source of the Lison **48**, 49–50, 51

S

Saintonge
Courbet at Rochemont 26, 27–8, 39, 53
exhibition in Saintes 27, 36
side-by-side views of 28, 29, 30
Salins
baths 77
Courbet in 69, 78
Gour de Conche 66–9, 76
geology 72–4
regional map **68**
Roche pourrie 14, 72–3
Rousseau's connections with 49
Le Salinois 14, 69, 77, 78
see also Franche-Comté
Salon paintings 10, 16, 17, 43, 53, 85, 129
seascapes
color in 103, 123–4
critical reception 90, 91, 102–3, 108
depiction of matter in 89, 90, 91–2, 94, 110, 163–4
of Eugène Boudin **88**, 89, 95, 104–5
vs. Hugo 108–10
as ink 111–14
of James Whistler 104, 105–7, **105**, **106**
of Johan Barthold Jongkind 95, **96–7**, 104, 105
vs. Le Gray 99–102
in literature 15, 90, 108–17
material equivalence of 92–4, 107
Mer, La (Michelet) and 117, 118–20, 123, 124
paint layering 92, 94–5, 103, 104, 107
in photography **99**
tourism 89, 105, 124
treatments of the horizon 98–103, 124
tripartite division of 15, 89, 95, 107
waves 94–5, 98, 99–103, 108–10, 125–6
Zola's critique of 158
Sickert, Walter 44–5
Source of the Lison **50**, **51**
compared to Rousseau 51-2
composition 52, 78–80
early sketch of 51–2
mark-making 23, 52, 58, 80–1, 163
period of 57–8
temporality of 81–2
Source of the Loue, The (series) **8–9**, **60–1**, **64**, **65**
anthropomorphic readings 18–19
as originary landscape 10, 14, 57–8
series of 59–61
still life
Courbet's work 39, 120
flower paintings 39–41, 120
relationship of landscapes and 12, 41, 120
Stream in the Forest **24**, **37**, **38**
framing elements 36–8, 53
mark-making 23, 38–9, 47, 49, 80, 81
tonal organization of 36, 39, 47
Stream of the Puits noir, The **6**, **86–7**
mark-making 26, 58, 163
as an originary landscape 7–10, 12, 14, 16, 19
period of 57–8
perspective 175
reception at the Salon 85, 129
series 88
site of 7, 12, 26
substance
Courbet's approach to the representation of 15, 42–5, 120, 123
in Michelet 118–20
the sea 15, 90, 108, 117
term 13
see also matter

T

technique *see* brushwork; mark-making; paint layering; palette-knife technique
Thoré, Théophile 47, 129
Thuriet, Charles 14, 63
Toubin, Charles 58, 66, 68, 69, 72–3
Trouville 10, 15, 88, 89, 105

U

Universal Exhibition 8, 25, 33, 44, 47

W

waterspouts 93–4
Whistler, James Abbott McNeill 104
Blue Wave, Biarritz, The 105–7, **105**
brushstrokes 107
Harmony in Blue and Silver: Trouville **106**, 107

Z

Zola, Émile
and Cézanne 23, 141, 152–3
on Courbet 129, 144, 158
ideas on temperament 152, 154
Thérèse Raquin 153–4

ACKNOWLEDGMENTS

The research and writing of this book were kindly supported by the Edith O'Donnell Institute of Art History at the University of Texas, Dallas. I would like to thank the faculty, staff, and students of EODIAH, and in particular Michael Thomas, Sarah Kozlowski, and Pierrette Lacour, for providing me with a welcoming home throughout the process.

Several people that were pivotal to the project are sadly no longer with us. Sarah Faunce, Linda Nochlin, Klaus Herding, and Rick Brettell each stepped in at moments of waning confidence, and it is safe to say that this study would not have come to fruition without their unflagging encouragement. This book is dedicated to their memory.

When I first encountered Courbet's landscapes years ago, little did I know that the naïve awe of a neophyte would lead to an entire book on the subject. The number of people who have since guided my way are too numerous to count. My utmost gratitude is extended foremost to readers of the earliest drafts: Matthias Krüger, Simon Kelly, Richard Shiff, and Jim Rubin scrutinized individual chapters, while Rachel Churner courageously reviewed the entire manuscript. I am also grateful to Laurence des Cars, Dominique de Font-Réalx, Daniela Stöppel, and Stephanie Marchal for my first opportunities to present publicly on the matter.

It is difficult in the genre of acknowledgment to thank one's interlocutors without descending into the tone of professional and institutional obligation, or worse, personal vanity. I nevertheless hope that what my words lack in originality is more than made up for in sincerity. From the beginning, Mary Morton, Petra Chu, Ségolène Le Men, and Jim Rubin graciously shared with me their vast knowledge of Courbet. I am forever in their debt. Lionel Gossman, Göran Blix, David Bellos, Denis Hollier, Pierre Georgel, Daniel Heller-Roazen, and Corey Miller helped me navigate unfamiliar disciplines. Holly Clayson, Frédérique Desbuissons, André Dombrowski, Ewa-Lajer Burcharth, Irene Winter, Nancy Troy, Noit Banai, Michelle Kuo, Meredith Martin, Jay Oles, David Rosand, Anne Higonnet, Jonathan Crary, Charlotte Eyerman, Henri Zerner, Molly Nesbit, Liz Childs, Margaret Carroll, Karen Leader, Linda Goddard, Dario Gamboni, Stephen Eisenman, Lisa Florman, Fabienne Ruppen, Claudia Denk, Harry Cooper, Thierry de Duve, Éric de Chassy, Eric Michaud, Viviane Alix-Leborgne, Noël Barbe, and Pascal Reilé have all contributed to this book either through direct conversation or moral support (and often both).

The gestation of this book took place almost as much in museum galleries and conservation labs as in the seminar and lecture hall. For those precious moments, I wholeheartedly thank Emily Beeny, Scott Allan, Emerson Bowyer, Gloria Groom, Joe Rishel, Isolde Pludermacher, Anne Dary, Carine Joly, Nicky Myers, George Shackelford, Charlotte Hale, Carol Christiansen, Bruno Mottin, Anthea Callen, Carol Mancusi-Ungaro, Ulf Küster, Michel Hilaire, Joachim Pissarro, Jodi Hauptman, and Maria Luisa Pacelli. Among the many institutions and persons that had helped me procure images, Jon Landau, Fred Bancroft, Jayne Warman, Jill Newhouse, Claude Aubry, Patrick Matthiesen, Bertrand Talabardon, and Bertrand Gautier were especially generous with their time and energy. My indefatigable editors at Yale University Press, London, Sophie Neve, Julie Hrischeva, and Rosalind Neely had to call upon deep reserves of patience throughout the process. I couldn't have worked with a more industrious and accommodating team. Thanks must also go to the anonymous readers of the manuscript for helping me better organize and sharpen my thoughts.

Finally, there are those whose names appear nowhere in the text but without whom this book would not have been possible. Norman Bryson, Rosalind Krauss, and Benjamin Buchloh, through the vigor of their teaching and writing, have been formative in my own thinking about art history and criticism in ways that I am probably not even aware of. My family, Marietta Galvez, Domingo Java, Marisa Galvez, and Christina Galvez have likewise been steadfast in their support. I extend a special merci to Yve-Alain Bois for showing me over the years that the vicissitudes of scholarship need not be incompatible with the pleasures of partnership.

PICTURE CREDITS

Albright-Knox Art Gallery, Buffalo/Art Resource, New York: fig. 2

Alfred Atmore Pope Collection, Hill-Stead Museum, Farmington, Connecticut/Anna Day: fig. 43

Bibliothèque nationale de France, Paris: figs. 13, 14, 22, 26, 28, 30, 31, 35, 48, 49, 50

bpk Bildagentur/Nationalgalerie, Staatliche Museen, Berlin, Germany/ Jörg P. Anders/Art Resource, New York: fig. 46

Brooklyn Museum of Art, New York. Gift of James H. Post, A. Augustus Healy, and John T. Underwood: fig. 59; Purchased with funds given by Dikran G. Kelekian: fig. 74

Carnegie Museum of Art, Pittsburgh, Pennsylvania: fig. 67

Chrysler Museum of Art, Norfolk, Virginia. Gift of Walter P. Chrysler, Jr. 71.505: fig. 70

Collection du Musée de la Grande Saline, Salins-les-Bains. H. Bertrand: fig. 29

F. Deval: fig. 8

© The Fitzwilliam Museum, Cambridge, England: figs. 7, 60

Fundación Almine y Bernard Ruiz-Picasso para el Arte, Madrid. © FABA Photo: Hugard & Vanoverschelde Photography: fig. 47

Galerie Talabardon & Gautier, Paris/Guillaume Benoit: fig. 5

Image © Lyon MBA–Photo Alain Basset: fig. 42

Institut Gustave Courbet, Ornans: fig. 19

Isabella Stewart Gardner Museum, Boston, Massachusetts: fig. 44

The Israel Museum, Jerusalem: fig. 62

Kunsthaus Zürich, Zurich: fig. 24

Laurence Graff OBE: fig. 71

© Maisons de Victor Hugo/Roger-Viollet: figs. 45, 51

The Metropolitan Museum of Art, New York: Catharine Lorillard Wolfe Collection, Wolfe Fund, 1916: fig. 40; Gift of John Goldsmith Phillips, 1976: fig. 41; H. O. Havemeyer Collection, Bequest of Mrs. H. O. Havemeyer, 1929: figs. 21, 52, 55, 56; H. O. Havemeyer Collection. Gift of Horace Havemeyer, 1929: fig. 36; Gift of Erwin Davis, 1889: fig. 57

© Musée des Beaux-Arts et d'Archéologie de Besançon–Photo C. Choffet: fig. 25

© Musée Gustave Courbet, Ornans. Photo: Pierre Guenat: fig. 27

Musées de Strasbourg, M. Bertola: fig. 9

Museum of Fine Arts, Boston: figs. 10, 11, 68, 69

National Galleries of Scotland, Edinburgh: fig. 61

National Gallery, London: fig. 71

National Gallery of Art, Washington, D.C.: figs. 3, 23, 33, 58, 63

National Museum of Serbia, Belgrade: fig. 6

Norton Simon Foundation, Pasadena: figs. 37, 38

Ny Carlsberg Glyptotek, Copenhagen. Ole Haupt: fig. 15

Philadelphia Museum of Art: John G. Johnson Collection: figs. 34, 72; The Samuel S. White 3rd and Vera White Collection, 1967: fig. 73

Phillips Art Holdings LLC: figs. 1, 54

Princeton University Library, Rare Books and Special Collections: fig. 39

Private collection: figs. 65, 66

Private collection, Minnesota Marine Art Museum, Winona, Minnesota: fig. 17

Provost and Fellows of King's College, Cambridge: fig. 64

© RMN-Grand Palais/Art Resource, NY: figs. 16, 18, 20, 32, 53

Toledo Museum of Art. Gift of Edward Drummond Libbey: fig. 12

© Ville de Liège – Musée des Beaux-Arts de la Boverie: fig. 4